That Inferno

*Conversations of Five Women Survivors
of an Argentine Torture Camp*

Munú Actis
Cristina Aldini
Liliana Gardella
Miriam Lewin
Elisa Tokar

Foreword by Tina Rosenberg
Translated by Gretta Siebentritt

Vanderbilt University Press
Nashville

10 09 08 07 06   1 2 3 4 5 6

This book is printed on acid-free paper.
Manufactured in the United States of America

Ese Infierno: Conversaciones de cinco mujeres sobrevivientes de la ESMA was
originally published in Spanish in 2001 by Editorial Sudamericana, Buenos
Aires, Argentina. *www.edsudamericana.com.ar* ISBN 950-07-2087-6.
Published by arrangement with Julie Popkin, Literary Agent,
15340 Albright Street #204, Pacific Palisades, CA 90272.

Readers may contact the authors at the following e-mail address:
eseinfierno@hotmail.com

Library of Congress Cataloging-in-Publication Data

Ese infierno. English
    That inferno : conversations of five women survivors of an Argentine
Torture Camp / Munú Actis . . . [et al.] ; foreword by Tina Rosenberg ;
translated by Gretta Siebentritt.
       p. cm.
    Includes bibliographical references.
    ISBN 0-8265-1513-4 (cloth : alk. paper)
    ISBN 0-8265-1514-2 (pbk. : alk. paper)
    1. Women political prisoners—Argentina—Biography. 2. Political
prisoners—Argentina—Biography. 3. Argentina—Politics and government—1955–1983. 4. Escuela de Mecánica de la Armada Argentina.
I. Actis, Munú, 1945–   II. Title.
HV9582.5.E8413 2006
365.45092282—dc22
                                                        2005026377

To the dead and the disappeared.
To the stolen children we continue to seek.
To Cristina, Elisa, Miriam, and Munú.
  (Liliana)

To Néstor, my compañero.
To Ceci and Diego, my beloved children.
  (Elisa)

To Alejo Mallea and Pepe Villagra.
To Sofía and Lucía and, through them, to all the sons and daughters.
  (Cristina)

To Juan Eduardo Estévez, Norma Matsuyama, and Patricia Palazuelos.
To the babies they were going to have in April and October 1977.
  (Miriam)

To Enrique Desimone, Norma Robert, and Adriana Barcia.
To the children of all of those who dared to seek a better world.
To Omar, for knowing how to be there.
  (Munú)

Contents

Foreword

by Tina Rosenberg

This is a book about a hallucinatory form of torture—unique in the annals of repression—that took place in the 1970s in the Mechanics School of the Argentine Navy. That navy—the most exclusive, sophisticated, and gentlemanly of the armed services in a country that prided itself on being the most cultured and civilized in Latin America—ended up running a torture chamber that became the most notorious in Latin America's history.

How this could happen is now, after Abu Ghraib, somewhat easier for U.S. society to understand. It's not simply what happened in that prison—the sexual humiliation, the dogs, the chains, the laughing abuse by twenty-year-olds, ordinary U.S. soldiers humiliating prisoners simply because they were given the authority to do so. It's the fact that U.S. society does not really want to know about it. The Pentagon has exonerated the chain of command. There is very little public outrage, little demand that the guilty be punished. We think of ourselves as a people who would never countenance torture. We are unwilling to disturb this self-image, even when the facts demand it. So we would prefer not to know, not to ask questions. As if it were second nature, U.S. military officers fell into torture and much of the rest of our country into willful blindness.

Is there anything we can learn from the Navy Mechanics School? First, we can learn that torture will not protect us. Raúl Vilariño, who had been a junior officer on the team that kidnapped supposed subversives for torture in the Mechanics School, said the following in an interview with the Buenos Aires weekly magazine *Semana*:

> I was probably responsible for the kidnapping of about 200 people. Let's
> say that half were guilty. Of the 50 percent who weren't, a quarter had
> a certain ideology, although just because they have certain ideas doesn't

Tina Rosenberg, an editorial writer for the *New York Times*, is the author of *Children of Cain: Violence and the Violent in Latin America* and *The Haunted Land: Facing Europe's Ghosts after Communism*, which won the Pulitzer Prize.

mean they'll do terrible things. . . . And the rest, well, how many times do people send you to a place and you have the address written down and you still have to ask if you are at the right place? We couldn't go around asking if guerrillas lived here. . . . I don't deny that we made five hundred thousand mistakes.

Everyone we arrested was always guilty. I thought we must be wrong sometimes. But no, everyone had done something. . . . I asked to watch a torture session to see if people really admitted to all those things.

There was a door where someone had written "The Path to Happiness." Behind that door was the torture chamber: electric shock machine, an iron band of a bed connected to a 220-volt machine, an electrode that went from zero to 70 volts, chairs, presses, and all kinds of instruments. . . .

Have you ever been shocked by a refrigerator or another electric appliance? Add a hundred and multiply it by a thousand. That is what a person feels when he is tortured, a person who might be guilty or might not. . . . I'll tell you about a case, a seventeen-year-old girl named Graciela Rossi Estrada. She was a sad-looking girl. Because they needed more hands, I was asked to be present. It began with the simple methods of the average villain in a grade B police movie: cigarette butts, poking her, pulling her hair, beatings, pinchings. As they apparently didn't get what they wanted to hear, they started with electricity. After a half hour of receiving blows and electric shocks, the girl fainted. Then they took her very delicately by the hair and legs and heaved her into a cell, into a pool of water so she'd swell up. Four or five hours later she was in terrible shape from swelling and they brought her back to the torture chamber. Then she'd sign anything—that she killed Kennedy or she fought in the Battle of Waterloo. That's why I saw the facts gotten from torture weren't real most of the time; they were just used to justify arresting the person. . . .

One of the lively systems [that the camp doctor] invented to torture a pregnant woman was with a spoon. They put a spoon or a metallic instrument in the vagina until it touched the fetus. Then they gave it 220. They shocked the fetus.

[Interviewer]: What did you do, watching that?
[Vilariño]: I vomited. What else could I have done?
[Interviewer]: Were there people who enjoyed it?
[Vilariño]: Of course.

As with the Mechanics School, two-thirds of those detained at Abu Ghraib were found to have no connection to terror groups—when they came in, anyway. It is not clear how many of them left that prison vowing revenge on the

United States or how many young people who learned about Abu Ghraib made the same decision. Torture in Abu Ghraib may very well have produced far more terrorists than it stopped. Nor is torture useful for extracting information that can prevent terrorist acts. It produces confessions, certainly—but too many confessions. The torture victim is not a reliable source.

Torture happens not because it must but because it can. It is an expression of power over those in bondage. This is the second lesson the Mechanics School can teach us. It is easy for U.S. society to say that the government knows what it must do in the shadows to protect us. But torture is not measurable, not controllable. It slips its leash. As such, it is a reflection of the full spectrum of human psychosis. Sadism is one manifestation, but there are others. The women in this book inhabited a surreal hell in which they were never sure that the knock on the door at midnight meant they were to be taken to the torture table or out for a steak. There were torturers who fell in love with their prey. Munú Actis says, "They'd come, they'd beat you to a pulp with a stick, and then at two in the morning they'd get you, put you in a car, and take you out to dinner. They'd sit you down at the same table, turn you into an equal: you ate the same food, they wanted to hear your opinions, and then back to Capucha you went. That would drive anybody crazy!"

The logic of life and death in the Mechanics School had nothing to do with whether one was really a Montoneros guerrilla or whether one broke under torture. The women in this book probably survived because they knew how to translate documents or could concisely summarize press clippings. These were skills of interest to Admiral Emilio Massera, chief of the navy, who was building his political career. Admiral Massera killed Montoneros as dangerous subversives or kept them alive as his political advisers. Or both.

But keep in mind that these women were the survivors. The main purpose of the Mechanics School, however, was not the production of survivors. It was to ensure that very few people survived. Every prisoner who came through the gates of the school was assigned a number. In the ninety-two months of the school's existence, the numbers topped five thousand. Several hundred survived—tortured and released after a few days. Fewer than a hundred were—like Munú Actis, Cristina Aldini, Liliana Gardella, Miriam Lewin and Elisa Tokar—kept for years in a bizarre, hellish zoo. The others who passed through the school—between four thousand and forty-five hundred, the vast majority of whom had never taken up a gun—died in torture or were thrown from an airplane into the sea.

The third lesson of the Mechanics School is that torture destroys everyone: the victims, surely—the women who tell their stories in this book are still prisoners of the Mechanics School thirty years later—but also the torturers. "I saw how people lost their sensitivity," said Raúl Vilariño. "They were so involved in the routine that it seemed normal. The victims were pieces of meat. . . . What happens to a person, to people who are used to seeing blood? What do they work in now? Selling real estate?" After the Mechanics School was closed down, many of its officers gnawed themselves apart. The French torturers in Algeria were the men who later staged acts of terrorism and tried to assassinate Charles de Gaulle and overthrow his government.

Argentina also suffered and suffers to this day. Argentines are still confronting the question of what their body politic was capable of doing, what their people were capable of supporting. In the United States, the damage of torture is more profound than the erosion of our image abroad, although that is considerable. In a nation where torture has become acceptable for the right purposes against the right people, smaller violations of everyday rights become more normal. Freedom in the United States is diminished. And the U.S. people now know that we are not the people we thought we were. Those who justify the torture in Abu Ghraib must now ask themselves, "If I were in the Mechanics School, can I be sure it would be as a prisoner?"

Preface

by the Authors

So then, to tell my story, here I stand . . .
You hear me speak, but do you hear me feel?
—Gertrude Kolmar (Jewish writer
killed in Auschwitz), "The Woman Poet"

This book is about Argentina during the 1970s, a time of social and political fervor in which the desire for transformation, the conviction and the resolve of much of the population made it seem possible to change the world. Argentina was not the only country immersed in this climate. It occurred in many contexts in the late 1960s and the 1970s: the anti–Vietnam War movement; the feminist movement; the sexual revolution; student protests in the United States, Mexico, and France; Prague Spring; the anti-colonialist struggles in Africa; and the liberation movements that swept Latin America. As in other countries throughout the world, young people in Argentina aspired to a politically, economically, and socially just society.

Argentina was a mobilized society in those years. Labor unions, neighborhood associations, sectors of the Catholic Church, schools and universities, professionals, artists, and political movements—some armed, some not—were galvanized. Fueling this mobilization was an educated, altruistic, combative, and vigorous generation, unified under leftist Peronist factions.

In 1973, faced with a severe social and economic crisis and unable to stem public resistance, the military regime in power was compelled to allow popular former president Juan Domingo Perón to return to the country from his eighteen-year exile in Spain. With Perón barred from running in the elections, ally Héctor Cámpora prevailed. After two months, Cámpora resigned to make way for an unrestricted presidential election, and so it was that in September 1973 Perón—with his wife, Isabel, as running mate—was elected to the presidency. Many Argentines believed that Peron's return would open the door to genuine social change. But on July 1, 1974, Perón died amid harsh, violent internal struggles between left-wing and right-wing factions of his broad-based movement.

By late 1975, the political situation had become critical. The government of Isabel Perón, who had taken over the presidency upon her husband's death, was discredited and corrupt. The country's day-to-day operations were, in fact, in the hands of former police chief, black magic devotee, and founder of the para-security force death squad the Triple A (the Argentine Anti-communist Alliance), José López Rega. The task of López Rega's Triple A was to eliminate the opposition, including congressional deputies, priests, labor unionists, lawyers, journalists, workers, and students. The tortured bodies of labor unionists and grassroots militants appeared daily in the cities and in the countryside. Control of the university was usurped. The guerrillas, including the Peronist guerrilla group, deemed the government illegitimate and opposed its authoritarian policies.

Meanwhile, the economic situation had become unsustainable. The value of the Argentine peso relative to the U.S. dollar was falling daily, even hourly. The official annual inflation rate was nearly 200 percent and rising. Savings evaporated, and small and medium-sized businesses were doomed to bankruptcy.

Against this backdrop, the armed forces resumed control of the government on March 24, 1976. Promising to pacify the country, the military junta launched the Process of National Reorganization, a plan that sought peace through submission and submission through force, illegality, and terror. The military junta designed its own strategy to annihilate the opposition: there would be no Triple A–style mass arrests, executions, or bullet-ridden bodies strewn about in broad daylight. Dissenters would be kidnapped, taken away by unidentified armed individuals in civilian dress, in unmarked vehicles under the cover of darkness. They would be savagely tortured to extract information, and then they would vanish forever. No one would be responsible; no one would have any information whatsoever about the crime. The victims would become the disappeared.

And so began one of the most far-reaching acts of genocide in Argentine history. The kidnappings and disappearances multiplied. The perpetrators were not renegade groups from the extreme right engaging in excesses, as the junta claimed; there was a centralized coordinating structure. Operations were conducted in the workplaces of the people who were targeted or on the streets, and they required that the police create a *free zone* in which to maneuver. Strangely, police patrols—which were everywhere, especially after the coup d'état—never intervened, even when a kidnapping took place just a few blocks from police headquarters.

Most victims were, however, kidnapped from their homes at night. The commandos would force their way into a house, terrorizing everyone in their path, even gagging the children and forcing them to watch. They would seize the targets of their search, brutally beat them, and drag the hooded victims to waiting vehicles. Meanwhile, other commandos burglarized the property, loading stolen items into trucks and other vehicles. Anything that could not be taken was destroyed, and the remaining members of the household were beaten and threatened. Even when a witness managed to raise the alarm, there would be no police response. Lawlessness reigned, and the futility of reporting the offenses soon became apparent. With so much of the population terrorized, witnesses became a rare commodity. Virtually no one saw anything. And more often than not, those who admitted what they saw would comment under their breath, "If they took them, there must have been a reason." In this way, thousands upon thousands of people—approximately thirty thousand out of a population of 30 million—joined the ranks of a phantasmagoric category: the disappeared.

In 1983, when Raúl Alfonsín was elected president and democracy was restored, testimonies given to the National Commission on the Disappeared (CONADEP) revealed the horror of the concentration camps where the disappeared had been held, camps with such deceptive names as Olympus, the Hotel Sheraton, and the Little Schoolhouse. One such camp was the Navy Mechanics School, the ESMA.

Alfonsín's government ordered the Supreme Council of the Armed Forces to prosecute members of the successive military juntas for murder, unlawful imprisonment, and torture. Months went by, and the military tribunals issued no rulings. Eventually it became clear that the Supreme Council would not prosecute its own. The matter was transferred to the civilian courts, and in December 1985 the Federal Court finally secured convictions against the majority of the members of the junta. Perhaps the most significant aspect of the verdict was Point 30, which recommended that midlevel officers be brought to trial. Shortly thereafter, more than fifteen hundred human rights violations cases were opened.

Yet the armed forces had not ceded power in 1983 because of strong internal resistance; they had done so as a result of a power base weakened by the Malvinas/Falklands War. And although they had failed at conventional warfare, they had succeeded in another task: the annihilation of a generation that sought to change the structure of the country. The armed forces retained their monopoly over power and pressured to ensure that they would enjoy impunity for their crimes. Two decrees sabotaged the efforts of those who sought justice: Punto Final and Due Obedience. The Punto Final decree—authorized by the Alfonsín administration ostensibly to pacify the country—curtailed the prosecution of new cases by establishing a date after which no more cases of human rights violations would be accepted. The Due Obedience decree absolved those who were found guilty of crimes that already had been documented and tried and asserted that because midlevel officers, unlike those in command, had no decision-making power, they had merely acted under orders. When Carlos Menem took the presidency in 1990, he completed the sabotage by granting pardons to high-ranking military officers who were serving sentences. With the exception of trials for crimes against minors, such as the kidnapping of babies born in captivity, impunity was sanctified.

Finally, in 2003, the National Congress revoked the Due Obedience and Punto Final decrees, paving the way for the prosecution of all those involved in the crimes of repression. On March 24, 2004, the Argentine government ordered the navy to vacate the campus of the ESMA, the most symbolic of the illegal detention camps. Today the ESMA facilities house the Museum of Memory and are being used for the defense of human rights.

In 1998, as members of the military were being imprisoned for the theft of minors—after having been shielded for more than a decade by the law and by a pardon that returned them to the streets—we felt the need to speak.

Twenty-three years had passed since we had been kidnapped and taken to the ESMA extermination camp. There we shared a horrific experience, one we long considered impossible to convey. Most of us had denounced our kidnappers and torturers in the courts, sometimes suffering reprisals for doing so. But it is not easy to relinquish the shelter of structured language, of formal testimony given before a judge or a human rights organization, to describe daily life in the concentration camp.

It means explaining how we existed on the inside, why and how we worked in order to survive, how we constantly feigned our "recuperation," our repentance, to navy personnel and many of the other prisoners. It means evoking our frustration at having been taken alive and our frustration at the cyanide pill as a symbol of liberation and sacrifice for others. And it means describing the torture, followed by conversation and coexistence with the torturers themselves. It means recalling the mass "transfers," followed by strange, untoward dinner invitations from our torturers; the family visits with and without supervision; the "outings" that were, in fact, fishing expeditions for new kidnap victims and the anguish of having to participate in them with former militants willing to turn in others. It means reliving our forced participation as witnesses to these kidnappings and as "covers" in street operations. It means eating dinner and watching television while pretending to feel nothing as you hear the screams from a torture session taking place in the next room. It means fearing former *compañeros* who joined the oppressors, and it means occasionally hearing the confessions of an oppressor who breaks down in tears. It means making love secretly with a *compañero*, and it means listening and trying to understand the experience of a prisoner involved in a contradictory love-hate relationship with an oppressor. It means resisting or crumbling several times a day. All of this it means, together and separately. All of this it means, encased in a single body, a single soul.

We are five women. We are still united after all these years. We needed to talk about these things again before they became diluted in our memories. We needed to write them down. We had to wait two decades to do so, until our internal timing coincided, among ourselves and with society's.

We know that much of what we relate will provoke debate, but we are prepared—some of us more than others—to face that test. We are already considered suspect for having survived. "If they took her, there must have been a reason" became, in the time of exile, "if she survived, there must have been a reason," a sentiment that resurfaces sometimes even today. For years, our own guilt also acted as a deterrent.

We decided to relate this anguish in the form of a conversation, sharing a cup of *mate* the way that affection is shared. Tears and anger were part of our conversations, but so was laughter. Some things can be exorcised only through humor.

We are not sorry to be alive.

We think that, ideally, everyone should hear our story, but our primary concern is those who have emotional attachments to the disappeared, particularly to disappeared children. We want them to understand the human dimension of this story and to use that understanding to reject a Manichean view of good and evil, because it is impossible to live up to the demands of absolute heroism. The truth is that, aside from brief episodes of heroism or saintliness, real history was made by human beings with all their inconsistencies.

Prologue

by León Rozitchner

And sorrow and sighing shall flee away.
—Isaiah 35:10

What we are about to read is the product of a long period of time suspended—that of a small group of women forever marked by having endured the limits of suffering against a backdrop of the tens of thousands who were murdered. "It took us twenty years to come together," said one of the women, describing the readjustment process they underwent before they were able to speak of the past. This long interval was necessary for them to recall, as a group, the experience of horror they had endured. The wound lanced by the tenacity of memory has not, however, brought them the healing they sought. The horror of genocide leaves indelible marks.

This book poses the crucial question: Is living in society possible when so many human beings, shielded by the impunity of power, delight in torture and murder? Where does one begin to conceive of a potential foundation for "homeland" in Argentina in the aftermath of genocide? Genocide is the matrix that exposes, with dark and monstrous evidence, the absolute evil that the authorities are capable of inflicting on their inhabitants.

We used to believe, "*That* (genocide) is something that happens in Europe, in Africa, but not in Argentina." Immigrants coming to Argentina distanced themselves from their own pasts, denying the tradition of hatred and death they had left behind, even that surrounding the American colonization. What happened in other latitudes could never happen in Argentina, on the other side of the ocean. We forgot the existence of international terror and death that had included Argentina in the not too distant past. And overlaying our forgetfulness was the innocence of recent generations of Argentines—until suddenly we were taken by surprise once more by the horror that still lingered deep in the bowels of Argentina's heirs.

We have had to reach this extreme in order to understand the criminal foundations upon which we stand, because all genocide, all gratuitous mur-

León Rozitchner, a leading Argentine intellectual and political activist, is the author of numerous notable works on contemporary philosophical, social, and political issues, including *El Terror y La Gracia* and *Freud y el Problema del Poder* (*Freud and the Problem of Power*).

ders pose the most fundamental question: What are the darkest and ever-present abysses of humanity into which our contemporary society has plunged its roots?

∾

This book transcribes meetings attended by several women who survived the ESMA extermination camp. It is inscribed within an extended debate over "the unexplainable": human criminality. It continues to be the most scandalous, the most paradoxical mystery, incomprehensible to many of those who ponder and suffer this ignominious reality that has characterized the twentieth century, in Argentine society as well: the genocide of millions of people apparently carried out in such a way as to be considered "banal." We believe, however, that underneath the apparent "banality of evil"—in the words of German-American political philosopher Hannah Arendt—crime and murder, whether individual or collective, by the state or by society, although they may be "normalized" and bureaucratic, are not and can never be banal.

The evil that leads one to delight in the murder and torture of another human being can never be, in our view, an indifferent experience for the perpetrator. Even the murderous routine of the torture and extermination camps must resonate, we believe, in the most obscure labyrinths of the personality of a murderer who takes pleasure and delight in the suffering and death of fellow human beings. Something deep inside those who kill and torture must die forever, leaving them worm-ridden by death even as they go through the motions of living. Making crime a banal act is the distance that the institution creates within the murderers to anesthetize their conscience and their feelings about the crime they commit. Could it be that this suspicion—that the murderers are turned into mere specters of themselves by the evil they commit—is the last hope that keeps us from despairing of mortals? We only have to believe that it exists to learn to conquer it with life.

This murderous force is not part of the universal "essence" of all humankind, although ultimately we must acknowledge that it is pervasive indeed. We cannot let ourselves believe that the violence of murdering others is among the most primitive "natural" instinctive forces fundamental to human life. The murderer may form part of a bureaucratic extermination machine; crime may be present in his or her daily life much like a career choice—like the hangman of yore—one of the many required by the modern state, sheathed in a thousand layers of superficiality and atrocious habit. But the enjoyment of torture and murder will always be a human fact that cannot be generalized. Not all people lend themselves to such acts, and many would face their own death rather than participate in them. But as for those who suffered these acts, can they possibly even consider the things we are saying?

Can we claim that there is "a human desire to spill human blood . . . an inexorable, human, and ominous logic of crime," as Jack Fuchs asserts? Or can we affirm, conversely, that "murder is against the normal desires and inclinations of most people," as Arendt writes?

I think we must place ourselves on the side of life. To say that crime has been banalized means that the deepest part of each murderer has been destroyed. But the society that tolerates it with indifference also is destroyed. Banality refers only to the institutionalization of crime, its routine, rather than to the profound metamorphosis it provokes in those who commit and accept it: there is always an underlying social institution promoting it. Even the most individual crime is collective. Humanization and its antithesis, criminality, are social products. Murderers sustained by an institution—imagined or real, present or past—are always individuals who believe in their impunity in committing the crime. They are always protected by a collective power. And that was true in Argentina, as it was in Germany, when the general population demonstrated its absolute indifference.

To ensure that crime does not keep sprouting, implacably, from the miserable figure of the murderer, we must trace its links to the power that requires it. This criminality would not have been unleashed without the support and strategic requirements of other groups and powers, because impunity and the absence of risk are the shields that cowards need to commit crimes. At the trembling point of the electric prod, in the darkness of the hood, in the death flights, the murderers were encouraged by the impunity created by the criminal influence of the United States and the Catholic Church in the training of military personnel. Could the craving for blood and the suffering of others have been unleashed without the protection of these two empires? Could it have been unleashed if the church had not contributed its millenary experience with bonfires, pillories, and lashings? Could it have been unleashed if soldiers had not, throughout the ages, killed the indigenous people and peons who dared to strike? No. The genocide would not have been possible without the training received in U.S. and European intelligence schools and war colleges and without the support of the powerful Catholic Church and economic interests linked to national dominance and imperialism. It is common knowledge that military regimes were a criminal response to feared social transformation, emerging in Paraguay in 1954, in Brazil in 1964, in Bolivia in 1971, in Uruguay in 1972, in Chile in 1973, and in Argentina in 1976. They shared more than similar characteristics: they were united under a common goal. The Argentine genocide is a criminal political strategy in a historic death-producing system. It is the triumphant neoliberal Fourth Reich, personified by the United States, which has replaced the vanquished Third Reich of the Nazis.

Our survivors live under the same insistent, implacable enigma: these women, obsessed, still question—and it is a question that will be with them throughout their lives, born of the need to comprehend the incomprehensible—

the mysterious design of having been among those who visited the extremes of horror and of having survived when so many thousands were killed.

How does one justify the privilege of having preserved one's own life when so many lives were lost? To experience the guilt of being alive is the cruelest way of all to annul life. It is hard to see oneself as a person "chosen" by destiny to survive when those doing the choosing were the torturers and murderers of one's relatives and *compañeros*.

Shall we suppose, perhaps, that it was pity on the part of the murderers that allowed the survivors to live? No. It was the murderers' interest in preserving them, after torture, as enslaved intelligence. The ESMA was the Argentine Navy's extermination camp except for the few survivors who could be used as "enslaved gray matter" for Admiral Emilio Eduardo Massera's political project. A sort of microworld was created that, on a small scale, synthesized and condensed the same forms of dominance and destruction that later were extended to the rest of the population. This project spread, with terror amplified, throughout a downtrodden society, and the Argentine people are still living with the consequences. This explains, in large part, the survival of the few who escaped not torture, which they suffered, but death.

> "I don't think the Montoneros officials kidnapped and taken to the ESMA were kept alive by chance. A group of naval officers, led by Massera, had a political project, and that's where the 'Montoneros Gray Matter' came into play."

> "They started to wonder, 'What can we do with these brains?'"

> "For us, the *fall* was the beginning of a new stage. For most people, however, falling into the hands of those murderers was truly the beginning of the end."

The feared public uprising, transformed into the "target" of the war, was the basis for this strategy in which the armed forces sought to take control of the ideological "weapons" of the "enemy." They wanted to redirect a transformative social passion, turning it into a successful "technology" to deceive the people. This stratagem, they reasoned, would enable them to effect a political manipulation by shifting from a murderous armed war to a more effective and destructive pacification policy, premised on the same underlying terror and contempt.

The impact that terror has on people reveals its destructive effectiveness, as a subjective technique, at the most subconscious, primal level of each human being. We repeat: the murder of souls and the torture of bodies at the ESMA spread simultaneously to the entire social body, which was restructured into submission or despair. It created the terrorized subjects of the postgenocidal, neoliberal society, with the devastating consequences that Argentina is experiencing today. Beyond the anguish brought vividly to life in the reading of this book, it is important to consider the political scheme underlying the extermination camps. There the mortal and bloody foundations of the forces of oppression in our society are laid bare. The conditions organized by terror constitute a microcosm of the threats that, in their amplified form, play a defining role in the lives of people today.

The women who survived the ESMA describe the personal transformations they suffered, transformations that also permeated society in their more diluted forms: the threat of death penetrated social subjects and obliterated civilian forces. We highlight four types of aggression—perhaps the cruelest of those experienced by these women—which in their expanded form persist as a latent threat in each Argentinian:

Stripping life of all meaning:

"I remember that I couldn't think . . . I couldn't conceive of a plan for my life."

"I began to believe that I had killed myself, that I had self-destructed."

"The only world was the present, with no expectation of a future—the absolute present, with no plans."

Total power over our own death:

"It drove them crazy when a prisoner tried to escape their power of decision over life and death."

Complicity of powerful institutions (in this case the Catholic Church):

"*Recuperated* for Western, Christian society . . . as TIGER [Jorge Eduardo] Acosta, who preached St. Thomas Aquinas, would say."

"He talked to baby Jesus every night, and baby Jesus told him who stayed and who was to be *sent up*."

Identification with the oppressor"

"Some of them identified very strongly with their oppressors. They copied them and even imitated the TIGER's tone of voice, his jokes, his way of standing."

"Ideologically they seemed to be totally identified. . . . Something changed inside them and they imitated them."

These four consequences—diluted but alive and festering—spread, dissolving the energies of each citizen and becoming the foundation for the political terror that persists in Argentina's "democracy." In order for neoliberalism to triumph, it was necessary for death to "pound the lesson into our heads"—a phrase we heard in school from the time we were little—leaving us alone, defenseless, and desolate within society itself.

"I didn't have anyone left! I started calling, and they were all dead."

That Inferno
Ese Infierno

Topography of Terror

The Building

Two repressive structures operated in la Escuela de Mecánica de la Armada:[1] the first was known as Task Force 3.3.2 (GT3.3.2), and the other was the Navy Intelligence Service (SIN).

Special groups within the regular navy chain of command carried out the repression. These groups were mainly composed of naval officers and noncommissioned officers (NCOs), although personnel from other forces also participated: the federal police, the coast guard, and the Federal Penitentiary Service.

In addition to performing specific acts of repression, the Task Force profited from the property and possessions of the kidnapped and served as logistical support for the political project of Admiral Emilio Eduardo Massera, Commander of the Argentine Navy until 1978.

The ESMA concentration camp is located in the northern zone of the federal capital. Its perimeter is defined by Avenida del Libertador to the west, Avenida Comodoro Martín Rivadavia and Avenida Leopoldo Lugones to the east, Calle Santiago Calzada to the south, and the Raggio Technical Schools to the north. Several buildings are located on the grounds: the Navy Mechanics School itself, the Navy War College, and on the northern boundary the Officers' Casino. The Officers' Casino, a three-story building with a basement and an attic, served as the base and operations center of Task Force 3.3.2.

The description of the detention center's internal layout is based on the reconstructions of survivors who were detained there during different periods;[2] for this reason, the accounts do not always match. The Basement (*Sótano*), the Ground Floor, the Third Floor (*Altillo*), and the Attic (*Sobrealtillo*), which were the areas used by Task Force 3.3.2, were rearranged regularly. The first and sec-

---

1. The Navy Mechanics School; ESMA

2. This reconstruction was created by the authors and was supplemented with data taken from the *Nunca Más [Never Again]* report and from survivors' testimonies.

ond floors were always used as officers' dormitories, and prisoners were never taken there.

Offices used for administration, intelligence activities, and planning operations were located on the Ground Floor. These areas were known as Jorges and Dorado. Some captives were taken to Dorado to work. Although captives usually did not work in Jorges, occasionally some were taken there.

∾

The entrance to the Basement was through Dorado and down two flights of stairs, where there was a heavy iron door. A guard armed with a rifle was always posted just outside this door. He was responsible for opening the door and monitoring the movement of people as they entered or left the Basement. The oppressors did not enter armed. An officer or NCO who wished to leave would identify himself, and the guard would look through the peephole and open the door.

The Basement was the first place captives were taken. Although they might remain there for some time, usually they were taken up to Capucha, the left wing, and brought back down to specially prepared rooms for interrogation or torture. There were few permanent walls in the Basement, and the space was constantly rearranged. Partitions were made of light materials so they could be easily set up and dismantled.

The torture rooms were furnished with only an iron bed, to which the prisoner was tied, a shelf for the electric prod, and a chair for the torturer.

An infirmary operated out of one of the rooms. It was equipped with two beds and two small, padlocked glass cabinets containing medications. For a certain period, wounded captives were treated there, as were pregnant women during delivery. The whole area stank of blood and filth.

There was no natural light anywhere in the Basement, which was illuminated by fluorescent bulbs twenty-four hours a day. Light vents located a few centimeters above the ground provided ventilation. The air was stale and thin. The torture rooms, where captives sometimes spent weeks, had no ventilation at all.

To the right, there was a huge iron door and three steps leading outside. Captives who were being "transferred" were taken out through this door. The Basement was rearranged on the occasion of the 1979 visit of the Organization of American States (OAS) Commission on Human Rights. For example, the stairway leading to Dorado was blocked off, and the outside door was used as the Basement entrance.

Recent kidnapping victims shared the Basement with captives who had been put to work. Working captives labored in specially prepared areas: a photograph laboratory, a document forgery room, a layout office, a printing studio, and a sound laboratory (the Egg Carton). There were also a dining area

PLANTA BAJA

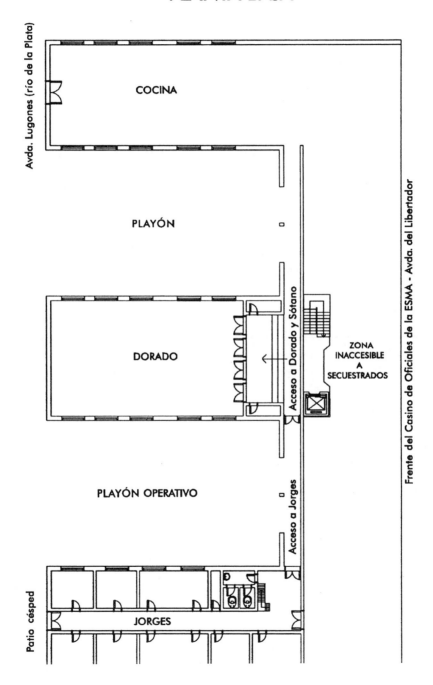

THIRD FLOOR [*ALTILLO*]

1 Central stairway
2 Armed guard
3 Entrance
4 Door and stairway to Capuchita
5 Ascending staircase
6 Iron door
7 Descending staircase
8 Dining room (formerly the Pregnant Women's Room)
9 Bathroom
10 Elevator motor
11 Ascending staircase
12 Bathroom
13 Room
13' Room (also used as the Pregnant Women's Room)
14 Windows facing Avenida del Libertador
15 Windows facing Río de la Plata
16 Iron door
17 Descending staircase
18 Light vents
19 Stalls [*camarotes*: literally, ship's cabins]
20 Shared living space
21 Library
22 Press office
23 File room
24 Office of the navy officer in charge

PLANTA ALTILLO

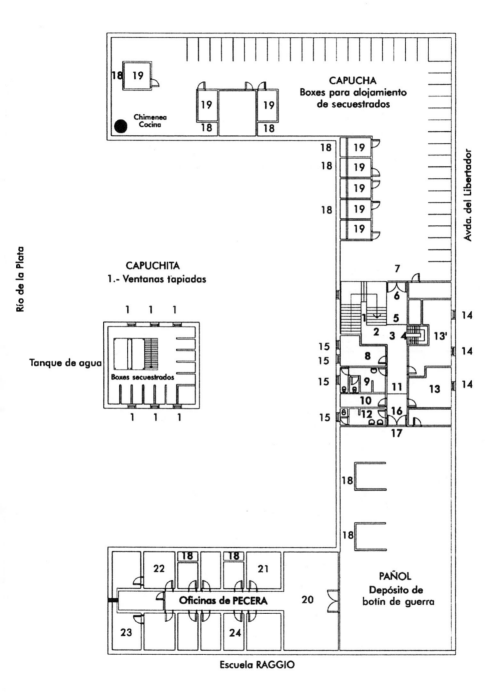

DORADO

1 Staircase to the Basement
2 Door leading to the courtyard
3 Elevator
4 Guard and control post
5 Staircase to Dorado
6 Living area
7 Living area
8 Telephone switchboard
9 Entrance to Dorado
10 Window extensions to the Basement light vents
11 Guard; closed circuit TV control panel
12 Office
13 Offices of intelligence officers
14 Offices of intelligence aides

BASEMENT [*SÓTANO*]

1 Staircase
2 Pantry
3 Electric generator
4 Armed guard
5 Iron door
6 Step
7 Layout office
8 Concrete beam
9 Documentation forgery office
10 Light vents
11 Photographic laboratory
12 Infirmary
13 Storage space for photographic laboratory
14 Guard desk
15 Torture rooms
16 Dining room for captives
17 "Egg Carton" [*Huevera*] audiovisual room
18 Large bathroom
19 Small bathroom
20 Staircase to courtyard
22 Exterior door ("transfers")

PLANTA DORADO

PLANTA SÓTANO

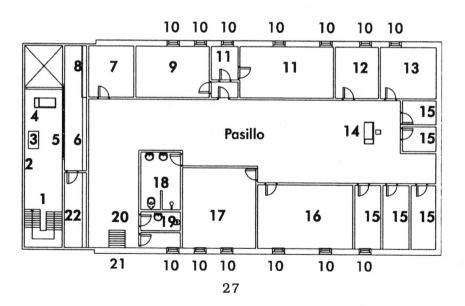

27

7

and two bathrooms. At all times, a guard was posted at the end of the main hallway.

Captives were taken to the Third Floor by means of a wide staircase. There was a huge iron door at the entrance to the Third Floor, where (as at the entrance to the Basement) a guard recorded in a notebook the comings and goings of the captives.

The Third Floor had two large wings monitored by closed circuit televisions located on the Ground Floor at the entrance to Dorado.

In the left wing, Capucha, captives were kept supine on the floor, hooded and shackled, separated by hardboard partitions one meter in height. There were some closed spaces called cubicles or stalls that had light vents. These vents provided the little ventilation in Capucha, which was reinforced by two very loud extractors. Artificial light was kept on all day. The floor was polished concrete.

The stalls were used to isolate certain captives. They were also used as sleeping areas for captives participating in the "recuperation process." These were furnished with bunk beds.

The Third Floor had a sloping roof with iron beams that, in some areas, reached the floor. A huge population of rats ran up and down the beams.

The central part of the Third Floor had two bathrooms and three rooms with windows, which were used, at various times, as a dining area, a room for pregnant women, and dormitories for some of the captives.

Offices were constructed in the right wing of the Third Floor, and some of the captives worked there. This area was known as the Fishbowl [*Pecera*], because since most of the partitions were made of glass, people could be observed as if they were in a fishbowl. The Fishbowl offices were used for, among other tasks, filing newspapers and magazines, writing essays and press articles, and translating documents. Guards were posted at the entrances to the Fishbowl and Capucha.

A storeroom, used to store objects stolen from the captives and seized during kidnapping operations—clothing, furniture, utensils, and appliances—was always located somewhere on the Third Floor.

Facing the entrance to the Third Floor was a small door that opened onto a staircase that lead to the Attic, which was known as Capuchita. There captives endured even worse conditions than in Capucha. At one time, captives of the Naval Intelligence Service were held there.

Oppressors

Included are legal names, photographs, and ranks of ESMA oppressors cited in the text. Ranks are those held while the oppressors were members of the GT3.3.2 (rank equivalents are listed at the end of this section).

ABDALA: Lieutenant Commander Luis D'Imperio, chief of SIN and later the GT3.3.2 (alias "Abdala")

AGOSTI: Orlando Ramón Agosti, air force officer

ANT: Orlando González, NCO of the navy (alias "Hormiga" [Ant])

BLONDIE: Lieutenant Junior Grade Alfredo Ignacio Astiz (alias "Ángel," "Rubio" [Blondie], "Cuervo" [Crow], "Gonzalo," or "Alberto Escudero")

CAT: Ensign Alberto González Menotti, intelligence officer (alias "Gato" [Cat] or "Luis")

CHAMORRO: Rear Admiral Rubén Jacinto Chamorro, director of the Navy Mechanics School until early 1979 (alias "Delfín" [Dolphin] or "Máximo")

COLORS: Juan Antonio del Cerro, oppressor in the Athletic Club, the Bank, and the Olympus camps

DUKE: Lieutenant Commander Francis William Whamond (alias "Duque" [Duke])

ESPEJAIME: Subprefecto Roberto Rubén Carnot, coast guard officer (alias "Ricardo" or "Espejaime" ["Gadget"])

FEDERICO: Assistant Chief of Police Roberto Oscar González, federal police officer (alias "Federico," "Obdulio" or "Gonzalito")

FELIPE: Lieutenant Alejandro Spinelli (alias "Felipe")

FRAGOTE: Carlos Generoso, NCO of the Federal Penitentiary Service (alias "Augustin" or "Fragote" ["Conniver"])

GERÓNIMO: Lieutenant Adolfo Donda Tigel (alias "Palito" [Stick] or "Gerónimo")

GIRAFFE: Lieutenant Hugo Damario (alias "Carlos" or "Jirafa" [Giraffe])

GRANDFATHER: An udentified GREEN, a young student at the Navy Mechanics School

HUNCHBACK: Lieutenant Fernando Peyón (alias "Giba" [Hunchback], "Gerardo," "Cuasimodo," "Eveready," "Mochila" [Backpack], or "Eugenio")

JUAN CARLOS: Sergeant Juan Carlos Linares, NCO of the federal police (alias "gordo [fat] Juan Carlos")

JUAN: Lieutenant Juan Carlos Rolón, intelligence officer (alias "Juan" or "Niño" [Boy])

JULIAN THE TURK: Julio Simón, oppressor in the Athletic Club, the Bank, and the Olympus camps

JUNGLE: Subprefecto Héctor Antonio Febres, coast guard officer (alias "Selva" [Jungle] or "Daniel")

LAMBRUSCHINI: Admiral Armando Lambruschini, commander of the navy and member of the military junta from September 15, 1978, to September 12, 1981.

LITTLE APPLE [Manzanita]: An unidentified physician

MAGNACCO: Jorge Luis Magnacco, a physician.

MANUEL: Lieutenant Miguel Ángel Benazzi Berisso, intelligence officer (alias "Manuel" or "Salomón")

MARCELO: Lieutenant Junior Grade Ricardo Miguel Cavallo (alias "Marcelo" or "Serpico")

MARIANO: Lieutenant Raúl Enrique Scheller, intelligence officer (alias "Pinguino" [Penguin] or "Mariano")

MASSERA: Admiral Emilio Eduardo Massera, commander of the navy and member of the military junta until September 15, 1978 (alias "Cero" [Zero])

PACO: Roberto Naya, NCO of the Federal Penitentiary Service (alias "Paco," "Hernán," or "Carretilla")

PEDRO MORRÓN: Víctor Cardo, NCO of the navy (alias "Pedro Morrón")

PIRANHA: Juan Antonio Azic, member of the coast guard (alias "Piraña" [Piranha])

PUMA: Lieutenant Commander Jorge Perren, chief of operations (alias "Puma," "Morris," or "Octavio")

RIVEROS: General Santiago Omar Riveros, commander of the Military Institutes, where an illegal detention center operated

RUGER: Lieutenant Jorge Radice (alias "Ruger" or "Gabriel")

SPARK: Gonzalo Sánchez, coast guard officer (alias "Chispa" [Spark])

THUNDER: Lieutenant Antonio Pernía, intelligence officer (alias "Trueno" [Thunder], "Martín," or "Rata" [Rat])

TIGER ACOSTA: Lieutenant Commander Jorge Eduardo Acosta, member of the GT3.3.2 from its inception until March 1979, chief of intelligence (alias "Tigre" [Tiger], "Santiago," or "Aníbal")

VIDELA: Jorge Rafael Videla, Argentine dictator

Listed below are GT3.3.2 personnel whose aliases are based on their role in camp operations.

GREENS [Verdes]: Students of the Navy Mechanics School (very young and usually of humble, rural origins) recruited to guard prisoners in sectors such as Capucha, Capuchita, and the Basement

GUSTAVS [Gustavos]: Young NCOs who worked as drivers for errands

LITTLE PAULS [Pablitos]: GREENS responsible for escorting captives—"*walled up*" and *hooded*—from place to place in the camp and transporting food from the kitchen to the detention center

OPERATIVES [Operativos]: Officers and NCOs from the Task Force involved in planning and carrying out *operations* including home invasions, raids, and kidnappings

PETERS [Pedros]: NCOs in charge of the GREENS and the LITTLE PAULS

ROTATIVOS: Navy officers who served temporary stints in the Task Force, who were rotated in as a way of implicating the entire force in illegal acts of repression

Rank Equivalents
Argentine Navy
    Admiral: Almirante
    Rear Admiral: Contraalmirante
    Captain: Capitán de Navío
    Commander: Capitán de Fragata
    Lieutenant Commander: Capitán de Corbeta
    Lieutenant: Teniente de Navío
    Lieutenant Junior Grade: Teniente de Fragata
    Ensign: Teniente de Corbeta
    Noncommissioned officer (NCO), enlisted man: Suboficial
Coast Guard
    Prefectura: Prefecto and Subprefecto
Federal Police
    Sergeant: Sargento

LAMBRUSCHINI:
Admiral Armando Lambruschini.

MASSERA:
Admiral Emilio Eduardo Massera.

TIGER [Tigre]: Lieutenant Commander Jorge Eduardo Acosta.

Chamorro: Rear Admiral Rubén
Jacinto Chamorro.

Mariano: Lieutenant Raúl
Enrique Scheller.

Juan: Lieutenant Juan
Carlos Rolón.

Manuel: Lieutenant Miguel
Ángel Benazzi Berisso.

Thunder [Trueno]:
Lieutenant Antonio Pernía.

Blondie [Rubio]: Lieutenant
Junior Grade Alfredo Ignacio Astiz.

Cat [Gato]:
Ensign Alberto González Menotti.

Gerónimo:
Lieutenant Adolfo Donda Tigel.

Marcelo: Lieutenant Junior Grade
Ricardo Miguel Cavallo.

Juan Carlos: Sergeant Juan
Carlos Linares.

Hᴜɴᴄʜʙᴀᴄᴋ [Giba]: Lieutenant
Fernando Peyón.

Pᴀᴄᴏ: Roberto Naya, NCO of the
Federal Penitentiary Service.

Pɪʀᴀɴʜᴀ [Piraña]: Juan Antonio Azic,
member of the coast guard.

Pᴇᴅʀᴏ Mᴏʀʀóɴ: Víctor Cardo,
NCO of the navy.

Slang Used by the Militants[3]

appointment [*cita*]: A place and time for several people to meet, usually including security measures.

bust up a house [*reventar una casa*]: To perform an operation in which repressive forces break into a home, detain and/or murder the residents, and destroy the property.

cell [*ámbito*]: An organizational entity associated with a specific function or area of action within the structure of the Montoneros Organization.

Column (e.g., West) [*Columna (Oeste)*]: A regional grouping of militants, based on the organigram of the Montoneros Organization.

compartmentalize/close up [*compartimentar/cerrar*]: To transfer persons to an unfamiliar location, taking measures to prevent them from seeing or recalling anything that would make it possible to reconstruct the route (for the purpose of protecting local residents or frequent visitors to the area who might *fall* (see below) and be forced to undergo interrogation).

control: A security measure; a mechanism to monitor the presence and status of militants following an event in which their security was placed at risk.

fall: [*caída*]: A capture, kidnapping, or disappearance. *To fall*: to be detained, captured, or kidnapped.

gang [*patota*]: A group of oppressors.

hook up [*enganchar*]: To carry out political activities based on a connection with other members of the Montoneros Organization or, minimally, to be in regular contact with other militants. *Unhook* [*Desenganchar*]: To lose or fail to have contact with fellow militants and political activity at some fundamental level.

lightning action [*acto relámpago*]: A political action carried out without prior notice in order to avoid repression. It entailed showing up unexpectedly in a certain place (generally an open area), distributing pamphlets, chanting slogans, and then quickly leaving the area.

nom de guerre [*nombre de guerra*]: An alias chosen by each militant for security reasons, to keep real names from becoming known within the Montoneros Organization.

pill [*pastilla*]: A cyanide capsule—and later other substances with equally lethal effects—which militants carried with them to avoid being taken alive.

*responsable**: the organizational and/or military head or chief of a group of militants functioning as a unit.

tapped telephone [*teléfono pinchado*]: Telephone monitored by the repressive forces using illegal wire-tapping devices.

under wraps [*guardado*]: Restricted to a safe house because one's security has been jeopardized.

---

3. *Translator's Note*: Spanish terms marked with an asterisk remain in the text.

vacate [*levantarse*]: To abandon or dismantle a residence or operational site because of the suspicion or certainty of its discovery by the repressive forces.

vise [*pinza*]: An armed forces control-and-intimidation operation carried out along public roadways. In general, it consisted of unexpectedly stopping public transportation or closing off access to stations or other public places in order to check identity documents and/or search luggage or other belongings, often resulting in detentions or kidnappings.

Slang Used at the ESMA

*chupadero** [*maw* or *gullet*]: A clandestine detention camp, a concentration camp (see "Suck up" [*Chupar*]).

dog pack [*perrada*]: A group of captives assigned to remodeling and maintenance tasks in the camp.

do KP duty [*hacer el rancho*]: Provide the basics, including food for lunch or dinner.

electric prod/machine [*picana/máquina*]: A device that produced adjustable electric shocks, used as a torture instrument; electric cattle prod. *To use the prod/to shock* [*Picanear*]: To torture using the electric prod.

expedition/outing/launch [*lancheo/paseo*]: A "fishing expedition," a search operation for potential detainees, without a specific target, that involved taking captives out to public places, usually in an automobile or a specially outfitted traffic vehicle.

finger [*dedo*]: The action and effect of pointing out or identifying a person whose detention or control would contribute to the advancement of the concentration-extermination project of the repressive forces.

flights [*vuelos*]: A mechanism used to make the bodies of the detainees disappear, consisting of throwing them from a navy aircraft into the Río de la Plata or the ocean after administering a pentothal injection.

free zone [*zona libre*]: A defined area or radius that was free of interference by legal forces, which facilitated a Task Force's actions during an *operation*.

get one's hands dirty [*poner los dedos*]: To collaborate, to participate actively in repressive actions.

hood [*capucha*] A covering made of dark cloth without eyeholes that was placed over a person's head to prevent him or her from seeing. It provoked a stronger sense of disorientation and isolation than the *mask* (see below).

mark [*marcar*]: To denounce, point out, and identify a person in sight, usually in the context of an *operation*.

marker [*marcador*]: Denouncer (see *finger*).

mask [*anteojito/antifaz/tabique*]: A type of mask made of dark cloth without eyeholes, used to blindfold people.

mini-staff: A group of captives incorporated into the navy's *recuperation process* (see below), implemented in the ESMA. They had a closer relationship with the oppressors than the rest of the prisoners and collaborated actively with the MASSERA project.

monta: A pejorative term used by navy personnel to refer to the Montoneros Organization.

operation [*Operativo*]: A procedure usually conducted either to eliminate people or to kidnap them and take them to the camp.

operations house [*casa operativa*]: A residential-type structure where captives were taken after an *operation* and temporarily housed until the decision was made to release them, send them to a camp, or physically eliminate them.

package [*paquete*]: A pejorative term used by the oppressors to refer to someone held captive in the ESMA.

penta/pentonaval: A pentothal injection—its effect is anesthetic rather than directly lethal—administered to captives with a *transfer* order (see below) before proceeding with the elimination of their bodies, usually by throwing them into the sea during *flights*. The term "*naval*," referring to the navy, was used for all medications administered there.

*perejiles/perejilas** [*Parsleys*]: Novices or low-level militants in the structure of the Montoneros Organization; small fries.

recuperation process [*proceso de recuperación*]: A plan implemented by navy personnel in the ESMA camp in which a captive gradually improved his or her conditions of confinement by demonstrating a change in militant behavior (based on the navy's parameters and opinions) and/or by contributing work or intellectual production to the MASSERA plan. Inclusion in this process did not follow any objective criteria. It represented a stronger probability—but by no means a guarantee—of survival.

send up [*mandar para arriba*]: To murder or eliminate, usually by lethal injection (see *penta/pentonaval*).

sing [*cantar*]: To provide information to the interrogators in the concentration camp under torture or by any other means of coercion.

suck up [*chupar*]: To kidnap or capture by force and without a legal warrant.

staff: A group of detainees incorporated into the *recuperation process*.

submarine [*submarino*]: A torture method consisting of cutting off the victim's breathing just short of drowning, through submersion—either total or the head only—in water. A variation of "dry" *submarine* was carried out using plastic bags to cut off breathing.

through the front door [*por derecha*]: Legal, official. Specifically with regard to detentions: through legal channels, and therefore recognized by the authorities.

through the back door [*por izquierda*]: Illegal, unofficial. Specifically with regard to detentions: through kidnapping, imposing the status of "disappeared."

transfer [*traslado*]: A euphemism for execution, murder, consummation of the detainee's death sentence; it was usually carried out by administering pentothal and then tossing the body into the river during a *flight*.

visit [*visita*]: A meeting between the detainee and his or her family members outside the camp, generally at the home of parents or other relatives. The detainees were transported by officers or members of the Task Force. At first the meetings were brief, with the oppressors present and watching, but they were gradually extended to several days without a guard present.

wall up [*tabicar*]: A concept equivalent to *compartmentalize/close up*, meaning in this case to ensure that detainees could not identify people or places when they were transferred from one area of the camp to another or as they entered or left the camp.

zumbo: Slang for noncommissioned officer (NCO).

Additional Spanish Terms

*compañero** (fem. *compañera*): A term used frequently to refer to fellow militants ("the *compañeros*") but which also indicates a spouse, partner, boyfriend, or girlfriend (my *compañero/a*") or a colleague or friend.

*marinos:** A generic term for navy officers and personnel.

*mate** (mah´ teh): A popular beverage similar to tea prepared by boiling leaves.

*milicos:** A derogatory slang term referring to military personnel.

"A Mantle of Memory"

Introduction to the Conversations

Only take heed to thyself. . . . Lest thou forget
the things which thine eyes have seen . . .
teach them to thy sons, and thy sons' sons.
—Deuteronomy 4:9

It was difficult to begin. We cannot remember whose idea it was. But the need to speak, to leave a record of what we endured in the Navy Mechanics School suddenly took hold of us as an almost physical imperative.

We are five women. Some of us were in captivity together: we have been friends ever since. Some of us knew each other only in name, because our time in captivity did not overlap. But having passed through that inferno was badge enough. Now we are sisters. We began meeting in 1998 to weave our memories, at a time when the twentieth anniversary of the coup still echoed and judges were sending military leaders to prison.

After surviving a concentration camp, it is possible to live a seemingly normal life. You work, take the kids to school, travel, shop, go to the movies. Until—sometimes forcibly, destructively, searing like a lightening bolt or else softly, stealthily, enveloping like a fog—the concentration camp resurfaces. And you become paralyzed: you distinguish the smells; you see darkness; you hear the chains dragging, the metallic clanging of the doors, the sparks from the electric prod; you feel the fear, the weight of the disappearances. And above all, you feel the void left behind by the disappearances. Occasionally over the years—sometimes triggered by specific events (a summons to testify at a trial, the news of a recovered infant, or the anniversary of a *fall*) or perhaps by an old photograph, a yellowed letter in a closet, a passage read—the memories, lying in wait, would ambush us.

For a while we were convinced that it was enough to testify before the judicial authorities. Some of us were able to do so in another country, immediately after our liberation; others testified at the trial of the juntas after democracy had been restored in Argentina; for still others the process took longer for various reasons. But we all knew that we had been through certain kinds of experiences that had yet to be told: stories of hate and solidarity; stories of attachments, cowardice, challenge, and resistance; stories of death but also of life. In the ESMA, as in any concentration camp, there were lights and shadows. We could die without ever sharing them or simply forget. But we decided that it was time to make sure these stories would never be lost.

It is uncomfortable to recall these stories—they are not easily told. They cause anguish, stir up pain. They bring us face to face with forgotten passions, extreme situations. Jorge Semprún, a survivor of the Nazi extermination camp Auschwitz, was able to put his stories to paper only after forty years had passed. To evoke them earlier, he said, would have kept him from living. For us—bridging the distances among us—this collective experience of systematic recollection was possible only after twenty years had passed.

The work of harvesting our experience in taped discussions over three and a half years was fraught with its own difficulties. Nonetheless, we were determined to do it. There had to be a record—other than the legal files confined to cold, objective facts—of what happened in the ESMA, perhaps the most Machiavellian of all the repressive projects of the last Argentine dictatorship.

We chose to remember together, because we believe that our survival in that place was a collective undertaking. Isolation was a tool that the oppressors used to force us to succumb, to break us: for those held in Capucha, partitions, "hoods," and injunctions against speaking to fellow captives were the rule.

We decided to limit our group to women, because our experience in the concentration camp was colored in special ways by our gender: nudity and humiliation, sexual harassment by our oppressors, relationships with our pregnant compañeras and their children. For our male compañeros, the time spent in the ESMA surely evoked different types of feelings.

For our meetings we chose a room in Miriam's house. We usually met on Saturday afternoons. At no time, essentially until our last discussion, did we have a clear idea of what to do with the cassettes, which we recorded on an ancient but noble tape recorder that Munú carried to and fro (along with cassettes and batteries) in a little plastic bag in her purse. "Maybe we should put them in a safe-deposit box," said one. "Turn them over to a human rights organization or to the National Historical Archive," proposed another. The decision to publish them was made almost at the end, after we had had numerous discussions and had managed to overcome many fears and misgivings. We had spoken only among women, with no witnesses other than ourselves, with our affection and our understanding—the kind of understanding that can be given only by someone who has been through the same experience.

Revealing experiences that we had silenced for so long left us feeling terribly exposed. At various times in our lives, each of us had faced the distrust caused by the fact that we had survived being in the hands of an enemy that had annihilated most of its prisoners. During our conversations, we asked ourselves the same question over and over again, like a litany: Why are we alive? Miriam did an interview with a Schindler's list survivor, who asks himself, "Why us? And the others?" He does not have the answer, and neither do we.

In the terrace room where we chose to meet were windows through which you could see the sky, sometimes clear and sometimes blackened by storm. There were rounds of *mate* and coffee, cigarettes and bills, and there were constant comings and goings. Even though we had set a recording time limit of an hour and a half per session, and even though we chased away the fear with laughter, we left the meetings with our wounds reopened. And one fine day, Liliana, one of those who had started out with the most determination, said she could take it no more. She took a leave of absence for more than a year, allowed the scars to form, and came back stronger than ever. We welcomed her with open arms and virtually no inquiry. United by the concentration camp in an almost blood kinship, we are used to giving each other companionship and accepting each other in good times and bad.

Over the years of these appointments with memory, life also shook us up. In the early days of our meetings, Elisa underwent the final phase of chemotherapy, which she faced with the same will to live that she had demonstrated in the camp. Cristina was elected councilwoman, and her schedule became increasingly full as, together with her colleagues, she faced corruption, political expediencies, and the challenges of building a collective project (illnesses of our times that are intimately related to this story). Liliana's only daughter, like many other girls her age, left Argentina to live with her father. Miriam toured the concentration camps of Europe as a journalist, working on stories of survivors of the Holocaust. In those stories she found correlations that left her more shaken than she had expected. Munú finally was able to create a plastic sculpture in honor of her disappeared partner, and she began to cry out her pain.

Each one of us went through unique, unrepeatable experiences. Our conversations do not necessarily reflect by debate the fact that we have different views on many of the situations that we lived through in the concentration camp. On the contrary, sometimes one of us would sink into a melancholic silence that the rest of us would try unsuccessfully to break. There were many days that we all fell silent, stunned into speechlessness by the confession of a member of the group.

But more often than not, laughter flooded the table. The group used humor as a tool to ward off the anguish that would have otherwise become unbearable and kept us from continuing. The distance and apparent coldness with which we related some events were also resources that we called on to defend ourselves against the blows leveled by the past.

We created a climate of affection and tolerance that made these conversations possible. There was no pressure: each one of us related what she felt able to recall. Our memory was an animal, sometimes rebellious, bucking, hard to tame. This probably would have been a different book entirely if it had been written several years or a decade earlier.

We were not always alone. Adriana Marcus[1] was also kidnapped and held in the ESMA. Today she is a physician living in Zapala, in southern Argentina. As part of her work through the public hospital, she provides services to suburban and rural populations, including Mapuche communities, visiting them in their homes in remote areas where there are few visitors. On several occasions, she left her job, took a bus to Buenos Aires, and joined our "tea parties" (as she, with her own particular irony, called them). She is one of us, even though she was not with us at every gathering. Her stories are an integral part of our testimony.

Mirta Clara's case was different.[2] Mirta, who was confined in an official prison for eight years, now works as a psychoanalyst for victims of repression. As a result, she was one of the first people to read our material, and she came to one of our meetings. After hearing her point of view, her piercing analysis of the similarities and differences between the prison and the concentration camp, we felt that it was essential to include her. Our intention was not, however, to enter into any psychological or philosophical interpretations beyond those that arose naturally in our conversations. Our intention was simply to harvest memories as best we could at that stage of our lives.

This book is just one small piece of the "mantle of memory" that Juan Gelman describes:

---

1. Adriana Marcus was born on October 12, 1955, in the federal capital of Argentina. She was kidnapped on August 26, 1978, when she was in her fifth year of medical studies at the National University of Buenos Aires. At the time, she was also doing a hospital rotation at the Castex Hospital in San Martín and was working as a nurse in a clinic. On April 24, 1979, she was granted supervised release and was subjected to forced labor until February 1980. Currently she is a general practitioner at Zapala Hospital in Neuquén and directs the Urban and Rural Program.

2. Mirta Clara was detained on October 9, 1975. She and her husband, Néstor Carlos Sala, were held incommunicado for one month in the Resistance Investigations Brigade in Chaco. Subsequently, she was held as a legally recognized prisoner in the Chaco, Formosa, Ezeiza, and Devoto Prisons, until her release on November 9, 1983. Her husband was executed in the Margarita Belén Massacre (Chaco) on December 13, 1976. Mirta is a psychologist who conducts research on the resources people employ to survive situations of extreme subjugation.

What a mantle of collective memory could be woven from those pieces of unspoken memory, fragmented and dispersed, that many witnesses and victims keep to themselves, as if immobilized in their former place. A mantle of solace and protection against possible recurrences. The crimes of the past inhabit what they have silenced within them in the present.[3]

There were hundreds of survivors; there are tens of thousands of families of the disappeared. Countless pieces must still be joined painstakingly so that this mantle, immense and paternal, may envelop us all, forever.

---

3. From an article by prominent Argentine poet Juan Gelman, "Del Silencio," August 13, 1998: www.pagina12web.com.ar

Identification of Actors Present in This Chronicle

Oppressors:

Oppressors are referred to by the aliases by which they were known in the concentration camp. Their legal names and, in many cases, their photographs are in included in the previous section, pages 9–15.

Captives:

Each author's statements are preceded by her current name or nickname.

Other captives in the text are identified by the *noms de guerre* by which they were known by their peers in the concentration camp.

Captives who played prominent roles in controversial situations in the concentration camp are identified by the initial two letters of their names only.

Although the actions and responsibilities of the detained-disappeared vis-à-vis the concentration camp authorities are currently the subject of a debate in which the opinions of the authors themselves conflict, they are in agreement that the incidents in question must be disclosed.

1

The Preceding Days and the Kidnapping

> What is going on, what mysteries are these, in what sort of fatal mechanism have we become enmeshed? The answer cannot simply be that we are all cowards. We are not that bad. We stand before a much deeper question.
>
> —Etty Hillesum (Dutch Jewish linguist, lawyer, and psychologist murdered in Auschwitz), *Letters from Westerbork*

Militancy had changed. It was no longer that rich experience, akin to happiness, that had taken hold of us. From 1976 on, danger, torture, and death loomed ever closer. Militancy was marked by exhaustion, abandonment, and fear. Terror closed doors that once were opened to militants. They were corralled, battered by the almost daily disappearance of loved ones. Some chose to commit suicide at the moment of capture. This, at least, ensured that (1) they would not turn in their fellow militants under torture and (2) they would posthumously deprive those responsible for the disappearances of the small victory of the decision of death itself.

Munú: Our history as militants evolved gradually. As the repression intensified, our type of militancy forced us to engage in a pretense with others that later helped us to resist inside the ESMA.

Miriam: Yes, maybe that's why we were able to develop a strategy of pretense to defend ourselves against the *marinos*.

Liliana: Outside, we already had experienced a clandestine life, hiding our militancy from others. Our family relationships also had been disrupted; there was a lot of covering up.

Munú: Every day I would put on my nicest face and go out to sweep the front walk of my house, just like all the other neighborhood women, and I'd chat with the woman next door, the one across the street. They weren't people I'd known since I was little; I had nothing in common with them. And when we went shopping, we always took the same basket with us so we could use it later to take out something we didn't want them to see. I think we had displaced our fear of death. We knew they could kill us at any moment, but it wasn't a constant or paralyzing thought: we worked, we studied, we fell in love, we had children, plans. And so, when we *fell*[1] in the ESMA, that fear was still displaced.

Liliana: That's probably how it was.

Elisa: I heard rumors about what was happening, but I said, "That much perversion just can't be real." Once, a colleague from the Actors' Guild who'd been *sucked up* and then released said that he'd seen the marinos and the captives in the ESMA toasting the New Year together.

Liliana: It must have been true.

Elisa: Of course! But when they told me about it—

Miriam: You said, "That's crazy!"

Elisa: Right! The worst rumors circulated about the ESMA. People said they cut off your fingers with a saw.

Adriana: So that would be why, when I *fell*, they motioned as if they were cutting off my hands!

Miriam: The rumor going around on the outside was that they put rats into your vagina in the ESMA.

Elisa: When I *fell*, during the torture, they asked me, "From what you know or what you've heard, where would you least like to be?" I said, "In the ESMA." And they replied, "You are in the ESMA." They must have asked a lot of people the same question.

Miriam: It was the same old line, the macabre joke.

Elisa: There was plenty of talk. When I *fell*, they explained to me that they didn't use the saw on detainees; they said they were doing construction, and that's where the noise came from. They were such great guys! [*Laughter*]

Cristina: Civilized people.

Elisa: And you, Cristina, had you heard any of this?

Cristina: I'd heard that there was some sort of *recuperation process*. Those were the rumors going around among the *compañeros*. You never really knew where those kinds of things came from. It was rumored that when people were detained in the ESMA, they immediately had them meet with other captives so they could see how well off they were.

Elisa: Of course, you *fell* later on.

Cristina: I *fell* at the end of 1978.

Liliana: By then there was a lot of water under the bridge.

Elisa: Were you a militant at that time?

---

1. *Authors' Note:* Terms used by the militants and terms used in the ESMA appear in *italics* in the text and are divided on pages 16–17. The oppressors' legal names and aliases appear in SMALL CAPITALS in the text and are listed on pages 9–15. *Translator's Note:* Additional Spanish terms are listed on page 19 and appear in italics at the first mention in the text (for purposes of clarity, "mate" appears in italics throughout the text).

Cristina: I had become disconnected from the Montoneros Organization in late 1976, when the repression became more systematic in the northern zone.[2] Later—at the beginning of 1978—my compañero and I stubbornly attempted to continue our militancy in the capital, but coordination had broken down completely and the security situation was terrible. After a few desperate and unsuccessful attempts, exhausted and disoriented, we decided to try to put our life back together, since by then it had been reduced to the most elemental existence. We tried to find jobs even though we were still underground, and we tried to contact others in the same situation to try to reorganize something. But we were virtually disconnected.

Liliana: We were in denial about what was going on. I think we couldn't stand the thought that the organization had fallen apart, and that's why putting our lives back together was so difficult.

Miriam: I was convinced that they killed everyone who *fell*; I never believed that anyone survived.

Elisa: So when you *fell* in the ESMA and they showed you people who were alive, what did you think?

Miriam: I *fell* in the air force, and they took me to the ESMA about a year later, in the trunk of a Ford Falcon, blindfolded, handcuffed, and shackled—in other words, completely immobilized. They left me there for only one day because there was going to be an inspection. The ESMA people told the air force officer who had brought me there that he had to take me back to the other camp;[3] they couldn't leave me there, because some foreign journalists were going to visit. That was in March 1978, the 26th or the 27th. I *fell* in May 1977. When they took me back to the air force, they opened the trunk, and a *zumbo*—the one who always cooked—asked the officer, "Is she dead?" just as if he were asking, "Is it raining out?" It gave me chills, because the guy knew me; he'd been feeding me for a year!

Elisa: He just passed by and asked, "Is she dead?"

Miriam: As if they'd taken me from the air force to kill me and had brought me back again. So if I still needed confirmation, that was it. The fact that a guy who'd seen me and fed me every day for nearly a year, someone who, since I was the only prisoner there, had had some sort of relationship with me—he would bring me the plate, and we'd exchange two words—should ask in such an offhand way whether I was dead led me to believe that they killed everybody there. Besides, I couldn't understand why they would let us live.

Elisa: We never could understand it, and we'll go on without ever finding an explanation.

---

2. In the Montoneros organizational structure, this refers to the northern zone of greater Buenos Aires.

3. "Camp" is short for concentration camp.

Liliana: You really do keep on being unable to understand it. It keeps on being irrational.

Elisa: When I was there, it never occurred to me to think about death or life. I couldn't conceive of a plan for after I got out. I think the compañeras who testified as soon as they got out of the ESMA had planned it while they were still inside. I spent a lot of time with all of them, but it never would have occurred to me to do it. Now I try to remember what I was thinking at the time, and the sensation I have is that I was sort of encapsulated; I felt as if those things weren't happening to me.

Miriam: It's really hard to recall exactly what we were thinking in there.

Adriana: I couldn't think about life or about death either. It was a chunk of time suspended forever; it was truly like the end of history. After that there would be nothing ever again.

Cristina: Before I *fell*, in conversations with the compañeros, we'd try to imagine what actually happened to the people who disappeared, and we came to the conclusion that they were out there somewhere. It was a defense mechanism; there was no accurate information about what was happening. I remember one compañero who said, "They must be in terrible circumstances, but they are there!" When I *fell*, one of the most painful things was realizing that it wasn't like that.

Elisa: That they weren't there.

Miriam: Before I *fell*, I was living underground, and I was taking certain security precautions, but they were very naïve. For example, my grandmother was dying at the time. I would call her every day to see how she was doing. I knew my parents' telephone might be *tapped*, so I always called from a different phone but in an area where there were only ten public telephones. They disconnected five of them, installed five guys at each of the others, and they hooked me. That's how I got *sucked up*. There were very few public telephones in La Matanza[4] in 1977.

Munú: It didn't occur to you that they could do that kind of thing.

Miriam: I doubt they would have set up that whole apparatus to kidnap me if they hadn't been looking for my friend Patricia, who was a militant and the daughter of a brigadier. I was a low-level militant, a *perejila*. They wanted to get to her, and they thought I would be the link. They wouldn't have used forty guys if I had been the target.

Munú: I'd always been in La Plata,[5] and when I came to Buenos Aires, I got

---

4. La Matanza is a municipality in the western zone of greater Buenos Aires.
5. La Plata is the capital city of Buenos Aires Province.

a contact in the southern zone,[6] in the province, so I could continue to be active in the militant organization. That would have been in April or May of 1997. In order to get *hooked up*, I wrote my life story in tiny handwriting on a very thin piece of paper, and at the bottom I wrote, in big letters, "*Hook* me *up!*" And I passed along the note. I wanted the compañeros who read it to know who I was; I thought maybe there'd be someone out there who knew me. Afterward the marinos made me read it there in the ESMA.

Adriana: How?

Munú: Someone had *fallen* with the note. What happened was this: when the compañeros in the southern zone described the activity they were planning to assign to me, I wasn't in agreement. The only thing left was the military structure of the organization. Besides, I would have been in charge—the *responsable*—of a *cell*, and I didn't feel capable of making decisions involving other compañeros. I could barely make decisions for myself. I kept in contact with them so I could collaborate in some way. As people *fell*, one after the other, the compañeros were becoming homeless, without pots and pans or clothes. So I would collect used clothing, and once every twenty days I would go to an *appointment* in that zone to deliver it. On one of those occasions two Ford Falcons appeared.

Elisa: And they *sucked* you *up*?

Munú: No, I didn't *fall* that time. I saw them coming up a dirt road, and I took off running across the fields. It was near the Alpargatas factory.

Miriam: So you tossed the clothes!

Munú: No, instead of throwing them away, I clung to them. And in the middle of my flight, it started to pour down rain. And I kept on running. I walked across Route 2 to General Belgrano Road. I couldn't get on a bus for the capital soaking wet in the middle of the night, so I knocked on the door of a house and told my story to the lady who opened the door. I asked her whether she would let me in to change out of my wet clothes, and I showed her what I had in the bag. She let me in, I changed, and I went to catch the Río de la Plata.[7] I'd gotten away one more time.

Adriana: A lot of us let down our guard about security measures. I had everything arranged to go to Paysandú:[8] I had a place to stay, and I even had a German passport, because, once I got to Uruguay, I planned to go to the German Embassy. I went to keep an *appointment* with La Flaca, whose mother-in-law was going to be there too, but they weren't there. I should

---

6. This refers to the southern zone of greater Buenos Aires according to the organizational structure of the Montoneros.

7. Río de la Plata is a passenger transportation company.

8. Paysandú is a city in Uruguay.

have left the country right then, but I didn't. I thought, "Something must have happened to her." And something had! When I tell it now, it seems suicidal, but I went home just the same. When I arrived, the *milicos* were waiting for me.

Munú: I did something similar. In November 1976, a huge number of people *fell* in La Plata, and they kidnapped my husband. It was the second big roundup. They'd been telling me for a while that I should leave because I was very well known, but I couldn't do it because my compañero had to stay. I thought about leaving after he *fell*, but then the leadership of the organization asked me to stay. A lot of new people had come in who weren't familiar with the zone, and they wanted me to help orient them. I went on vacation in January, and when I came back, all the members of my *cell* had *fallen*. I went into a state of paralysis; I couldn't leave the city. I felt that if I left, I'd be abandoning all those who had *fallen*. I was alone, shut up inside a house. I lived on what I could knit by hand, one sweater per day. Once a week I would go to a boutique, they'd give me a bag of yarn, and I'd hand over a bag of pullovers. I'd go back with the yarn, and I'd knit and knit. So what was I doing in La Plata?

Elisa: You couldn't leave.

Munú: No. Eventually I was able to, and I came to Buenos Aires in April 1977. I stayed in the province for security reasons.

Elisa: What security?

Munú: I was afraid of the *vises* in the capital. They had a special device here that they used to check your identity documents.

Adriana: The Digicom[9] that the patrollers had.

Munú: And I wasn't sure about mine; I didn't know whether or not they had a file on me. When I was able to leave La Plata, I began to think about leaving the country too. It was very hard for me to leave everything behind. In any event, you were supposed to stay and die. I never believed what a lot of people thought, that the people who had disappeared were alive somewhere; I thought they were all dead. Maybe it was because in La Plata they had killed so many people in the street and that was where they threw the bodies of the compañeros who had disappeared. So I started to do the paperwork to get a passport. I had heard that if you were applying and they told you to go to the second floor, you had to leave right away. I started the application process, they sent me to the second floor, and I . . . out I went! And while all of this is true, I'm not sure to what extent I really was doing everything necessary to leave. I had those papers with me when I *fell* in the ESMA, and during the torture I used them as part of my story, which they believed at first.

9. The Digicom was a centralized information system in police mobile units.

Elisa: I didn't consider leaving. I really didn't have any way to do it or anywhere to go. Even after I *fell*, I still thought that the people who left were traitors.

Munú: It was one thing to consider leaving in 1976 and quite another in 1978. It seemed as if ten years had passed, and it had been only two!

Elisa: You didn't know where the organization was, what had happened, how to get yourself *hooked up* or *unhooked*. You were the living dead. Everything beautiful about the militants, the custom of getting together with the compañeros, the activities you participated in, all of that was disappearing. You couldn't sleep in your house or have your things.

Miriam: There were many times when I didn't have any place to sleep!

Adriana: There was an absence of support from the whole apparatus of our militant organization.

Elisa: So you started to criticize, asking, "Where are the compañeros now, when I need them? How do I keep going?"

Adriana: I never criticized; at that time I thought everyone had *fallen*. We got together at my parents' house for Christmas in 1977: Andrea, her husband, the baby, La Flaca with her little girl, their brother-in-law (Chango), a friend of his, and me. As we were leaving, they kidnapped Andrea's husband. The following month we went on vacation to Villa Gesell with our *responsable*, and when we got back, they *sucked* him *up*, along with Chango and the other skinny guy. We three women were left alone without any contact with anyone, trying to live a normal life and not succeeding. You had to stick to the story that you yourself had invented—explain to the neighbors who you were and what you did, and make sure everything sounded consistent with the fictitious person you were pretending to be. You had to be careful to avoid contradictions. It was a schizophrenic situation that had become intolerable. We were no longer active in the militant organization, yet we had the stigma of having been, and we felt the moral obligation, the desire, the need, the commitment to continue our militancy even though we knew we could not. I think this also contributed to the big roundups.

Elisa: It was as if you were dead in life, with no militant organization, no plan whatsoever.

Adriana: It was all or nothing. And if it wasn't all, it was nothing, and that's how you saw it.

Elisa: That was our existence. You didn't consciously register what was going on, or you didn't want to. In my case, all of my compañeros in the militant organization had *fallen* except for Víctor. I was *unhooked*, and I saw him only occasionally until we lost contact. And I don't even know how I ended up in the northern zone, which I had nothing to do with. At the first meeting, they invited me to Mantecol's birthday party.

Miriam: I can't believe it!

Elisa: That's where I met Roque, and Mantecol, and Bichi. They *fell* during the same raid as I did but a few days earlier. They were my reference points during my first days in the ESMA.

Liliana: Before my capture, I felt a sense of irritation toward society. I was angry. I think it was a consequence of the isolation, which, perhaps because of my own immaturity, turned into resentment. It would be worth doing a political analysis on the feeling that society didn't include you. And it didn't, because ultimately there was a problem in the political project.

Miriam: The virulence of the repression also played an important role. I remember that my compañero, who'd been underground since June 1976, gradually lost his rear guard, places where he could stay. People would tell him, "Look, if I were single, I'd lend you the apartment, but now I'm married, and I have a baby, and I'm scared to." Or you'd ask relatives whether they could wash your clothes, and they would get furious, or you'd lose contact with even your parents, because they still had teenagers at home and they were afraid they'd be *sucked up.* You had the feeling that they'd take anyone, not only militants: they'd take people who were committed, those who weren't so committed, friends, relatives. And the stories of repression that were going around were so savage that the people who loved you, who otherwise would have opened the door to you, closed it instead. You ended up completely alone. People felt as though even a telephone call from you could be compromising.

Elisa: We had given up. I remember experiencing that, toward the end. My loneliness was so extreme that I sank into depression, into my sorrow over the loss of the people I loved. One night I felt as though I didn't have any place to sleep, so I joined a wake.

Liliana: For someone you didn't know?

Elisa: Of course. There was a funeral home on the corner of Deán Funes and Chiclana. I thought, "Where can I spend the night? I don't have anywhere to go." It wasn't really that bad; I guess if I'd rung the doorbell of any of my friends from high school, from the neighborhood, they would have let me in.

Liliana: You don't know that.

Elisa: But they were school friends who weren't even aware of my militancy.

Liliana: With what was going on, people in any family home were likely to be afraid that some acquaintance would knock on their door and say, "I want to sleep here."

Elisa: I didn't even try to knock on a door to see whether or not they'd let me in. I took myself down to that funeral home where they were holding a wake for a man, and I sat down and started to cry. I cried all the pent-up tears from all those deaths. I even started to become the center of attention, because I was crying harder than the widow.

Liliana: And no one asked you who you were?

Elisa: No one dared.

Liliana: I think they knew, and it didn't bother them.

Elisa: They were unwitting allies. They were immersed in their own sorrow. No one asked me whether I was a colleague from work or a neighbor. They served me coffee. And I cried until I was tired of crying, and then I left.

Cristina: Something like that happened to me, but it was after I got out of the ESMA. I went to the countryside, and when I came back, a friend of my parents died, a wonderful person. I cared about him, but he wasn't my best friend or anything. I went to the wake, and I was in anguish—as if it were my father instead of a friend. I couldn't stop crying. I think I did it to make up for all the times before when I hadn't been able to cry. Before we *fell*, so many times we choked back the pain of losing compañeros! You couldn't just break down and cry in the middle of the street.

Miriam: A lot of strange situations arose for lack of a place to stay. I was living with a compañera in a rooming house in Ciudadela,[10] and they kidnapped her. We'd set a time limit on waiting for each other: if she didn't come, I had to leave. I waited for an hour and a half, and finally I *vacated*. I had no place to sleep. I got in touch with my boyfriend, and we decided to go to a little place we'd rented and were fixing up, a little apartment behind a house in Villa Madero.[11] We arrived at the empty apartment at night in a torrential rainstorm, and we lay down on the floor. The owner, a widow, upset because she had heard noises, sent her son, and he came in with a flashlight. Those people, in their solidarity, brought us a mattress. I don't remember what excuse we invented—something like we'd forgotten the key to the place where we were living or the lock had broken and we couldn't find a locksmith. Sometimes you would sleep with a compañero at a hotel and of course nothing would happen. I remember once when they had kidnapped the girlfriend of my *responsable*, and he didn't have any place to sleep. So we decided that I would go with him to a hotel. I know compañeros who did it all the time.

Liliana: Yes, that happened to me too.

Miriam: I remember that it was really funny; I went in and lay down on the bed, and he threw his jacket on the floor to sleep there. I told him, laughing, to stop screwing around. Poor guy, his girlfriend had been kidnapped.

---

10. Ciudadela is located in greater Buenos Aires.

11. Villa Madero is located in greater Buenos Aires.

Afterward we found out that they kept her alive for a long time before they killed her. You had nowhere to go, and you were just running scared in the streets. You had to work it out any way you could.

Liliana: That final period in La Plata—the last weeks before I went to Mar del Plata—since I'd studied nursing, I had a lot of friends working in the hospitals. I'm not sure whether or not they believed me, but I would tell them I wanted to do the night shift with them.

Elisa: They didn't know about your militancy.

Liliana: No, they didn't know. I told them I did it to learn, and I would spend the night—worn out because all I wanted to do was sleep—on the cots for the hospital night shift.

Miriam: And you slept?

Liliana: I slept when they slept. You usually sleep during the night shift. If something urgent came up, I worked with them. But I felt worn out and incredibly isolated.

Elisa: For me there was a before and an after. All of us intuited that ferocious repression, but I experienced it differently. And when my compañeros *fell*, it distorted my reality. I began to feel a terrible weight and horrific fear. I was constantly thinking, "Should I go to this house? Is it safe? And if I leave, where will I sleep? Where will I bathe?" I worked in the northern zone of the capital, and every day I would go to work wearing the same clothes. I took along deodorant and a change of underwear, and that's how I lived.

Miriam: In general, we had very little clothing. When I moved to that apartment, those last two weeks, the closet was empty. I had a jacket, a pair of pants, and two shirts. And half of those clothes weren't even mine; they belonged to compañeros who had lent them to me. When they raided your house, you weren't about to go looking for your stuff—you couldn't; it was too risky. And sometimes the *gang* took your things.

Cristina: So many times you lost the little that you had in one of the places where you ended up! Maybe you had been staying there for a while and you had to leave suddenly, for security reasons, and the little that you had was left behind. Entire households were lost; they were modest, but they were all we had. I was in those situations where you wandered about aimlessly with no place to sleep, trying to get a little work to buy food for the day. Sometimes we didn't have anyone to turn to get a meal.

Elisa: And to keep on living.

Cristina: I remember my sister and I went a whole day on one café au lait.

Miriam: I had an assignment at that time. I was working; I kept a little cash for the basics, and I gave the rest to the compañeros who were clandestine and didn't have jobs. I was clandestine too, but I had a job. I worked under the table in administration in a furniture factory. Salaries stretched a little farther then than they do now, but I turned over 80 percent of that money to people who had no place to live.

Cristina: You could get work, which would be impossible today. We couldn't show up on the books because we had problems with our identity documents, but you'd take a temporary job to get by. I had the experience of having one job end and going out and getting another one in a day. It wasn't easy to have a more or less stable job and a place to stay where you could relax and live a more normal life, but that's what helped you recover a little.

Miriam: I got work through the newspaper; I'd go out, and within two or three days, I'd get a job.

Elisa: I always took up with the same agency.

Miriam: But you were always careful not to show up on the books; that was dangerous. You had to ask them not to register you, to take you on for a probation period, because you weren't sure what you were going to do. You always made up some story, so they wouldn't write your name down in the books. In my last job, the excuse was that I was about to get married, and my fiancé wanted us to go to Rosario, so I didn't know how long I'd be staying in the job. Always the smoke screen. But the lying didn't affect me so much; what got to me were the deaths every day. You started with a group of seven people, the next day there were six, and within a week only two were left. They all *fell*.

Liliana: But you also formed very intense relationships. Groups came together and gradually fell apart, and you *hooked up* with others. And when you looked back, you realized that you'd developed incredibly strong bonds with someone you'd seen four or five hours a day for a month, someone you suddenly never saw again. Because we were so isolated, our conversations with those compañeros were very intense. Those last days in Mar del Plata, we had nothing to do, so we actually got together just to talk. You ended up spending hours talking to someone you'd met just two days before. That doesn't happen to me now.

Elisa: I remember that six months before I *fell*, I would get together with Petisa, a compañera who had been a militant but who had never had problems with her identity documents. Taking advantage of her legal status, she rented an apartment in her name, so that Pipo, my *responsable*, and his family would have a place to live. She had to implement *controls* practically on a daily basis to make sure everything was all right; otherwise she'd have ended up clandestine herself. When Pipo *fell*, she stayed in touch with Ela, his wife, and they were able to cancel the lease with the real estate company. The bond between Petisa, Ela, and me endured and became very strong. We needed to see each other every week. We'd go to the theater, to the movies. When Ela found out about my *fall*, she broke off that bond, and to this day we don't know what became of her. We think she went to Spain with her mother-in-law.

Miriam: The other thing is that we were relating to people who had suffered huge losses. My *responsable* had a little girl, I think she was two, and his wife was disappeared. Since he was underground, he couldn't see his little daughter, because she was living with her mother's family. Thank God. He had to call a neighbor, go through a whole process, in order to say two words to her by telephone once every two weeks. Imagine the situation that man was living in. He had an enormous need for affection, for someone to hug him, to listen to him.

Cristina: The context was state terrorism.

Elisa: Society was held hostage. Our compañeros who were less active in the militant organization, who were just collaborators, vanished from their usual settings; they left the university, their jobs, because it was too risky to stay. If you were young, you were dangerous.

Cristina: It was my experience that people who hardly knew me would lend a hand, and I think that some compañeros were able to escape the repression thanks to a lot of "anonymous" people. I also had the experience of going to a house and having them refuse to let me in out of fear. And I remember understanding it, because I knew what that was. At varying levels of consciousness, the entire society lived in fear.

Elisa: It was a subjugated society, a generation forced to forgo its plans. Some compañeros left in fear, while others had to change their way of life.

Cristina: A short time ago, I found a tape of a speech given on March 24; I think it was on the twenty-first anniversary of the 1976 coup. I had gone to the speech, and to illustrate the different faces of state terrorism and how it imposed its disciplinary action on society as a whole, I'd taken along some documents that had circulated at the time, alerting people to subversive elements in the educational system: how to detect them, what the signs were, what precautions parents should take, which words to use and which raised a red flag. Words like "commitment," "dialogue," "exploitation," "Latin America!" and group theory, team work, "which impede people's individual development and conceal other ideological interests and concepts." And a text in which MASSERA speaks of the ills of the twentieth century: Freud and psychoanalysis, Einstein and the theory of relativity, and Marx.

Liliana: Concepts that questioned the order of things.

Cristina: The concept of western, Christian life.

Miriam: The genius and words of the admiral.

Munú: I think that *falling* was like saying, "Well, that's that." I imagine it must have been different in 1977, in 1978, and in 1979. As the years went by, you had been resisting longer and becoming more and more worn out, especially if you were no longer active in the militant organziation for whatever reason. In the meantime, they kept on killing everyone around you. You had to hide under the rug for more years, increasingly alone. You arrived at the moment of capture already deflated, finished. We had no structure available to leave the country; we couldn't even consider it. That's why I think that, for a lot of people, the *fall* was like saying, "That's that; it's over." If it had been in 1973 or 1974, even if it seemed utopian, we would have had more spirit; we would have fought differently.

Miriam: Your morale had changed! When we *fell*, our morale was one of defeat. We were defeated internally. That's what many people questioned about the *pill*; it meant that you wouldn't even face the torture, because you just assumed that you wouldn't be able to take it. That's what you assumed, even though later you discovered that, yes, you could. So to protect the rest, the best thing was self-immolation.

Elisa: I think everything had an influence. But your relationship with the Montoneros Organization when you *fell* had a particular influence.

Miriam: But the organization didn't exist!

Munú: It did exist. You knew it was there.

Miriam: And that tomorrow it was going to fall totally to pieces! The organization was defeated, unfortunately.

Elisa: Who would I have found from the organization if I had escaped in 1978? Before I *fell*, the basic structure that I belonged to no longer existed. Out of twenty compañeros, only two of us had survived; the rest—they weren't there! Never again!

Munú: What still existed was outside the country, plus a handful running around in circles here.

Miriam: When I *fell*, in the Western Province,[12] only seven compañeros were left. Every day someone else *fell*; every day there was another casualty. One afternoon in 1976, I arrived for an *appointment* twenty minutes late, and I found my *responsable's* comb lying in a pool of blood; the neighborhood was in an uproar, and the *gang* was whirling about with their rifles outside the Falcons. It was just a matter of time before I *fell*. For me, to have killed myself with the *pill* would have been—the way I saw it at the time—a dignified death, in consideration of others, like the death of Jesus, dying for your friends. That's what I wanted.

Elisa: A dignified death!

---

12. The Western Province was, in the organizational structure of the Montoneros Organization, the western zone of greater Buenos Aires.

Miriam: I was desperate when I couldn't do it; because the *pill* I had was homemade, it was wrapped in half a centimeter of insulation tape.

Elisa: Mine was like that too. Once I put it in my mouth to go to an *appointment* that I was afraid might have been *sung*, and it gave me an infection.

Miriam: The leaders had a glass one that cut the tongue when you bit it so that the cyanide entered the blood stream right away.

Munú: I didn't know whether the glass one even existed; I had a little plastic one.

Cristina: I had a plastic one too, but when I *fell*, it was already ruined, because I'd been carrying it around in my purse for so long.

Miriam: I made mine with my own hands. You know those cotillion lipsticks for little girls? You had to break the black tape around it with your teeth and open the capsule to swallow the cyanide. The black tape was to protect it from the light.

Elisa: Oh no! Mine was wrapped in Scotch tape!

Cristina: Mine was a capsule like the ones used for medication.

Munú: Mine was a capsule too. I covered the regional *appointments* in La Plata, so I got to have one of those.

Miriam: Those were the good ones; ours was just a toy.

Munú: If you only knew how often I went around with the *pill* in my mouth! I'd put it in to go to the *appointment*. Compañeros came from all over, and in the midst of all the chaos, you couldn't tell whether or not the *appointment* had been *sung*. I felt safe that way; my only goal was not to be taken alive.

Liliana: We usually carried it in our purse.

Miriam: A group of us from the Western Province made my *pill*. We used cyanide that we bought from a laboratory. Jewelers use cyanide to detect silver, so I had half a kilo of cyanide at home in the cupboard. [*Laughter and comments*]

Munú: Chiqui told me that when they were captured in Uruguay, she didn't have the *pill*, because she didn't have any information and she didn't want to have it anyway. I didn't know that another girl in the same house had taken the *pill* and died.

Elisa: The children were all in that house?

Munú: Yes, Elena's daughters, Chiqui's, and the daughter of the other compañera. They were all really little.

Liliana: I remember now. That compañera took the *pill* with a baby bottle.

Elisa: Now, from this distance, it seems so horrific to us.

Liliana: The level of madness in which we were immersed.

Elisa: At the time, we were caught up in that whirlpool; we believed it was the best way to defend our project, by saving the other compañeros.

Liliana: What madness!

Munú: Two weeks before I *fell*, I had the *pill* in my mouth because the army was conducting a sweep[13] of the neighborhood in Valentín Alsina,[14] where I was living with a friend, and they were searching all the houses. They arrived at night, surrounded the area, posted themselves in the streets; they came in through the courtyard, taking over every block, inside and out. It was horrible! Everywhere you turned, there was a rifle pointed at you.

Elisa: And did they search your house?

Munú: Yes, they began around dawn; they searched everything. They opened drawers, they looked through the books, they asked us what we did, and they copied the information from our identity documents onto pieces of paper. Our house was on the inside; you had to go in through a hallway, and there was a courtyard beyond that. At one point, the one in charge of the raid grabbed our documents and went back out to the street, I guess to check and see whether we had a record or appeared on some list, so . . . Just remembering it gives me goose bumps! My friend was sure that she wasn't being sought, and I didn't know what my status was. I put the *pill* in my mouth just in case. I stood in the middle of the courtyard, so they'd be able to see me if they came in, and from there I gave La Negra the orders: "If they come running in from the street, I'm going to swallow the *pill*. I'll run in this direction to draw their fire, and you throw yourself to the ground over here."

Elisa: It all seems so terrible now.

Liliana: How could we have been so insane!

Elisa: I don't experience it as insanity.

Munú: I don't either.

Liliana: I experience it as insanity because it seems so impossible, so removed from what I would do with my life now. Maybe insanity isn't the right word, but it's the feeling I have right now when I look back on that time.

Elisa: At the time, it was the natural thing.

Munú: It was a decision.

Liliana: It implied a series of prior choices—all choices that would be absolutely impossible for me to make now!

Elisa: I think at that time, at the height of our militancy, we had a different life project, and we thought accordingly. We were totally convinced that the right thing to do to save the project was to take the *pill*, for fear of not withstanding the torture and turning in compañeros.

Munú: We were involved in a kind of militancy in which each of us was one grain. The social was more important than the individual, than the

---

13. A sweep operation [*operativo rastrillo*] is a procedure to conduct an exhaustive search of a predetermined area.

14. Valentín Alsina is in the southern part of Greater Buenos Aires.

personal. I think that only from that standpoint, in the context of that thought process, can you conceive of risking your life in the militant organization.

Elisa: Yes, that was the militant's belief, and that's what we thought.

Liliana: Evidently that's how it was. The thing is that you look at it from this distance, and what you see are acts that are impossible to imagine.

Munú: Because you see them from the individual perspective, as isolated acts.

Elisa: Of course.

Munú: I still defend the *pill* to this day, even though I'm alive. If I'd managed to take it, I'd be dead, but I still feel that way, at least up to now.

Elisa: It was a way of protecting the compañeros.

Munú: There's that, but also, since I believed they killed everyone, the *pill* protected me from going through the torture, from the death that the milicos chose for me. I remember perfectly well that when they found it on me, the guy torturing me yelled that it showed I had a philosophy of death. And I told him it wasn't like that at all, that the *pill* was what enabled me to choose the moment of my death and that instead he would be the one to decide from then on. I'm alive. It didn't happen to me, because of that damned luck that you have sometimes and that I'll never be able to explain.

Elisa: To keep on living. Did you all think about that on the inside? Did you think about how life would go on outside?

Liliana: I don't remember whether I thought about it.

Adriana: I don't either. I couldn't even imagine it.

Elisa: I remember that I couldn't think; I forced myself not to think.

Munú: You didn't think about anything?

Elisa: I couldn't conceive of a plan for my life.

Munú: It was impossible. I wonder what it was like for people who had children; maybe they were forced to think about the future.

Elisa: Probably.

Munú: In the ESMA, there was just one time when I thought they were going to kill me—and they took me out to dinner! I didn't even know where I was, much less that from there they could take you out to dinner. It made more sense to think they were taking me out to kill me! I gradually learned that logic and coherence didn't exist there. I remember that I was shaking all over. I was shaking and I asked, "Where are you taking me? Where are you taking me?" I could feel that my face was distorted, my eyes unhinged. So I don't know to what extent you displaced reality, the fear.

Liliana: The efforts at dissociation were tremendous.

Elisa: I still think, from listening to your stories, that I experienced everything in a subconscious way, always pretending that nothing had happened to me.

Munú: When you *fell*, it was a lot harder; a lot more people were *falling*.

Elisa: I was in a state of complete subconsciousness; I didn't think. I think I recovered consciousness later. I kept that *hood* on for years! I spent a lot of time like that.

Munú: I don't know whether I'm still wearing the whole *hood* but definitely several pieces of it.

Elisa: I was shaken up by the trial of the juntas; that's what made me start to take it off. And at the same time, I realized that I couldn't remember anything. I knew only a few *noms de guerre*, and I couldn't relate them to individuals. The anguish set in after that and asking myself why I was alive, why they had let me live if I was like a dead person. At that moment I began to think that I had killed myself, that I had self-destructed. It was only after I started therapy that I began to understand that the marinos had destroyed a part of me.

Munú: How did you overcome that anguish?

Liliana: Those blows are for life. Your identity has been so sequestered that it's hard to find a way to rebuild it, although every case is different.

Cristina: I was thinking about talking about my suicide attempt in the ESMA.

Miriam: It was more common for us to attempt suicide before *falling*. Once they got you on the inside, there weren't as many attempts.

Elisa: The feeling was that you wanted to live, and that's the memory that stayed with me.

Liliana: During the first few days, I had a lot of fantasies about killing myself. They were constant. I was always plotting, inventing strategies to do it. Later the obsession faded.

Munú: The first days, when they still had you in Mar del Plata?

Liliana: Yes, afterward the feeling went away completely, and it didn't come back again until eight or nine years ago. But at first it seemed to me that there was no reason to live; from that moment on, there wouldn't be a single instant that was not one of absolute suffering. I didn't see any way out. My only alternative was to think about how to kill myself. And I couldn't figure out how, since I didn't have any concrete way to do it. Everything I imagined was absurd. I never figured it out during those first days, and I don't know what I would have done if I had. I probably would have done it.

Miriam: And what did you imagine?

Liliana: Putting a spoon down my throat, suffocating myself with a rag, taking off my clothes and hanging myself with them. Everything that occurs to you when you don't have access to anything.

Munú: Everything had to do with your throat?

Liliana: Yes.

Munú: Now I remember the time you choked in the ESMA; you felt as though you were dying.

Liliana: But it had to do with the throat because I felt as though that was the only thing I could work with. I couldn't fantasize about cutting myself or taking *pills*, because I didn't have any.

Miriam: This happened when you were still in solitary?

Liliana: Yes, in solitary at the naval base.[15]

Miriam: Because later, in the ESMA, we had access to knives, glass bottles.

Liliana: Yes, but by then I was no longer obsessing about suicide.

Miriam: Suicide probably wasn't common, or else they wouldn't have let us have all of those things.

Cristina: I was desperate. I had just gone through the loss of El Negro, my husband, and the experience of torture. My house had *fallen*, and in the house they'd discovered lists that we'd made of people, stupidly. At the time we were cut off, but we were interested; we wanted to meet up with some people, and that's why we'd made the lists.

Elisa: You wanted to get back into the militant organization?

Cristina: No, but we did want to get back in touch with people.

Liliana: To be among compañeros.

Cristina: To assess our situation and think things through together. The suicide attempt came out of feeling destroyed. I didn't know what to do in order to escape that horrible scene in which they were torturing me. I knew I had a limit. So I had a ring, and I'd noticed an electrical outlet in the bathroom. It occurred to me that I could break the ring in two and use it—

Miriam: To electrocute yourself.

Cristina: Right.

Miriam: Electricity again, like the *electric prod*.

Cristina: With the same electricity. Let's just say there weren't a whole lot of options.

Miriam: And what happened?

Cristina: And I did it. But it gave me a kick that threw me against the wall behind me. I needed two metal prongs, and that's why I had decided to break the ring. It took me several days to do it.

Elisa: How did you break it?

Cristina: I kept bending it until I finally had two little pieces.

Liliana: And you plugged yourself in.

Cristina: Yes.

Munú: Were you in Capuchita at that time?

Cristina: I think I was in Capucha, when they sent me to spend the holidays there as a punishment.

----

15. The naval base located in Mar del Plata was the site of a clandestine detention center.

Liliana: Did anyone realize what you had done?

Cristina: No. In the moment, I behaved normally with the GREEN who had taken me to the bathroom. I fixed myself up as best I could; it had left me very disoriented.

Elisa: But you knew what could happen to you.

Munú: Do you suppose that, in that instant, you got scared and subconsciously did something wrong to save yourself?

Liliana: She thought it was going to kill her.

Cristina: I thought so, but I always assumed that some subconscious mechanism stopped me; something like the survival instinct, something stronger than a rational decision.

Miriam: You don't always get stuck. Sometimes electricity kicks you. It gave you the kick.

Cristina: Of course.

Munú: When you told me about it, back then, I think you said they'd taken you for a shower, and there was an outlet in the shower stall.

Cristina: I don't remember very well, but it wasn't inside the shower stall. There was a wall, the door, the outlet on one side, and the shower on the other.

Munú: And it gave you a kick that threw you to the floor?

Cristina: It threw me against the wall, but I wasn't hurt. Afterward I composed myself as best I could.

Elisa: And you didn't tell anyone?

Cristina: Yes, I did. When they took me back to the Basement, I think I told you, Munú, and Andrea. MARIANO was putting a lot of pressure on me at the time. He wanted to get at some people I knew, and that was worrying me. I didn't know what to do to stop him, and at some point we were talking among ourselves about what suicide meant to them. My memory is contradictory because our assessment was that it drove them crazy when a prisoner tried to escape their power of decision over life and death. But on the other hand, Andrea and I also had discussed it, and we thought it would be useful if I told MARIANO about it.

Miriam: For what?

Cristina: We had evaluated that one potential strategy was to gamble that it would have a strong enough impact on him to make him lift the pressure.

Miriam: To make him stop using the *electric prod* on you.

Cristina: Of course. I thought that I could manage to strike a chord in him, so that he would stop bothering me. And that's what happened too. I don't know whether it was because of that or a confluence of reasons, but he didn't torture me anymore.

Elisa: So you told MARIANO? Didn't it occur to you that he might punish you?

Cristina: He didn't go crazy, and he didn't take any measures. And afterward he told me that he wasn't going to keep on torturing me, because he trusted me; he believed I was telling the truth.

Miriam: And when you told him that you had wanted to kill yourself, how did you explain why you'd tried it? Because you couldn't take the torture? Or did you spell it out for him: "I don't want to turn people in?"

Cristina: No, the part about people no, but I did tell him what it meant to be there inside, that nothing had any meaning for me anymore. I told him the truth even though, at that moment, I actually was defending myself from his continuing to put the squeeze on me to get to other compañeros.

Munú: I told him something similar, and I think I was able to put a stop to certain things. They wanted to go out looking for a girl who'd been a sympathizer of the militant organization. I knew someone who supposedly might have a connection—those things they made up when they didn't have anything better to do.

Elisa: Yes, they did intelligence work.

Munú: I knew that this girl was about eight months' pregnant. I remember talking to MARIANO for several hours in Dorado. I told him, "If you go looking for that girl and she dies for any reason, I'll kill myself. And you know it's true." I think that conversation had some influence, to keep them from doing it. They knew that before I *fell*, I had two houses in La Plata. I had the deeds, and they took me there to confirm that it was true. We went by car, some of them got out, and they left me alone with this guy who held a gun to my ribs the whole time. While we were there, I fantasized about opening the door to escape so the guy would kill me. I was handcuffed, and I debated whether or not to move. I wanted to, and I didn't want to. I told MARIANO about it once, and he said, "I knew you were going to try it, and that's why I ordered them to keep the gun trained on you the whole time." I think that's why later, when I told him, "If you go looking for that girl and something happens to her, I'll kill myself," he believed it, or at least he thought it was possible.

Liliana: You'll never know whether what you did influenced his decision.

Cristina: They were attempts.

Munú: I don't know whether other people considered suicide on the inside, much less whether anyone tried it or actually succeeded in doing it.

Elisa: I know of some people who tried it in the moment they were *sucked up*.

Munú: But that's different. Liliana thought about how to go about it. Cristina actually tried it, and I considered it at a given moment. I wonder whether everyone had those moments.

Miriam: I remember once they took a girl to the Basement, and she had long, raised scars on her neck and hands. She had cut herself with a bottle. I have no idea how they saved her.

Liliana: It seems to me that they'd taken her there from the Bank.[16]

Elisa: And later they killed her.

Miriam: Yes. I don't know why they took her to the ESMA or in what circumstances I saw her. I think I went to talk to her while distracting a GREEN; someone must have told me, "Go and take this to her." I said two words to her. Her neck was covered with red scars, like mouths. I remember she gave me an unfriendly look, full of rejection. She had come from the Bank and, seeing me there alive, walking around in relatively good shape, she must have thought that I'd turned completely, that I was collaborating with the military. Who knows? I tried to tell her that it would be good for her to stay there, that she should request it, but she hardly said a word to me.

Elisa: It drove them crazy that someone would choose her own death.

Munú: If she had scars, she must have been captured a long time before.

Elisa: And they treated her.

Miriam: They treated her, and then they killed her. She never appeared again.

Elisa: Gabi attempted suicide three times with three different *pills*.

Munú: When she *fell*?

Elisa: Once when she *fell*, and twice on the inside, in the Infirmary. She had two *pills* hidden on her, one I don't know where, and the other in her bra.

Munú: And they didn't strip her?

Elisa: She took a *pill* when she *fell*; they got her out of that one, and she took another one. They didn't have time to strip her. She had another one hidden away, and she took it. And they resuscitated her again.

Miriam: Sometimes they used a regular siphon to pump the stomach. How long did they have her?

Elisa: For one year.

Miriam: What was she like? Unfortunately, I never had a chance to meet her.

Elisa: Gabi's conduct on the inside was exemplary.

Munú: I never met her either. I put her on a pedestal.

Elisa: I met her when I *fell*. After about three hours, they asked, "Do you know a certain Gabi? Norma Arrostito?" I said, "Only by name." "What do you know about her?" "That she died in a battle."

Miriam: Of course. That's what came out in the newspaper.

Elisa: And they said, "No, it's a lie. See, you believe all the idiotic things you hear. Do you want to see her?" I said, "But I don't know her" and then— "Hey, go get Gabi." And they brought her in shackles.

Miriam: And the cannonball.

Elisa: No, not the cannonball; she wouldn't have been able to walk. Gabi

---

16. The Bank was a clandestine detention center located at Camino de Cintura and Riccheri Highway in greater Buenos Aires.

came in, already fed up because she was a symbol, and they showed her off to every good soul who *fell* around there.

Munú: And there were a lot of good souls who *fell*, unfortunately.

Elisa: She took off the *mask*, and she looked at me as if to say, "I'm decrepit." Or at least that's how I interpreted it. It was terrible. I didn't know her, not even by sight. Then they took her away. I saw her in Capucha. She was in the cubicle at the far end, alone, and even then, in September 1977, she still had the cannonball. She was shackled, handcuffed, and with the cannonball.

Munú: When did she *fall*?

Elisa: In December 1976. That's when it came out in the newspapers. They reported that she had died in a battle.

Munú: And what you're talking about happened in September of '77.

Elisa: Of course, she was alive until January 1978. She talked to all the GREENS.

Cristina: Without watching what she said.

Elisa: Not in the least. She knew perfectly well what her fate was. She had long talks with CHAMORRO. All she asked was that they kill her with the same dignity with which the Montoneros had killed Aramburu.[17] But none of them had the guts to do it. Those cowards couldn't kill her face to face, as she asked.

Miriam: They killed her with an injection?

Elisa: Yes, with an injection. The only redeeming aspect of the whole thing was her conduct—always firm in her convictions. She was like everyone's ideological mother, even the GREENS. I remember that when they asked me whether I knew how to type, to offer me a job, she came over to my cot and said, "Don't ever doubt it; you're just a *perejila*," as if to say that I had nothing to lose, that working would offer me a chance to survive.

Miriam: Ca's attitude, when I got to the ESMA and was confined in the little room at the far end of the Basement, was to come in, stand up on his tip-toes—which I later found out he did to imitate the TIGER—and tell me to take off the space *mask*: "So you were in the *Monta*, asshole! Here you have to *get your hands dirty*, because anyone who doesn't *get her hands dirty* is *sent up*! You have to fuck up those sons of bitches!" It was two o'clock in the morning; we were alone; there was no guard, no officer, no micro-phone, no camera. Why did he have to treat me like that? I couldn't believe

---

17. On May 29, 1970, the nascent Peronist guerrilla organization, the Montoneros, kidnapped and executed General Pedro Eugenio Aramburu, former president of the military dictatorship (Revolución Libertadora) and the person mainly responsible for the executions in José León Suárez. Norma Arrostito was part of the group that carried out that action.

that he wasn't a *marino*! Four days later they were still insisting that he was a *compañero*, and I didn't believe it. And on the other side, there was Roque's attitude, saying, "You're so thin! Where do you come from? Do you feel okay?" He stroked my head.

Cristina: Shortly after I *fell*—I can't say exactly when, because it was a time of enormous confusion—they were taking me somewhere *hooded*. I couldn't see anything, and suddenly I felt someone take my hand in a different way than you might have expected in there. It was like a ray of light in the middle of the night! When you felt that human warmth, it was so powerful! I think I lifted the *hood* a little, and I saw him there. It was Roque. That Roque is incredible! He took my hand, and he gave me a Coca-Cola. For me a Coca-Cola in that place had to be a hallucination; I didn't understand anything, but I didn't need to understand to receive that gesture.

Munú: Something wonderful!

Cristina: He said something to me, very briefly, because we were in the middle of the hallway in the Basement. They were taking me from one place to another.

Elisa: You had just *fallen*?

Cristina: A short time before. After the torture, they took me to Capucha. I was there for a while, in a state of complete confusion. They took me down; they took me up.

Munú: But the part when Roque gave you his hand happened in the Basement?

Cristina: Yes, in the Basement.

Elisa: In my time, there was a lot more supervision. They left me downstairs for several days, in one of the little rooms. I'm not sure whether it was 13, because the Basement was changed around a lot afterward. It was one of those little rooms they made out of hardboard. La Chinita came over to me and said something that I didn't understand at that moment but was able to decipher afterward, something like "Ultimately, the choice is yours." She was referring to each person's attitude from that moment on, although I don't remember the exact words she used. During those first few days, Em also came over and said something about how I had to collaborate; he talked like someone who had been completely *recuperated*.

Munú: *Recuperated* according to the *marinos'* criteria.

Elisa: Right. He told me, "You're lucky you *fell* here." By then he was convinced that he would survive.

Munú: He was crazier than we were!

Elisa: Serafo was another one who came by, in a joking mood, and didn't compromise himself with what he said to me. The Greens were there, and he came over to me and said, "These boys are fabulous." At that moment I was confused by his words; I couldn't understand his having such a trusting relationship with his oppressor.

Munú: It was his way of being, of handling himself inside there.

Miriam: Probably at that time, there was still no room for any other gesture.

Munú: When I *fell*, Serafo was still like that; he joked with the GREENS just as he did with us. But it was clear that he was one of us, that he was on our side.

Elisa: Of course, but at that moment, just a few days after I'd *fallen*, in September 1977, everything was so confusing. I *fell* on September 21, and they were all coming back from a picnic.

Miriam: From a picnic?!

Elisa: Yes, a prisoners' and officers' picnic.

Munú: Who had they taken?

Elisa: Serafo, Em—I don't know who else. They were all bronzed, because they'd improvised a little soccer match. I know about them, because they were brought to my interrogation,[18] since they had been my compañeros in the militant organization. They were all tanned and gorgeous.

Miriam: Torturers against prisoners—that would've been some match! [*Laughter*]

Elisa: There were compañeros who would come over to me and say, "Well, what are we going to do about it—we *fell*," but there was no opportunity for them to bring me a piece of candy, a lollipop, whatever. I also feel as though, during the time I was there, distrust predominated. Or maybe I was in such bad shape that I couldn't feel a gesture of solidarity. In the Fishbowl, the air you breathed was very thin. Certain complicit looks were exchanged, but I don't remember that we shared any huge gestures of solidarity. Everyone was polite, but we didn't seem at all like compañeros who had been fighting for a common ideal just a short time before.

Munú: Did the marinos send any of you to talk to someone who had just *fallen*?

Miriam: Yes, me. To you!

Munú: To me?

Miriam: Yes. I don't remember what I said to you, but MARIANO, my interrogation officer,[19] took me to talk to you in the little room with the telephone—that little place without windows, next to Dorado, all paneled. He said, "I want you to meet someone."

Munú: And I was that someone!

Miriam: It was you! You were sitting down. There were two chairs and a coffee table.

Munú: I remember the place.

Miriam: You said, "I'm Munú." He went out and left us to talk by ourselves.

---

18. This was a form of information gathering using different levels of coercion that do not involve physical torture.

19. In the ESMA an interrogation officer had direct responsibility for a captive.

I felt your distrust, but at the same time, I distrusted you. Who could you be? Besides, that little room was made especially for installing microphones. I don't remember what we talked about; I think it was religion. [*Laughter*]

Elisa: How long had it been, Munú, since you had *fallen*?

Munú: I don't know; I don't even remember that it happened.

Miriam: She had just *fallen*.

Munú: It couldn't have been that recently if I was sitting there.

Miriam: It was during that time. He wanted me to meet you and tell you about my experience. I don't know what I said to you. I think that was the only time they took me to talk to someone who had just *fallen*. Later what you did was to go when no guards were around to try to take a little extra food, calm nerves, explain things if you could. The marinos did it so that the new prisoner would see people who'd been there for a long time and were still alive, to show that it was possible to survive. A total travesty, and that's what disgusted you about those situations. They used us to deceive the *fallen* compañero. They would tell the individual that he or she might survive through collaboration. But we knew that there was no guarantee you'd live whether or not you *sang*. In fact, not even being selected to work was a guarantee.

Liliana: We've talked a lot about the issue of victims and victimizers, about not confusing the two. And I think that compañeros who have been kidnapped never stop being victims, no matter what they do, no matter what attitude they adopt, because of the pressure placed on them by the captors. You know you do things out of terror, under pressure, because it's what comes out of you in that extreme situation. But you never stop being the oppressor's victim, a subjugated person.

Miriam: I draw a line. It's one thing to break down under torture, to give a name, or two names, or a place, but systematic collaboration and harassment of other compañeros is quite another. You can't deny that there were people who harassed others. The night I arrived at the ESMA, I didn't know where I was, I didn't understand anything, and Ca came over to pressure me to turn people in, to threaten me. Naturally I thought he was an oppressor. And then you have Roque's solidarity and Chiqui's advice. From inside that little room, I could hear laughter. I heard a voice that I later recognized as Chiqui's.

Munú: I also heard Chiqui's laughter.

Miriam: She was one of the few girls downstairs. When I got there, I think Chiqui and Rosita were in the Basement. Chiqui came to see me in the little room where I was being held, and she was wearing an embroidered tunic and some little bead bracelets. I was a total mess, wearing a black shirt and a pair of pants that was too big and fell down when I stood up. She was all fixed up, made up, meticulous. She explained to me that the marinos liked it when you dressed well, because it was a sign of *recuperation*.

Munú: She was wearing a Mexican smock, I believe, because the embroidery must have been Mexican.

Liliana: She had her embroidered smocks.

Miriam: And then FRAGOTE came to see me. I thought he was a compañero! "Do you feel okay? Do you need anything?" he asked. "Were you able to sleep, get some rest?"

Munú: He was so gentle; he acted so sweet. I don't draw the same line as you do regarding the captives' behavior, and I place a lot of weight on the fact that they were captives. However, I often asked myself, for example, about the girl who *marked* me: Why did she do it if she was in a situation where she didn't need it to survive? One day I said this in front of a friend, someone whose opinions I respect, and he asked me, "How do you know by what yardstick she measured whether or not she needed to do it?"

Liliana: Of course.

Munú: Without doubt, the crucial, the extreme moment is the physical torture, with the *prod* or any other method.

Liliana: But the pressure is always there, because you carry the terror inside you. As long as you're a captive, or you're dependent on them, they don't have to be physically present for you to feel the pressure.

Miriam: No, don't tell me that the pressure is always there. That's not true!

Munú: It isn't the same, but the pressure exists, and everyone experiences it differently. I'm not saying this to justify the attitudes of certain compañeros; I'm not saying anything goes.

Miriam: When Ca came to put the squeeze on me, there wasn't a single milico in sight. Why couldn't he have said, as we all did, "Look, stay calm; you know that here there's a chance you'll survive. Try to talk to a marino, and see whether they'll put you to work. That's how things are here." Chiqui told me right off, "Try to ask for nice clothes; we'll lend you some; we'll give you some makeup, so they'll see that you're better." It sounded like nonsense to me, but that was the internal code, and she was revealing it to me. It was a caring gesture. She told me, "Here we sometimes get to see our family; we have a little girl—our parents have her." Something! It sustained you; it showed you a light.

Munú: I find it almost impossible to admit that someone who was a compañero would stop being one at a particular moment and would turn into an oppressor. I don't have any scientific explanation to offer, but I think that there must be a very complex mechanism involved for someone to undergo a transformation of that magnitude. I'm not trying to defend Ca, that's not my intention, but I am trying to understand his behavior. I think he was playing a character; he was trying to be just like the TIGER. He imitated him all the time.

Liliana: Possibly that was his way of surviving.

Munú: Maybe he did it so that if we talked to the marinos about him, we would describe him in that way. I saw him assume some really screwed up attitudes, maybe the worst, but I also saw him break down two or three times. Once or twice I saw him drunk, crying in despair. Another time he dotted the "i"s for a compañera who was standing up to the milicos, answering them in a nasty way, and he told her how things were on the inside: "Look, it's like this, and this is like this, so stop acting like a spoiled girl, because they'll *send* you *up*, with no problem at all, just like so many other people." He said this to her in front of me; in a way, he put himself at risk to help her.

Adriana: Running into people like that was confusing and painful for me—not knowing who was still a compañero and who wasn't anymore. Serafo was the one who took a chance on me. FEDERICO made him come by to see me, because he knew that we knew each other. He explained how things were there, and it was a risk, because he didn't know where I was coming from. I remember his gesture with so much gratitude.

Munú: I think there's one thing that we shouldn't lose sight of, and it's that the vast majority of compañeros acted with great solidarity and upheld the standards of the militant organization. There were a few who didn't, and because it's so incredibly painful for us, we talk more about them than about the rest. I've always thought that, for whatever reason, those were the ones they succeeded in destroying more completely.

Munú: There's one thing that surprises me, and that's how, in a place as terrible as that was, more people didn't go insane. I've heard thousands of explanations, but I can't help comparing it to the fact that excombatants from the Malvinas are still committing suicide, while the camp survivors are not.

Miriam: I think there are more psychologically ill people than you might think among the camp survivors. I think the fact that we are able to be more or less okay has more to do with our psychological makeup before the kidnapping and the support afterward—and also the fact that we understood. The people who went crazier were the ones who ended up there without knowing why. You could withstand what was happening better if you were prepared ideologically; if you understood that they were repressing you because you were a threat to the system. But the elderly mother of a militant—how could she comprehend the *electric prod*, the *hood*, the shackles? It would drive anyone insane.

Munú: The only girl I knew who went crazy in there had nothing to do with it; she had not become a militant.

Elisa: She went crazy?

Munú: Yes.

Miriam: The thing is that being there made sense if you were a militant. It was comprehensible from the oppressors' perspective and also from ours. But it could be absolutely devastating for someone who had nothing to do with it, for someone who had never been a militant, who'd never thought about the possibility of *falling*. We were very rigid, and some of us still are; we have a very solid mental structure in terms of values.

Munú: We also were experts at pretense. We had spent years acting one way at home and another way outside! And we kept on doing it in there. Because of our experience, it came easily to us, knowing how to face up and have an answer ready. You were experienced at lying to all your neighbors. It's not that living a pretense as militants or lying to the neighbors as a choice that you made as a free person because of your militancy is the same as dissociating yourself from the marinos' pressure or lying as a defense mechanism in a situation of subjugation. But let's just say that you already were familiar with some of the behaviors you needed to fake it.

Miriam: We also pretended at work. No one knew about our real lives; no one knew we were militants, what we carried in our bags, what we hid among the files at the university. At home we said we were going out dancing, and we would go to a *cell* meeting, or to a demonstration, or to a *lightning action*.

Elisa: Those of us who survived had a habit of dissociation, a certain agility. Without that skill, we wouldn't have been able to survive.

Munú: Do we still have it?

Elisa: Yes, in a different way; we have the agility to adapt to new and difficult situations.

Miriam: We're all professional con artists! [*Laughter*]

Cristina: Do you remember the group that *fell*, and there was a girl who didn't want to be released if her boyfriend didn't get out too? She was really young; she didn't understand anything; she had no idea where she was, poor thing. We tried to help her understand, to convince her to leave. At the time we thought that if she left, while it was no guarantee, it could increase the chances that they'd release the boyfriend.

Munú: There were two couples. Did they *transfer* all of them?

Cristina: Yes, in the end they did. I never knew exactly how it happened, but we found out that they had *transferred* them.

Munú: That girl, the one they wanted to let go, she's the one who went crazy; she would sing and walk on top of the beds in Capucha.

Miriam: When was that?

Munú: At the end of 1978. They were going to let her go on two or three occasions. The boyfriend's uncle, who was in the army, had been looking for him. They had denied having him, and so they were going to kill him. They wanted to let her go. They told her she was to leave and must not report it, must not tell anyone that her boyfriend had been kidnapped. FRAGOTE told me that they asked the boy to persuade her to go and not to talk. They told him to tell her that he'd never loved her, that he'd deceived her—all that, knowing that it was because they were going to kill him! She didn't want to leave without her boyfriend; it was the only important attachment she'd had in her life. I know this because I read it in a document they forced her to write, although I don't recall how it came into my hands.

Elisa: I experienced the feeling of utter defeat in a brutal way. Keeping that *hood* on for so many years was my downfall. It's true that I was able to build a family that I love deeply and that has sustained me all these years, but that was not my life plan. I've only just started to reemerge, but I feel as though I'm a loser. They killed me, and this other Elisa emerged— lighter, flimsier.

Liliana: They killed me too; that's how I feel.

Miriam: Why?

Liliana: I felt the blow crushing what had been my life plan at the time, my motivation, my way of relating to people. Now it's very difficult for me to find any continuity with my experiences before the kidnapping. I lost my spontaneity in that moment, and I never recovered it. At forty-six, I've become a completely manufactured being—one whose every action, thought, or word, whose every connection to someone else is the product of an extremely complicated construction process. I have to probe, ponder, manufacture everything. And this has nothing to do with what I'm like. I've lost my naturalness, my spontaneity, and therefore my identity. And this is the case because what's missing is the plan. Since I no longer have a plan for my life, I have to deal with everything through questions: So what do I do now? Why do I have to do it? In order to preserve what? I can't find myself. Daily life is a terrible effort for me. I never know what I'm about. It takes an enormous effort to find meaning in what I do, to figure out the ethics, to make room for affection. It's an enormous effort because I can't be natural. They don't kill your body, but this is also dying. You continue to function—you have feelings, experiences, emotions, desires, and sexuality—but the same old question cuts through all that functioning: Where am I? What do I do with this? Who am I? The moral questioning is constant. I'm always wondering whether what I am doing is right or wrong, and that didn't happen to me before. I just did what was right, and I didn't do what was wrong, period. Now I never know.

Munú: I think that these feelings of being destroyed, which I share, didn't start in the ESMA. It seems to me that they gave us the final blow there, the strongest one, but we were already defeated, already losing the project.

In the ESMA I also felt as though they had killed me. The person I was died. It's one of the feelings that I recall most intensely from the entire time we were on the inside: I felt death. You never completely return from that point.

Elisa: I took refuge in the affective aspect, in building a family, but I still retain the sense of loss and of being a loser. That history contains the absence of my beloved compañeros, whom I still miss. And when I imagine them, they're not twenty-five years older. The image I have of them, and of myself, is from that time. And it is an image of defeat.

Cristina: I felt something very unique in the early eighties, when I went to visit a compañera who had been in the ESMA. She was in theater, and at that time she was presenting a one-woman show in which she played various characters. When it was over, I was extremely moved, because it seemed to me that they hadn't succeeded in killing her totally. She was re-creating something that had been in her from before, and she was letting it out, offering it to others. I went there thinking something else entirely, but what I found was that evidence: that they hadn't been able to do it with her.

Munú: Maybe it's similar to what happens to me. I've painted all my life, since I was a little girl, and when the killing started, I couldn't keep on painting. I couldn't create in the midst of anguish. A lot of years had to go by before I could return to my brushes, to my collective murals. I know that I can work out the technical aspects fine, but my imagination still lacks passion, a passion that I'm recovering little by little. I rarely feel the pleasure that my beloved profession always gave me. The loss of the project and my compañeros is a load I carry around with me every day. I've learned to live with it, but I rarely allow myself to feel pleasure. There's too much pain.

Miriam: I didn't feel as though they'd killed me, but at first the guilt kept me from giving testimony. I felt unworthy for even having flicked on a light switch in the ESMA. People who knew me before and saw me afterward would say I seemed different, a lot calmer, more mature.

Elisa: Assimilated into the system.

Miriam: I don't know . . . more settled, they said. Sometimes, when I meet people who are like I used to be, I remember. I have sparks of memory: passionate, impulsive, very talkative, very vital. After that, I think I began to view everything relatively, and I can't even feel the more intense emotions. For example, when my uncle died, I was the only one who went to identify the body. My uncle was like a second father to me, but as I was comforting my mother, I said, "But Mom, he was almost eighty years old; he lived a full life." And my brother asked, "How can you talk like that?" And so I explained to him, "I lost friends who were seventeen years old; they were just beginning to live, and they killed them. To me, the death of a person who is fifty years old, sixty—"

Liliana: Is normal.

Miriam: We had bought the whole book of raffle tickets; we had gambled on making a priesthood of our lives. They asked me to leave journalism, which was what I loved best—I dreamed about the smell of ink on newsprint. "Devote yourself to the militant organization," they told me, and I gave myself over 100 percent to the militant organization. And when they told me, "Leave the university, because it's dangerous, and go live in the western zone," I went to live in a room with a tin roof, a rooming house. I didn't care, because I couldn't be happy if that project we wanted so badly didn't crystallize. I believed I could never live in peace knowing that all around me were people who didn't have food to eat, didn't have a job, didn't have a roof over their heads. I wanted a more just society for everyone; that was what was going to make me happier.

Elisa: And that project was cut short.

Miriam: The intensity of that love for the project of creating a more just society combined with the intensity of the defeat, of having lost so many compañeros—in my case two compañeras, who were gunned down when they were nine months' pregnant, my two best friends, my boyfriend, the people I loved best. After having suffered and loved so intensely, I'll never be able to feel anything as strongly again. My psychologist always said that everything I told her about my personal or professional achievements seemed as though it was coming to her through a mattress. "Now I'm going to cover the elections in Israel," I'd say. "But that's great!" she'd say. "Yes," I'd say. "Now I'm going to do a fellowship in Atlanta." "That's great," she'd say. But nothing seemed important.

Munú: It was a project full of ideals that enveloped our lives. It was the fulcrum for what we were and what we wanted to do: study and have a job, a partner, children. It had to be for everyone if it was going be for us. Now it's hard to accept the fact that each one of these things is a separately functioning project, and each one of us individually is the fulcrum.

Miriam: After I left the ESMA and my mother would complain that she didn't have enough money to pay for gas, I'd say, "Cook with a heater." All the day-to-day things seemed so pointless, the everyday worries so stupid. Maybe in a way it was enriching to stop caring about mundane things.

Elisa: But isn't it a loss?

Liliana: It's enriching, but it's loaded. It's lethal.

Elisa: That's what I feel as though I've lost: spontaneity.

Liliana: What we were before.

Cristina: Enthusiasm.

Munú: Everything is more relative.

Elisa: A life plan.

Liliana: A plan that wasn't destroyed in an innocuous way. What they did was to mine our ideals, force us to adapt to their behaviors in order to survive. It's true that nobody's life turns out just as he or she imagined it at the age of fifteen. But there are different ways of not having your life turn out as you thought, and this is a terrible way.

Miriam: It's the worst.

Cristina: Even with my current political involvement, I sometimes feel I don't know how I got here. It seems so removed. It's very hard for me to find enthusiasm for what I do, and I do a lot of things just because they have to be done, sort of like what Miriam was saying.

Liliana: I feel as if I do things because there's a script. What should a forty-six-year-old woman be interested in doing? She should want to get along with her daughter, she should want her daughter to get along with her father, she should want to work, and she should not be indifferent about what kind of work she does. And so she has to choose, and compete for her position, and not let them send her just anywhere. But it's all a script, as if I were buying somebody else's life, even though clearly these are still my own situations.

Cristina: I have moments when I connect with something that must relate to something from my past, and I get enthusiastic. But everyday life is harsh; I find it very difficult. Even though I have goals, rationally speaking, I don't have that enthusiasm, the joy of doing things. I have to keep inventing all the time. Fortunately, since I didn't arrive at this place alone, I also have my compañeros and a project that, although totally different from the other one, gives meaning to day-to-day activities, because despite this sadness that none of us can hide, I still believe that it's worthwhile to search and to work with others to transform this unjust reality, even if we never, as Galeano[20] says, reach the horizon.

Liliana: Lately I've become a sad person, and I can't tell you how peaceful and relieved I feel.

Cristina: Ah!

Miriam: Why?

Liliana: Because I'm so much more comfortable in that role. I don't laugh anymore, I don't bother to get involved in things I'm not interested in, and I'm much more at ease. I no longer make any effort.

---

20. Eduardo Galeano, born in 1940, is a Uruguayan poet and writer. He is the author of several works, including *The Open Veins of Latin America*, *Book of Embraces*, *Upside Down*, and *Soccer in Sun and Shadow*.

2

Detained-Disappeared

Many were the ways devised and put into effect by us in order not to die: as many as there are different human characters. All implied a weakening struggle of one against all, and a by no means small sum of aberrations and compromises. Survival without renunciation of any part of one's own moral world—apart from powerful and direct interventions by fortune— was conceded only to a very few superior individuals, made of the stuff of martyrs and saints.

—Primo Levi, *If This Is a Man*

Torture and abuse served as an initiation rite for captives in the ESMA. After that came the *hood*, the shackles, the loss of identity. For members of the *staff*, however, this suffering was compounded by the need to stage a continuous farce. If you wanted to survive, you had to pretend to the oppressors that the incessant kidnappings, the screams of the interrogated, the *transfers*, all meant nothing, did not move you. It was forbidden to cry for someone else in the ESMA. You were allowed to express neither sorrow, pain, nor the repugnance induced by the disappearers' bizarre attempts to "get close" to the disappeared: the New Year's toast, birthday parties, movies, dinners, outings. The ESMA had no bars to separate the victims from the victimizers. As a result, it was even harder there than in a prison for captives to maintain their integrity.

Elisa: I have a very high physical tolerance, and for many years I maintained that they had not tortured me in the ESMA. "What did they do to me?" I'd say. "They punched me a few times; they used the *electric prod* on me." What was that to me? The other pain was so much stronger.

Liliana: And you think it's because of your high tolerance for physical pain? I have no tolerance whatsoever, and still for many years I denied that they had tortured me.

Elisa: I suffered other, much more intense kinds of pain than physical pain in there, and they still hurt today.

Liliana: Emotional pains?

Elisa: Pains of the soul, which have been much more lasting over the years than the physical pain.

Liliana: I wonder whether it's because you downplay or don't recall the physical pain of the torture, or maybe everything that happens in those moments is so much more intense and terrible than the physical pain. That's why sometimes we don't remember the physical pain or we lose our memory of the specific sensation. In contrast, when you experience physical pain in a normal situation, the pain is the main thing: your stomach hurts; your head aches; you're injured; they do a surgical procedure on you, and the anesthesia doesn't kick in. In those situations, the physical pain is at the center, and you're focused on it, and no one is enjoying it.

Miriam: I compare it with delivering a baby. During delivery, the physical pain is very intense, but everything is geared toward soothing you, supporting you, and buffering that pain. And besides, you're having a baby. On the other hand, during torture, everything is geared toward destroying you.

Liliana: When I gave birth in Italy in 1980, I had a hallucination: I was alone for eight hours in the labor room, convinced that the guy sitting there watching me with indifference, a typical obstetrics nurse, was enjoying my physical suffering. And when I had surgery in 1987, I went berserk; they couldn't get near me. I crouched in a corner of the bed and covered myself with pillows. I was more or less calm until the moment I entered the operating room. And there I was able to bear it, because the guy who was going to operate on me, who was someone I knew through references, was calm, warm. I wouldn't let them give me the epidural, so he came over and asked me what was wrong. I told him that I had been tortured before, so he had me talk with the team's anesthesiologist, and he gained my trust. They gave me the epidural, and the surgery went smoothly. But when I came out of the operating room, I threw myself off the stretcher while my legs were still paralyzed. And the upheaval continued throughout the three or four days I spent in the hospital. They couldn't give me injections; they had to change all the medication. They had to give it to me orally because I wouldn't let the nurses near me.

Munú: I lose control when I have to allow other people to do things to my body. So the first thing I do is to tell the people who are treating me that I was tortured; I ask them to handle me with care, and they always do. I remember once when they excised a polyp without anesthesia and the doctor helped me through the moment. I feel my face get distorted; I make guttural sounds. I close my eyes, because they move all over the place. The doctor put his face very close to mine, he took me by the arms, and he said over and over, "Open your eyes, and look at me; I'm the one who is treating you." As soon as I was able to look at him, I started coming out of that state. When these things happen, I'm left devastated for several days. Even though I can't conjure up the pain of the torture, it's definitely recorded inside me, and any similar situation carries me back to that moment. The torture happened only once, but it lasts a lifetime.

Cristina: After being kidnapped and imprisoned in the ESMA, one of the first ordinary situations that I associated with torture arose when I had to go to the dentist. Coincidentally and fortunately, our family dentist was connected with the human rights organizations. For years I'd kept the reasons for my apprehension to myself, but when I was sitting there and he was holding the drill, I had to keep repeating to myself that what this person was doing was for my well-being.

Liliana: You need to know that the other person isn't sadistic.

Cristina: Another thing was that for a long time I couldn't stand to hear a baby cry. It's still hard for me; it upsets me terribly, but before it was worse. I think it's because a newborn baby is so defenseless. Crying is such a primal mechanism that it must trigger a kind of identification.

Liliana: You don't gauge other people's suffering, and any sort of suffering seems like torture to you.

Cristina: But it happens to me particularly with babies. That's why I associate it with something very primal.

Miriam: I can't stand to watch torture scenes on television or at the movies. I close my eyes.

Munú: I can't even watch them on the news. When the police arrest someone, and they cover his head and handcuff him, in my mind they put the *hood* on him and take him away, and after that comes the torture and everything that I understand as subjugation.

Adriana: Not only am I unable to watch suspense or chase films but I'm also unable to listen to the audio track that accompanies these scenes, even without watching them. The other thing that happens to me is that when I have to treat hospitalized patients, it infuriates me when they are referred to by bed number or when I see them lying there half naked while I'm standing up fully dressed. It gives me a sense of imbalance that is very upsetting to me.

Cristina: What's happened to me before is that when I'm in a situation of serious confrontation or in the middle of a conflict and there's someone there with psychopathic characteristics, I associate the person in some way with the torturer. In these situations I feel something very peculiar, although it tends to be subtle. In general, this feeling hasn't left me paralyzed, but I register it, and I've even transferred these daytime remnants to a dream in which it's all replayed as a torture scene.

Miriam: I had my first child not long after I was tortured, and it was easy for me to distinguish between the two situations. Torture is geared toward breaking you. The torturers seem determined to let you know that they enjoy what they're doing to you. It's like a diabolical ceremony. In the air force, where they tortured me the first time, the room was very large, and there was a light shining on my face. I was naked, my eyes were blind-folded, my hands were tied, and no fewer than ten people were yelling at me. "Bitch!" they yelled. "You have to collaborate," and they asked me about my friend Patricia. Meanwhile, another one stroked my hair, took my hand, and whispered in my ear, "Stay calm, and if you collaborate, nothing will happen to you." It was a truly demonic scene. There were yells, insults, obscenities. At one point, one of the guys lifted my *mask* and another one lowered his pants. I was naked and tied up. He brought his penis close to me, while the others threatened, "We're going to go at you one by one, bitch." The truth is that I would have preferred an actual rape. I would have taken it as something more human, more comprehensible than the torture. At one point during the session, the power went off because they were staging a boycott over the disappearance of Oscar Smith.[1] The Light and Power Union was conducting blackouts. And I . . . when the power went off, I laughed.

Elisa: Because they couldn't use the *electric prod* on you.

Miriam: The situation struck me as funny. The guys said, "Oh, this is fucked up!" and they brought in a portable, battery-powered *electric prod* that I didn't even know existed. When I screamed, they said, "Come on, you dumb ass, cut the crap. This is nothing; you got off easy because the power went off." I don't know whether the other one was more potent. I was lying on a wooden table, and later they took me somewhere else, where there was an elastic belt and a metal cot, and they also wet me down to help conduct the electricity. And after the *electric prod* in my womb, in my vagina, in my eyes, on my gums, one of my most vivid memories is of how afraid I was that they would torture me again. They shut me in a cell, and they gave me the usual warning that I shouldn't drink any water. They cov-ered me with a blanket, and they left me there with one guy. I asked him right then whether they were going to kill us, and he said yes, because if they let us live, we would go right back to doing the same thing—that was his reasoning—and if they sent us to prison everything would continue. I asked him not to leave me alone. I was terrified of being left alone. I pre-ferred to be with one of them, even though he was surely one of the ones who had tortured me. When I was alone and heard someone approaching the cell, which they evidently did on purpose—they would pound on the door and yell—I felt like a scared little animal.

Elisa: You remember that feeling very well.

Miriam: I remember that feeling. And I also remember that at one point, in the middle of the torture, they made me sit up on the bed, and they told

---

1. Oscar Smith, the leader of the Light and Power Union, was kidnapped in the area of Wilde (in the southern zone of greater Buenos Aires) on February 4, 1977.

me to lift up the *mask*. So I saw all their faces. There were six or eight of them, and one of the things that struck me was that they looked just like militants.

Elisa: They wore jeans, mustaches?

Miriam: Yes, they were very young. Some were twenty years old, and they were all wearing checked shirts and suede boots. They smoked the same brands of cigarettes that we smoked, Particulares, Parissienes, and they themselves drew my attention to it. "So, up to now we've been asking you questions; now ask us something," they said. And so I asked them why they tortured, and they replied that if they just gave me a soda and asked me what they wanted to know, I wouldn't tell them. They said I seemed surprised by the way they looked, and I said, yes, that I was worried about how much they looked like us. "When you want to fight an enemy, you have to infiltrate and mimic it," they replied. That gave me a feeling of tremendous vulnerability—for all the people still on the outside, because of how exposed they were. I had the impression that I'd have handed a flyer to any one of them at the university; I'd have tried to persuade him join our militant cause, without any qualms at all. That didn't happen as much in the ESMA. There were fewer similarities. No one would have mistaken fat JUAN CARLOS, or JUNGLE, or MARIANO.

Munú: But MARCELO or SPARK you would.

Elisa: Or BLONDIE.

Miriam: But there were fewer of them.

Munú: They belonged to a different age group, so you saw them differently. There weren't very many who were twenty years old.

Miriam: One of the things that made me feel worse, after the torture, was to hear them torturing other people. I heard it constantly, and in contrast to what happened in the ESMA, I was alone and shut in a cell with absolutely no contact with anyone. In this sense, we had more company in the ESMA. When we were in the Basement and heard the screams from the torture, we could take the hand of the compañero next to us.

Munú: Another prisoner.

Miriam: Another prisoner. It was still terrible, but it was more bearable than being alone in a cell and hearing the screams.

Munú: I lived in the Basement during the eight months I was in the ESMA, and I know that it's too painful and distressing, unbearable. "Too much" is the exact term. Every time they tortured, we would look at each other, all the compañeros, and we wouldn't say a word. The silence was dense and profound, and each of us relived our own story in the screams of the one being tortured.

Elisa: In my case, after a really long torture session—it had been extended because CHAMORRO had arrived—they moved me to the room next door; I'm not sure for how many days. From there I could hear them beating and using the *electric prod* on people who had *fallen* in a neighborhood in the northern zone. I remember this as being more painful than when they were subjecting me to electric shocks.

Munú: To this day, I can still see myself tied to that metal bed, the water on my naked body so the current would be stronger. I see myself, but I can't evoke the physical pain.

Liliana: Not even the other type of pain, the other sensations? What happens to me is that I reconstruct the scene, and I can see it from the outside, and when I put myself inside it, I can recreate absolutely all of the emotions: what I felt, how I reacted to their faces, the confusion. But my memory of the physical pain is very vague. Maybe, in the midst of so many things that happened, the physical pain got filed away.

Miriam: It gave me a feeling of being split in two; I left my body, and I watched it from the outside.

Munú: I think that isn't something that happened in the moment; that's how you remember it now.

Miriam: No, it happened to me in the moment.

Liliana: Yes, you dissociate yourself.

Miriam: It's a defense mechanism.

Elisa: In addition to the emotional shock you suffered when you *fell*. And on top of that, they showed you compañeros you thought were dead, and there they were, alive.

Liliana: So much happened in such a short time.

Elisa: And in the midst of all the confusion were those questions that you had to really think through in order to answer. For example, "Where do you live?" I wasn't about to say, "I live with Petisa," so I said, "I live in a rooming house." They responded, "You live in a rooming house, just like all the other Montoneros bitches." Those words, "Montoneros bitch," were a constant throughout my torture and the following days. I heard them all the time. It's painful for me to think about it, because I couldn't say anything. I felt humiliated, and I cried.

Munú: I didn't cry. I answered. They started saying bad things about my compañero, who had already disappeared. They said he was a son of a bitch because he had gotten me into the militant organization. I told them that when I met him, I'd already been in the organization for about three years, that it wasn't true. I always answered them, to the point that MARIANO, who was the one using the *electric prod* on me, would say, "How can you be so calm? If I were in your shoes, I'd be crying and begging for mercy." And I said, "Why should I beg you for mercy, why should I cry, since you're just going to kill me anyway?" Later someone else came in and spoke to me in a very soft voice. He said he was a lawyer; he acted like the good guy.

Cristina: Who was he?

Munú: He was a prisoner. I recognized him later by his voice. He asked me to tell him everything I knew, because that way they wouldn't torture me anymore and they would send me to prison. And then the wild yelling started again and after that a whole bunch of people all talking at once, including the TIGER. And the radio was turned up all the way. At some point, the torture stopped, and a few days later it started up again. I have memories of very denigrating situations. At one point they untied my hands and feet. I was sitting on the metallic bed frame, naked, *hooded*, wrapped up in a filthy brown blanket. My whole body was trembling. It was uncontrollable, and I felt as though I was going to pee on myself. I asked whether anyone was there, and no one answered, and I wet myself. It was like the final blow.

Miriam: Something similar happened to me. In the middle of the torture, I said I needed to go to the bathroom. And they answered, "Do it on yourself." Another guy came over and ordered, "Take her." They made me go down the stairs with the *mask* on, shoving me. They took me to a bathroom with a latrine, and they said, "Turn around and do it with the door open." One more abuse among so many abuses.

Elisa: Now I ask myself, "How did I manage not to say where I lived and so many other things?"

Miriam: What you did, in the middle of being asphyxiated by the *submarine*, the *electric prod*, the pain, was think about how to lie, how to protect the compañeros who were still on the outside.

Munú: In the midst of all the confusion, they stopped torturing me, and they made me lift the *hood* and write down what I'd said. It was a lie, and I stuck to it. I'd go to sleep, and they would wake me up and make me write the same thing again. And they did the same thing over and over again, obviously to see whether what I wrote was always the same. I think you got the feeling that someone else's torture was more painful than your own because you were outside of the situation and you could let yourself feel what you had experienced at that moment.

Liliana: Or because when it was your body on the line, you were focusing on other things; in other words, you were thinking about how not to talk, how much information they actually had, always on the alert.

Cristina: It's so painful because you "relive it" through the other compañero. We are the ones who are in there. It's a terrible we. Just hearing the radio can bring back the horror. For a long time, I found it impossible to listen to the radio. Now I can. But in my mind it was associated with the radio in the Basement.

Munú: It was on all the time.

Cristina: And they turned up the volume when they were torturing. And with the torture itself too. They were always playing whatever was popular at the time. When I hear those songs, I get goose bumps. Besides, I think it's very hard to be objective about the torture situation. The only thing you can do is convey your own experience, what you went through, and there must be as many experiences as there are people. Variables, personal traits, each person's past, each person's circumstances at the moment of capture intersect. But I identify with Miriam, in her evocation, in her story of torture, because I do remember the physical pain, and I have the image of being outside it and inside it at the same time. I feel the sensation of lying there tied down, face up, covered with the *hood*. Sometimes I can't sleep in that position. I've had dreams of being bound and standing up, like those dreams where you're in a dangerous situation and you fly away. But I think what weighs on you most about the torture is that there are human beings—apparently that's what they are, your own kind—who are doing the worst thing that one person can do to another: inflicting the worst possible damage to obtain something that is a treasure for that individual, the most valuable thing the person has. That surpasses the physical pain, but it's related.

Liliana: The terrible thing about it was that ultimately you had to relate to those dreadful beings. You ended up talking to them. The memory I have is that in the midst of all that confusion, you even thought that you could negotiate the pain—say to them, "Torture me less."

Cristina: You couldn't help believing they had something human in them.

Liliana: Maybe some people were able to cut themselves off from them completely from the start. That didn't happen to me. I feel as if I had a relationship; I tried to gain their sympathy so they would spare my life, so they'd torture me less, so it all wouldn't be so terrible. Without realizing it, after the torture you ended up talking to the same guys who had tortured you, which was nothing more than a continuation of the suffering. But you didn't just start talking about little birds, as if nothing had happened. You ended up asking them whether or not they were going to kill you. And they lied to you. They would say that someone who was disappeared was alive and living in a beautiful apartment with an ocean view.

Munú: One thing that made a strong impression on me was to see the face of the torturer, to see MARIANO. I'd been there for days, always *hooded*, and since I was sure they were going to kill me, I talked a lot with that guy about what I thought, my ideals, how you had to live "on the edge," take risks. I knew his voice, and I had made up a face for him resembling Palito Ortega.[2] When they took off the *hood*, it was hard for me to match that voice to his face.

Elisa: You appealed to all the resources you could.

Munú: Another very powerful thing that happened to me, something I was never able to explain, was that at one point one of my hands came loose and I asked the torturer to give me his. He was talking, shouting, asking

---

2. Palito Ortega was a famous Argentine singer turned politician.

about this, that, and the other. I interrupted him: "Will you give me your hand?" And he asked, "What for?" And I said, "Nothing. I need it." And he gave it to me! I remember that I took his hand, squeezed it, and let it go. I said, "Thank you," he tied me up again, and everything continued. How do you explain that?

Miriam: Probably, in the midst of so much pain, of something as inhuman as the torture, you needed to feel as though there was a human being there, even on the other side of the *electric prod*.

Liliana: Those things leave more lasting effects than the physical part.

Miriam: On the issue of *singing* or not *singing*, I make a distinction. I think it's one thing to break down under torture, and quite another to be drinking *mate* with the marinos six months after you've *fallen* and say to them, "You know what? I remember a certain guy called Skinny who lived in such and such a place, and maybe if we go there right now, we can grab him"—in other words, really collaborate with them. On the other hand, every experience was different during those first days; each torture process was unique. What happened to that guy who watched while they applied the *electric prod* to his twenty-day-old baby? What happened if they tortured a relative right in front of you? They did that to the brother of a friend of mine: they shocked his father with a television wire right in front of him so he would tell them where his militant brothers were. The boy told them where they lived. And what of it? Is he a son of a bitch? How do you withstand that?

Liliana: I need to believe that all the captives were victims. I think there are different ways of clinging to survival. It was a situation of pressure, and under pressure people did different things. I don't make that distinction, because otherwise you never come to the end of dividing out the good and the bad. In my view, the marinos are the bad guys. Everything else has to do with the different ways that someone under pressure adapts to a terrible situation. This is all above and beyond the fact that I wouldn't want to run into some of them as people. My feeling is that you never know how far you would have gone had the pressure been stronger.

Munú: My opinion is very similar, and I think it's a very complicated subject. I start with the fact that we were all victims. They succeeded in destroying some people more than others, and at certain times those people acted in ways that were similar to the victimizers. But I cannot forget that the very same person, before *falling*, was a compañero, a militant at my side, even if I didn't know him or her. I also agree with what you're saying about the pressures; you went through it, and you still don't know the limits.

Miriam: There are different degrees of pressure—that's true.

Elisa: I do make the distinction. How can it be that there were people who, many months after *falling*, went on an *expedition* and *marked* someone who had been a compañero—someone they hadn't seen for months and therefore someone they weren't even sure was still *hooked up*, was still in touch with people?

Liliana: That distinction upsets me a lot. It hurts me, and I make every effort to dissolve it.

Cristina: It's also true that when we were inside, our intuition was really honed.

Liliana: The alert!

Cristina: You put it into practice with the other captives even though later you wouldn't judge them to save your life. Once you've lived through that experience, you're very careful not to judge. But I do think that we did it in practice without realizing it. You knew which people you could talk to, speak frankly with, and which you had to be careful with, because that was also part of survival.

Liliana: Of course. Personally, I never felt as though I could speak frankly with anyone in there.

Cristina: No?

Liliana: I never spoke frankly with anyone inside there. Never!

Cristina: Not with any of the compañeros?

Liliana: With no one. Never!

Cristina: Because of distrust?

Liliana: No, I don't know whether it was distrust; it just came out like that. That's why I say it was a terrible effort. I spent fourteen months encapsulated, isolated from everything around me, when I was inside and also when they took me for a family *visit*.

Munú: That honing of your intuition that Cristina described, I think it was always operating. I feel that I got to know the people in the Basement and that I knew what to say to each one and how to say it.

Cristina: I was there during a different period. I worked in Dorado with Andrea and Adriana, and we shared a cubicle in Capucha for a while. I already knew Andrea. I was a close friend of her compañero's, who was disappeared. I met Adriana through mutual friends. We were together during the last part of your captivity, Munú. We established a trusting relationship, and we kept on seeing each other when we were under supervised release. You and I saw each other less often inside, Miriam, but we would run into each other every once in a while when we were working on the outside. I knew Roque.

Miriam: On the inside I talked a lot with Viki, Chito, and La Negra. In the Fishbowl you could talk to pretty much everyone, except for a few of the more slippery characters.

Elisa: Yes, in the Fishbowl you could talk to anybody, but I don't recall speaking in depth with anyone. I usually related to people through games: cards,

TEG [a game called Strategy and Tactics of War]—we loved to play that one.

Miriam: Once we were outside, toward the end, Diego was sort of our delegate.

Cristina: I think I owe the fact that I'm here to Diego. That time they sent me to Capucha as punishment, he took steps to defend me and prevent my *transfer*.

Elisa: When was it that Diego began to play a bigger role?

Miriam: Once we were under supervised release. We discussed all our strategies with him, about leaving the country, getting a passport, everything. He was our authorized spokesperson, and since he talked directly to the marinos, he knew what they were thinking and whether or not it was a good time to ask for something, depending on their mood.

Munú: I never had shackles, but even so, I don't know whether I'll ever in my life be able to forget the sound they made when people walked around in Capucha.

Elisa: You mention shackles, and it hurts me here—my ankles hurt! Wearing shackles was a heavy subject in more ways than one.

Munú: During the time that you were there, did they use them on everyone?

Elisa: Yes, everyone. In 1977 if they took off the shackles, it was a step up for you.

Munú: You had a better chance of survival?

Elisa: Exactly. You couldn't be in the ESMA without shackles, except when you were going to take a shower. That was the only place where they took them off.

Miriam: Did you have to wear them when you slept? Did you sleep in chains?

Elisa: Yes.

Munú: And didn't they remove them when someone was working?

Elisa: The Fishbowl didn't exist yet when I started working, and they would take me down to the Basement in shackles.

Munú: Three flights of stairs with that noise?

Elisa: Yes, down the stairs shackled and blindfolded. And when they took us on an *outing*, an *expedition*, we were shackled, and the officer in charge of the *operation* had the keys in case we had to get out of the car. Once they took me on an *expedition* with Ca Apparently, he had the address of a compañero from the JUP[3] at the Law School. I realized this when we got to the alleged house, on Garay and Catamarca. Up until then I'd thought

---

3. The JUP was the Juventud Universitaria Peronista [Peronist University Youth], a university-based wing of the Juventud Peronista [Peronist Youth], both if which were political groups espousing the political positions of the Montoneros Organization.

it was just another one of the regular *expeditions*. At the corner, FRAGOTE, who was leading the *operation*, came over and removed the shackles right there in the car because he wanted me to go up and identify the compañero. They were all very nervous. After they took them off, they told me to hurry up and get out, but I had a cramp in my leg, and I couldn't move it. FRAGOTE grabbed me by the arm, pulled me out of the car, and practically dragged me toward the house. As we went inside, Ca and some officers came out cursing because although there was a resemblance, the guy in the house had absolutely nothing to do with the guy they were looking for—luckily, and for my peace of mind! The terrified look on that boy's face is etched in my mind, sitting there in his living room watching television when, in true ESMA style, fifteen guys appear and start asking name, activity. Naturally they were shouting and waving their rifles. Some of the others to one side were saying, "It isn't him." Poor kid. When the circus was over, they put the shackles back on me. It was instantaneous: I got into the car, and they put them right back on.

Munú: They would thrust you into a terrifying scene from one moment to the next. Why don't you tell us what the shackles were like?

Elisa: They had two steel rings.

Miriam: Handcuffs.

Elisa: Exactly, they were cuffs for the feet, except that they had some adhesive tape, supposedly a protective covering, wrapped around the rings.

Munú: So what you had around your foot was a ring about four or five centimeters wide?

Elisa: Yes, five centimeters more or less. It was very heavy.

Munú: Because they were dragging a thick chain, a chain about one meter long.

Elisa: No, it was shorter. It was very uncomfortable—you couldn't walk. When you went up the stairs—since each step was about 30 centimeters high—you lifted one foot, and the other pulled you back down. You felt the weight. The situation changed over time. They would take the shackles off to go up or down the stairs and put them right back on afterward.

Munú: How long did you wear them?

Elisa: I *fell* in September, and I think they had only just taken them off in February. They removed them when they took me on my first family *visit*, which lasted about forty minutes. And when I returned, they put them back on.

Munú: When they put them back on you, did they give you any explanation?

Elisa: No, it was so natural inside there. It was like a little present; you went in, and they gave you the shackles, the *mask*, and the *hood*.

Miriam: And the case number: "090, here is your *mask*, your kidnapped person's gear." When we were there, they just gave us the *mask*.

Munú: I wore the *hood* for a few days and then the *mask*.

Miriam: In the ESMA, I was wearing the *hood* when they put me in the little room next to the interrogation room, on that cot, the first night. I was still wearing the *mask* they'd put on me when they brought me from the air force, so they put the *hood* on top of it. The compañeros teased me; they called it the "space *mask*." It was completely different: a layer of foam three inches thick with an angled opening for the nose, covered in jean material. The one I had in the ESMA was just like the one you use to sleep on airplanes; it was the same shape but made of black cloth. I never wear them when I fly now, and I get upset if someone near me puts one on. So I wore the space *mask* with the *hood* over it during the first nights.

Elisa: The shackles were like an extension of our feet.

Munú: Everyone was like that?

Elisa: Yes.

Miriam: They injured a lot of people.

Elisa: When I had an X-ray taken, the marks showed up on my anklebones.

Miriam: After twenty years?

Elisa: Yes.

Munú: Gabriel still has the marks.

Elisa: I don't have any.

Miriam: No external mark you mean.

Elisa: On the X-ray it shows up as an injury. In the workup, the mark left by the shackles is described as a nonspecific injury to the ankles. All of us from 1977 wore them for a long time. Everyone in Capucha was shackled, even those who went to work.

Munú: Those who worked and those who didn't? Everyone was shackled?

Elisa: Later on they started using them less. The ones who didn't wear shackles were the pregnant women once they were assigned to a room. They were shackled at first, while they were in Capuchita. By the time I *fell*, the Pregnant Women's Room already existed, and they weren't shackled. You heard that infernal noise every time the GREENS took someone to the bathroom.

Miriam: Now that you mention it, I think they also used them when we were there, although it wasn't as common in 1978. I saw people being brought down from Capuchita with the guards, *hooded* and shackled, and I remember it caught my attention.

Munú: In November 1978, a group of around sixty people *fell*. They were all in Capucha. We slept in beds, and they slept beside us on thin mattresses on the floor. They were separated by those hardboard partitions about one meter high, and some of them were shackled. There were people in Capucha before that big roundup, but no one was shackled. It seemed as if they'd designed a harsher punishment for that group.

Miriam: They kept you chained as a way of showing that they considered you dangerous. You were their property; they could do anything they wanted to you. They tortured you; they bound you in chains.

Elisa: So you would remember where you were—it was a way of bringing you down.

Munú: It was a form of subjugation. In 1978 it seems as though it was a more selective thing.

Elisa: Not in my time. They could select you for work, which meant you could go downstairs and have the chance to eat better and spend less time lying on the cot. But you still had to wear those shackles!

Munú: On July 9, 1978, when they still had me shut in a tiny room, the people from the Fishbowl came down to the Basement to drink their Independence Day hot chocolate. They brought in big cauldrons, and it was the same hot chocolate that the students from the [Navy Mechanics] School drank. Some officers came down and drank hot chocolate with the captives. They must have done the same thing the year before, and many of the prisoners would have been shackled.

Miriam: The marinos celebrated Independence Day with *sucked-up* people wearing shackles!

Elisa: I *fell* on September 21, and on November 14, I was working in the Fishbowl, and in came JUNGLE with little crustless sandwiches, pastries, and soft drinks to celebrate my birthday.

Munú: Your birthday?

Elisa: My birthday, on November 14; that's how I spent it, with little sandwiches, but manacled. I was turning twenty-four. Looking back on it now, it was more a punishment than a celebration.

Munú: The purpose of the handcuffs, the shackles, the *hood* was not to keep us from escaping. There was no way to escape from there; the only door to the Basement and to Capucha was made of iron, and there was a GREEN armed with a FAL standing behind it.

Cristina: Wearing the shackles obviously made it hard to get around: you had no speed; you had to take short steps; you couldn't move around freely. It also made it possible to cart you back and forth like a *package*.

Munú: I remember them shouting, "Here goes a *package!*" and the *package* was one of us being taken from one place to another.

Cristina: Besides, everything had its symbolic value. Being trussed hand and foot—like an animal that had just been broken in—meant they controlled our bodies and movements even in their absence.

Munú: When you were there, Elisa, when you were all shackled, did they remove the handcuffs so you could work?

Elisa: I wore them while I was in Capucha. When I started working, they took them off.

Munú: Diego told me that they made him write with the handcuffs on.

Cristina: I was handcuffed when I was in Capucha.

Elisa: That was at the beginning, in the early days of your *fall*.

Cristina: In the early days and also on other occasions when they sent me to Capucha as a punishment.

Elisa: People said they punished Fat Casildo at the end of 1978, when almost everyone from the Fishbowl was leaving, and they handcuffed and shackled him.

Munú: Yes, we were very afraid because they also put him into solitary on another floor. We sent him food with the LITTLE PAUL.

Elisa: When I was there, the people in Capucha who weren't working usually weren't handcuffed. There were compañeros who swept the floor shackled, but they weren't handcuffed. You gradually earned small privileges: first you could go around without handcuffs, then you wore the *mask* but not the *hood*, and after that . . .

Munú: Everyone followed the same process then?

Elisa: No, there were people who were considered much more dangerous who were still chained to the ball. From the talk going around Capucha, I found out they took the ball off Gabi in November 1977.

Miriam: How did they put the ball on you?

Elisa: They didn't put the ball on you; they attached you to it.

Miriam: In addition to the shackles?

Elisa: The ball was stationary.

Miriam: Was it a cannonball? How did they attach it?

Elisa: I think it was attached to the leg iron.

Cristina: The famous iron ball.

Munú: The same as in the Middle Ages.

Elisa: Exactly. Luci spent months like that. According to the stories they tell about 1976, everyone had the ball. There were so many people that they kept them standing up and attached to the ball. They even attached several people to the same ball. They say that in Capucha everyone was handcuffed and attached, with their arms raised, to a pipe overhead, and below, on the floor, they were attached to the cannonball.

Cristina: I remember that they took me to Capuchita first, and I was handcuffed and shackled.

Elisa: From the Basement they sent you to Capuchita?

Cristina: They had me in the Basement, then they took me up to Capuchita, and after a while they took me back down to the Basement until the end of the year, the end of 1978.

Munú: It had been about a month since you had *fallen*.

Cristina: I *fell* on December 5. I don't remember now; it's all a blur. After the torture, I spent several days in a state of total confusion. I was on a mattress—I don't know where—with the *hood*, the shackles, and the handcuffs. Then they took me downstairs, and shortly after that they punished me, which is why they took me back up again. I remember walking around shackled at that time. It was the same when they took me to the bathroom. I have some memory of that, of moving about with difficulty. The second time they punished me was when they caught me trying to read the files from the 1000 Cases,[4] which was expressly prohibited, so they ordered me back to Capuchita.

Munú: So by then it was March 1979.

Cristina: It was already summer, February or March, I think; I was shackled.

Munú: That time it was part of the punishment for what you had done.

Cristina: Right. Later they took me downstairs. My grandmother had died. They didn't take me to the wake, but I found out because they let me talk to my family on the telephone. They took me down shackled but not handcuffed. In some places, in Dorado and in the Basement, they took off the *mask* but not the shackles. I spent many days like that because I was being punished.

Miriam: You weren't *recuperated*!

Munú: And you went around Dorado like that?

Cristina: The whole time. They would take me to Dorado, and it would take me a century just to walk across that huge room. I could take only very short steps, and it hurt.

Elisa: When you were in a hurry, you got hurt; if you wanted to walk faster, you got tangled up.

Cristina: Later on they removed them. I can't tell you how many days I wore them, but it was a long time.

Munú: You see how it is? I *fell* earlier, and they didn't put them on me. And they left me sleeping in the Basement for a long time; they didn't take me to Capuchita. Then Andrea *fell*, and they didn't put them on her either. Then Adriana and La Flaca *fell*, and they weren't shackled either. They held Adriana and La Flaca in Capuchita for a long time, and then they moved them to a stall. They left Andrea in Capuchita for several weeks.

Miriam: It was completely arbitrary. There were no rules.

Munú: After you, Cristina, a whole lot of people *fell*, and they shackled some of them.

Cristina: The group you're referring to *fell* before I did, in November.

Munú: You're right. There were a lot of people in Capucha then. They took up all the space from the beds where we slept, four or five women, all the way to the beds—turning the corner—to where Chiquitín and Roque slept. They were lined up side by side, separated by those partitions, thrown down on a mattress, *hooded*, handcuffed, and some were shackled. I remember Three Kings night in 1979. The GREEN on guard duty—I am

---

4. These were files located in the Intelligence Offices, numbered from 1,000 on. They were not about navy kidnap victims; they were usually denunciations.

seeing him as I speak; his face must be different now because it was a long time ago, or I'd still recognize him—this GREEN had promised the people in Capucha that if he had guard duty on January 5, he would give them a Three Kings night.

Elisa: What did that mean? Was he going to take the shackles off?

Munú: No, the Three Kings night he gave them was to allow them to sit up. They were each on their own mattress, but when they sat up, they could see each other. He let the couples be together, sit beside each other. They were all telling stories, and the laughter rang out. They took me up to sleep at around three or four in the morning, the usual time, and when I went into Capucha, I could hear the laughter from one end to the other. I didn't understand what was going on. The GREEN told me, "I promised them that if I had guard duty, I was going to give them a Three Kings night." He must have arranged to be there. He let them talk and tell stories all night long. One person told a story, then someone else told another one in a loud voice so that everyone could hear, and they laughed. They laughed. The next day everything went back to normal.

Munú: We've always talked about being kidnapped, and I know we were. But for the rest of humanity, we were disappeared, and there's a big difference. We were kidnapped by the navy, but for the 33 million inhabitants of the country, we were disappeared, and this also was operating inside of us. So I ask myself, "How did we experience that situation? How did we feel when we looked out the upstairs dining room window, knowing that the people outside thought we no longer existed?"

Elisa: And we still were disappeared, even after they released us. Maybe you stopped being a disappeared person from the moment you testified. In my case I was still disappeared, at least to myself, until the first time I testified before a human rights organization ten years after my release.

Munú: Those are two different things. When we were in the ESMA, we were disappeared persons. Afterward, as you said, you still felt as if you were.

Elisa: The first time I read my name in the newspaper, I felt as though I reappeared.

Munú: With regard to testifying and feeling guilty or not, we have to be very clear. Maybe each person has his or her own individual guilt, but in general when we talk about guilt, we're talking about the guilt of having survived, of being alive when the rest are dead, as if we could have done something to change that finale. I guess those of us who spent time in the camps aren't the only ones who feel guilty about being alive. I imagine it must be the same for all of us who were militants during that period and especially for the people who went into exile.

Elisa: The people you cursed because they left.

Miriam: Because in our minds, the people who left were traitors. That's what we believed—that they'd turned their backs on their commitment.

Elisa: You said, "How could they leave at this moment?" And now I say, "How lucid of them!" [*Laughter*] We are a destroyed and guilt-ridden generation. We were kidnapped or disappeared, and those who remained in the country, in hiding and scared, were also disappeared in a way. They couldn't live their lives! In 1986, after a march, I was walking down Corrientes Street, and I ran into a fellow militant from the law school. We hugged each other, and I decided to tell him what had happened to me. And he said, "Can you believe that I stayed in the country, and this is the first time I've set foot on Corrientes Street in twelve years?" We were all disappeared!

Munú: Internal exile was a terrible thing, and it still is to this day. If you were living abroad, even though you missed a lot of things, at some level there was a social acknowledgment: "Poor thing, you had to leave," they'd say. The people who stayed behind had to just swallow it all the time. Those of us in exile could talk—we needed to talk to survive; those who stayed in the country had to keep quiet to survive. Among the people who stayed, there were those who disappeared from the place where they lived, left their families and friends, and reappeared somewhere else with a trumped-up story to explain why they'd turned up there. And today they are not acknowledged.

Adriana: In part, that's what happened to me when I went to work in Neuquén in 1982. When I watched the trial of the juntas on the hospital television set in 1985, it was like something completely foreign to me. It wasn't until 1989, when I saw my name in the newspaper on a list of people who had been pardoned and I rejected it and denounced the maneuver, that I was able to take off my *hood*, as Elisa says. I emerged from a two-layered clandestine existence: that of my militancy and that of the kidnapping.

Munú: Excuse me, but I want to go back to the time when we were inside. Were you all truly conscious of the fact that for the rest of humanity we were disappeared?

Liliana: It drove me crazy that my name would appear on a list of disappeared persons. I had a very clear sense of the difference between my name and that of other mortals. Mine was a *sucked-up* name. I was aware of the deep chasm between the names of the rest of the human beings on the planet and the names of those of us inside. They were two different worlds. Eight or nine years ago, a colleague and I went to conduct a survey in El Calafate.[5] We surveyed a woman, a ranch owner, who was very eccentric and arbitrary in how she wielded her authority. All of her laborers were undocumented Chileans. We couldn't finish the survey, because she

5. El Calafate is in Santa Cruz Province near the Perito Moreno Glacier.

threw us out. My colleague left cursing her out, and I felt awful. A few days later, when we were returning to Río Gallegos, we went to take the commuter plane, and this woman showed up in the airport with a couple—Chilean laborers—and a baby. She was taking them to Río Gallegos to get identity documents for them. She had decided to "legalize" them. She was going to talk to the government officials. I got very upset when this woman wrote down the names of the couple under her own name. It made me feel as though they'd been kidnapped. Their attitude was one of absolute submission. I was very upset when I got back to Buenos Aires.

Elisa: To you it symbolized the kidnapping.

Liliana: Now I realize that when I was inside, I felt as if they had installed a glass window that separated me from the world. I knew that my name wasn't worth as much as before; it was a disappeared name.

Elisa: I'd never be able to find the term that could explain what happened to me or to describe it in that way. My name in the militant organization was Monica. When they took me to work at the Foreign Ministry, there was another woman there with the same name, and when somebody said, "Monica," we'd both answer. I was Elisa Tokar, but I was still Monica; I couldn't answer to any name other than Monica.

Liliana: They must have thought you were crazy.

Munú: And you would explain that they called you Moni.

Elisa: I told them that they called me Moni, short for *monigote* [rag doll]. [*Laughter*] It went with my happy-go-lucky image. And so I was Moni, short for monigote. It was a perfect fit.

Miriam: You identified the name Moni with the militant organization and with being inside.

Elisa: Sure, at the Foreign Ministry I was still kidnapped, and so I was still Moni; I answered to that name.

Munú: That's what they called you every day, because they took you from the ESMA to work there. Nobody in the ESMA called you Elisa.

Elisa: But my co-workers at the Foreign Ministry did.

Liliana: The "regulars" at the Foreign Ministry called her Elisa.

Munú: Of course, but to her it was abnormal for someone to call her Elisa. She was Monica in her everyday life and had been for a long time. When she went to work at the Foreign Ministry, she was Elisa, and then she went back to the ESMA, and she was Monica.

Elisa: Afterward I had a serious identity crisis, because I thought, "I can't be Elisa Tokar, because it's dangerous." So it occurred to me that I had to get married. My full name is Beatriz Elisa Tokar, but I only used Elisa Tokar; Beatriz didn't exist.

Liliana: Your family called you Elisa?

Elisa: Always. Everyone called me Elisa. When I met Nestor, we thought that getting married would be the solution for my life: I was going to become

Beatriz Di Tirro. I even wanted to change my signature! [*Laughter*] Actually, by then no one called me Monica anymore.

Munú: For me, those years seem so long. You talk about one thing or another, and in the interim it seems as if years had gone by. Speaking of identity, I don't know what your experience was, what it meant to you—the fact that they gave us each a number and used it to identify us.

Miriam: The number thing didn't really bother me that much.

Elisa: Me either.

Miriam: I was 090.

Elisa: It made me feel more comfortable. I was 481. When I went in or out of Capucha or they took me on an *expedition*, they said, "481!" It was good for me, because I needed to feel that I was a prisoner. It was a way of distancing myself from the naval officers.

Munú: The need for bars.

Elisa: The famous bars that we didn't have!

Miriam: You went to the Basement, and you said, "090," and the GREEN at the metal door wrote it down in the logbook.

Munú: It was the same in both places, upstairs and down.

Elisa: And when we were in Capucha and asked to go to the bathroom, we also had to use our number: "481 needs the bathroom."

Cristina: "481 needs a door!" [*Laughter*]

Liliana: "481 needs a plane to Switzerland!"

Cristina: I know they gave us a number, because I've heard it from other people, and from our conversations I've recovered some fuzzy images of going through the door announcing it. But I don't have my own memory of it, and I can't even remember the number they assigned to me. I have these gaps and clouds in my memory in other areas too; I guess it's a subconscious mechanism.

Munú: My number was 125, and at that time a new car model had just been introduced, the Fiat 125. They found that very funny.

Elisa: But it didn't bother you.

Miriam: The thing is that with all the other things they did to you, calling you by the number was the least of it. You were inventoried, and you just put up with it.

Munú: It had to do with the lost identity.

Elisa: At the time I wasn't aware of having lost my identity. I still didn't feel that a name could be worth so much, but maybe that's how it is.

Munú: I want to ask a very personal question. Not long ago, Liliana, you told me that you had accompanied me to the apartment where I had been living with a friend when I *fell*. At some point they took me to get a little

suitcase with some clothes. I have a vague recollection that while I was doing that, someone was standing there beside me.

Liliana: Yes, MARIANO and I.

Munú: MARIANO was there too?

Liliana: I couldn't swear to it. I'm not sure whether MARIANO went in or
waited for us below.

Miriam: And what was the reason for that? I don't get it.

Liliana: It was for her to get her clothes. What I don't know is why he took
me along.

Munú: So that you would go up with me, most likely. So that I would feel
as though I was being watched. I didn't know you. What I do remember
is that I had to write a note to my friend saying that I'd come to pick up
some clothes and I was leaving. They had created this whole circus so no
one would report my disappearance, so that a writ of habeas corpus would
not be presented.

Miriam: You had to leave a note for the girl in the apartment?

Liliana: To avoid arousing any suspicions—a reassuring note, let's say.

Munú: Of course. Supposedly, I was leaving.

Miriam: That's why you were taking the clothes.

Liliana: That was another fucked-up thing the marinos did. They kept insisting that what they were doing was for your own good, so your family
wouldn't be alarmed. They said that if the habeas corpus came up, there'd
be nothing else they could do for you.

Miriam: That was going around on the outside too. I remember that when
many of my boyfriend's—my compañero's—friends disappeared, the
families didn't submit a writ of habeas corpus, because they thought it
would make things worse. A habeas was the mark of a politicized family.
The other rumor going around was that if the *sucked-up* person's family
had a contact in the government or an influential relative in the military,
this contact wouldn't be able to help them if the family submitted a writ of
habeas corpus.

Munú: They gave Adriana a lot of trouble on this issue. She had an aunt in
Amnesty International in Germany, who immediately denounced her disappearance. Her parents, who have a history of persecution, didn't want to
have anything to do with submitting a habeas corpus petition. The marinos said they were going to *send* her *up* because there was an international
search for her. Those were the things they did "for your own good," so that
no one would denounce a case.

Miriam: They took you only to that friend's house?

Munú: No, they took me other places. When I *fell*, I didn't realize that I was
being kidnapped because of my political militancy. At first I thought they
were thugs and then slave traffickers. I had been part of the militant orga-

nization in La Plata, and I'd been *unhooked* for about two years, although I'd had a few contacts. I figured that no one knew me here, in Buenos Aires. It never occurred to me that they'd be able to *mark* me, so I wasn't taking precautions. There I was, *hooded*, and my fantasy was that they were slave traffickers!

Elisa: Slave traffickers?

Munú: Yes, it's absurd but true. Just recently, a friend who was also kidnapped told me that she'd had the same fantasy. In the Basement, when they asked me who I was, where I worked, where I lived, who my friends were, I told them. In any case, none of them had anything to do with the militant organization. Then came the torture and the realization of why they had *sucked* me *up*. A few days after I was kidnapped, they took me to see these friends in order to ward off a denunciation. They wired me with a microphone. I'll never forget it—a microphone taped to my chest! Mil taped it to me.

Miriam: Mmmm.

Elisa: How sophisticated. I never experienced or even heard of that.

Liliana: She was the only one they did it to. I think it was Al's invention. In his obsession with undercover espionage, he'd offered the marinos that marvelous contraption.

Munú: Since I was wearing a microphone, I couldn't warn people.

Miriam: That you were disappeared.

Munú: Right. And I also had to be careful about what they said!

Liliana: The responsibility for others—making sure they didn't say anything foolish.

Munú: They took me to the workplace of the friend I'd lived with until twenty days before, because they'd taken down everybody's information during a *sweep operation*. They'd given me a piece of paper stating that they had searched the house, and I had it in my purse as if it would work in my favor if I got caught in a *vise*. The address of the house was on it. The people from the ESMA had gone there and told La Negra that they were looking for me. I didn't know that. They took me to see her at work, wearing the microphone. I had to go say hello to her. La Negra cried and said, "I thought something had happened to you; they came to the house looking for you. I tried to file a complaint, but they wouldn't accept it at the police station." And I was saying, "No, nothing happened to me, I'm doing great."

Liliana: Where was that?

Munú: Here, in Buenos Aires. They took me out of the car and sent me over with the microphone. I was walking along all by myself.

Miriam: But you could write when you were with La Negra.

Munú: No, I couldn't. Those guys were standing twenty meters away! We were outside. And, besides, I had to control her reaction! I told her I was staying with friends. Since she told me they'd been searching for me, I went ahead and told her I was leaving. After that, they took me to the house of some friends from my hometown.

Elisa: Did you see them again afterward?

Munú: Yes, I see them all the time.

Elisa: And they didn't suspect anything?

Munú: No, they believed me totally and absolutely. While I was with them, trying to fake the situation, the microphone came unstuck and fell into my clothes. I was desperate. I was thinking, "These milicos aren't going to hear anything else I say, and they're going to come, and these people have nothing to do with anything." So I went to the bathroom and stuck it back on. In the meantime, I told my friends not to look for me; I said I was leaving, and I'd call them later. I get really upset when I think about how anguished I felt.

Miriam: What a horrible situation!

Munú: It wasn't until a year ago that it really dawned on me how complicated and traumatizing it all was. I was reading something about extreme situations and the feeling that there is no way out. I was trapped! I couldn't tell them I'd been kidnapped, because I had to avoid provoking a reaction. If I talked, they'd take us all to the ESMA, and if I didn't talk, I'd be going back to the ESMA. They were going to kill me either way. I didn't know they kept people alive there. I didn't know anything about anything. I guess I still didn't even know I was in the ESMA.

Liliana: How horrible! What evil people!

Elisa: Did they also take you to your own house in the town?

Munú: No, because I usually communicated with my family by letter or by phone. They made me call them at some point, and I always wrote to them. I wrote to them from the ESMA, and the marinos monitored what I wrote and sent the letter.

Miriam: Why do you suppose the marinos never *sucked up* those people? It's very strange that they didn't take them to the ESMA to find out whether it was true, as you said, that they weren't militants.

Munú: I guess they believed me. Not only did they never go after them; they never even asked me whether they were militants. They never questioned that they were just friends, and later on, during a *visit*, they would take me to their homes. When they started to torture me and question me about the militant organization, my attitude changed completely. I clammed up, and that must have given them an indication that it was true. I don't know; that's how it happened.

Munú: Liliana, tell us about the place where you were kidnapped in Mar del Plata and how long you were there.

Liliana: It was the naval base, the one in front of the golf course.

Munú: Is that the place they call the submarine base?

Liliana: I think so. In fact, there were submarines. You can see this perfectly well from up above, from the golf course.

Munú: Could you get there from the beach?

Liliana: No, if you walk or drive from Playa Grande to the Port, heading down, you pass alongside it. You can't see the sea anymore, and you begin to see a very high hedge, three or four kilometers long.

Miriam: There's no more hedge; now you can see the buildings.

Elisa: Did you see other people there?

Liliana: Yes.

Elisa: Liliana Pereyra and Patricia de Rosenfeld?

Liliana: They were both there.

Elisa: Did they take you to the ESMA with them?

Liliana: No, they took me alone from the base to Buenos Aires. I don't remember whether they took them before or after that.

Munú: What was the place like? Were there lots of people?

Elisa: Were there men and women? Their husbands must have been there.

Liliana: I was alone in a room the whole time. I believe there were some larger rooms where people were mixed together. It seems to me that I saw one room where there were several people sitting in chairs. There was an open space about five hundred meters wide between the hedge and the buildings on the base. It was completely cleared and had a lawn. At that time there was only one entrance to the naval base, one big door, and I remember that we entered through there.

Munú: You could see?

Liliana: I was just able to see that we went in through that door and we went to a building that I later identified. It was different from the others, like a white cube.

Elisa: In other words, they *sucked* you *up*, and you knew where they were taking you.

Liliana: Yes, I figured it out. Maybe because I was very familiar with Mar del Plata, I knew perfectly well where we were going and that it was the entrance to the naval base because of the distance we traveled, the avenue, the open space, the way the sun hit.

Munú: You didn't have the *hood* on?

Liliana: No, they put me in the car, and they threw me down on the floor. And once inside, I immediately began to hear the noise of the boats, the sirens. I knew I could be in one of two places: the naval base or the ESIM,[6] which surrounds the Punta Mogotes lighthouse. When I heard

---

6. In the ESIM, a school for navy NCOs, a clandestine detention center operated.

the boats, I knew that it was the base, because no other place in Mar del Plata has those boats. Years later, I identified the building, because it was the only white cube. The torture room and offices were down below. There was a small stairway outside that led to the first floor, where we captives were held. If you look at the cube from above, from the golf course, on the side facing Juan B. Justo Street, that's where the big room was where I have the notion that I saw more than one person sitting in chairs. On the side where the Playa Grande jetty is, at the far end, adjacent to the golf course, there was a large bathroom and several small rooms. We were confined alone. I spent several days there. During the day, I was sitting and facing into the room not the door, and at night they tossed in a mattress. You had to spend the whole day in the little room. The guys paraded in and out trying to get information out of you. They talked to you; they confused you.

Elisa: And in the morning they removed the mattress?

Liliana: They took out the mattress, and you had to sit there.

Elisa: How long were you there?

Liliana: It must have been about two weeks. No, less, because they captured me on November 25, 1977, and I was already in the ESMA when they kidnapped the French nuns,[7] and that was around December 8.

Elisa: What was your number in the ESMA?

Liliana: 041.

Miriam: How did they transport you? By car?

Liliana: Yes, by car. Liliana Pereyra and Patricia were at the base. Liliana's daughter's father was also there. I can't remember whether I saw Walter, Patricia's husband, or whether he was already in the ESMA.

Elisa: Walter was never in the ESMA; he was in another camp here in Buenos Aires.

Liliana: I guess it was just my imagination, then, that I saw him again.

Munú: But in between the base and the ESMA, they took you someplace else.

Liliana: I spent only a few hours at that other place, and I don't recall seeing anyone I knew.

Miriam: Did they ever explain to you why they transferred you to the ESMA?

Liliana: I never did understand it very well. They took me in a car with three guys.

Elisa: And you never found out who they were?

Liliana: I was never able to find out their names.

---

7. French nuns Alice Domon and Léonie Duquet were detained illegally with a group of relatives of the disappeared. The *operation* was carried out in December 1977, under the command of the ESMA Task Force.

Elisa: Did you ever see them again? Or did they just drop you off and leave?

Liliana: Once, a couple of months later, they showed up in the ESMA. I was working in Dorado, and they came in to say hello. I was terrified at the very thought that—

Elisa: That they'd come to take you away.

Munú: It must have been when they came to interrogate me.

Liliana: No, not that much time had passed. They took me to the ESMA in December, and you *fell* in June, and they showed up before that.

Munú: People came to interrogate me from the La Plata Naval Base, the army in the southern zone of greater Buenos Aires, and the Mar del Plata Base. The ones from the base mentioned a compañera they were holding there; they told me she sent greetings. Apparently they had her in a situation similar to ours. I don't know whether it was true. I believed them, and I sent her greetings. They asked me some very specific things that only her compañero and I knew. He was dead. Apparently they kept her alive for quite a while.

Liliana: I haven't been able to reconstruct completely whether or not they had people there they'd kept alive for a long time. It was just a couple of days, and I was left with the feeling that everything they said was a lie. After many years, I realized that they lied to us all the time, and so I'm very confused about the things they said to me. I've never made the effort to try to figure out what was true and what wasn't.

Elisa: And did you eat alone?

Liliana: Always alone. Once I ran into Liliana Pereyra in the bathroom; by then she had a huge belly.

Miriam: You realized it was Liliana later, in the ESMA?

Liliana: No, I knew her from before. I knew her, Patricia, and their husbands from the outside.

Munú: Were there any survivors from the base? You always hear about people who *fell*, but I've never heard that anyone might still be alive.

Liliana: I think not. When those guys went to the ESMA, I was in Dorado, and they came to say hello to me, and I was terrified that they were going to take me back to the base. They put on a big show just to terrorize me. They said I actually was supposed to go back, but MARIANO had arranged for me to stay in the ESMA. They did all that to scare me. Those were five minutes of absolute panic. I never saw them again.

Munú: So what they told me about having my friend probably wasn't true.

Liliana: I can't begin to tell you what big liars they were. It was a terrible thing. They never admitted to you that they'd killed someone. No matter who you asked about, that person was alive someplace.

Munú: And you always believed it.

Liliana: And I believed it. I needed to believe it. That's probably why it took years for me to be able to admit that all those people I'd asked about were dead. You never got them to say anything other than that they were all alive.

Elisa: In the ESMA they would say, "They've been *transferred*."

Liliana: Not only did they not admit that they'd killed them; they'd tell you they were fine. They'd tell you anecdotes, repeat conversations. They didn't say, "They're in Devoto Prison" or "We took them *through the front door*." They'd say they'd taken them to a house: "Yesterday I was with so and so, and she says hello." It was awful! They insisted that people were alive, in good health, and that they were on good terms with them.

Miriam: What was the context for those conversations?

Liliana: They'd come by, hang out, show up.

Elisa: And they'd give you the chance to inquire about some compañero.

Liliana: You ended up talking about anything. They came by a lot. For instance, sometimes they would show up during the night, tie me up, and say I should get ready because the next morning I was going to tell them everything I knew. And they'd leave me tied up all night long.

Miriam: And the next day, nothing.

Liliana: The next morning they'd untie me, sit me down in a chair, and give me breakfast.

Munú: This is the first I've heard of the chair part.

Liliana: I had to be sitting in a chair. I wasn't allowed to stand up or lie down on the floor.

Munú: Were you handcuffed?

Liliana: I don't think so.

Miriam: I had a little cot in the air force.

Liliana: They went to the trouble of taking out the mattress and giving you the chair.

Cristina: But there was a reason for that.

Liliana: Of course. It was so you would spend the whole day staring at the wall. It wasn't because they had read the protocol. It was to force you to stay in one position.

Munú: Not standing up, not walking, not anything.

Liliana: No, and once when I asked for the mattress during the day, they said no. I wasn't allowed to sleep during the day; I had to sleep at night. It was discipline.

Elisa: Where did they take you before they took you to the ESMA?

Liliana: They were taking me to the ESMA, but there was something they had to do on the way. And that's when it occurred to them to deposit me at the Athletic Club.[8] Those were hours of sheer terror, when the guys from the Athletic Club took control of me.

---

8. The Athletic Club was a clandestine detention center located in the capital, at the intersection of Paseo Colon and Juan de Garay.

Miriam: And what did they do to you?

Liliana: They didn't torture me, but they took me to the torture room. They took me through all of the situations that I'd supposedly be in if the others didn't come back to get me.

Miriam: So as not to waste the opportunity.

Liliana: The guys from the base came back to get me after a few hours. The guys at the Athletic Club had me in shackles, and naturally they couldn't find the keys to take them off. So they took me to the ESMA wearing the shackles. They had to cut them off me. They filed them off and then put on the ESMA shackles, this time with their own key.

Munú: You wore shackles in the ESMA?

Liliana: Of course. I don't really remember how they removed the ones I was wearing when I got there. I know they worked on them for a while, and then they put their own shackles on me. I was the property of the navy and not that conglomerate, that nefarious mixture of police and army that was the Athletic Club!

Elisa: So you didn't even spend one whole day in the Athletic Club?

Liliana: No, hours. Afterward the guys from the base cursed out the other guys because they had disrespected them, yet they were terrorizing me all the while. It was nerve-racking being in the hands of two different *gangs*. They were all just one big mob of torturing murderers, but you ended up feeling as though one side was protecting you.

Elisa: Your savior.

Munú: Did you see people in the Athletic Club?

Liliana: I have some vague memories. People were being taken, shackled, to the bathroom and to eat, all lined up, holding on to one another. One of the things they did was take me up to the line to show me what it was like. They took me up to one of the boys, pale, very white, tall, very thin, covered with bruises. They said, "Tell her why we had to do this to you," and he said, "Because I wanted to save a friend."

Munú: How horrible! How incredibly painful!

Elisa: And by then was it all the same to you whether or not the guys from the base came back for you?

Liliana: No, I wanted them to come back and get me.

Elisa: But you didn't know where you were going either. Did they mention the Navy Mechanics School to you?

Liliana: No, never.

Miriam: I think there's an explanation for why everything in the ESMA seemed to be less chaotic, more organized. There was a project behind all of it. Massera's political project, which was to use the abilities of certain prisoners to further his ambitions.

Munú: How far does that go in explaining why they let us go in the end?

Miriam: Once he retired from the navy, MASSERA no longer had enough power to keep us imprisoned. He held on to some of us longer; he could control one group but no more than that.

Munú: If there had been a policy not to let us go, they wouldn't have released the first compañeros who went to Europe. They could have killed us just as they killed the rest.

Elisa: Their objective was to destroy us; they knew we were totally fucked-up. They took a piece of our life away from each one of us, so they had killed us in a way. For us to say it took us twenty years to be able to meet together . . .

Munú: Twenty years to say what we're saying now—but the denunciations happened immediately, and after that there was the trial of the juntas, and people found out about what had happened. Half destroyed or whatever, some able to talk and others not—but at least the bulk of it came out very quickly: in 1979 the first testimonies, in 1984 CONADEP,[9] and then in 1985 the trial. We were fucked-up, we still are to some extent, but they didn't destroy us completely. I don't think they let us live because we were no longer good for anything.

Cristina: They also had to go through the process of deterioration of the dictatorship itself, and, besides, it was part of their insanity, their own inconsistencies.

Miriam: I think in the end, for the most part, they let us live because they couldn't stand to kill us. It's one thing to kill someone when there's no day-to-day relationship, no familiarity, and quite another to kill someone when you know his or her little boy, his or her mother. I think we shouldn't rule out a certain "human" side to those murderers.

Munú: In addition there was the omnipotence of thinking that very few people would talk because they had us convinced.

Miriam: Convinced of what?

Munú: Of the "blank" face that we wore on the inside and of the success of their *recuperation process*, making us people who were—

Elisa: Decent!

Munú: *Recuperated* for Western, Christian society, with the fitting middle term, as TIGER ACOSTA, who preached Saint Thomas Aquinas, would say.

Cristina: I don't think the "human" side was the determining factor. But the people they put to work entered into a different sort of dynamic; life in Capucha was different from life outside Capucha. You related more; you

---

9. CONADEP (Comisión Nacional sobre la Desaparición de Personas), the Argentine National Commission on the Disappeared, was created by the government on December 15, 1983, to clarify acts or events associated with the repression carried out under the state terrorism instituted following the military coup. The dictatorship lasted from March 24, 1976, to December 10, 1983. This period is known as the Process of National Reorganization.

were face to face. We knew that people who started to work had a better chance—no guarantee, but a better chance. The thing is that one would be hard-pressed to call it "human" in that context, but it is true that the direct relationship with the other person had a strong influence.

Elisa: It would be very difficult, virtually impossible, to describe what happened inside there in terms of feelings, from the emotional standpoint.

Munú: We lived a life of alienation.

Elisa: Exactly. Was there any feeling?

Munú: Things happened to us.

Elisa: Do you know what you felt in that moment? I know that I had to act, to do.

Munú: I don't know what I felt, just like I still can't feel the horror of the torture. When I say, "They tortured me," I see the body of a woman, and it's me, thrown down on a bed, but I can't put myself inside that body and feel the pain; I describe it from without. The psychological explanation is that one needs to dissociate oneself to be able to survive such situations, to split off the actual feeling induced by that reality. You separate it out, and then you have to travel a long, cluttered road to put the two things back together again. We probably still haven't finished traveling that road, and I don't know whether we ever will, because there must be stages that are closed off forever. You aren't supposed to be able to bear them.

⸙

Elisa: I think that one of the hardest things to tolerate was the perverse relationship with those men, the oppressors. Apparently that didn't occur in the other camps, or at least not in the same way.

Munú: There were kidnapped people in a lot of camps, but the people they brought in from other places usually said that the ESMA was much better, because they could see some of us walking around with an appearance of normalcy. That's what was so perverse. We were kidnapped, the marinos owned our lives, yet we moved around and had to talk to them as if nothing were wrong, as if the daily life in the camp were "normal."

Elisa: What we have to try to understand is that permanent state of confusion. In order to grasp what happened in the ESMA, you have to understand that everything inside there was dehumanized and each person defended him- or herself as well as possible. You have to try to put yourself in the captive's position. Once I ran into a survivor from another camp, and she said, "You all have so much to tell. So many things happened in the ESMA!" In other camps, people were taken, they were tortured, they couldn't see anyone, they were in the dark.

Miriam: I wonder why it is that people understand why some Jewish women prisoners slept with the Germans to survive and they are shocked that the same thing happened here in the ESMA. They can't comprehend it. I just read the book *Literature or Life*, by Jorge Semprún, where he describes how it was inside Auschwitz, and he says there were happy occasions even in the midst of death. But in the ESMA it seems as though it was a sin to laugh!

Elisa: Do you know why people understand the facts about World War II? Because someone told the story. But no one has talked about what it was really like in the ESMA. People understand what happened in Germany, because somebody told the tale, it was discussed, and it's still talked about.

Miriam: In *Schindler's List* you see how the head of the camp falls in love with the prisoner he's chosen as his servant. They don't show it in the movie, but it's obvious that he had relations with that woman and that it made him angry; he despised himself for desiring her. He was supposed to hate her. Semprún describes how imprisoned intellectuals met and listened to music on Sundays in an isolated barrack in the camp. It was a sort of respite, a way to connect with the outside world, with the spirit. They helped each other. One of them, an old university professor, died shortly before the liberation of Auschwitz. Semprún recalls his conversations with this man on his deathbed and how, even in those circumstances there were moments of joy, of solidarity. Surely when they looked out the window, they could see that people were being burned in the crematorium, prisoners were being sent to the gas chamber. But in the midst of all that adversity, they rejoiced at being together, at being able to sustain each other, and sometimes they smiled. Why is it that they've been able to talk about all that, while we seem ashamed to do the same?

Munú: I don't feel ashamed.

Elisa: Some compañeros believe that "some things can never be told," and I disagree with that. We can't let the true story die with us. Sadly, all kinds of events took place in that story. Some captives even fell in love with their torturers!

Miriam: That's been analyzed enough. It's nothing new. There are psychoanalytic theories that pick it apart completely. I think that in the midst of adversity, darkness, in the midst of being alone, tortured, and isolated, a "kind" hand—someone who offers you a plate of food, who asks you how you're feeling, who in your imagination has the power to protect you or at least to stop the torture with the *electric prod*, who lets you send a note to your parents, your kids—well that can disarm you, confuse you. I can understand the compañeras who felt that way. Fortunately, practically none of those relationships lasted any length of time.

Elisa: It's just that in the midst of the dehumanization in that place, people just defended themselves as best they could. That has to be made very clear. And if we laughed once in a while, that doesn't mean there were good torturers.

Miriam: And just because there were some relationships, it doesn't mean that the oppressors deserved our love! When you explain to people what happened to us, they understand, no matter how absurd and perverse the situation. A while back, a Chilean television station came to interview me as part of a documentary on disappeared children. After the spot, one of the reporters said to me, "They say that you were well off, that it was a luxury hotel, that they even took you out to dinner." And I said yes: "It's true that they took us out to dinner, and I'll tell you something else. Once they took a group of girls out dancing, but I'm going to give you the context: they had just murdered the husband of one of the girls, and they took her out dancing at one of the most "in" nightclubs in Buenos Aires. You tell me that wasn't psychological torture at its most sophisticated—that your husband's murderers, who had beaten you and tortured you with an *electric prod*, should then take you out dancing."

Munú: "They took her" doesn't mean "they invited her." You didn't have a choice; they just said, "Let's go!"

Elisa: "Get dressed!"

Miriam: "Hurry up and get dressed, get ready, and let's go." A "no" meant the *hood, transfer,* death. "Either you get ready and we're going dancing or else it means you can't be *recuperated.* I'll give you a *pentanaval,* and I'll *send* you *up,* you Montoneros bitch!"

Munú: How the hell do we convey what happened to us when they took us out, took us into that world, and then brought us back—when the LITTLE PAUL came with the order "You have to go out," and afterward they brought us back to that inferno? The outside world became even more unbearable, the subjugation was laid bare in all its cruelty: "Go out, see the world, see life, and now, go back to the Basement; I own you."

Miriam: What did it mean to us, for example, when they took us out to celebrate the World Cup Soccer match in '78? For me it was terrible! It was torture! To see people hugging in the street, while I was a detainee in a concentration camp who didn't know whether they were going to kill me from one day to the next and who knew that compañeros were being tortured at that very moment. And they took me to a pizzeria on Avenida Maipú! People were shouting in the streets with Argentine flags, "We Argentines are right and human!" And they were kissing each other, all excited. The marinos were elated. And we were kidnapped!

Elisa: And also being afraid that you'd run into someone who might recognize you and you'd have to look the other way. How could you explain that you were kidnapped, standing there in the street?

Miriam: It was denigrating! I can't ever forget the rage I felt. Even now the World Cup gives me a combination of visceral revulsion and melancholy.

Cristina: My experience was different from yours.

Munú: We were all in different circumstances at the time of the World Cup.

You were captives, Cristina was with her compañeros, and I was free and celebrating at first, and then I was kidnapped, all during the course of the World Cup.

Cristina: We were all in the same place. How could we ever have imagined it?

Elisa: That we were kidnapped!

Munú: The kids celebrating the victory in the streets were yelling and chanting their slogans to the same tunes as the political slogans.

Cristina: I was with my compañeros at that time. We had made a sign with a sketch of "Clemente"[10] on it that said, "Let's go Argentina, damn it!" and another with a huge hand making the "V" for victory sign. In the midst of so many losses and so much pain, disconnected from our collective spaces, feeling as though the project we'd fought for was becoming more of a chimera every day, to be able to go out and yell in the middle of a crowd, even for that stupid World Cup, seemed like a dream.

Munú: It wasn't about celebrating the World Cup but about contributing a grain of sand in that context. Cristina was with other people, and I was cut off. But I was with the kids who hoisted up the flag in the obelisk, and I sang, louder than the rest, "Or swear to die gloriously!" They were just the kids from the neighborhood, sweating in their T-shirts, and I was singing the national anthem with them at the top of my lungs, "Or swear to die gloriously!" I wasn't celebrating the World Cup; I was coming together with a whole bunch of people.

Miriam: It was a personal celebration, inside you, because the political and commercial exploitation of the moment was something else altogether.

Munú: Right!

Miriam: I think we need to tell everything that happened in the ESMA. Why are we afraid they won't understand us? Especially when there have been other very similar experiences throughout history. The more I read about the Holocaust, the more I read about the Nazi concentration camps, the more I understand that this is nothing new and that human behavior has gone on the same.

Elisa: I want to talk about what happened. The truth. I don't want anyone to applaud my behavior, and I don't want anyone to say, "Poor thing" either.

Miriam: None of us considers herself a heroine! My heroism ended the minute they pulled the cyanide *pill* out of my throat. The order was that you weren't to be taken alive, because you couldn't be certain that you wouldn't turn someone else in. As I was taking the *pill*, I remember that my final reaction was to look at the sky and thank God, or I don't know whom, for allowing me to die with dignity. For me, that would have been a moment

---

10. "Clemente" was a comic strip character created by "Caloi" (Carlos Loiseau), an Argentine humorist and cartoonist.

of happiness. When they took the *pill* out of my mouth, I felt defeated. "Now what do I do?" I thought. "How am I going to face this?" I never dreamed I would be taken alive. What are you crying about, silly [Munú]?

Munú: [*Crying*] Because I felt the same as you did, and in a sense I still feel that way. I feel it even though I was able to survive. I'm here; I've been able to see everything I've seen. And the mere fact of having been able to give testimony about what happened in there seems so much more worthwhile than if I'd died at that moment. But even so, I'm still torn up about their having won that final battle. The feeling that the *pill* protected me from having someone else subjugate me, destroy me, kill me—with the *pill*, I was the one who decided when I would die! I remember that when they discovered it on me, MARIANO yelled, in the middle of the torture, "Why do you have the *pill*? The *pill* is a sign of death!" And I said, "Because that way, I got to decide when to die. Now you decide!" And to me, that was like my last chance to say, "I define when and how, and screw you!"

Liliana: It took me years to accept that the disappeared were no longer there, that they had killed them.

Munú: You never thought about it in the ESMA when they took people off in those trucks?

Liliana: No.

Elisa: The *transfers*—what did you think they were?

Liliana: I didn't know—people who weren't in that place anymore.

Munú: If you believed that those people were someplace else, then the possibility of your own death didn't dawn on you.

Liliana: Of course. Then it wouldn't happen to me either.

Munú: That was no small thing.

Liliana: And besides, I'd inquired about certain people, and a marino had told me they were free. And even after I was on the outside, I stuck to that conviction for a long time, to the point of arguing with people I knew who said it wasn't true. I'd say to them, "They have to be alive somewhere, because the marino told me so."

Elisa: He told you they'd been released.

Liliana: Right.

Miriam: How?

Liliana: I would ask a marino about someone I knew who had *fallen,* and he would say, "He's free; we let him go." I was so convinced that this had to be the case that in my desire to make it true, I'd argue with mutual friends of that person who said, "He isn't here. The family says he isn't here; he never came back." And I would insist: "Stop talking nonsense. He just never got in touch with the family for some reason." Total denial. I couldn't accept it! It went on like that for years.

Munú: When you say years, how much time do you mean?

Liliana: I don't know, after Alfonsín,[11] two or three years after that.

Miriam: That long?

Elisa: After the trial of the juntas?

Liliana: After the trial I still believed that there were people who were alive somewhere.

Munú: But not all of them.

Liliana: Not all of them. It was horrible for me to have to start killing them off one by one. Horrible.

Miriam: You never thought about why?

Liliana: Clearly I didn't accept that they were dead. I didn't accept it. I think part of it was that if I admitted they were dead at the time, then I died too. It was like accepting the possibility of my own death. If that marino was lying, and the compañero wasn't alive, then I was going to die too. So that compañero had to be alive until 1987—until I finally accepted that he or she was dead and I was alive. That's why I had those arguments with mutual friends, people who argued with me because they felt what I was saying was cruel, that it was cruel to the family. They would ask me, and I would insist that they were still alive.

Munú: I've never heard that before. What was very hard and painful for me—and I'm still in the process of doing this—was being able to adjust my image of the compañeros who are disappeared to an image of them as being dead—to really feel that they are dead.

Elisa: That you'll never see them again.

Munú: That's been hard for me, and it still is. A disappeared person isn't the same as my mom or dad, who died. They are there, in the cemetery. A disappeared person is someone you don't see anymore, someone you never see again but who isn't anywhere. To me, that person is floating in space.

Adriana: Well, they didn't think up this macabre method for nothing.

Liliana: I still say there's another side to the issue, which is that while you were still in the camp, the disappearance or death of the other person raised the possibility of your own disappearance or death. If the person you love is dead, then you too could die at any moment. And you dragged this around with you, even on the outside. Evidently I dragged it around with me for more than ten years.

Elisa: One of the times we met, we talked about the absence of a sense of future when you were inside, about the sensation that life was ending. I couldn't have plans; I didn't know what was going to happen.

Liliana: Of course. You didn't make any plans, because if you did, it was extremely painful.

---

11. Dr. Raúl Alfonsín was the first constitutional president following the dictatorship.

Adriana: It was a microworld, where everything that happened was magnified. The only world was the present, with no expectation of a future—the absolute present with no plans.

Munú: But another thing was to think you were going to die. Not having a plan and not being alive are two different things.

Elisa: To feel that you're going to die! When I asked fat JUNGLE about a group of people, including my compañero, he said, "They were all *transferred*." When he said, "*transferred*," I understood, "dead." I didn't think they were someplace else, in another camp. I took it like that. To you, Liliana, the word "*transfer*" didn't mean death.

Liliana: No.

Elisa: It did to me, and I remember that every *transfer* was terrible. I felt tremendous anguish.

Miriam: Is it true that some people asked to be *transferred?*

Liliana: That's what they say.

Elisa: Yes, in Capucha.

Miriam: But why? What were they thinking?

Elisa: That they'd be better off somewhere else.

Miriam: They were probably told they'd be taken *through the front door*—sent to an official prison.

Liliana: Of course—the possibility of a change in circumstances.

Elisa: Even in the case of El Negro Ricardo and Loli. Ricardo was in Capucha, but Loli was working. One day they told her that CHAMORRO wanted to see her. We gave her the nicest clothes to wear. She had to show that she was *recuperated*. Up until that moment, a lot of us thought they were going to take her *through the front door*. What actually happened was a clear example that if they wanted to cut you down, they'd cut you down. It didn't matter whether you were in the Fishbowl or still in Capucha. It was all the same to them.

Munú: Loli is the girl they killed.

Elisa: Yes, they say they gave her 220 volts and killed her—downstairs, in Jorges.

Miriam: They killed her in Jorges?

Elisa: Or else in Dorado. I can't remember who told us, but we found out. They killed her right there; they didn't take her someplace else. And Ricardo too. They said that Ricardo kept on cursing the milicos, no matter what they did to him. Everybody there found out about it shortly after it happened.

Munú: We knew that "*transfer*" meant "death," and they knew we knew it. When I *fell*, they made me sleep in the Basement for about five months, in the Infirmary. There were some medicine cabinets there. The names of all the medicines ended with the word "naval" or something like that. For the first few days, I couldn't figure out what it all meant. I still hadn't

94

realized that they gave people an injection and took them away. I think I never knew about the *flights*, but I did know that they gave them an injection, put them to sleep, and took them away. Before I found this out, the marinos were joking around, and they said, laughing, "Put a lock on the cabinet just in case this one . . ."—in case I injected myself. They were joking among themselves and I just stared uncomprehendingly.

Elisa: Funny guys.

Munú: A long time after that, they *transferred* four compañeros who were in Capuchita: one was called Yacaré, Cafati the Turk, a girl from Santa Fe, and her brother-in-law Bicho. That would have been late November 1978. I didn't see them when they were taken away. The next day MARIANO came into the Basement. The word was out that they'd been *transferred*, and I was in the little office where I worked. He stood in the doorway and screamed at me, "Well, don't give me that shitty look, because that's how it is here." As though I were going to reproach him—

Elisa: For killing them.

Munú: I don't know, something like that. I had spent a lot of time talking with Cafati the Turk. He wrote me some beautiful poems for my birthday. He had *fallen* just a short time before, and we knew nothing about his life. We'd see him when they took him *hooded* to the bathroom. That night, October 18, PEDRO asked me whether I wanted to say hello to him, and I took him a cup of some sort of dessert that the compañeros had made for me. I went into the torture room where he was and gave him a kiss. I told him it was my birthday and that he should be strong, that we were going to get out of there. Later they took me out of the ESMA to phone my family. I bought a magazine and passed it to him. The next day, a GREEN gave me back the magazine, and he told me there was a paper inside it for me. I went into the small bathroom and found two poems. I read them, and that was the second and last time I cried inside there. Supposedly you weren't allowed to talk to the Turk, but since I stayed down there until late at night, depending on which GREEN was on duty, we would talk for hours. The GREEN was at the desk, I was standing in the doorway of the room, and he was inside it, so that if some officer came into the Basement, the Turk would just shut the door, and I would keep on talking to the GREEN. We kept this up for days. What could the three of us have been talking about at three or four in the morning in the Basement of the ESMA?

Liliana: The Turk was always downstairs?

Munú: He was downstairs for a long time. Later they took him to Capuchita, and occasionally they'd take him back downstairs again.

Miriam: They made him write his story.

Munú: They made him write his life story, and Andrea and I were given the task of typing it up and doing a style edit. The Turk wrote beautifully; he

18/10/78: Aguantame este presente para tu cumpleaños. Pa
ra echar un poco en el festejo y agradecerte — a vos, a
todas las pibas y a los muchachos — la mano que dan. Gr
acias.

PARA TODOS TUS DÍAS

PRIMERO FUE TU VOZ, ENTRE OTRAS VOCES,
ENCENDIENDO EL PASILLO, ILUMINÁNDOLO.
DESPUÉS TU CAMINAR, TU PASO ALEGRE,
TUS GANAS DE VIVIR, DE AMAR,
TU CANTO.

SIN CONOCER TU NOMBRE, ESPERABA TUS OJOS,
CUALQUIER DÍA,
ASOMÁNDOSE AUDACES POR LA PUERTA,
CUALQUIER NOCHE, CON VOS, SE APARECÍAN
A PERFUMAR MI PATIO,
EL DE ESTA CELDA,
CON SU CELESTE FRESCO DE GLICINAS.

¿QUIÉN SOS?
YO QUISIERA JUNTARTE TUS RAYUELAS,
TUS MANCHAS Y TUS RONDAS. TUS MUÑECAS.
CONTARLES MIS PICADOS, MIS BOLITAS,
MI BARRILETE AZUL, AQUELLA ESTRELLA.

DESPUÉS ¿FUISTE CRECIENDO?
¿QUÉ VISTE? ¿QUÉ NO VISTE?
¿QUÉ APRENDIERON TUS PECHOS? ¿QUÉ, TUS MANOS?
¿QUÉ BEBIERON TUS OJOS? ¿QUIÉN ROBÓ SUS GLICINAS...
...HOY LO SABÉS: EL HUMO DE LAS FÁBRICAS
NO SE VENDE AL CONTADO EN LIBRERÍAS.

— — — — — — — — — — — — — — — —

Poem written by Cafati the Turk for Nilda Actis (Munú), inside the ESMA, on the occasion of her birthday.

10/18/78: Allow me to give you this present for your birthday. To join in the festivities and to thank you, and all the gals and the guys, for extending your hand. Thanks.

For All Your Days

First it was your voice, among other voices,
Brightening up the hallway, illuminating it.

used a lot of street slang. What he did was fantastic, and those barbarians wanted to change his words; anything that came from the people bothered them that much. We explained this, and they left it as it was. He wrote about his grandmother, his mother, his childhood, the vineyard.

Liliana: What they really wanted was the money from a kidnapping in which he allegedly had participated.

Munú: Yes, that's what they were interested in.

Liliana: Once they resigned themselves to the fact that the Turk was not going to tell them anything about that money, they *transferred* him.

Munú: The officers used to say that when they stopped torturing him for a moment, he started to sing a tango, and they decided, smiling, not to touch him again. They liked his reaction; they thought it was funny, and they realized that he wasn't going to tell them anything. The Turk was delightful!

Liliana: I remember that the CAT talked with Cafati a lot. I was working in Dorado, and I would see him come and go. They must have sent several different people in to talk to him to see if anyone could get out of him where that money was. I was struck by the stunned look on the CAT's face when MARIANO, or someone in Dorado, told him that Cafati wasn't there anymore.

Munú: I have the poems he wrote for my birthday, in his own handwriting. He wrote another poem for Andrea, where he talks about Roque, about

---

Then your walk, your joyful step,
Your desire to live, to love,
Your song.

Not knowing your name, I awaited your eyes,
Any day, showing up boldly at the door;
Any night, with you, they came
to perfume the garden
of my cell with their fresh celestial blue of wisteria.

Who are you?
I would like to sound out your hopscotches,
your freeze tags and rings-around-the-rosy. Your dolls.
Tell them about my soccer matches, my marbles,
my blue kite, that star.

Later, did you grow up?
What did you see and not see?
What did your breasts learn? What, your hands?
What did your eyes drink in? Who stole their wisteria . . . ?

. . . Now you know: the smoke from the factories
is not sold cash down in bookstores.

Serafo, and about me, and he alludes to how they're going to take him away. I don't know whether he thought they'd take him somewhere else or whether he knew they were going to kill him. After the *transfer*, the GREENS found the drafts of his writings inside his mattress. We weren't even supposed to know each other, and we appeared there in his poems. They warned me that the drafts were in the Intelligence Office, and I got scared. That night I waited in the Basement for Roque until they brought him from the printers, and I said, "You know, such and such happened." And he said, "If they'd decided to let the Turk go, then there'd be cause for concern, but they killed him; they *sent* him *up*. What do they care who he knew!" And that's how it was. They never said a word to us. They held him for about two months, and they *transferred* him. It was a moment of absolute anguish.

Liliana: What a story! So much anguish and pain!

Munú: That's why I say that once I started to circulate a little, it was always clear to me—

Elisa: That the *transfers* meant death.

Munú: That the people who weren't there were dead.

Elisa: We discussed these subjects in the Fishbowl; maybe you weren't there.

Liliana: There were people who understood it better and said so. Maybe I had such an attitude of denial because I was so young. I have the feeling that there were people who were older than I was who understood everything much better than I did. I always think of it as a matter of age.

Elisa: How old were you?

Liliana: Twenty-three.

Elisa: I was about the same age as you were, one year older. Miriam was younger.

Miriam: Yes, I was twenty. I was nineteen when I *fell*, but I had turned twenty by the time they took me to the ESMA.

Munú: It seems as though it was more a matter of denial than age, because you still felt it after you got out. It wasn't as though you got out and there was some big revelation.

Elisa: Maybe I didn't register the subject of my own death. I didn't think about my own death.

Munú: I didn't either.

Miriam: I did, especially when I was at the air force. I thought about how sad it would be to die at nineteen, without having done what I'd dreamed of doing in life, without having children. I cried. I also thought a lot about how they were going to kill me. I never could have imagined the *flights*—I thought about a bullet; I even picked out my executioner. I asked one of them to be the one to shoot me.

Liliana: It wasn't only that I didn't think about my death; I had a big fantasy about how much time I would be imprisoned: ten years, fifteen, twenty. The issue was how old I'd be when I got out of there: twenty-five, thirty, forty. I imagined that I'd be there until I was forty. So then, the few times I tried to think about my life, I'd think, "Well, what does one do with a life that starts at forty?" Just think how completely into denial I was that I had decided that they were going to give me twenty years. I had put together my own scenario. When they killed my compañero, El Gringo, I'd decided the same thing, right up until his body turned up: he wasn't dead; he'd be in prison for twenty years, and then we'd be together again. I don't know why, but I thought everything got worked out in twenty years. Maybe it was because of the tango that goes, "Twenty years is nothing." I had decided that people disappeared and reappeared after twenty years, and therefore, that's just what would happen to me.

Miriam: I think it's hard to understand what we're talking about when we describe our experiences in the camp; you really have to have experienced that proximity, that contact with the kidnapper to understand it. Some people consider that daily contact with the jailer, the torturer, the murderer obscene.

Elisa: When I went to Spain to testify as a witness to the crimes against humanity perpetrated by the juntas, I spoke with a girl who was kidnapped and held in the Bank for a month and a half. She said, "You didn't have bars. That was worse!"

Cristina: The bars seen from a different angle, the bars that separated and, in fact, would protect you.

Elisa: She said the bars helped her keep her sanity. She talked about the symbolic bars that defined who was who. The jailer was the jailer.

Munú: They constantly distorted the situation. They'd come, they'd beat you to a pulp with a stick, and then at two in the morning they'd get you, put you in a car, and take you out to dinner. They'd sit you down at the same table, turn you into an equal: you ate the same food, they wanted to hear your opinions, and then back to Capucha you went. That would drive anybody crazy! Except for us! [*Laughter*]

Miriam: We're brimming with mental health!

Munú: I'm gradually realizing how unsettling that situation was. That phrase "You didn't have bars" was like a revelation. Besides that, we couldn't express what we felt. Every time I think about what you were telling us before, Elisa, about how they told you, "Don't cry!" and you never cried again, it fills me with sorrow.

Cristina: How did they tell you not to cry?

Elisa: When the first *transfer* happened after I *fell*, I started to cry like a madwoman, and Quica and Chiche came up to me and said, "You're digging your own grave. Don't cry. You can't cry here." It was a lifelong curse, and I never cried again. I still can't.

Munú: Merque told me that she cried for an entire year when she was working on her thesis, her research on the "concentrationary power." "You're lucky," I'd tell her. Last year I started to cry a little. In other words, there were several of us who never cried.

Cristina: My daughter helped me with that, when we suffered another terrible loss just when I thought my plate was full. In October 1987, Pepe, my second husband and Sofia's father—she was eighteen months old at the time—died of an aneurysm. We'd gotten married in 1985, trying to pick up the pieces of two histories traversed by loss and pain. Sofi and I lived alone at first, but then we moved in with my family for three years. When we moved again, just the two of us, she was seven years old, and she felt her father's absence even more strongly. One night she got very upset, and she asked, "Why did my daddy die?" I gave her all the possible explanations, the same ones I'd been able to offer all those years—the truth—but she wasn't satisfied with that. She kept insisting that "there's a reason for everything in this world" and there had to be one in this case too. It got to the point where I couldn't take it anymore, and I went off to cry. And then she said, very surprised and relieved, "You're crying. I've never seen you cry." And it did us good to be able to cry together.

Miriam: To survive in there and bear the suffering, you had to suppress it. And you were already out when you were widowed, but you kept on suppressing it. Sometimes I wonder how it was that most of us who survived were able to stomach it, to endure so much horror.

Elisa: You can't set out to explain the unexplainable. They put you in there, and everything that was human was relegated. It was all a travesty. We were defenseless, primitive beings at the mercy of lunatics. We didn't have any rights!

Miriam: When one person kidnaps another person and confines that person in a little room, then that person eats when the other person wants, speaks when the other person wants, does what the other person wants all the time. They had enslaved our will, even though there were small opportunities for rebellion that took on a wide variety of expressions.

Elisa: You need to explain the unexplainable—to find an answer for why what happened happened. Each one of us did the best we could. Faced with the reality of kidnapping and disappearance, we each reacted as best we could.

Munú: And we're still reacting as best we can.

Top (inset): Nilda Actis (Munú), photograph from official identification card (supervised release, January 12, 1979). *Bottom:* Nilda Actis forging the watermark on a federal police identification card as one of her jobs in the ESMA, October 18, 1978.

3
Daily Life in Captivity

Work sets you free.
> —Writing on a door in Auschwitz

The camp is an infinite spectrum, not of gray, which implies a combination of white and black, but of many colors, always a spectrum in which there are no clear, pure tones but rather multiple combinations.
> —Pilar Calveiro, ESMA survivor, *El poder desaparecedor*

To be chosen to work in the ESMA was, for the detained-disappeared, a step in the direction of life. But taking part in that sinister production machine had other costs: it required constant pretense, dotted with the oases of small everyday acts of more or less silent rebellion. Through such acts, the disappeared mocked the power of the disappearers. Relationships among prisoners, with death rubbing up against them at every turn, were charged with tension and distrust but also with solidarity.

Munú: Sometimes I start thinking about our acts of resistance.
Elisa: I resisted on the work side. When they took me to work, I started making spelling errors that I'd never made before; I couldn't remember how to spell words. This caused serious problems with the compañera who was dictating to me: I'd write, I'd make a mistake, and she would get angry.
Munú: You did it all wrong!
Elisa: You don't know how wrong!
Munú: That was a subconscious form of resistance, unpremeditated.
Elisa: But I thought, "I'm going nuts." It wasn't something that usually happened to me. It happened only there, and afterward it stopped.
Munú: Another thing we did, even though we knew we weren't supposed to, was to talk to the compañeros they had thrown down on those filthy mattresses in Capucha.
Elisa: Yes! And with the pregnant women. I'd be walking by, and I'd turn automatically into the room where they were held.
Munú: I remember roller-skating around in the Basement of the ESMA, which of course wasn't allowed, and now I see it as a sign of life. I had a

pair of borrowed skates when I *fell,* and when they took me to get clothes, I grabbed them so as not to leave anything of mine in that house. One time, Andrea and I put them on late at night, and we skated up and down the hallway from one end to the other. There were no captives in the torture rooms, of course. We laughed a lot. Another time, they gave the two of us an intelligence job: to locate the house of a compañero, who I hope never *fell.* It was terrible when they made you do a job like that, because you didn't want to collaborate with a kidnapping but you also couldn't risk having them find out how you felt. In this case, they had information that someone had been taken from a house *compartmentalized;* they'd driven for about fifteen minutes and crossed a street, and he'd gotten out, walked five blocks, and arrived at a particular location. I didn't know the capital at all. They gave us a map, and our intelligence job was to figure out where he'd started from, based on where he'd gotten out—where the house of the compañero they were looking for was located. And it was obvious! [*Laughter*] You left from here, you went twenty blocks, you crossed the street, and there was the house.

Liliana: But you two didn't realize it!

Munú: Nooo!!

Liliana: You guys thought you'd have to go to Paris! The compañero was in Paris! [*Much laughter all around*]

Munú: You had to go anywhere except where the compañero actually was! We were in the Egg Carton, looking at the map and saying, "What do we do?" "What can we invent?" To make matters worse, we had to present a written report! We described how the car had traveled in I-don't-know-which-direction, the range of movement was such and such, and after four blocks, something or other. They were going to end up in hell!

Elisa: Of course!

Munú: MANUEL had assigned us the task. Why did they give us those intelligence jobs? To test us? Well, we arrived at various and sundry conclusions, analysis, and description—everything perfect. When MANUEL saw our report, he said, "This is a disaster."

Liliana: You're no good at this—off to the kitchen with you! And you said, "That's what we were hoping you'd say." [*Laughter*]

Munú: We always had these conscious attitudes of resistance.

Elisa: I don't know whether I did. I acted like a robot! I did a lot of the things you describe, but I didn't see them as conscious resistance; on the contrary, I acted on instinct. For example, I collected the telephone numbers of the compañeros in Capucha so that when I went out, I could call their relatives and tell them that their sons and daughters were being held captive in the ESMA.

Munú: You didn't do that on instinct!

Elisa: Yes, I did.

Munú: Today, sitting here in your house drinking *mate,* are you aware of the risk that was involved?

Elisa: Yes, but I wasn't conscious of it at the time; it wasn't a conscious resistance. I didn't think, "I'm doing this to screw the milicos!" My bad spelling, for instance, just happened to me spontaneously.

Munú: Maybe you did some things more consciously than others.

Elisa: In my case, I think that everything was absolutely subconscious. At that moment, I just couldn't do battle with them.

Munú: How can you say that getting the phone numbers and notifying the families was a subconscious act? No, you decided to ask for the numbers and take the risk!

Elisa: Probably. In fact, I didn't call from my house; I'd go to a public pay phone.

Munú: I stole the sheets! When they took me on a *visit,* I'd take along the sheets that I knew had belonged to the compañeros and had been pinched by the marinos when they ransacked the houses. In Buenos Aires, they took me two or three times to the home of some friends, and I took the sheets with me to leave with them. In the ESMA Storeroom, the system for changing the sheets consisted of turning in two dirty ones for two clean ones. I would go to great lengths to turn in one and get two back! They couldn't find out.

Elisa: Was it automatic or deliberate?

Munú: Deliberate! I stole anything I felt belonged to someone.

Miriam: You didn't steal them; you recovered them.

Munú: You're right. You're comment is right on. I took a little watch, and I still have it. I figured that someday I would find its owner; obviously I didn't find him. I took a leaf from a tree outside; I put it where I worked, and I called it my "external reference." Taking a sheet was less risky than getting a telephone number as Elisa did, but it was a risk nonetheless.

Elisa: But you were conscious of the fact that you were doing it to screw them?

Munú: Yes, I was taking something that belonged to my compañeros. What I don't know is why I focused on the sheets. I never stopped to think that the washing machine and everything else there also had belonged to the compañeros.

Elisa: And you didn't take them with the thought that they would serve as testimony either.

Munú: No, I took them because they belonged to my own!

Elisa: Of course.

Munú: I hadn't even begun to think about giving testimony. The feeling I had in there was of being suspended in time; you were just "there."

Liliana: I remember going to the Fishbowl once, and you, Elisa, were reading the newspaper and looking at the performance supplement.

Munú: [*Laughter*]

Liliana: And you asked me whether I liked to read about movies. And I said, "The truth is that I don't pay much attention to that." And you replied, "But don't you think about the prospect of all the movies you'll be able to see?" It was probably your way of resisting, your desire to live. There are three situations that I recall as planning for the future. One was that conversation with you. Another was a conversation, also in the Fishbowl, when Merque was there, you—Elisa—and I don't know who else. And Merque was talking about her daughters, and she was saying something about how you weren't going to spend the rest of your life raising your children based on what had gone on inside there. You had to try to move on however you could. And another thing I remember is MARIANO and his obsession with planning your life. MARIANO had a certain—I don't know what to call it—irony, cynicism, idiocy. I don't know—I never understood it.

Munú: Sometimes it seemed as if he really didn't grasp our situation. Maybe it was cynicism.

Liliana: Basically he was stupid about certain things. He was always reminding you that you had to enjoy life. He used to tell me that I wasted a lot of time and that if he were in my shoes, he would take advantage of the chance to study history, for example. I would just look at him. [*Laughter*] The life of the captive, nothing to do all day, and he would have used the time to study history. I said, no, not history—what I was going to do was work out. [*Laughter*] So from then on, I had to spend hours pedaling on the stationary bicycle upstairs, stolen from who knows who. And whenever Mariano passed by, he'd say, "Very good, very good."

Elisa: How awful!

Liliana: And I'd just pedal away.

Miriam: What do you remember about the food? I came from the air force, where I hardly ate.

Munú: They didn't feed you?

Miriam: I had boiled *mate* only in the morning, when they gave me that much, and a plate of something or other at noon, usually noodles or a piece of burnt meat.

Liliana: So who do you think they were fixing that food for?

Miriam: They weren't fixing it for other prisoners, because there were hardly any others there. It was an *operations house*. The food would have been for them.

Liliana: But then why was it so bad?

Miriam: I don't know. Either they didn't give me the same food, or they went out to eat.

Elisa: There weren't very many of them; it wasn't like the ESMA.

Miriam: It was an intelligence center. Sometimes, a zumbo was there, a non-com who cooked, and other times he wasn't. There was no cook at night or on Saturday and Sunday. So I didn't eat, or they might bring me a yogurt or a slice of pizza.

Munú: You were starving to death.

Miriam: I lost 26 pounds. I weighed 125 pounds when I *fell*, and by the time I got to the ESMA, I weighed 99 pounds. I never weighed so little again in my life.

Munú: Well, I'm glad it didn't happen again!

Elisa: We didn't all eat the same food in the ESMA. Being in Capucha wasn't the same as being chosen for the *recuperation process*, to work.

Liliana: The food in Capucha was horrible. I don't know where they got it. The meat was half raw.

Elisa: Sandwiches with a lot of bread and very little meat.

Miriam: And boiled *mate*.

Elisa: The meat was rotten. It smelled sickening.

Munú: When I was sleeping upstairs, I was in the Capucha sector, except I was in a bed, next to yours, Miriam, and Chiqui's and María Eva's. Roque would pass by on his way to bed, and he'd say good night to us. And from there I could see the GREENS fixing sandwiches on a big table. Sometimes they left bread out, and the rats would run off with it. I'd fall asleep watching them.

Miriam: There were lots of them. And they were huge. They crawled down the beams, very close to our heads. They'd grab the bread out of the baskets and run back up the beam with it until they hit a turn and bumped into something and it dropped. Then they'd go back down to the basket for another piece. What did you see the GREENS fixing?

Munú: Some meat with bread, some kind of dried beef.

Miriam: It resembled scallopini, half boiled.

Liliana: Yes, it was boiled!

Miriam: Grayish.

Elisa: It looked like boiled scallopini. They made it into sandwiches. They'd come at ten or eleven in the morning, and, depending on the guard rotation, they fed you whenever they felt like it—at twelve, twelve-thirty. If it was really hot, the meat was already rotten.

Miriam: That's why it smelled rotten. But those of us who were working ate better. After having eaten so badly at the air force, I was surprised when I got to the ESMA—to walk into the third-floor dining room and find a can of sweet potato pudding with chocolate they'd bring out of the kitchen every so often. Do you remember how we'd bring food back from our home *visits*?

Elisa: We'd bring those cookies—*alfajores.*

Miriam: Or that rolled, stuffed meat. Or cold cuts.

Liliana: Sometimes they gave us sweet potato pudding and cheese in the Basement too.

Munú: I guess I wasn't in the ESMA, because I have no memory whatsoever of cheese and pudding.

Liliana: Maybe you didn't notice, but they brought it and passed it around.

Munú: They brought it to the Basement?

Liliana: Yes.

Miriam: Maybe there was less of it downstairs, because the "proletariat" was in the Basement, the manual laborers.

Munú: They brought us boxes full of apple halves, all rotted. There was never a whole apple. In very special cases, some charitable GREEN around there would steal something from the Officers' Casino. For example, on my birthday one of them stole a tub of cream and brought it there. But I don't remember them sending us pudding or a slab of cheese.

Elisa: The food came on big platters.

Liliana: Huge tin trays, enormous platters.

Miriam: What was the regular food like, the everyday food?

Elisa: Bad.

Miriam: It was the food for the Mechanics School students.

Elisa: Do you remember that chopped meat with potato, egg, and string beans—that mishmash of leftovers?

Liliana: And the pulverized chicken—chicken "a la grenade."

Munú: It was dreadful. They brought chicken a lot.

Elisa: It was prepared badly.

Miriam: Pulverized, nearly disintegrated—you couldn't identify the parts. They also served those crepes topped with a pile of cold cuts. What were they called?

Liliana: German cold cuts.

Miriam: Yes, or "primavera."

Munú: I don't remember those crepes.

Elisa: No, they weren't crepes. It was a batter on this big tray, a gigantic heap of crepe batter, and on top they put—

Miriam: Mayonnaise.

Elisa: Mayonnaise with the cold cuts, but mixed cold cuts, not salami with cheese for instance, but salami with ham, with the stuffed meat rolls, all topped with a gigantic layer of crepe.

Miriam: And what did we drink?

Elisa: Water.

Miriam: They didn't have juice concentrates—did they?

Liliana: No.

Miriam: I remember seeing some large cans of juice in the freezer in the Fishbowl, but someone must have brought them from a home *visit*.

Elisa: The same as when some of that gin or rum appeared. It came from the family *visits*—things people brought from home and hid so they wouldn't be found.

Miriam: On one of my first nights in the ESMA, one of the GREENS went to buy ice cream, and Roque brought me some.

Elisa: Were you in Capucha?

Miriam: No, before that they kept me for several days in one of the interrogation rooms in the Basement.

Elisa: And they gave you ice cream there?

Miriam: Yes, but it was a transgression. Once in a while a GREEN would give you chocolate or a piece of candy, or we'd go to Capucha and secretly give candy to those who weren't working, the ones who were thrown down on the mattresses.

Munú: I did that a thousand times.

Miriam: When you went home, what foods did you bring back?

Liliana: I didn't bring back food.

Munú: I didn't either.

Elisa: The compañeros would ask me to bring back gin or "spirits" as we called it there.

Munú: I never brought back anything.

Liliana: I didn't either.

Miriam: I'd bring back cakes.

Elisa: I'd bring some kind of dessert, a ricotta cheesecake, things like that.

Liliana: I would bring back personal items, toiletries. That's what I wanted—more than food. I couldn't enjoy my food in there.

Miriam: We did it to entertain those who stayed behind, like when you go on a trip and bring back a souvenir.

Elisa: To share after a meal. You usually brought back something sweet. The important thing was to bring them something.

Miriam: Once someone who'd gone to one of the provinces brought back avocados. I also remember the alfajores—those cookies they brought from Santa Fe.

Munú: I don't remember anyone bringing food back from the *visits*.

Miriam: Do any of you remember the day they made fritters?

Liliana: Yes, Elena made them when she was still in the Basement, before they moved her up to Capucha.

Munú: The prisoners in the Basement gave me a birthday party. They made a cake, which was actually applesauce with lots of cream on top. That's why I remember the GREEN who stole the cream from the Officers' Casino.

Cristina: I remember that whenever Adriana went home, she would bring back cookies or German cakes, which were her mom's specialty and had a lot of sentimental value. But I have absolutely no memory of the mealtimes. It's strange. I know I lived those moments, because I remember the huge rectangular trays and the crepes, but I can't conjure up images of the dinners or lunches; they're erased from my memory. In fact, I have only a few memories from daily life. Earlier I jokingly said I didn't have a day-to-day life. Maybe it was because, as you all were saying, I was moved back and forth—from the Basement to Capucha, then back to the Basement, to Dorado, and over to Capuchita. There was too much moving around. I do recall our chaotic schedules; sometimes I didn't even know whether it was day or night. Something could happen at any moment. We lived in a state of alert, even though we pretended otherwise or we'd gotten used to it.

Liliana: Why did we fight over food so much? It was chaos. Once I had a run-in with Em over this issue.

Elisa: I remember a fight that came to blows between two compañeros, a guy and a girl. There were sliced oranges, and they were topped with caramel. The fight was over spoonfuls of the caramel—"You're taking too much; you're not leaving any for anyone else; give me some of that caramel"—and it came to blows. I think that the fights were associated with the enormous anxiety.

Munú: Mealtimes were horrible for me; I couldn't bear them. Once I started the *recuperation process*, I ate as fast as I could, so I could get up and leave. Every day, I'd automatically go straight to the Egg Carton, over to the side, because I couldn't stand the laughter of the prisoners at the table. If only one or two people were there, I could laugh and talk perfectly normally. For years after I got out, I could talk to only one or two people at a time; with three or four, I'd be struck dumb.

Elisa: You couldn't speak?

Munú: No, I couldn't say a word. Now I can talk, but I couldn't before. I never figured out why I reacted like that at mealtimes—being all together, the laughter, the conversation. And besides we always talked about horrible subjects. Everything descended into dark humor using the slang from that place. There was a TV in the Basement dining room. I wonder whose it was.

Liliana: Yes, there was a television at one point.

Elisa: I experienced something similar at mealtimes. I would stay awake at night, with some excuse about work. I would go to bed at six in the morning and sleep until two in the afternoon, and that's when my day started. That way I avoided contact with the marinos and also the lunches and the constant fighting. The fights weren't over the best serving, because we all ate the same crap.

Liliana: What could they have been about?

Elisa: I don't know, but upstairs the fights were constant.

Miriam: Once they found a compañero's homemade stuffed meat sandwich in a desk drawer, and it caused a scandal.

Munú: Who started it, the others?

Miriam: Yes, the other prisoners. He'd brought it back from his house, hidden it, and forgotten all about it. The sandwich rotted in the drawer before he could share it with anyone.

Liliana: I'd have lunch with Jorgelina, in Dorado, Monday through Saturday, and evenings and Sundays I ate in the Basement.

Munú: And was it the same food?

Liliana: No, it wasn't the same. They took different meals to Dorado. We ate chicken a la milanesa, but prepared differently, and beef. It was the same food but prepared better.

Elisa: That's what they gave the *mini-staff* people. In 1977 and early 1978, when they left the door to their room open, you could see what they were eating. It was the same food but prepared differently.

Miriam: Where did the *mini-staff* eat?

Elisa: In what later became the Pregnant Women's Room, on the third floor, in Altillo. Those were the *mini-staff*'s rooms; they had a dining room and a dormitory.

Munú: Which ones were they? The large ones, facing the entrance to Altillo?

Elisa: Right.

Miriam: Those rooms faced the street; they faced Avenida del Libertador.

Elisa: Yes, there were two large rooms.

Munú: With some small ones around the corner, on both sides.

Elisa: What were they like?

Munú: The doors of the big rooms opened into the hallway in front of the dining room, and the small rooms were located on the way to the Fishbowl and Capucha. They held Patricia Roisinblit in the small room on the Fishbowl side when they took her to the ESMA to give birth. On the Capucha side there were other little doors where they stored the men's clothing.

Liliana: I don't remember that.

Munú: What were those places called?

Liliana: The storage rooms.

Munú: No. The Storeroom was opposite. They were little closets where they stored the clothes of the men who didn't sleep in stalls. The lockers! I'm referring to the end of 1978, when they took me upstairs to sleep on the third floor.

Elisa: All of that changed over time. It was very different before.

Miriam: Do you all remember the fight over the cactus?

Elisa: Ah, yes!

Munú: What happened?

Miriam: María had a plant in the dining room. She took care of it, and one day it was found all slashed up.

Munú: How awful!

Liliana: Horrifying!

Miriam: People said the plant brought misfortune, bad luck, and she insisted that it wasn't so.

Munú: And, with a "stroke of luck," someone went and destroyed it!

Miriam: Sure! It was all cut up! And the knife was sticking out of it, like some kind of ritual murder. We never found out who did it.

Munú: What assholes!

Elisa: The circumstances there brought out the meanest, the worst in you.

Liliana: We were under pressure.

Elisa: The worst kind of meanness known to human beings came out in the fight over something so insignificant. Now we can see it clearly. Maybe we weren't even suffering deprivation or hunger at that exact moment, but we were connected to death.

Miriam: But wasn't there enough food? Why did we fight?

Munú: I don't remember fights in the Basement. Sure, when the big tray came out, everyone pounced on it. But they weren't looking for a fight. The composition of people downstairs was different.

Elisa: Yes, I think that has something to do with it. Upstairs, people fought; there were confrontations.

Munú: Or maybe it had to do with our activities.

Elisa: I think it was a matter of human misery. It just came out of you naturally. Maybe the cause was the connection with death. We wanted to maintain our hold on life through the bread.

Munú: Are you saying that the people upstairs were—

Liliana: Crazier than the ones downstairs?

Elisa: There was a higher degree of craziness. Although I never worked in the Basement, I think the pressure in the Fishbowl was very strong. Those lunatic marinos would come in with a different idea every day—make notes, speeches, reports—and you had to have it done by whenever they needed it.

Munú: The jobs downstairs were less intellectual—printing, forgeries, videos, construction—and even though we had the same insane deadlines for the work they ordered us to do, I think we experienced the pressure differently.

Munú: Now that more than twenty years have passed, when I remember that there was a washing machine in the bathroom, I think that washing machine must have belonged to—

Miriam: To someone! It was stolen!

Munú: What an amazing degree of denial. It never occurred to me while I was there.

Elisa: The washing machine we used upstairs was Chiche's.

Munú: I'm speaking about the Basement, not upstairs. You were talking about how you fought upstairs. Did you also fight when you lined up to take a shower or use the washing machine, or only at mealtimes?

Elisa: I never fought with anyone over the stationary bicycle; no one made me get off when I was using it. There was more solidarity when it came to clothes. If I had clothes to wash, and someone said, "Let's combine our loads," then we did.

Liliana: I can't remember what I did with the clothes.

Elisa: We washed them.

Liliana: Where?

Elisa: Those of us upstairs, in a washing machine.

Liliana: I can't remember! And where did we hang them?

Munú: Did you keep your clothes downstairs or upstairs? When you wanted to change your clothes, where did you go to get them, downstairs or upstairs?

Liliana: Upstairs, in a stall.

Munú: So you did your wash upstairs.

Liliana: No, if I washed, I washed downstairs.

Munú: I did my wash in the little bathroom downstairs.

Liliana: I think I did my wash downstairs in the Basement, because I never spent time upstairs. I went up there only to sleep.

Munú: They washed our sheets.

Liliana: I can't remember. I can't remember!

Elisa: I never had any sheets. I always slept in Capucha on a little mattress. When did they start having sheets?

Munú: When I started sleeping upstairs, there were sheets. There weren't any for the five months before that, when I slept in the Infirmary.

Miriam: Were there sheets on the bed in Capucha?

Munú: Yes, on the bed, in the area of Capucha next to the people who were thrown down on the mattresses handcuffed and wearing *hoods* or *masks*.

Elisa: I never did sleep in a bed in the ESMA. I went from the mattress to my house, with no layovers! [*Laughter*]

Munú: Some of the sheets had a navy emblem on them. The brown blankets too—the ones that stank. I still smell them; they always stink of filth, even when they're new. Sometimes I was given a sheet with a little flower print or polka dots, and those were the ones I took.

Liliana: Naturally, it was part of their booty, the things they stole. Everything was pinched!

Elisa: The chair you sat on—everything was stolen.

Munú: The furniture?

All: Everything was pinched!

Liliana: Anything that wasn't navy issue was stolen.

Elisa: The desks in the Fishbowl and everything in the front part of the room—the table, the chairs. Do you remember the hammock—the Fishbowl hammock?

Munú: I never went into the Fishbowl. They wouldn't let me.

Elisa: A hanging wicker hammock and two armchairs—they belonged to Chiche.

Munú: And she was detained there!

Elisa: It was terrible! The outside inside! Her husband and children were left homeless.

Liliana: Where did we hang our clothes—downstairs?

Munú: Liliana is still dwelling on the clothes. We put the clean clothes in the Egg Carton.

Miriam: We hung the clean, wet clothes in the area where they later put the printing press.

Munú: Yes, at the entrance to the Basement.

Miriam: There was a staircase there, with a big door leading outside to an area where they parked a trailer truck. They would inject people with pentothal, with *pentonaval*, downstairs and then take them out through that door.

Munú: Yes, they made me go in through that door to get to the Basement when I went back to the ESMA before leaving the country. I'm not sure whether they'd already changed things around or whether they took me that way for some other reason.

Elisa: I never knew anything about that door.

Liliana: The printing press was at the entrance.

Munú: Of course. The two small bathrooms were there and the big outside door, and we had hung two clotheslines there. The printing press was on one side, and in the middle there was an empty space where a lot of pretty filthy stuff was always piled. There was a machine we called the "crocodile" that shredded whatever you put into it, which was used to destroy identity cards and such. Later they started to do woodworking there.

Liliana: Of course! They did woodworking there.

Munú: Serafo, Roque, and Tito.

Liliana: They set up a carpentry shop of sorts, and they cut wood. Now I remember.

Elisa: I don't remember where we hung the wet clothes upstairs when I was there. It seems to me that in Capucha we hung them between the partitions. Miriam, you mentioned the small bathroom?

Miriam: Yes, there was some sort of hanging rack. I never saw a lot of clothes hanging there.

Elisa: We didn't have a lot!

Miriam: I remember that people hung up their clothes in the stalls; they strung a cord from the bed to a hook in the wall and hung them up there to dry.

∽

Elisa: Adriana, where did they put you when you *fell?*

Adriana: In the Basement, in the Infirmary, facing the dining room. They also took me to the far end.

Elisa: There were a lot of changes. When you *fell*, Munú, did 13 exist?

Munú: When I *fell*, they tortured me in a little room, and I don't know whether it was 13 or whether that room no longer existed by then.

Elisa: There were three rooms together, if you could call them that—actually it was one room, partitioned with hardboard. When I was there, all three were used for the same purpose—torture.

Munú: There was a large room with big sinks in the back.

Miriam: When I was in the Basement, we washed the dishes there. We did *KP duty.*

Munú: We never washed dishes there; we washed them in the bathroom.

Elisa: We didn't. Once, when they took me downstairs, I caught a glimpse of a really nice bathroom; it was brand new.

Munú: That's where we washed the dishes. We used it as a bathroom; some compañeros used it *"de telo."*[1] Everything went on in that bathroom. When I *fell*, they were building new little rooms. Adjacent to the dining room on one side was the Egg Carton, and they built two rooms on the other side. At the far end, facing the entrance, they built a third. Those three rooms were for torture.

Miriam: For torture or where they kept you for a few days right after you *fell*, before they sent you to Capucha.

Munú: Lita was there, Victor's wife. I taught her how to cross-stitch to keep her from going crazy.

Adriana: You also taught me how to embroider. And you gave me the needle.

Munú: You're kidding!

Adriana: You had two identical needles. One had sentimental value, and the other didn't; they both looked the same to me. [*Laughter*] You gave me the one that didn't have sentimental value.

---

1. *"De telo"* is slang for use as a pay-by-the-hour motel room for romantic encounters.

114

Elisa: The one that hurt her less.

Adriana: But it started to have sentimental value for me. [*Laughter*]

Cristina: The "sentimental value added tax."

Adriana: I used that needle to embroider a little black cat for Chiqui's daughter.

Elisa: A crochet hook?

Munú: No, an embroidery needle. I was teaching them how to do it: her— Chiqui—and Lita.

Cristina: Occupational therapy.

Munú: Right. They held Lita in the Basement for at least twenty days. I have a memory of her talking to me about the baby, but I never saw the baby. Actually she had just given birth.

Miriam: She was still swollen because the baby had been born just a short time before.

Munú: I had to explain to Victor, her compañero, how to make the stitches, and he would pass it on to her. I couldn't see her, but it wasn't very strict. I'd talk to her in the little room next to the dining room, where they were holding her.

Miriam: I was remembering the other day how the whole idea of modesty was completely blurred in there. In the air force they always made me shower with the door open. A guard was posted at the door to make sure I didn't commit suicide or break a mirror and cut his head off or something. I tried to shower quickly, with my back turned. Someone was always there; the door was always ajar. They never left me alone.

Elisa: There was a curtain in the ESMA, but—

Cristina: No, in the ESMA, you showered with the guards present at first.

Elisa: There were showers and a curtain you could close, but it was torn and filthy. The guard was always there, and if a prisoner wanted to go in to use the toilet beside it, he'd let the prisoner in and stand there staring at you.

Miriam: That's why I say that the notion of modesty was blurred.

Munú: So there was a guard at the door, and you had a little curtain pulled across?

Elisa: The curtain was a rag, and you could see everything through it.

Miriam: It was the same as nothing at all. Besides, after having been naked during the torture . . .

Munú: They didn't do that to me in the bathroom in the Basement; that's why I'm asking. They didn't make me, and to me that's an important difference.

Elisa: Munú, but that was a different time. In late 1977, if you were in Capucha and had to go to the bathroom, you had to call a GREEN. If the guard was decent, he'd take you right away; if the guard was mean, you had to wait until he felt like taking you.

Munú: But Cristina *fell* after me!

Elisa: Cristina, are you talking about the large bathroom upstairs?

Cristina: Yes.

Miriam: There were two bathrooms: the one for the *mini-staff* and the one for the *staff*.

Elisa: Right.

Miriam: The washing machine was in the one for the *mini-staff*. It was smaller, with yellow tiles. It had only one shower, and it was nearly always clean. The other one was usually filthy.

Elisa: The *staff* bathroom was the same bathroom as for Capucha. There wasn't any bathroom just for the *staff*.

Miriam: But we could use the other one.

Elisa: Only when the *mini-staff* left and that bathroom was assigned to the *staff*—not before that. There was the bathroom in Capucha, which was like a soldiers' bathroom: it wasn't tiled, and there was a mirror, a large sink, two open showers, and to one side a toilet with a door.

Cristina: And a sanded glass window.

Munú: This was next to the place where you ate?

Miriam: Of course, next to the dining room. Did they always make people in Capucha take showers with a Green present?

Cristina: I can't generalize; in my case it was like that at first, a couple of times, I think. There was no room for modesty among so many other feelings, but I'll never forget the first time. The guard was the least of it; the most painful thing was the violation of intimacy, to find yourself so exposed, like raw flesh.

Munú: When I *fell*, they left me for several days in the same room where they had tortured me. Ant came in one day with someone else, and they said they were taking me to shower. They told me to grab the blanket I was lying on and use it to dry myself. They took me into a bathroom, *hooded*. I recognized it later: it was the large bathroom downstairs. The shower was very small, and it had a door. When I tried to close it, Ant said, "No, you have to shower with the door open!" I came out of the shower, and full of bravado, I said, "Then I won't take a shower!" He answered, "It was a joke." I think that was the only time I took a shower with the door closed, because later I couldn't stand it; I felt as though I was suffocating. So some compañera, usually Chiqui, would make sure no one came in.

Elisa: Now I remember that when they took me from the Basement up to Capucha, they gave me some pants and a T-shirt so I could change out of the clothes I was wearing, which were also borrowed. When I put on the clothes they'd given me, I discovered that they fit very snugly, and because of the whole . . . protection . . . thing, I asked them to give me something larger. I kept myself covered up from then on. And I kept it up the whole time I was there.

Munú: Protection from the sexual issue.

Elisa: Exactly! In fact, I didn't have a period the whole time I was in the ESMA. I menstruated on the first day they took me to work at the Foreign Ministry—after ten months.

Munú: Oh, Elisa!

Cristina: No!

Elisa: We all looked out for ourselves as best we could. I was afraid of being exposed, of showing my femininity—not my beauty, my femininity. I covered it up; it didn't exist.

Munú: You didn't exist much at all.

Elisa: No, you didn't. [*Silence*]

Miriam: For a long time in the ESMA, it was forbidden for us prisoners to share any kind of relationship as couples. I can't remember whether they even allowed married couples who had *fallen* together to have sexual relations in there. In fact, they didn't sleep together. As time passed, I think that maybe although they didn't allow it, they came to tolerate it. But they always preferred that a female captive sleep with a marino rather than a prisoner. Would it have been seen as a sign of *recuperation?* In any case, I don't know about all of you, but the whole time I was in the ESMA, I had no sense of my sexuality. I was in love with a compañero in the Fishbowl, but it was a totally infantile love. I don't recall any physical attraction. One night, shortly after they installed surveillance cameras in Capucha, I was already in bed when Roque passed by on the way to his bed, which was at the far end, and as usual he sat down to visit for a few minutes. He tried to kiss me, and I panicked!

Munú: Why?

Miriam: I don't know—the cameras, the GREENS, the place. I couldn't imagine a romantic situation there! No one could kiss with all that. Anything that happened in that context struck me as obscene. I pulled that filthy brown blanket up over my head and asked him to go away. And to think that he later became my husband and is the father of my children!

Munú: Something similar happened to me, but it wasn't the same for all the compañeros.

Miriam: No, of course not. I remember being a lookout for Liliana and Tano in Capucha, so they could be alone in one of the stalls. Merque and I would sit down to chat on the beds right at the corner. We'd keep watch to make sure no GREEN came around.

Munú: It appears as if all of us acted as lookouts for Liliana. There was a fairly large area in the downstairs bathroom where there were the sinks and the washing machine, a little room with a door for the toilet, and another little room with a door for the shower. Liliana and Tano would duck

117

in there, and Chiqui and I had to run the washer so it would make noise, and we had to sing. If we stopped singing, it was because some GREEN or officer was approaching. It was hilarious. And I hope they had a good time. We laughed a lot and enjoyed the situation just like errant teenagers.

Elisa: I don't remember that they tolerated relationships between couples. I do have the sad memory of seeing them go to the Pregnant Women's Room to get Susanita. They'd take her to a small Storeroom in Capucha and bring her husband, Marcelo, there too. They had no more than fifteen minutes together, with the door open and the GREEN looking on. They couldn't even caress each other. At least they knew they were still there; maybe that was enough for them.

Munú: I don't know whether it was enough, but it was very important. Weren't they *transferred* together after the baby was born?

Elisa: I don't remember.

Munú: And, Elisa, what was your experience with love in there?

Elisa: I admit there were some very appealing compañeros, but I couldn't get involved with any of them. I donned my armor in there, and that's how I functioned.

Munú: I have the feeling that for me the whole subject of love had remained outside the ESMA, along with a whole lot of other feelings; it was part of my dissociation. There, I was a captive, and all of my energy was put toward the most basic survival. I regret it because it must have been very beautiful to be able to merge with someone else, to have at least some plan about how to see each other, how to meet up, the complicit looks. A kiss and a hug inside the ESMA must have acquired infinite dimensions.

Miriam: And when we were working on the outside, was it still the same for you?

Munú: More or less. Another compañero who was also on supervised release kept saying he was in love with me, but I didn't feel the same way. He wrote me poetry, and once he wrote something so beautiful that I never forgot it: "I want to reach out to you and you'll be my horizon."

Elisa: That is lovely; we had so many poet compañeros in the ESMA, and we're just now realizing it. [*Laughter*]

Munú: There were certainly ephemeral relationships inside the ESMA, but others endured. Some compañeros got married, had children. They were love affairs that were born in captivity and were able to endure in freedom. It really moves me.

Miriam: Do you remember how we celebrated birthdays?

Elisa: I remember mine. It was two months after I *fell*; I'd been in the Fishbowl for a week, and fat JUNGLE found out it was my birthday. He ordered some little crustless sandwiches and brought everything necessary for a snack to the Fishbowl, and they sang "Happy Birthday" to me. I was ashamed, especially when I went back to Capucha. I always felt that way when I went back to Capucha.

Munú: The shame of guilt because there were others—

Elisa: Who couldn't do that.

Cristina: Spend a part of their day in a better situation.

Munú: They had more parties upstairs.

Liliana: We also had parties downstairs.

Miriam: Munú, don't keep going on and on about the class issue, about the differences. I was in both places, and they also had parties downstairs in the Basement.

Munú: During the whole time I was there, only once did I see them bring in a cake from outside, and that was when they took me upstairs for someone's birthday. They had decided they would convert me quickly, through an intensive course, into a "semi-*recuperated*" person. So that first month they took me back and forth like an inanimate object—out to eat, to a birthday party upstairs. I didn't know anyone at that birthday party; I didn't know who were captives and who were marinos. I watched without comprehending. They were all singing "Happy birthday to you, happy birthday to you," and I was thinking, "What is this?"

Miriam: But you talked about one of your birthdays when they made you applesauce.

Munú: Oh, yes! But those were my compañeros! It's not the same as the cake brought in from outside with the officials included.

Elisa: And the little crustless sandwiches.

Miriam: But the officers didn't always come. Juan, the chief of the Fishbowl, was there but no one else.

Elisa: Not all the officers came to offer their best wishes.

Adriana: I was still in Capuchita on my birthday, and a Green brought some cream, and Andrea whipped it with handcuffs on.

Miriam: I remember that during the first few days I was there, they must have been celebrating a birthday, because someone brought me a piece of cake. Did they pass it out to the people in Capucha?

Elisa: It depended on the guards. Actually, we passed stuff to the compañeros in Capucha whenever we could.

Miriam: I remember being surprised because after the dry bread with rotten meat, suddenly there was a piece of cake with strawberry jam.

Munú: And a lot more surprises were still in store for you. We had parties, but I don't recall that the officers brought anything. Cristina, you said you remember one?

Cristina: I remember one that they took me to after I was out; I wasn't sleeping in the ESMA anymore.

Munú: That was in Abdala's time, not the Tiger's.

Cristina: Right. Under ABDALA. I don't remember why they had taken me there, but whenever it happened, I'd make sure to visit Ana, whom I had met when I was still sleeping there. So I went down to the Basement, where they were celebrating a birthday. Victor was there, and Ana, and several other compañeros I'd never seen before, and a few marinos—I don't remember which ones. There was a cake and a guitar. It was a very bizarre scene. I felt bad because I was out and they were still there. They asked me whether I would sing a song, and I couldn't refuse. Since my repertoire was never very broad, I sang "Chiquilladas," but this was a very sore issue because I used to sing it with my friends, many of whom disappeared before I did. Despite my efforts, halfway through the song, I felt my hands start to tremble, and I was finding it increasingly difficult to pluck the strings, so I faked an early finale.

Munú: Of course. Going in and leaving was very hard.

Miriam: We sang a lot. I remember that we'd congregate in the Fishbowl or in the dining room. And whenever we had a birthday party, we celebrated by singing. Merque sang tangos. I think that's where I learned to love the tango, because I'd never paid any attention to it before. I learned to love it listening to Merque sing in the ESMA. Someone would bring a cake or pudding with a little candle in it, and we'd sing.

Munú: In that dining room?

Miriam: Yes, or in front of the Fishbowl. We'd sit around and sing, usually in an office or in the hall, which was spacious and had some little chairs.

Munú: You sang whether or not there was a birthday.

Miriam: Pelado sang folk songs—*chamamés*—with really funny lyrics, the traditional shouts and all. La Negra sang songs by Mercedes Sosa or Victor Heredia—very sweet. Maria Eva always sang *zambas*;[2] Merque had her tangos—"Fangal," "Chorra," "Muñeca Brava,"—gorgeous tangos, with a lot of street slang, gangster talk. Chiquitín, Chito, and I always sang sui generis songs: "I need someone to patch me up a little." We were fantastic! Or "Country Mornings" by Arco Iris. We were the "young" act. Elena also sang tangos, but she wasn't as into it as Merque was.

Munú: There was a guitar downstairs, and we would sing in the Egg Carton. Chiqui and Andrea played and sang.

Cristina: After you all had left, Danielo played the guitar, and Adriana and I sang. We had some songs that, not coincidentally, were a little melancholy, like "The Little Music Box." There was another one she sang in German, and she taught me a little bit of it.

Adriana: Yes, that was when we were working, but before that, when I was still in Capuchita and there was an accommodating guard, I'd sing with my neighbor, Veronica. They *transferred* her later. We sang "Rin del An-

---

2. *Zambas* are very melancholic traditional songs from Argentina.

gelito," by Violeta Parra, and several other songs. Whenever I sing it now, I remember Veronica.

Cristina: I'd told Danielo that I liked "Becho's Violin," but he didn't want to sing it and for good reason, because it's very sweet and sad. When I had that confrontation with the GREENS in Capuchita, they put me in solitary in a little room at the far end of Capucha. There I was, thrown down, handcuffed and shackled, and suddenly I heard a guitar. It was Danielo playing that song. I was isolated but not alone.

Munú: SPARK showed up in the Egg Carton a number of times, wearing his checked shirt and jeans. He'd grab a guitar and sing rock songs. One day he was singing, and someone with more stripes came along and dragged his ass out of there. Apparently he wasn't even supposed to go into the Basement. Luckily we never lost our laughter and song, inside there and outside of there. Even though the anguish and grief occasionally pass over our heads, they still crush us.

Miriam: Who remembers the Mother's Day cards?

Munú: I do, and I still have one. Mother's Day was coming up, and those of us working in photography and design, forging identity cards, passports, and such—Tito, Roque, Chiquitín, and I—decided to make a card for all the compañeras who were mothers. We looked for a picture, and we chose a Picasso sketch of a mother holding a baby. Onto that we superimposed an excerpt from a poem by José Pedroni.[3] You had to test the limit. We all knew very well who Pedroni was and why we'd chosen him. The marinos probably didn't, but, just in case, we didn't use the author's name. He wrote a poem that goes, "Woman: in a silence that will taste of tenderness to me." So beautiful!

Miriam: "For nine months your waist will swell. And in the month of reaping you will be the color of wheat."

Munú: We were going to use that one, but we ended up picking another one.

Miriam: I knew it by heart: "You will dress simply."

Cristina: "And you will move wearily."

Miriam: It's very lovely.

Munú: It was a beautiful moment. We made enough to give to all the compañeras who were mothers and to all those who were free but whose compañeros were imprisoned with us. We had to print the cards on the navy printing press, where Chiquitín and Roque were taken at night. That was where they printed the forged documents and who knows what else.

---

3. José Pedroni (1899–1968), originally from Santa Fe Province, was an Argentine poet with openly leftist affiliations. He published several volumes of poetry, including *Gracia Plena*, *Poemas y Palabras*, and *El Pan Nuestro*, and was known for extolling motherhood and work.

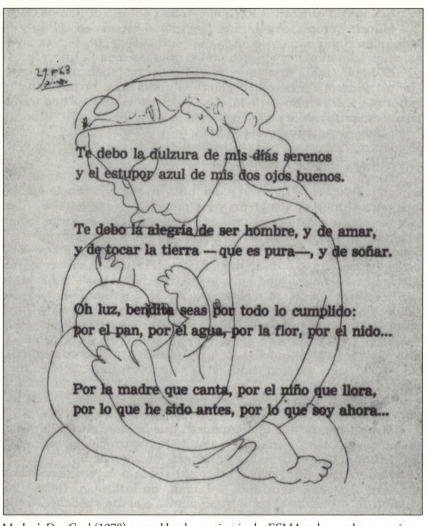

Te debo la dulzura de mis días serenos
y el estupor azul de mis dos ojos buenos.

Te debo la alegría de ser hombre, y de amar,
y de tocar la tierra —que es pura—, y de soñar.

Oh luz, bendita seas por todo lo cumplido:
por el pan, por el agua, por la flor, por el nido...

Por la madre que canta, por el niño que llora,
por lo que he sido antes, por lo que soy ahora...

Mother's Day Card (1978) created by the captives in the ESMA to honor the compañeras who were mothers. (Drawing by Pablo Picasso and poem by José Pedroni.)

I owe you the sweetness of my serene days
and the astonished blue of my two good eyes.

I owe you the joy of being a man, and of loving,
and of touching the earth—which is pure—and of dreaming.

Oh light, for all that you have brought about, be blessed:
for bread, for water, for the flower, for the nest . . .

For the mother who sings, for the child's wail,
for what I was before, and for that which I am now . . .

Miriam: You printed them in the Liberty building![4] [*Laughter*] An act of resistance!

Cristina: There were so many mothers among the compañeras that you had to have them printed?

Miriam: There were quite a few: Merque, La Cabra, María Eva, Chiqui, Laurita, Rosita.

Munú: And what happened was that the marinos saw the card, and they thought it was so beautiful that they asked us to make more for them to give to their wives. I'll never forget it. So if some marino's wife who has that card reads here—

Miriam: That it was the Montoneros card! Dear Wife of a Marino: If you are reading this and you have a card of a Picasso mother and a poem by Pedroni, I want you to know that your husband was a murderer!

Cristina: Madam, rummage through your keepsake trunk!

Miriam: Your husband might be a police officer, a member of the coast guard, or a prison official. [*Laughter*]

Elisa: It reminds me of Christmas 1977, when we made the booklets. The idea originally came up as a gift to share among ourselves. Then production became so efficient that we had enough to give to the people in Capucha. The booklets were formatted like a *Patoruzú* comic book.[5] We had spent days clipping out of the newspapers comic strips like "Clemente," "Inodoro Pereyra," and "Diogenes y el Linyera," and we made booklets out of the strips.

Cristina: You did that!

Elisa: Of course, with the shackles clinking, sssc . . . sssc . . . sssc. At one point the guards let us pay a visit to the people in Capucha. Pelado had *fallen* only a few days before. I went up to him, I kissed him, and I handed him the book. He was moved by the humanity of the gesture, and he said something to me like, "Those bastards might break us, but they won't be able to break the people." I felt a chill run up my spine for fear that the GREENS might have heard him. I couldn't tell him to be quiet or that he was right; I just felt that chill. Then Nose and Beto came up to say hello to him. When Pelado describes this encounter in the book *Recuerdo de la Muerte*,[6] he says, "The girl's pupils contracted in terror. Then she averted her gaze and began an inane conversation, as if she were at a family party." And I remember that's how it was. I couldn't stop playacting.

Munú: He could see you?

Elisa: He raised his *hood*. I was terrified by what he'd said.

---

4. The Liberty building was a navy facility.

5. The format was wide and rectangular.

6. *Recuerdo de la Muerte* [*Memory of Death*], by Miguel Bonasso, was based on the testimony of an ESMA survivor.

Munú: Talking to people in Capucha was rough.

Elisa: Yes, and those things happened. However, I could relate more easily to the compañeros in Capucha than to those who were able to move around the place. When a good Green was on guard duty, I'd make my little escape and run over to talk to someone. Or I'd take them some dessert left over from a family *visit*.

Liliana: What were the booklets like?

Elisa: They had a hard cover lined with silver foil. Everything was very rustic at that time. When we ran out of cardboard, we glued together a stack of paper and wrapped it in foil. We attached comic strips to the pages.

Munú: Was every booklet different?

Elisa: Yes, because we made them out of any newspapers we could get hold of.

Munú: Was that the Christmas when you had a party?

Elisa: It wasn't a party. On the afternoon of December 24, after saluting the troops, the marinos went up to the third floor wearing their dress uniforms—the whole ESMA officer corps, with Chamorro at the head, accompanying Massera!

Munú: And what did they do?

Elisa: I don't remember it as something that was planned. There were ten or fifteen captives in the Fishbowl. They gathered us all together, and Massera started to speak right then and there. He said something about how history had brought us together and we had to deepen our commonality. After he left, we commented among ourselves that he had come because he wanted our compañeros to create the platform for his incipient Social Democratic Party.

Munú: I had heard that it was some kind of festivity.

Elisa: This is what I remember. There were no official preparations. After that, we ate what we'd brought back from the family *visits*—cakes and things like that. And since we had a decent guard, that December 24 we were able to go to Capucha and take the cakes and the booklets.

Liliana: I remember the night of the 31st. I spent it in the Fishbowl, and we danced. I danced in shackles.

Miriam: You danced in shackles in December 1977?

Liliana: Yes, but I don't remember the 24th. I couldn't say whether they took us to the Fishbowl, or whether we stayed in the Basement, or whether I was with the people in Capucha. I don't remember the booklet either.

Elisa: I also remember dancing with shackles on. We were there with the Greens; there were no officers.

Munú: And what did you dance to?

Liliana: Upbeat music.

Munú: Do you remember the parties for the patriotic holidays?

Miriam: Yes, they served hot chocolate.

Elisa: The hot chocolate didn't make it to the Fishbowl.

Munú: They didn't let me participate, but I know that on July 9, 1978, they took people down to the Basement to drink hot chocolate. They had me in the Egg Carton, by myself, and they brought some hot chocolate to me there. MARIANO brought La Negra to visit me that day. I was ecstatic because I knew her from La Plata and I felt as if I could hold on to that face, but she acted as if she didn't know me. I remember being upset, and I asked her, "But don't you remember?" And La Negra replied, "No, actually I don't." I didn't get it at all, and I thought, "What's wrong with her?" Later I understood that it was better to pretend you didn't know each other so they couldn't compare notes and suddenly come up with a contradiction between the lies each person had told.

Miriam: Do you remember the time there was risk of a gonorrhea outbreak and they ordered us down to the Basement for a gynecological examination? I didn't go, because I didn't know what it was for. I probably would have gone if I'd known. Another prisoner came to the stall to get me, and I told her, "No way am I going to spread my legs down there." I made an excuse, and they didn't push it.

Munú: Ca was there that day. What was he doing? Why was he there?

Elisa: Was he drunk or sober?

Munú: It's like I can see him, standing on tiptoes.

Miriam: What did they do to you?

Munú: They did a gynecological examination, a laboratory test.

Elisa: They had all the instruments—the speculum and all that.

Munú: Of course, since they did them one after the other, if one person was sick, it was passed on to all the rest.

Miriam: And none of you protested the presence of Ca, a prisoner who had no reason to be there?

Munú: I don't know whether Ca was there the whole time, with everyone, or whether he had a—

Miriam: A particular curiosity about you.

Munú: The examination was done in the Infirmary, where they had set up a sort of examination table, by pushing some tables together, I guess. Apparently, when the time came, I must not have seen anything wrong with their examining me—maybe because going to the gynecologist had been a regular part of my life. I don't know. Now to go into a place where a doctor is going to examine you and find a prisoner there . . . I guess I must have thought he was there to help.

Miriam: He's a nurse, you thought.

Elisa: MAGNACCO was the doctor?

Munú: Yes, it wasn't Little Apple with the round face; it was the big one, Magnacco.

Miriam: With his kind look.

Elisa: Ah!

Cristina: An icy stare.

Miriam: I can't imagine a woman who would voluntarily allow herself to be examined by that son of a bitch. He was the one who attended Patricia Roisinblit's delivery. He could perform deliveries only in a concentration camp!

Munú: I don't recall his look.

Miriam: Once, a television producer came over to my house because she thought she'd located him, and she showed me a videocassette to see whether I could identify him. When she pressed play, I said, "That's Magnacco!" without hesitation. "Are you sure? Look, no one is ever sure." she said. "Yes, I'm sure." I answered. "One hundred percent sure." I'll never forget those eyes.

Liliana: I remember my fights with Ca. He tormented me because I didn't work.

Munú: You ate in Dorado, and you didn't do any cleaning.

Liliana: I ate in Dorado at noon; I went down to eat dinner. I'd stay there for a while, and then I'd go to bed. Ca started resenting me, telling me I was slacker who didn't do any work. So he got Mariano to put me on the list of people who had to wash the floor.

Munú: Yes, at night.

Liliana: So Ca persecuted me; he told me that I didn't scrub enough. I don't remember fights over food, but I remember his malice toward me over the cleaning issue. Maybe he felt bad because he had to wash floors and it made him lash out at everyone else.

Munú: Downstairs we had a work schedule with all the chores distributed. You had to set the table with whatever was available; there weren't always enough plates and silverware.

Miriam: Yes, you had to borrow a knife, a fork.

Munú: We had to serve the food when they brought the tray in and wash the dishes.

Miriam: How often did you have to do it?

Munú: More or less once a week. We split up into pairs. We did the chores at lunchtime and in the evening, and in the evening we also had to wash the floor of that huge hallway from one end to the other, from the entrance to the torture rooms.

Elisa: I don't remember ever washing floors. What I do remember, and it nauseated me, was washing the dishes in the same sink where people brushed their hair and washed their clothes—with the flies, the hair, and the food scraps. It was filthy. It backed up all the time.

Munú: We also cleaned the bathrooms.

Miriam: Upstairs, in Capucha and in the Fishbowl, the GREENS washed the floors. But we cleaned the stalls.

Elisa: When I was there, when the guards were more lenient, the prisoners in Capucha swept the floor. That way they could move around a little and talk to the others. But I never saw a GREEN washing floors. When did they wash them?

Miriam: At dawn, when everyone was asleep.

Munú: The GREENS never did anything downstairs; we did it all ourselves. We cleaned the offices—if you could call them that. Chiqui cleaned the photography laboratory. I cleaned my layout office.

Elisa: Maybe there was more camaraderie downstairs, more organization.

Liliana: I have a very warm memory of Mantecol. He knew I always went downstairs on Sundays, and he'd be waiting for me with a cup of *mate*. I loved it.

Munú: Even though we spent every day in the Basement, Sundays were different. There was something different about them; some people didn't work.

Liliana: Yes, but every so often the atmosphere in the Basement would pall because people were being kidnapped. It was horrendous! There were days when it was more relaxed; you'd settle down into a routine, and all of a sudden, it started! Also, certain people would hang around there, like ESPEJAIME, from the coast guard, who showed up drunk at night. You had the strong feeling that there were moments when you were left in the hands of people who were even more out of control. Or when that other guy showed up, the one with the flashlight—what was the guy with the flashlight called?

Munú: Oh! He was crazier than—

Liliana: Than everyone else there. We called him HUNCHBACK.

Munú: Just as she was saying, one minute everything was more or less calm and then—bam! bam! bam!—they'd come banging on the doors, and they'd put us all in the offices or in the Egg Carton.

Liliana: There were guys who never lost control when they were torturing. FEDERICO, for example, could torture for five hours straight, and then he'd come out as if nothing had happened. It drove you insane, because it ended up giving you a feeling of security.

Elisa: A feeling that everything was okay.

Munú: I remember how out of control MARIANO was, for example.

Elisa: When they *sucked up* somebody?

Munú: Yes, you'd see him come in yelling, with his face contorted, his eyes fixed. It reminds me of a werewolf, the transformation: he would go down the hall, yelling and kicking and insulting you. And they'd turn that radio up all the way—it wouldn't stop screaming either, just as the people they were torturing screamed, as I surely screamed, as everyone must have screamed. We were always immersed in that suffering and in the interminable anguish of knowing that a compañero was going through what we had gone through. We watched them come and go, enter and leave. All of a sudden, the one doing the torturing would leave, and then two, three, four more would come, and it would all start up again. And when some compañero went into cardiac arrest, LITTLE APPLE would come running to stabilize the person and to say when they could start torturing him or her again. How could we have lived with that nightmare? How come we didn't go insane? And when they brought in old people! Or children! It can't be.

Elisa: And then everything settled down again, as if nothing had happened.

Munú: You knew that the compañero who had *fallen* was there; you didn't know who it was, so our inquiries would begin.

Liliana: To try to find out who it was, to get close.

Munú: What he said, what he didn't say. I see him; I don't see him. PETER's there; PETER isn't there. They'll let him go; they won't let him go. He came alone; others *fell*. And after that first moment, or the next day, we'd try to get something to the person, food, a reassuring word, or just an open door so the person could see you—an instant, a smile—and all the while we'd keep that "nothing" face on. This could happen at any hour; it might be two o'clock in the morning, eleven, during a meal, or at three in the afternoon.

Elisa: Upstairs, in the Fishbowl, the prisoners' experience was different; you didn't have that happening right in front of your eyes.

Liliana: Downstairs you did.

Munú: You were further removed from . . . the particulars, the moment.

Elisa: We experienced all of it differently upstairs. When we received news of a captive, the atmosphere would start to heat up. If no officers, GREENS, or *mini-staff* were in sight, the prisoners who knew the *sucked-up* person would meet and come up with a strategy—for example, to say that when they *fell*, the compañero wasn't *hooked up*. In any case, even though we didn't see anything, we'd wait for news, and the tension would rise with each passing minute.

Liliana: When there was an *operation* to go kidnap someone, you had to act as if everything were normal even though inside you were dying. I think much of what we did was connected with finding out what was going on around us, but the thing is that we weren't really conscious of doing it.

Munú: You would go around asking questions to find out what was going on and even to find out whether the person who had *fallen* was a friend of someone you knew. Each person who *fell* was a point of reference from the outside world.

Liliana: I feel as though part of my head thought about whether or not I would survive and the other part tried to reconstruct what was going on inside there. And I suppose that if I wanted to know about it, it was so I'd be able to tell the story at some point. Everything was so dizzying and exerted constant pressure. I have the feeling that the way we functioned as people wasn't normal.

Elisa: It wasn't.

Liliana: You did everything at once, as if you were five people in one: one who stupidly wondered whether she would survive and didn't care about anything else; another who was still a militant gathering information to use tomorrow; another who believed that it would all pass and that, once she was out, she'd be able to go to the movies.

Munú: We tried to find out what was happening, because whether or not you would keep on living, whether or not your history would continue depended—or you thought it depended—on that knowledge.

Liliana: That's what I have the least memory of, I mean of going around gathering clues to figure out where I had ended up.

Munú: To find out, for example, whether the TIGER had gotten angry or whether or not MASSERA still had power—we had all the neurons trained on that, even though I'm not sure to what extent we were conscious of the risk we ran.

Elisa: If we had been totally conscious, we couldn't have endured it!

Liliana: We would have gone crazy.

Munú: Something I did in the ESMA that I am now able to recognize as an act of resistance but that I experienced as a necessity at the time was to copy on an old typewriter poems by Juan Gelman and Mario Benedetti.

Elisa: When did you copy them?

Munú: At night. I'd stay awake until very late. At that time of night, the officers usually weren't down in the Basement. I'd go into the Egg Carton and copy them. I'd somehow gotten hold of some very thin paper. I cut it into smaller sheets, like the pages of a book, and I'd transcribe the poems. I don't recall whether all the poems were from just one book by each author or whether I selected them from different books. A compañero who worked in the Fishbowl had given the books to me.

Elisa: Of course. The oppressors had stolen them, along with everything else, during the raids and kidnappings. They belonged to the compañeros.

Munú: Right. Now I have all the poems together in an envelope that I also took from there. I don't recall where I hid them or whether I sneaked them out a few at a time. I just know that I absolutely treasure them. The envelope is all yellowed and rust stained. The poems got mixed up, so I don't know which ones are by which author. I don't care. In any case, a new book was created, written by both.

Cristina: And you never told them? I'm sure they would have liked to know.

Munú: In mid-2000 I attended the presentation of a book written by another compañero who had survived the ESMA. I knew that Juan Gelman was going to be one of the speakers, so I got up my courage and went with my envelope. I waited for him after the event. I went up to him and said that I was an ESMA survivor and that I wanted to tell him something. My voice broke, and I couldn't speak. When I regained my composure, I said, "I want to thank you, because you are one of the people who helped me survive in the ESMA." He looked at me with surprise, and I told him the story. We stood there in silence, and I had a sense of profound emotion. Juan said, "I'm going to tell Mario about it." I thought that was fantastic. As he was leaving, he turned around and said to me, "Thank you for having survived." I went into a bathroom and started crying. Later I went out into the street and walked; I walked a lot, feeling a mixture of anguish and joy.

Miriam: When they took me to the ESMA in 1978, Chiqui came to see me in the little room in the Basement where they were holding me, and she said, "Here you will have the opportunity to see your family in the future. We are doing different kinds of work." She didn't explain what they were, but I understood that it was not intelligence work but something more concrete.

Elisa: To work was to prolong your life.

Miriam: Of course. To use whatever skills you had. A while back I read about the dissident scientists who were sent to the Gulag Archipelago[7] in the former Soviet Union and how they kept laboring away, producing scientific works from inside the prison—one more example of the utilization of the labor force.

Elisa: Slave labor.

Miriam: Of slave labor, of the intellectual capacity of the prisoners.

Adriana: When I was in Capuchita, Veronica told me that they were going to offer me work and that I should accept it, because it was the only way to survive and eventually tell the tale of what happened in there. It seemed

---

7. The Gulag Archipelago was a Soviet prison.

dishonorable to me, but she was adamant. It seemed contradictory coming from a militant who seemed so committed, so solid, so firm.

Elisa: The first prisoners to work worked in intelligence. Apparently they did intelligence work by *marking* people. Later, in October 1976, there was a huge roundup. Practically the entire high command of the Montoneros Organization *fell*. I think that's when they started to wonder, "What can we do with these brains?"

Miriam: With this gray matter.

Elisa: Exactly! And after that they started to keep alive the compañeras whose husbands were still free and working for the militant cause, because they figured that they could use those women, the wives of Montoneros officers, to *suck up* the men. In other words, they were holding them as hostages.

Miriam: There was a small group of captives that promoted creating jobs for other prisoners. None of us belonged to that group; they were people who had been higher up in the Montoneros Organization.

Elisa: They asked me only whether I knew how to type.

Munú: I knew how to draw, so they had me making maps and forging documents; I spoke French, so they ordered me to translate newspapers.

Miriam: I also translated articles from French and English. They were interested in the *New York Times*, the *Financial Times*, *Le Monde*, but they were particularly interested in the *Latin American Newsletter*, which was published by Rodolfo Terragno[8] in London and distributed throughout Europe. He had very good information, usually about the military's inner workings, and he would publish denunciations. That little newsletter drove them crazy. It made them feel so vulnerable! As soon as they received it, they ordered me to translate it urgently. And I'd take great pleasure in the commotion it caused. Sometimes those of us working in the press office in the Fishbowl had to write pieces that later would be read on the Channel 13 news station, which had been taken over by the navy, or on Radio Argentina's international broadcast.

Elisa: I don't think the Montoneros officials kidnapped and taken to the ESMA were kept alive by chance. A group of naval officers, led by MASSERA, had a political project, and that's where the "Montoneros Gray Matter" came into play. Some compañeros had developed increased bargaining power by demonstrating their ability in their work, so they asked for the necessary infrastructure to carry out their assigned tasks. And that's where the archival work began. I remember that we would select the

---

8. Rodolfo Terragno, a lawyer, writer, and journalist, was exiled under the dictatorship. He was a congressman, a government minister, and a cabinet head. He is currently a member of the Radical Civic Union.

issues and clip articles from the print media. For example, one of my jobs was to mark news stories and then prepare a news synthesis.

Munú: The compañeros who were assigned jobs were able to prolong their lives. By the time I *fell*, the *staff* was already functioning. I rarely saw the people who had promoted that structure, since they were upstairs in the Fishbowl and they were beginning to leave.

Miriam: So a group of captives influenced the marinos from the Task Force[9] to create an opportunity for *sucked-up* people to work. They encouraged MASSERA's political plan so there would be a growing need for labor, because that meant more lives could be saved.

Elisa: I remember that after I had been in Capucha for a while, fat JUNGLE came to visit me. He didn't ask me whether I wanted to live but whether I could type. One of the jobs was to write "The O Report." It was a newsletter designed to change Argentina's international image. It was to be written in several languages and then distributed through the embassies. Since they didn't have enough typists, they took me out of Capucha. A compañera told me that she remembered seeing me writing on the composer. She said the other women assigned to the same task wanted to clobber me because I was constantly making mistakes. It really was true: I didn't get a single one right. I was always making mistakes. Maybe, as I said before, it was a subconscious form of boycott or resistance, but it disrupted everyone else's work.

Munú: When the conflict with Chile started over the Beagle Channel,[10] that same group of captives encouraged the marinos to get involved—according to them, to distract their attention from the kidnappings and focus it on resolving the Chilean question, so they would stop hunting people down. I don't know whether that's how it happened. What is true is that they made me trace and superimpose maps of Beagle, indicating where the bases were.

Elisa: Maybe it is true that when the project first began, the people with the best chance of survival were the Montoneros officers, because they could use them even to write MASSERA's speeches for him, to give him a different political vision.

Miriam: Of course. MARIANO himself told me that the best of Argentine youth had died in this war. So they would have thought, "Since they're the best, let's use the ones who survived for our project!"

Elisa: I think the marinos asked for the newspaper clippings at first, and then

---

9. Repressive groups were referred to as the Task Force during the dictatorship.

10. The Beagle Channel, located in southern Argentina, is an area of ongoing dispute between Argentina and Chile.

they must have requested the news synthesis, and since they liked it, they kept on requesting it.

Munú: Was that the goal when they put together the *mini-staff*?

Miriam: No, the people who joined the *mini-staff* survived for very different reasons.

Elisa: The *mini-staff* had intelligence functions. The objective there was to find a way to *suck up* more people. I don't know whether or not it's true, but Go, one of the captives who was part of the *mini-staff*, used to brag that he was the one who invented *fingering*.

Munú: I came from La Plata, and they used it there too. I doubt he invented it in the ESMA and then later on they moved the system to La Plata. Those people, as we all know, had taken several intelligence courses here and outside the country.

Elisa: What happened to Go was terrible. When he *fell*, he didn't *sing* about anyone. He endured fourteen days of the *electric prod*.

Munú: And then he broke?

Elisa: Right. And people disappeared, and no one understood it.

Munú: I find it irritating to ascribe the invention of the *fingering* system to one of the kidnapped. That would require believing that the marinos were a bunch of dimwits and that they'd gotten nothing out of the intelligence courses they'd taken. They had a bunch of kidnapped people, under torture and the pressure of imminent death, who knew a bunch of other people. Nothing made more sense than to use them and take them out to *mark* people. When I was there, they knew very well who would *mark* people and who wouldn't. They knew who to take on the *expeditions*.

Elisa: They knew?

Miriam: I think so.

Elisa: It's true, because they had a *marker* on every *launch*.

Munú: What do you mean on every *launch*?

Miriam: In every vehicle, there was someone who would *mark* people for sure.

Munú: I never heard of the *launch*, and there wasn't always a *marker*. They took me out four times and only once with people who *marked*.

Miriam: They took me on only one *expedition*. They took me to Lomas de Zamora,[11] and I wasn't worried because I'd never been to that area. There was no danger.

Munú: You didn't know anyone.

Miriam: I didn't even know where it was! La Cabra and I were on the same *expedition*, and neither of us *marked* people. But another captive went along too, and apparently he did know people there, and we didn't know what he was going to do. Let's say that he was the centerpiece, and we were

---

11. Lomas de Zamora is a location in greater Buenos Aires.

the padding, just in case, because it was always a good idea to take women along.

Munú: They took women along as cover. One time they took La Cabra and me to Lanús.[12] During that *expedition* I shoplifted a spatula used for pottery making.

Miriam: That was stupid!

Munú: And not only that; I went back to the ESMA talking about it. I not only stole it; I didn't try to hide it at all, and it caused a huge commotion. They sent me back to Capucha again, punished, because according to them, they were outside their jurisdiction and hadn't gotten the green light, and if the people from the shop had found out, they could have called the police. Everything is so clear in hindsight. Time helps you see just how absurd everything was that we experienced then. They sent me to Capucha for stealing a pottery spatula, yet they stole everything, including babies!

Elisa: They did, not you.

Munú: Another time it was really bad. They took me, along with a captive who *marked*, to some bars located in the subway under the obelisk. They divided into two groups, one in each bar, with the crowds milling around in between. All of a sudden, down the stairs came an old compañero from the militant organization, who saw me and came up to say hello. It was excruciating. I knew very little about him, because we had been so *compartmentalized* in the organization, and I had to keep on talking the whole time; I couldn't let him make any reference to our past. I was the idiot who just kept rattling on about everything. Three OPERATIVES were sitting at the same table listening to every detail of the conversation, and I had to convince them that he was just a friend.

Miriam: And what happened?

Munú: I was able to do it, but while that was going on, the guys at the other table took off running. They went down a stairway, and we started to hear the screams of a woman as they were dragging her back up. She was screaming that they were kidnapping her, that she was looking for her kids. It was so horrible. It was like watching your own kidnapping and participating in it. They passed right by us, and she never stopped screaming. The guys with me said, "Let's go," so I said good-bye to the compañero I was speaking with, who had turned as white as I had, and I left with them.

Elisa: And they had her in the ESMA.

Munú: They kept her there for a few days. They said that they had let her go home and that they had intended to keep her under surveillance because

---

12. Lanús is a location in greater Buenos Aires.

they wanted to talk to her husband but that she had gone into hiding in some embassy.

Miriam: I wonder whether it's true.

Munú: Yes, it's true, because in 1982, I went to Barcelona to visit some compañeros whom I hadn't seen since La Plata. They had planned a cookout for my arrival. There were about ten Argentines I didn't know. They asked me about the ESMA. Very little was known at that time, and at one point someone mentioned the *expeditions*. I told this story, and one of the women there said, "I was that woman."

Miriam: Ah!

Munú: It was very moving. She was alive; she was there; I was too. I hugged her tightly, deeply; my skin was covered in goose bumps. Clearly it was something totally ours. None of the others could have felt what that hug contained.

Cristina: When I was given the opportunity to work, it wasn't easy for me to dissociate it from the notion of "collaboration." However, it was dawning on me that it was a way to be able to move around—with risks, of course, since a task could come up that might affect some compañero on the outside. I lived in constant fear of that. They assigned me to Dorado, where I had to make photocopies and type up documents and mostly assemble copies of the famous Dossier.[13] Worst of all, I had to transcribe *tapped* conversations, which were impossible to understand, but there was that overriding fear of unknowingly causing harm to someone. Most of the time we did routine office work, except when some particular demand came up that might turn out to be inoffensive or might create enormous tension over the risk it implied. Once they made me place a call to a school that someone they were trying to locate was associated with. I got so nervous that, besides acting like an idiot and failing to find out anything, my strange phone call must have set off alarm bells. Another time they assigned me the task of going through a suitcase they'd taken from the house of a couple that had just been kidnapped. I was reluctant to do it, but then I thought it was better that I do it than some marino. The whole time I was doing it, I felt an overwhelming grief. There were a lot of photographs depicting the daily lives of these compañeros—who fortunately survived—and thousands of papers. How to know which ones were compromising! I ended up classifying them into those that might have sentimental value, which I later secretly returned to the couple; those that

---

13. This was a report prepared for foreign distribution, which contained largely fabricated information about Montoneros actions.

I would destroy; and those that, with great effort, I separated on unlikely premises in an effort to justify the whole classification system. It was also very upsetting to be in that place because the OPERATIVES congregated next door, right there in Dorado, and you lived with the constant comings and goings of the *gang*. That's one of the strongest memories I have of impotence and anguish. Even so, working effectively represented an opportunity for personal survival and for influencing those in charge in order to save other lives.

Elisa: I don't know whether I've ever talked here about the experience I had in the ESMA—I mean in the Foreign Ministry, when I had these two GREENS guarding me.

Munú: The ESMA and the Foreign Ministry were one and the same to you!

Elisa: Yes, it was all the same thing—it was the same to me. If you want the psychological interpretation, I'll give it to you. Besides, when I first worked at the Foreign Ministry, I was still sleeping in the ESMA.

Cristina: To her, the Foreign Ministry was merely an extension of the ESMA.

Munú: I think that working with them had the same meaning for all of us.

Elisa: I was still kidnapped.

Miriam: You still answered to your *nom de guerre*.

Elisa: Preferably! Once, when I'd been there only a very short time, two GREENS were standing guard at the door of the Foreign Ministry Press Office when the mother of Teresa Israel, a disappeared lawyer, came in to inquire about her daughter.

Liliana: She was there to report the disappearance?

Elisa: No, she asked me whether she could speak with Captain Pérez Froio, who was the director of the press office at the time. She knew the navy had kidnapping victims, and she wanted to ask him about her daughter. This woman didn't have the faintest idea of the risk she was taking. They were there, and they could have seen her—DUKE, GIRAFFE, FELIPE. I asked her to leave, saying I didn't know anything about it. I could have said, "I'm a kidnapping victim; don't say anything," but I knew she wouldn't be able to keep that sort of assertion to herself. In mid-1978 it would have been a real revelation. But for her own safety, I said I didn't know anything and suggested she go look somewhere else. She looked at me beseechingly and said, "What do you think? Can I go to the ESMA?" And I said, no, she should go somewhere else, like a church. And she told me she was trying to find out what was going on. She was going from military base to military base, and she hadn't gotten any answers. What a story!

Miriam: Was her daughter in the ESMA?

Elisa: I don't know. I think this is the first time I've talked about this.

Miriam: That girl was with the Communist Party, a party lawyer.

Elisa: I can't even begin to describe how anxious and desperate I was. She hadn't come all the way in. She was standing in the doorway, very close to the GREENS. I had her sit down, and I spoke to her in a very soft voice so that she would do the same. The GREENS could have been listening. I was so nervous! And there was the other fear too—wondering why they'd asked me to receive her. The permanent staff of the Foreign Ministry had sent her to talk to me; in other words, they knew.

Miriam: They knew what?

Elisa: That I was different, that I wasn't a regular employee.

Liliana: What did the Foreign Ministry staff know? Was it ever discussed?

Elisa: No, absolutely not. I was able to tell a couple of compañeros whom I later came to trust a lot. I told them that I had worked there when I was kidnapped by the navy. I couldn't tell them much more than that, because they froze. I'm sure that some of them knew or at least must have imagined it. Some of them had a lot of seniority and were close to the diplomats, who, in turn, were very close to the armed forces. Others must have thought that we were the marinos' women. They didn't know what our connection with them was or why we were there. But obviously the marinos had a power relationship with us that was unlike their relationship with the rest of the staff in that department of the Foreign Ministry. To the others, they were just their bosses—which is what I wanted to achieve—but to me, they were also my torturers. I can never forget that my first "boss" there was DUKE, my torturer.

Munú: Try forgetting that! I think some of the employees knew.

Elisa: I don't know whether or not they knew. If they did, they were shrewd enough to keep quiet. I stayed on after the marinos left the Foreign Ministry. I still had my *hood* on; I didn't want to ask them anything, for fear they'd send me somewhere else. And since I'd always tried to keep my distance from the other people from the ESMA, the other kidnapped people, it was easy for me to join another office.

Liliana: But did you have legal documents?

Elisa: It was a job. I was an employee! By then they had given me a job that had absolutely nothing to do with the ESMA. I was even going to get a promotion!

Liliana: You were going to be a diplomat!

Elisa: All the marinos left, and I stayed! My co-workers didn't know where I came from; they didn't know that I was a disappeared person taken there by the marinos. So then the air force people came in.

Liliana: They were divvying up the ministries among the different armed services, right?

Elisa: Of course. The air force people took over the Foreign Ministry after the navy left. And I was still an employee.

Miriam: Highly regarded. [*Laughter*]

Elisa: Commodore Boittier became my immediate supervisor as the director of the Foreign Ministry Press Office. When the navy left, the department heads were career people, and so I related to them. This commodore wanted to appoint me as his secretary. [*Laughter*] So people reacted; my colleagues from all those years in the Foreign Ministry asked me who I thought I was to take that job. And I figured that the first people to raise the hue and cry were the ones who knew my background.

Munú: Naturally!

Elisa: They could have said, "She's one of the people *sucked up* by the navy." They could have been more direct. But they simply said I'd been brought in by the navy, and it was counterproductive. So they left me in the same position.

Liliana: You were saved by envy!

Elisa: Imagine how crazy I was to stay in there! It was 1980 then. Being there enabled me to find out what was happening abroad, because the Foreign Ministry Press Office received correspondence, including the earliest reports.

Liliana: What was your status when the air force came in? Had you been given permanent status?

Elisa: I had every possibility of fighting for a permanent position, but evidently my craziness didn't go that far. Somewhere deep inside me, I knew I had to leave there.

Liliana: And who paid you?

Elisa: The air force paid me. They paid me under the table, from reserved funds.

Munú: The marinos also had set up an office that had something to do with videos. The word was that they had taken the photos from *Noticias* there.[14] Do you all know anything about that?

Elisa: There was always talk about that, but I don't know for sure.

Munú: Did that file contain only politically related photographs, or was it that I looked only at the Peronist Youth activities? That file used to be in the Egg Carton.

Elisa: When I was there, it was in the Fishbowl. The compañeros would use it to get information to write an article or a speech.

Munú: When they began to let me move around the Basement, let's say August or September 1978, it was already there. I slept in the Infirmary, and they would put the *mask* on me and take me across to the Egg Carton. I would look through the file, since I didn't have anything else to do. At the

---

14. *Noticias* was a newspaper with a Peronist bent, politically aligned with the Montoneros Organization.

time, I didn't know what *Noticias* was, and I thought, "Damn, they have a lot of pictures of us!" I don't remember seeing written text, only photos.

Miriam: Where did they *suck up* that file?

Munú: I don't know.

Elisa: That file was already there when I arrived.

Munú: When did *Noticias* fall? There must have been a raid, and the ESMA had a hand in it. I don't think they bought it! [*Laughter*]

Elisa: Bought it?

Munú: Another Task Force must have *sucked* it *up*, and the ESMA paid money to get hold of it. It was a catalog of faces! We were all in there.

∽

Adriana: In November 1978, I was in Capucha, next to Danielo and I don't know how many other people. Afterward they moved La Flaca and me to a stall. They'd given us a typewriter to practice on, so we wouldn't get bored. [*Laughter*] I dictated tangos to her, and she dictated things to me. We tried to learn to type without looking at the keys, and that's how we spent the day.

Elisa: Always inside the stall?

Adriana: Yes.

Elisa: In other words, you never worked?

Adriana: I worked. In December they took La Flaca on her first *visit*, and she had a seizure just as she was arriving at her house. She had epilepsy, and she had the good fortune to have a seizure right at that moment; it turned out that they got scared and never went back to get her. Every so often, they would talk about how they were going to get her or how they were going to leave her there. Even they laughed about the situation. It was so absurd, so arbitrary.

Cristina: And we would lay it on them about how serious epilepsy was.

Munú: They left her there for so long that she ended up staying at her house.

Miriam: Unfortunately, it was a double-edged sword. If they had believed they'd triggered the disease through the torture, they might have disappeared her so no one could accuse them of having scarred her physically. Who knows how it could have gone for her if that's what they'd believed. They were unpredictable; you never knew how they were going to react.

Adriana: Luckily, it didn't happen like that. They fed their version to the father, to the whole family. The mother was grateful that they'd taken such good care of her.

Cristina: The woman next to me in Capucha was of very humble origins, a domestic. They went out to kidnap someone else, and they brought her back. She'd had an epileptic seizure while she was in Capuchita.

Adriana: I helped her.

Cristina: You remember?

Adriana: First they looked for Andrea, who was studying nursing. Andrea wasn't there, so they took me, because I'd done my fifth year of medicine. They took me, *walled up*, to a room next to the bathroom, heading toward the Fishbowl. They made me go in, and the woman was on the floor having a seizure. I assisted her, and I explained to the GREENS how to manage a person with epilepsy. They were there alone. After I gave them the official lecture on managing a person with epilepsy, they got scared and took me out of the room. Apparently, they weren't supposed to let me assist anyone.

Munú: It was a transgression.

Adriana: They pulled me out of there, and very roughly they took me back. Later, once I was back downstairs in Dorado, my job was to translate into German that dossier that some other compañeros had written about the history of armed [left-wing] organizations in Argentina. Does anyone want to tell me why?

Miriam: You weren't about to question the need. Into German? You were happy as a lark.

Adriana: But I told them, "If you don't bring me a dictionary, I'll have to call my Dad." I called my old man every day!

Miriam: Ah! To ask him questions!

Adriana: Sure. How do you say this in Spanish; how do you say that in German? Every single day, Monday through Friday, I called my old man!

Miriam: That's great! He must have been standing next to the phone waiting. The parents endured so much anguish!

Adriana: Speaking of that, when we were there typing, we came across a letter. It was written by a hairdresser who was a single mother. They had *sucked* her *up*, and her son, who was very young, was left in the streets with no one to take care of him. I believe she was Uruguayan, and she was in the hair salon when they *sucked up* the mother of a militant. The letter was heartrending; we all cried.

Munú: So she *fell* because she was the hairdresser?

Adriana: Yes, because she was there and saw the incident. She wrote that letter saying, "Please, let Christmas arrive. I alone care for my son. I am the only one who can protect him. What will become of him without me?" They released her later.

Cristina: Yes, yes, she was next to me in Capuchita. I remember how desperate she was; she talked and cried all the time. I'd *fallen* only a short while before.

Munú: She didn't have anything to do with anything, so they'd have kept her in Capuchita so she wouldn't see or hear anything. Poor woman—to end up in Capuchita.

Elisa: At first the only people in Capuchita were those who'd been *sucked up* by the SIN.[15]

Miriam: Of course, those were two different periods. A while ago, I was thinking that if some ill-intentioned person decided to compare the testimonies without taking into account the chronology, a lot of contradictions would emerge, because things were always changing. They were constantly changing things around—building and remodeling.

Elisa: Right.

Adriana: I memorized one detail: there were nineteen steps from Capuchita to the Capucha floor. I thought that even with the remodeling, they wouldn't add or remove a step, and I figured that piece of information might be useful someday.

Miriam: We all had different survival strategies in the camp. Each person took on a role, a personality. I don't know whether there was a correlation between the selection criteria they used to put us to work and give us a remote chance of survival and the role each of us ended up playing. But I think that, in general, there was a correlation. Internally, perhaps instinctively, you intuited why you had been selected and you adapted to it. You froze into position; you adjusted to that role.

Liliana: But not only the role in terms of work—that adaptation also compromised our internal world, our personality. Our entire subjective experience was acclimated to the relationship with them. You knew that agreeing to work meant having the chance to survive, so you tried to adapt. But I am convinced there's more to it than that. I never did a concrete task; I never served a useful purpose inside there. Jorgelina and I spent all day gossiping in Dorado. What we did was of absolutely no value. Maybe other people—the ones who worked in design or in the print shop, the intellectuals in the Fishbowl—did things that were useful to someone. I'm convinced that my terrible effort to adapt was more on the emotional side, adapting day after day to whatever seemed as though it wouldn't bother them, trying to be what they expected me to be.

Elisa: Constant playacting, with all the internal burden it entailed.

Liliana: Which had to do with an overall attitude and not just a particular job. It was a terrible effort for me, more than for those who perhaps were convinced they were doing some useful work.

Miriam: Since you all worked in the intelligence office, we thought you were doing something terribly important for them. That's why I never asked

---

15. The SIN is the Navy Intelligence Service.

you what you did. We talked about our work with the other prisoners, but with you all never!

Liliana: They weren't about to have Jorgelina and me do intelligence work. They weren't that stupid!

Miriam: But what did you do?

Liliana: We typed things up, the little pieces of paper that were flying around there. Maybe I'm underrating the work Jorgelina and I did because I can't bring myself to think that all those things we were typing were ever useful for any serious intelligence work. That's what it was like there, and I can't bear to think about it.

Miriam: What was a typical day like for you in Dorado? What time did you arrive? What did you do?

Liliana: We got there between nine and ten in the morning. Then we spent a long time drinking *mate* and straightening up. If Mocho was there, we talked, chatted. We also had to organize and classify papers from interrogation sessions by one of the other branches of the armed forces.

Miriam: They gave you interrogations from the other branches of the armed forces?

Liliana: Yes, we had to classify them, put them in a file, then move them to another file, and so on. For a while, they made us transcribe telephone conversations. They were *tapped* conversations that didn't have anything to do with political intelligence. They had to do with commercial matters, their business dealings, surveillance in matters of infidelity. I spent weeks on end transcribing conversations between women and their lovers.

Miriam: They had their own women followed?

Liliana: They were private business matters, as if it were an agency. I'm not sure about Mariano or Jungle—they were very busy with logistics— but they probably had their buddies in private intelligence who went in on the take fifty-fifty.

Miriam: Do you remember any names?

Liliana: No, it was all completely unfamiliar to me.

Miriam: And you gave that stuff to whom?

Liliana: Always to Mariano or Jungle. Then the other officers would ask them for the materials. They were private business matters. I also transcribed interrogations.

Elisa: Interrogations of our people?

Miriam: Of torture sessions?

Liliana: Yes, I transcribed interrogations with torture.

Miriam: They taped them?

Liliana: Yes, they taped them. It was terrible.

Miriam: People who were in Capucha?

Liliana: Yes.

Miriam: And what do you remember?

Liliana: I don't remember anything specific. What I do recall is that they would evaluate whether or not the interrogations under torture were useful. The information was fragmented, so MARIANO would read it and say, no, it was better to find other ways to persuade people to collaborate. Those were the intelligence jobs. I guess our work was useful, but my feeling was that the gargantuan effort was in adapting to them.

Miriam: And when they were planning an *operation*, did they discuss it in front of you or behind closed doors?

Liliana: Behind closed doors. Sometimes Jorgelina and I could hear the racket from the other side of the partition. El Dorado was divided.

Miriam: I went in there only a couple of times.

Liliana: There was a room divider. The offices were on one side, and they planned *operations* on the other side.

Cristina: There were enclosed rooms.

Liliana: Yes. And they had a big blackboard. El Dorado was a very large space, with a partition. The front part was like a meeting room, and that's where MASSERA was. There was an entrance on the right and another on the left. The left-hand one was communications, where you could hear the radios they used to maintain contact. I never went in there; we just heard the noises. To the right was the central office, which was for MARIANO or JUNGLE, depending on who was in charge of the whole Task Force. There was another little office, where they kept supplies. They used room dividers, which they often moved from place to place. So sometimes Jorgelina and I would find ourselves in a large office and other times a small one. Those idiots would take it into their heads to change the place around, and they'd move them. There was a little kitchen next to the entrance.

Miriam: And where were the OPERATIVES?

Liliana: That I don't know. Most likely there was another enclosed area in El Dorado that I don't remember. They weren't there.

Cristina: But they passed through there.

Liliana: Yes, they came and went.

Miriam: Where did they keep the weapons, in Los Jorges?

Liliana: In Los Jorges, I guess. There was a closet filled with weapons in El Dorado, but I don't know whether they used those for *operations*. They would take them out and clean them. They didn't make us help them with that, thank goodness. That's how the four zumbos on guard duty entertained themselves—MOCHO, deaf JULIO . . .

Elisa: Who is deaf JULIO?

Cristina: He was a zumbo who worked in intelligence. One time they made me clean out a refrigerator, and they brought me a big glass bowl filled with water and detergent. I stopped dead, because it was the salad bowl my grandfather always used to make his famous fruit salad. It was unmistakable! Seeing it there drove me crazy. They'd stolen it from my house. Deaf JULIO noticed it and asked me what was wrong. So I told him, and to my great surprise, he emptied it, wrapped it up, and put it on top of a closet. A few days later, ANT discovered it and threw it out.

Munú: What a nightmare to find your things in the hands of those sorts. Your story describes deaf JULIO and ANT perfectly. Luckily there was always someone who was less of a bastard than the rest.

Liliana: Deaf JULIO was a character. I never knew whether he was really deaf or just faking it. I guess he must have been deaf, because at one point they were talking about how he had to have ear surgery. He was very nice to Jorgelina and me. ANT was the most fucked-up.

Cristina: One day I was with several compañeros, and ANT came in and showed us a photograph that he was going to enter in a contest. It was no coincidence that he showed us the piece of work and even less of a coincidence that he had come up with it. It was black and white, very lugubrious. In the foreground, there were several figures resembling the Ku Klux Klan, except they were wearing black robes. Behind them, against a grayish background, you could see some trees, cypress or poplar, black and vague. It was a depiction of the horror of death. It gave you chills. So, in a bantering tone, he said he didn't know what to call it. I said, "That's the Parcae." I said it to throw him off, because I knew he'd have no idea what it meant. Months later, I was at my family's house reading the *Clarín*, and guess what I found? Nothing less than a small but unmistakable reproduction of the photograph taken by that despicable human being. That son of a bitch had won! And I admit feeling sick to my stomach when I read the caption. It was called "The Parcae."

Munú: He also showed me photographs once when they were taking me to Dorado. He was really fucked-up. Once when I went into the Fishbowl, which I was forbidden to do, he saw me on the closed circuit television that they used to monitor movements. He sent LITTLE PAUL to get me, and he lit into me as if he were the superior officer of the Task Force.

Liliana: He was the worst. There was another one who made us clean; he was a tormentor, but in a silly sort of way. And then there was MOCHO, with his whole saga of love for Jorgelina. MOCHO would talk to her, and I'd be sitting right there.

Elisa: You didn't even offer an opinion.

Liliana: I gave my opinion only when he asked for it—otherwise, no. But I had to be there. He said that his love for her had cleansed the blood from his hands.

Miriam: How horrible!

Liliana: "Thanks to you," he would say, "my hands, drenched in blood . . ."

Miriam: And how did she react?

Liliana: I don't remember very well. What struck me most were the things he said.

Miriam: The only time I went into Dorado, I went straight to Mariano's office to talk about Anita. He took me there one night to show me the photograph that saved Anita's life. It was a photo of her on her father's sailboat; he was a sailing instructor. Mariano showed me that photo, which they'd picked up during the search. "Does this girl sail?" he asked. "She loves the sea!" I lied. "She's always sailed, ever since she was a little girl." I'd run into Anita in the little Storeroom when I was looking for sheets. We knew each other from the militant organization. She told me that Mariano had been impressed when he saw the photograph of her sailing. Something clicked inside. I realized she could save herself, and we cooked up that story together. The marino saved the *sucked up* woman because he believed she loved the sea just as he did! That was the only time they allowed me into Dorado.

Munú: So you weren't there for Massera's farewell?

Miriam: Ah! Yes! The day that Massera went to say good-bye, because he was retiring, they took us there to see him. He was wearing his dress uniform, all in white. He told us that this had been a war but that he hoped to be able to sit down and visit with us over coffee in the future. Before that he'd decorated those who had fought in that war, his *gang*.

Munú: When I recall that scene, it seems like part of my fantasy world. He said things like, "When a group of people feels oppressed it may legitimately take up arms," and "We were in different trenches, but if Argentina ever goes to war, I hope we're on the same side." He must have been practicing his speech-making skills on us, since he was launching his political career.

Elisa: I was no longer in the ESMA by then.

Munú: Lambruschini came in when Massera retired, and a few days later he came to visit the Task Force. The delegation included at least ten people, in uniform, who went around the Basement inquiring about what activity was done in each of the rooms where we were working. I remember that I was standing at the drawing table wearing my little blue twill dress. They stayed the longest in the document forging area. They went everywhere, including the torture rooms.

Miriam: Going back to the subject of survival strategies, Liliana, you were saying that you acted in a very infantile manner and that you were Mariano's little girl, who worked in intelligence, steeping *mate* and cleaning. You embodied the image he had of you, which in a way, guaranteed that you would be protected.

Liliana: I was MARIANO's little girl. Fat JUNGLE was the only one who saw me as a sexually appealing adult woman, but his hands were tied, since I was the little girl under MARIANO's protection.

∽

Miriam: There were different levels of identification among the *mini-staff*. Some of them identified very strongly with their oppressors. They copied them and even imitated the TIGER's tone of voice, his jokes, his way of standing up on tiptoe and showing his talons.

Liliana: Maybe the only way they could endure the situation was through total identification.

Miriam: And then there was another group that followed a grayer path, and even though they were women, they too acquired the habit of imitating them. In their case, it wasn't so much in the physical aspects, or the gestures, but ideologically they seemed to be totally identified. I worked with Co in Social Welfare. She looked right through you. She had a crafty, sidelong look, suspicious; it was depressing to see the transformation in that woman. I don't know—something changed inside them, and they imitated them.

Elisa: I worked with Ne in the Foreign Ministry, and she'd say to me, with that invariable distrust, "And to think that we fought without knowing everything we know now. Realizing the degree of corruption and moral bankruptcy of these guys leaves you drained and without any desire to keep on fighting. We fought against them without realizing how morally bankrupt they were." She would give me this spiel, and I would look the other way. I would put my "nothing" face on. I also remember the story Go and Pe concocted.

Miriam: They pretended to the marinos that they were a couple in order to save Pe.

Elisa: They slept in the same bed and absolutely nothing went on. Their case was an exception. They never authorized prisoners to sleep together, and at that time they didn't allow couples.

Miriam: Pe was pregnant when she *fell*. He must have known their plan for pregnant women, and he must have told her, "Here they remove the kid, and then they kill you. I'm useful to them. If we say we're a couple, then you have a chance to save yourself." Virtually the entire *mini-staff* adopted a strategy of intense identification, of using that mechanism to save themselves and to become almost a force unto themselves. Among us, among the *staff*, there were different . . . there was your method, which was to become very infantile. I didn't need to act infantile because—

Elisa: You were a little girl.

Miriam: I was still a little girl. I kept on playing the role I had when they brought me from the air force. The role of the good girl, the family girl, the one who'd *fallen* because her grandmother was dying and she called home every day. This lent me an aura of sensitivity that stood in contrast to the stereotypical impression they had of the guerrilla woman—hard. Mariano told me this. There was a group of leaders from the Montoneros Organization who operated on a different plane in their relationship with the marinos, almost as if they spoke commander to commander.

Liliana: As if between equals, a chief negotiating with another chief. I'm not sure whether it was really like that. I doubt there was a free and democratic dialogue among peers.

Elisa: I remember how Chacho, smoking a pipe, would stop in front of the Tiger as if they really did have the same level of power. "After you," he'd say, and he'd usher him into his office in the Fishbowl.

Miriam: Maybe they were the ones who, in their conversations, engendered this apparatus, this enormous travesty of collaboration, to try to save themselves and to save lives. There were different types of behavior among them too. There were the most argumentative ones. And then there were the ones, like Diego, who obeyed and acted in a more submissive way but retained a certain margin of negotiation and came a long way toward the end.

Cristina: Once, in there, someone remarked to me that the milicos thought we had a strong internalized notion that things had to be done right—as if, in spite of ourselves, we had this propensity for fulfilling certain obligations properly. Regardless of our profiles and the fact that many of us were just small fry—*perejiles*—they appreciated our work ethic.

Miriam: When you analyze the spectrum of the people who survived, there was an acknowledgment of political hierarchy but also of the widowed spouses of prominent combatants.

Elisa: And other compañeras were hostages because their husbands were Montoneros leaders who hadn't *fallen.*

Liliana: But all of this occurred after the captive had entered into the logic of survival.

Miriam: No, I think that's why they were chosen.

Liliana: You think so?

Miriam: Yes, I think that the selection criteria included the fact that they were "famous widows."

Elisa: I still maintain that we can't explain this insanity. It's out of our hands. I also believe that something emanated from inside us, which was that we had chosen to live.

Miriam: No, that's not true!

Liliana: The majority of the kidnapped must have chosen to live.

Miriam: What are you trying to say, Elisa? That of the five thousand people who passed through the ESMA, only a hundred wanted to live?

Liliana: There were a lot of captives who could have been just as useful to them, and yet they didn't survive.

Elisa: I think that the selection was random but that there also was something about us; if not, why did they pick me to type?

Miriam: Because they needed someone who knew how to do it.

Elisa: So why didn't they pick some other clerical worker among the many there?

Liliana: That was random.

Munú: The only common thread I see in the selection of people is its arbitrariness. To that I can add personal characteristics, skills, having a certain political level within the Montoneros Organization, life history, the moment of capture, but arbitrariness is always the starting point. They were the absolute owners of those of us who were kidnapped. They could choose what to do and with whom.

Cristina: In that context of arbitrariness and insanity, almost everything is uncertain, except for one option: if you wanted to choose death, you could die in there. You couldn't choose to live and have any guarantee that you would live no matter what you did. But you could guarantee your death. If you wanted, they'd kill you. I was conscious of discarding that alternative at a particular moment in time. If I'd kept on hurling insults at them, as I did when I *fell*, or fighting to the bitter end, I wouldn't be telling this story.

Munú: I agree completely. You couldn't choose for them to grant you the chance to live, but the chance to die, yes.

Liliana: Wanting to die when you could live?

Cristina: I think so. Surely some compañeros must have opted for that denouement or just lost it completely. There were people who drank water from the toilet after torture. That is choosing to die, without any euphemisms. I don't rule it out; it was an option.

Miriam: There were ways. One was for you to refuse when they offered you work, so that they'd kill you.

Cristina: Or just continually hurl insults at them.

Munú: I never heard of a compañero who reacted like that to an offer of work; in terms of insulting them, it's more likely that happened.

Miriam: Failing to pretend was a guarantee they would kill you, although some compañeros had a certain amount of leeway to tell them the truth to their faces.

Elisa: But that also had to do with how, and to whom, you said it.

Cristina: Telling the truth to the extent possible, without provoking an outright confrontation, was a survival strategy. It was an attempt to preserve your mental health on the inside.

Munú: It helped you to know who you were and to have some semblance of control over the confusion.

Elisa: In principle, the selection criterion was random.

148

Miriam: But not the survival strategies. The compañeras who were widows with "famous" last names and the ones who bore a special burden of pain—for example, Quica, whose husband and two children had been killed—made them feel . . . I can't say it was guilt but definitely some combination of pity and guilt.

Elisa: I'm not sure about pity. But I would say respect.

Miriam: Respect for the pain. Respect for the enemy's widow, for the widow of a superior officer with two militant children who had died as teenagers.

Cristina: These are hypotheses.

Miriam: And how did Quica behave with that weight on her shoulders? What I'm getting at is that I wonder whether the selection criterion had anything to do with each individual survival strategy.

Liliana: We don't know. We don't know what that random selection criterion was through which, out of a hundred people who might have been there at any given moment, two or three ended up participating in a project that included the possibility of survival.

Elisa: Gabi's case and that of the widows make me think of war trophies. Do you know what it meant to have Gabi, whom they considered a real bitch, alive and in shackles? It was a real trophy.

Miriam: But did they all really think she was a bitch? Because CHAMORRO admired her.

Elisa: It may be that CHAMORRO admired her, but even so, any army man who showed up there was taken to see her—look, we have her, and we also have so-and-so's widow. They kept them there so they could denigrate them whenever they pleased.

Miriam: Let's think about the *dog pack*. Bichi and Mantecol were there, selected to do manual labor because they were from the shantytowns.

Elisa: And they were really nice.

Miriam: Yes, but Chiquitín was also in the *dog pack*; he was selected for it, and he bought into the role. And he was a student and the son of a middle-class doctor. You kept your ear to the ground: "I wonder how they have me catalogued? How can I come across to them as useful and nice?" And you kept going down that track, sticking to it like a locomotive. Elisa would say, "I'm the silly little girl with the insipid face; I went out on September 21 clutching a bouquet of flowers, and they *sucked* me *up*." Liliana would say, "I'm infantile? OK, I'm infantile."

Elisa: If you don't want me to understand anything, I don't understand anything. I don't hear, don't see. That was my position.

Miriam: Here's what I think: our survival strategies had to do with the image they had formed of us, which maybe, in an obscure and indirect way, could have had something to do with the selection criterion. We just don't know.

Elisa: I can't put myself inside their heads enough to have a categorical opinion.

Cristina: I think there's a point of convergence. At a certain moment in time, those strategies that you intuitively put into play converged with some random factors and your own weaknesses. I am a person who before, during, and after that experience, inspired, and inspires, trust. I have a sort of nice person certificate. And I think that somehow worked in my favor.

Liliana: Each person is probably convinced that some personal characteristic rendered him or her selectable, but it must have to do with what you want to be and not how you acted at that moment.

Elisa: You think it was totally random.

Liliana: Yes.

Cristina: I don't know. I think it's very complicated. There was a dose of randomness, but I think that our personal traits also had some influence. MARIANO told me, "I trust you; I'm not going to torture you anymore."

Liliana: The question to ask is this: What made the oppressors talk more with certain captives? What was it that created that space? Or did they do it because a selection had already been made? That's what I don't know. And I don't know whether they had the same long conversations with the people who didn't survive as they had with us at the beginning.

Miriam: Yes, they did. With El Sordo, with Cafati the Turk, with Loli.

Liliana: So that doesn't work either—thinking that they were swayed because there had been more extensive dialogue.

Miriam: No, it doesn't have anything to do with that.

Liliana: Out of thousands of people, one hundred survived. Why did they choose us?

Miriam: I was searching for some logic, to bring some order to the chaos.

Cristina: That's impossible. I don't believe there is a pattern, which isn't to say that each individual experience might not have an explanation; it just can't be generalized to other cases.

Munú: I still say it was all part of the same plan; everything was arbitrary— the selection of people and the vast majority of things that happened. Some of us were able to behave in ways and say things that others couldn't and vice versa.

Miriam: The leaders didn't always survive. They had El Sordo, who was a superior officer, and they killed him.

Liliana: Of course, it wasn't enough to be a Montoneros leader.

Miriam: That's true. It wasn't enough, but how did El Sordo behave? Surely they would have offered him the chance to collaborate. I remember that they made him write something before they killed him. They probably determined that the document hadn't been sufficiently useful or didn't go far enough, or they perceived some duplicity. They had sent him to Campo de

Mayo,[16] and they tortured him there—him, with his colostomy! And since he didn't die, he ended up back in the ESMA, and they killed him.

Elisa: In El Sordo's case, they must have been under pressure from other branches of the armed forces. The same with Gabi. We could go on talking for days trying to figure out the reason that they let us live, but the question should really be this: Why did they kill so many people?

---

16. Campo de Mayo was an army regiment located in greater Buenos Aires where a clandestine detention center operated.

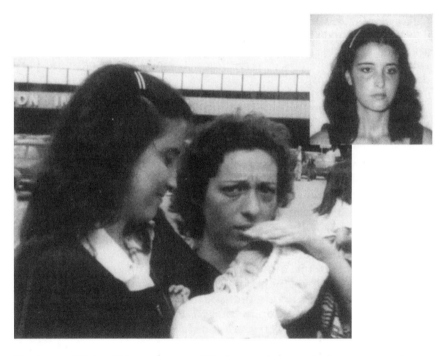

Top (inset): Cristina Aldini, government ID photograph (supervised release status, January 18, 1980). *Bottom:* Cristina Aldini with Adriana Marcus and nephew (supervised release status, September 1979).

4
Torturers

The past is here with its laments
Now it is still here but laments no more
There are visages of shame and ruin
the needle threaded with horror
the traps of derision and doubt
We shall not forget a single millimeter
Nor waste ourselves on hate
The past is here and it is enough.
                    —Mario Benedetti, "Diálogo con la memoria" in *Preguntas al azar*

MASSERA himself said that JORGE EDUARDO ACOSTA had an atomic bomb in his head. The TIGER, lord and master of life and death in the ESMA, was unpredictable, Machiavellian, and perverse. He placed his imprimatur on everything that happened in the Task Force. ACOSTA and his subordinates interacted with the disappeared people who were at their mercy in the concentration camp in the course of events that ranged from the cruel to the bizarre. There were, however, variations in the conduct of the oppressors: in most cases their conduct was characterized by extreme violence and distrust, but it was also characterized by vacillation, isolated—usually guilt-ridden—acts of solidarity, and an irrepressible admiration for the courage and dignity of some of their "enemies."

Cristina: After you all were gone, I lived through an incredible episode. One day this guy showed up, a very high-ranking officer, and he "adopted" me.
Munú: What do you mean he adopted you?
Cristina: He adopted me. It was a horrific experience! It's mortifying to even talk about it! He had a very high rank; I'm not sure what it was. He was completely insane and an alcoholic besides. Shortly before I was to be released from permanent confinement in that place, MARIANO sent me to make a mountain of photocopies, with the assurance that they'd let me go as soon as I'd finished the whole job. All I did was make photocopies.
Munú: You didn't even go to the bathroom!

Cristina: I hardly slept in order to finish it!

Munú: Wishing you could read all the photocopies but unable to do so, for the sake of finishing faster!

Cristina: No, I read some things that I always regretted not having taken with me. They were documents about the methods of repression that were later bound into notebooks. I was able to talk about them later, but I wasn't able to keep the evidence. One day I was in Jorges making photocopies, and this guy showed up ranting and raving. It seems that I reminded him of his niece who had disappeared. He came in and asked me what I was doing, and I said as little as possible to him. All of a sudden, he started saying that the people who'd been detained there weren't dead. He said they were in the South, and they'd been taken there in helicopters. Because he was so crazy, the others would take him away whenever they could. But they're so hierarchical—"subordination and valor" above all—that the guy could ask for anything and they'd all jump to attention.

Munú: Was that under Abdala?

Cristina: Yes, the guy had become obsessed with me. I reminded him of his niece, and he'd talk to me about her. He said he was delighted to have met me, and for that reason, he was going to organize a dinner in my honor.

Miriam: No!

Cristina: And he did!

Munú: Oh, no, Cristina, please!

Cristina: It was in Jorges, in one of those offices where the Tiger always was.

Munú: In Jorges there was a wide hallway and offices along the sides.

Cristina: I didn't want to hear a word about it. So they came to talk to me— Espejaime, fat Jungle—to persuade me to go.

Miriam: This guy, the nutcase, had he participated in the repression? Was he part of the Task Force?

Cristina: Apparently not, but he was aware of everything that happened. He'd suddenly start chatting with the prisoners, and this had created problems with his visits on more than one occasion. The thing was that he organized the dinner, with a waiter and everything—and the high command! The Tiger was there; Chamorro was there, I think; Marcelo was there; and two or three other marinos were there. The situation was—I don't know what adjective to use—bizarre and sinister in the extreme. The guy was saying all kinds of irrational things, and everyone would just go along with him.

Miriam: What was his rank—do you know?

Cristina: No, I never knew his rank or his name.

Munú: One step above the Tiger evidently.

Miriam: How old was he?

Cristina: Around fifty. And to top it all off, he wanted to dedicate a piano piece to me.

Munú: You, on your own with all those monsters! Were they standing or seated around that table?

Cristina: Seated. And there was an embroidered tablecloth on the table, wineglasses, silverware. A marino was acting as the waiter, "in costume." And everyone was going along with it. Just when I was on the verge of insanity, they took me to a place where there was a grand piano.

Munú: In Jorges?

Cristina: No, they took me by car to a huge hall in some other ESMA building, outside the camp.

Munú: How terrifying.

Cristina: Total insanity! The guy started to play a classical piece, and he asked me to stand beside the piano. The others contemplated this ceremony with such an exaggerated show of pleasure that it was even more outrageous than the insanity of the pianist himself. Just when I thought I couldn't take any more, MARCELO orchestrated my exit. He said I had to go, and he had to take me. Without saying a word, he put me in a car and took me to my parents' house. It's very hard to describe the state I was in when I got there, like being in shock. And on top of that, I couldn't tell them what was wrong. It was one of two episodes I experienced in the ESMA after which I had to take a sedative, something I'd never done in my life.

Miriam: I'm coming from a dinner in my honor!

Cristina: Where a crazy marino dedicated a concert to me! I found out later that he'd been discharged. I think they hospitalized him.

Miriam: It was all a vindication of his niece, to give homage to her.

Cristina: Ana once told me that she had related this story to a writer friend of hers, and he wrote a story based on it.

Munú: The truth is he didn't have to add much to it.

Cristina: I never read it.

Miriam: And at the same time, they were still kidnapping people. One floor below they were torturing somebody, no doubt!

Munú: They could go from dinner straight to the torture room with no trouble at all.

Cristina: Yes, that was the most deranged part.

Munú: Several days went by from the time he saw you making photocopies and told you he was going to organize the dinner to the dinner itself.

Cristina: Several days went by, and the guy would come and install himself next to the photocopier. That's how I found out about his niece. It was a fixation.

Munú: Was he looking for a relationship with you as a woman?

Cristina: No, absolutely not; to the contrary, he treated me very paternally, with a sort of tenderness. Honestly, I felt more pity than hate. After all, something inside him had stopped him from directing horror and driven him insane instead. The guy started talking in the middle of the dinner, with the others acting derisively. He said he was happy to have met me; he gave a speech. [*Protracted silence*] Then he sang something for me that I didn't understand because it was in German, I think. And you know what I did? Overcome with nerves and anxiety, I sang a song for him. You know what I sang? "Alfonsina and the Sea."[1]

Miriam: Oh, Cristina!

Cristina: Maybe no one will understand it. I don't understand it myself, but that's how I felt, so I sang. [*Long silence*]

Munú: [*Crying*] What insanity! [*Silence*]

Cristina: I don't know why I did it. It wasn't to screw with him. I didn't do it on purpose. I don't know.

Munú: You just stood up and sang!

Cristina: No, I sang sitting down.

Munú: I imagine it must have been some sort of reaction.

Miriam: That song—it's a sweet death. [*Silence*]

Munú: It's amazing to me that in the middle of that tragedy you were able to sing. I imagine it must have been a way of leaving that reality behind and entering into a profound state of communion with yourself. I don't know how to explain it—like rising above it all.

Miriam: Yes, but that song!

Munú: I see it as a life-giving act, even though you sang what you sang.

Cristina: I swear to you that I have no idea why it happened. Maybe it was a subconscious recourse, since I couldn't speak, or maybe it was in homage to his niece, a compañera I would never know. And besides, I can tell you that since leaving the ESMA, I think I've related this episode only in very exceptional cases. As you can imagine, I feel pain every single time I hear that song.

Miriam: Did any of them ever try to sleep with any of you?

Liliana: It happened to me. Fat JUNGLE was always looking for houses. He had to rent locales, or properties, and he would take me along with him. There was a motel around the corner from the ESMA, in one of the adjacent houses. During one of those excursions, he turned the car around and stopped in front of the entrance. He didn't even have enough imagination to go very far. I can't remember whether he said something or just looked at me, and so I don't know whether I said something to him or just motioned, but—

Munú: There was a "no" from your end.

Liliana: Resounding.

Miriam: There was retching. [*Laughter*]

---

1. "Alfonsina y el Mar" is an Argentine ballad about a girl who drowns herself at sea.

Liliana: Yes, there was no insistence. The pick-up attempt began and ended there. After that my whole love story with Tano developed. MARIANO is actually the one who handled that, because at no time did I abandon—

Munú: His protection.

Liliana: MARIANO's protection. I'm not sure whether fat JUNGLE asked MARIANO's permission to take me around Buenos Aires. In any event, it was evident that fat JUNGLE—

Miriam: Was wounded.

Liliana: Was wounded, because one day he called me into the Fishbowl, and he said—[*Laughter*] it's such a ridiculous thing, please!—well, he said he was admitting defeat. He thought he was going to win that battle because he rode the sheriff's horse, because he was an officer and Tano was a mere prisoner, but he actually admitted defeat. I still believe I never said anything at all. The same way that I feel that I didn't utter a sound at the motel entrance, I don't think I did after that, that . . . [*Laughter*] that gentlemanly . . . amorous . . . resignation from fat JUNGLE.

Munú: And Diego helped you, Miriam, to dodge the TIGER.

Miriam: When we were working in RUGER's parents' house in Núñez,[2] where they took all the materials from the Fishbowl archive after MASSERA's retirement. Relatives of RADICE, GREENS, were guarding us, and every so often the TIGER would drop by. Once he said to me, "Oh, Michi,[3] you are so beautiful! One of these days we'll have to go out to dinner." I was terrified. The next day, he arranged a night out with Diego and Co, a dinner for the four of us. I don't remember where we went. It was always horrible to have dinner with him, but that night was even worse. I had a knot in my throat; I felt queasy, which always happens to me when I get nervous. I was living alone across from the School of Agriculture, in the apartment my parents had rented for me. I took Diego aside and said, "Please don't leave me alone, because I think the TIGER has ulterior motives." Diego paled and he said, "Yes, I noticed. Don't worry." When we finished eating, the TIGER announced, "I'll drop you two off in Núñez, and then I'll take Michi home." And so Diego said, "No, TIGER, let's do it the other way around: let's take Michi home, and then we'll head straight for Núñez." And that's what we did. They dropped me off first. When I got home, I was shaking; I locked the door with all four locks, and I was prepared not to respond to the buzzer in case he came back. He was quite capable of doing so.

Munú: My experience in this regard was that every time the TIGER saw me talking to MARIANO, he'd start insinuating, he'd make jokes about our

---

2. Núñez is a neighborhood in Buenos Aires.

3. Michi was the prisoners' nickname for Miriam, derived from the Yiddish word "*meshuge*" ("crazy").

relationship. I'd put on a "nothing" face, MARIANO would laugh as if he felt flattered, and the three of us knew it wasn't true. Whenever he found me alone, the TIGER would say, "You're such a vixen." A lot of officers, and even some of the prisoners, thought something was going on between MARIANO and me, and I always figured it wasn't in my interest to deny it. It was a matter of survival.

Miriam: Yes, and only now, twenty years later, am I able to tell you that at the time I believed you were involved with MARIANO, but I never would have considered asking you. You didn't talk about that kind of thing in there. You felt a certain modesty, respect for the other person's privacy, embarrassment. And what happened with you, Cristina?

Cristina: It was surreal. Andrea, Adriana, and the DUKE were there. We were a little group. They put us all in a car and took us—guess where? We couldn't believe it.

Munú: Where?

Cristina: To Mau Mau.[4]

Miriam: To Mau Mau?

Cristina: Just as we were. I'll never forget it as long as I live. I was wearing the same light blue dress I wore night and day. It was insane. Just imagine, an evening in Buenos Aires, the women all dolled up, and there we were, four or five prisoners from the ESMA. The TIGER was there—the famous Lata Liste, the owner, greeted him at the door as if he'd known him all his life—and someone else. We all just stood there stiff as boards; people were dancing. Then the TIGER started pestering Andrea, Adriana, and me to dance. No one wanted to do it, and we all had these asinine expressions on our faces. The TIGER was enjoying the tension between him, with his outrageous power, and us, with nothing but our humanity. So I decided I had to do something unexpected. I donned my armor, and off I went. I danced with TIGER ACOSTA.

Munú: That is too much!

Cristina: I danced like a robot, feigning indifference, even though I was trembling inside. Until they put on a song that had a special meaning for me and I couldn't keep it up any longer. Still playacting, I casually said, that's enough, and then I went to the bathroom and broke down crying in the corner, next to a toilet, drowning out the screams that rose up in my throat. Afterward, I didn't know what to do about going back out. I was fit to be tied. I washed my face. I have no idea how I pulled myself together. Beside me was this woman, all gussied up. We stayed a while longer. I don't understand what the TIGER was trying to do, why he did it.

Munú: It was just like when they took you out to dinner.

---

4. Mau Mau was a famous nightclub frequented by show business celebrities and social elites—locale of the classic "evening in Buenos Aires" of the seventies.

Liliana: Right.

Cristina: No, it was different—a perverse game.

Munú: And the dinners weren't perverse—taking you to a restaurant when all the while they kept on killing people as if it were nothing?

Cristina: I was also familiar with that experience, but this one was more intense.

Munú: It probably was. That type of place, the dancing . . .

Miriam: When they were the same people who'd killed your compañero.

Cristina: It was a subworld within a world.

Liliana: That's right. The subworld of those nightclubs is oppressive. They're horrible even under normal circumstances.

Cristina: But he couldn't leave it at that. Afterward he organized a return visit, and he fixed it so that I'd go alone with him in the car. So he starts telling me all about his life. You had noticed that he liked to talk.

Miriam: Yes.

Cristina: About his wife and about how he needed new ambrosia and I don't know what else. So I asked him what had happened to his wife's ambrosia.

Liliana: Again, you! [*Laughter*]

Cristina: The thing is that to me it was inconceivable, repulsive; I guess I was reacting straight from my heart and my stomach. And then he went crazy, and he said I was insolent and he was going to *send* me *up*. And he was also going to keep in mind my younger sister, who was fifteen at the time. So I said, "That doesn't fit with what you're always saying, that you're the gentlemen of the sea." He drove past the ESMA, spun the car around, and made as if to drive in, and then he said, no, he wasn't going to do it, and he took me to my mom's house.

Munú: He made as if he was going to drive you into the ESMA to *send* you *up*.

Cristina: But then he kept on going straight, and he took me to Martínez.[5] He stopped in front of the house and said that despite everything—

Munú: He admired you!

Cristina: Yes, that I was very up-front and I don't know what else. He opened the car door for me. I rang the doorbell at four o'clock in the morning, and my blessed mother opened it. Obviously, I couldn't tell her what I'd just been through. "I'm okay. Please, just give me something to drink," I said. And I went up clinging to the walls for support.

Liliana: Oh, my God!

Munú: Oh, how awful! [*Silence*]

∾

---

5. Martínez is an area in the San Isidro section in the northern zone of greater Buenos Aires.

Miriam: The TIGER was obsessed with Luis Brandoni![6] He wanted to *suck* him *up* at any cost.

Elisa: What happened?

Adriana: One night they took us, as they had on many occasions, to have dinner at El Globo,[7] a place where I always chose my meal based on the price. In an absurd act of childish resistance, I would always choose the most expensive item [*Laughter*], which was nearly always the fried calamari. So I've had my fill of fried calamari. I don't eat it anymore.

Munú: They took you out to eat at El Globo often?

Adriana: Too often for me. It wasn't very pleasant to have to share a table with those sorts.

Miriam: It was horrible!

Elisa: It was torture.

Miriam: You'd watch them chatting and eating, and you'd imagine them with the *electric prod* in hand, and you couldn't let them see the repugnance you felt or the fear. You had to treat them like normal human beings.

Elisa: That kind of thing didn't happen as often during my time. It must have been ghastly! So much interaction with those sorts. When I hear you talk about it, I feel that I was saved from that brand of torture. They took me out to dinner on three occasions. One of those times, I was already at the Foreign Ministry.

Miriam: Terrible! The TIGER's favorite places were Los Años Locos, El Globo, El Imparcial, El Hispano, Fechoría, and a club called Spiagge di Napoli.

Adriana: I remember how they'd wake us up at all hours of the night: "Girls, get dressed. You're going out to dinner."

Elisa: Girls and guys.

Adriana: No, with them it was always the girls.

Cristina: The guys went sometimes.

Miriam: In our time, the outings were mixed; Chito would go. The truth is I don't even remember what we talked about. I just remember that I didn't want to be sitting next to any of the marinos, because I wouldn't have known what to talk about. I couldn't look them in the eye, and I didn't spend much time looking at the people at other tables either.

Munú: The groups were mixed. They took me out with Gabriel and Tito.

Cristina: I guess when it was just the three of us, once most of the people you mentioned had left, it was different.

---

6. Luis Brandoni is an Argentine actor who played in the film *La Tregua* [*The Truce*], screenplay by Osvaldo Bayer, based on the novel *La Patagonia rebelde* [*Rebel Patagonia*], by Uruguayan writer Mario Benedetti, and other film and theater productions with social content.

7. El Globo, Los Años Locos, El Imparcial, El Hispano, La Cabaña, Fechoría, and El Tropezón were well-known restaurants whose fine cuisine, structural features, and/or prime location gave them a certain prestige. The Embers, located in exclusive areas, was the first chain in Argentina to sell "Yankee style" hamburgers and fast food.

Elisa: It was Cristina, Adriana, and who else?

Cristina: Andrea.

Adriana: You had to get dressed up, and if you put on make up, so much the better. The more paint you wore, the more *recuperated* you were. No cowboy boots, suede shoes, or moccasins. Lots of teardrop earrings and necklaces, like a Christmas tree. One night we went out—I think the TIGER was driving, and there were two of them—and I don't remember whether you were there, Cristina, or whether it was Andrea.

Munú: Were you still inside the ESMA?

Cristina: Yes.

Adriana: Yes, that was the last time they took me out to dinner. We were driving down Nueve de Julio Street, and on the radio we heard, "We have Brandoni *x* number of meters away." So the TIGER clicks on, saying, "I'm an OPERATIVE!" and he starts driving. We were all caught up in the *operation* to *suck up* Luis Brandoni! Once again that feeling of extreme danger, replaying the feelings I had when they *sucked* me *up*—the image of the weapon to your head, the blows to your body, the boot on your back, the *hood*, the handcuffs, the yells, the darkness.

Miriam: The TIGER detested Brandoni. He was his obsession. He considered him a dangerous enemy.

Adriana: Cristina, were you there?

Cristina: They took me one time, but I don't know whether it was the same one. I wanted to slit my wrists! What I remember is that I was walking along with someone, and Brandoni was somewhere. There was a signal that had to do with a briefcase. I know they followed him, and when he reached a corner, they signaled which way he was turning by switching the briefcase to the right or left hand. Luckily, nothing happened. I can't remember the details; I'm confused about the whole episode.

Adriana: No, this one was in a car. I can't remember whether they said, "Get down" or whether we decided to get down on the floor to protect ourselves. They were all going at high speed, giving orders back and forth on their walkie-talkies, which weren't very common at that time. At one point someone said, "We've lost sight of him," and the TIGER started to curse. We ended up at El Globo as usual.

Elisa: Toasting and talking about some idiotic thing. And what were they going to do with Luis Brandoni if they *sucked* him *up*?

Miriam: Kill him!

Munú: I don't know. If they'd really wanted to find him, they could have waited for him outside the theater.

Elisa: I remember BLONDIE's gripe with Charly García. He said he was an instigator of violence, but I never heard him mention Brandoni.

Adriana: We would always get to El Globo just when all the famous actors finished their performances and went there for dinner. We'd be surrounded by a whole bunch of people that I didn't recognize, naturally, because I'd never had a TV and I never went to the movies. So they'd be whispering to me, "That's so-and-so, and over there that's so-and-so."

Munú: One night they took me out to dinner. Chiqui and Tito were there too. MARIANO was there, and the TIGER, and JUAN. And there were others, but I don't remember who they were. We went to El Tropezón on Callao and Sarmiento. There were seven or eight of us, and we sat at a table in the back. Brandoni, his wife, and several others were seated at another table, in front of the window by the entrance. They were celebrating his birthday, because you could hear "happy birthday" and all that. The TIGER said to MARIANO and JUAN, "There's Brandoni. Shall we *suck* him *up* on our way out?" So just like that, we found ourselves in the middle of an *operation* that they were concocting. My guts knotted up.

Miriam: Why did they hate him so much?

Munú: I don't know. There they were: they'd take him; they wouldn't take him; they'd *suck* him *up*; they wouldn't *suck* him *up*—until finally Brandoni and his party finished eating, got up, and left. And the TIGER didn't get up to go after him, to our relief. This happened at the end of 1978. I went to Venezuela in 1979, and in 1980 or 1981 the Open Theater was founded in Argentina.[8] They always held the International Theater Festival in Venezuela, and so the Open Theater group went, and Luis Brandoni was with them. On the first day that he was going to be performing, I stationed myself at the theater entrance to wait for him. I was thinking, "This happened two or three years ago, but he's still living there. He needs to know what I know."

Miriam: Of course. You couldn't just keep quiet about it.

Munú: So Brandoni arrives for the performance, and I stop him at the door.

Cristina: With a very reassuring message! After that he gave a brilliant performance.

Elisa: What did you say to him? [*Laughter*]

Munú: I said, "You don't know me. I'm Argentine, and I want to tell you about something that happened to me that also involved you. I was kidnapped." He looked at me, and we went to get coffee. I told him the whole story: "I don't know whether or not you're going to believe me; do whatever you want. I was in the ESMA; I got there on this date, and I left on that date. And on one occasion, such and such happened. It was your birthday." He asked me the date it had happened, and I told him. "Yes, that's true," he responded. I told him that five tables away, they were talking about *sucking* him *up* right then and there. So he told me the story of his kidnapping.

Elisa: He was kidnapped?

---

8. Teatro Abierto [Open Theater] was a theater movement that emerged during the final years of the dictatorship.

Munú: Yes, for a short time, I believe. Afterward he left the country. He spent some time abroad, and then he went back. "I thank you very much," he said, and he left to perform in *Gray of Absence*, a play by Roberto Cossa. I'll never forget it. We were exiles, and he was talking about the gray of absence. We had agreed to meet the next day, and he introduced me to his teenage daughters.

Miriam: I'm not sure whether this was the same incident, but I remember they came to get the TIGER because Brandoni was premiering in something and they'd figured out where he was going to have dinner after the show. The idea was to *suck* him *up* as he was leaving there.

Munú: It can't have been the same time, because they were very surprised when they saw him.

Cristina: It was pure luck that saved that guy!

Munú: He was a public figure; he was in the union; everybody knew him. If they managed to track us down, bottom of the barrel *perejiles*, surely they could find him.

Cristina: But they made several attempts. Why did they go out on all those ridiculous *expeditions* if not to *suck* him *up*?

Munú: It gives you the impression that the sight of him would get them all riled up and they'd go dashing out after him.

Munú: Once, at a dinner, I got into trouble with the TIGER, and I have no idea why he didn't kill me.

Elisa: Why?

Munú: The TIGER said something like God was the one who decided who was *sent up* and who wasn't. And in an effort to be ingratiating, since he was looking right at me, I answered, "Oh! But your little God must be pretty bad, because there are very few of us here."
[*Sighs and interjections of horror and laughter*]

Elisa: And what did he say?

Munú: "And why do you think you're still here?" he shouted. "Do you think you'd be here if it weren't for Jesus? You'd have been *sent up*! I don't know what's wrong with you!" It was horrifying; I thought he was going to kill me. I'd said it to be ingratiating, and it didn't come out like that! I couldn't believe that he actually believed what he was saying. I thought he was joking.

Adriana: Your career: diplomacy.

Munú: Definitely. I did another one in El Globo, and it also came out wrong. I was always doing things to ingratiate myself.

Elisa: With the TIGER again?

Munú: Of course. The TIGER was my problem!

Elisa: Oh, God, he was so evil!

Munú: While we were eating, I said to the Tiger, "I really don't understand why it is that all of you stay at the ESMA when you could go home every night. Surely your families must need you; your children must be growing up without a father figure."

Adriana: "God, Country, and Family."

Miriam: What you were saying was part of the image of *recuperation* that they had for us as family-oriented women.

Munú: They always went on about how we destroyed the family. If they always stayed at the ESMA, then they were destroying it too! They could go home on their days off, and they didn't. So what was the enraged Tiger's response? Shouting so that every single person in El Globo could hear him, he said, "Don't you realize that it's your fault we don't want to go home?" He kept looking at Mariano, as if he were asking for approval, and Mariano would nod his head in agreement.

Elisa: Confirming.

Munú: And the Tiger was yelling, "With you, we can talk about movies, the theater, about anything. We can talk about politics. You know about raising children; you can play the guitar; you know how to handle a weapon! You know how to do everything! You are the women that we thought . . ." —all this time Mariano and Juan were nodding their heads—"you are the women that we thought existed only in novels and movies, and it has destroyed our families! Because now what are we going to do with the women we have at home!" He kept yelling like a wild man.

Cristina: Are you serious?

Munú: I swear it.

Elisa: We discussed these things among ourselves, and we couldn't understand why some officers lived as if they too had been *sucked up*. But I didn't know that they expressed it.

Munú: It was too dramatic to be theater—and all at the top of his lungs. He kept asking the others, "Right?" and then he'd go on. "What can I share with my wife? I go home on Saturday, and we talk about whether or not we'll go to the club on Sunday, whether to take the picnic basket or not take the picnic basket, whether we're going with someone else. That's what I share with my wife. And on Sunday we go to the club, and the subject is 'Did you bring the umbrella?' 'I don't have the chair; that guy over there took the chair.' There is nothing else I can share with my wife!"

Elisa: The Tiger said that to you?

Munú: Not just to me. There were other people there who certainly would remember it. It was all our fault they were having problems with their wives.

Adriana: Thunder and Marcelo also talked about such things. I remember that Marcelo had a crisis with his girlfriend, and after we'd been released, he'd often come by to get Ana and me. He'd take us for a drink or to eat something, and he'd talk to us about personal matters.

Elisa: As if you were friends!

Adriana: We were under his responsibility. He had to monitor us, ensure our satisfactory *recuperation process*, keep track of what we were up to.

Miriam: Like the "parole officer" in Yankee films. [*Laughter*]

Adriana: Sometimes I had the feeling that some of those guys, in whatever sliver was left of their humanity, were broken, not just by their own evildoing but also because they had met other people—people like us, atypical women to them, and the compañeros. We shook some of their beliefs.

Munú: MARIANO often told me things. Once, very despondent, he told me, "I got home, and my wife showed me the latest steps she'd learned, because she's learning how to march. I leave here, I go home, and I find my wife marching! I look at her, and I think I don't belong there. I'm sharing this history with all of you, not with her."

Miriam: Except they *sent up* most people for sharing that history.

Munú: A minor detail.

Elisa: That type of relationship between captives and torturers didn't happen in 1977.

Munú: No, of course not. In mid- and late 1978, they had more time; they didn't have so many people left to kill.

Elisa: You were saying that the TIGER said it to you openly, but we often discussed the fact that they didn't go home. It seemed to us that they stayed there because they shared a world with the captives that they probably couldn't explain at home. I'm sure they didn't tell their wives what they were doing. What could MARIANO say to his wife? "Today I was torturing three women, and I shocked them with an *electric prod.*"

Miriam: Adriana, you were saying earlier that in their free time they would shock each other with the *prod.*

Munú: How did they do it, with a weak current?

Adriana: Of course, testing it.

Munú: So they could see what it was like? I can't imagine any of them tied to a bed, naked and *hooded*, retching.

Cristina: Of course not!

Adriana: I didn't ask for details, because I really couldn't stand it.

Munú: And there was a fundamental difference: they were equals. It wasn't as if one of them were using all his power to subjugate the other. It was totally different, even if the intensity of the current had been the same.

Elisa: No, they played around.

Miriam: A pretty . . . sadistic, perverse game.

Cristina: It must have been some kind of defense mechanism.

Adriana: Of course, it's the same with doctors. During their shifts they pull some pretty heavy stunts, and sometimes they turn out badly. I never could stand those stunts. Less so now! Maybe those guys couldn't stomach someone else's pain. Bah, I want to believe they had something human in them.

Munú: Sometimes I've thought exactly what you just said, and frankly I never could come to a conclusion. It's a very complicated subject.

Cristina: MANUEL had tortured me. If he had to go into the room in the Basement where I was, he wouldn't look at me. On other occasions, he'd open the door, and if he saw me there, he'd close it again and leave. He avoided me the whole time I was in the ESMA. He didn't say a word to me. A few months after leaving there, I was at my parents' house—

Munú: Were you still working with them?

Cristina: My memory is a little confused. I think I was about to leave for the provinces, because it completely threw me. He came to get me, and, of course, I went. He took me to a pastry shop nearby, and we spent about two hours there. He talked to me about his childhood. [*Laughter*] I never understood what that had to do with anything! Afterward he deposited me at my house, and I just stood there petrified.

Munú: We could publish it—publish MANUEL'S *Childhood*.

Miriam: The childhood of a torturer!

Cristina: My only memory of what he said is an image—when he and his cousins climbed trees or ran among the trains.

Miriam: Like any normal boy.

Adriana: He wanted to convince you that he was human.

Miriam: Once the TIGER got my parents to invite him out to eat at La Cabaña, and my Dad took him a bottle of Chivas Regal as a gift.

Munú: What?

Elisa: Miriam, tell that story again, because I never heard it!

Munú: Since he usually didn't take captives to their homes, he wanted to know what the families were like, and he'd invite himself over.

Miriam: He invited himself, of course. In November or December 1978, when they were about to release me—which ended up being supervised release, because I slept at home but I worked at the Ministry, which was run by the navy, or in MASSERA's press offices or at RUGER's parents' house—the TIGER sent me to tell my parents that he wanted to meet with them, that he'd like to go out to dinner at a restaurant of their choosing. In other words, he was saying, "Me—the guest." My parents asked me where they could take him. I told them that the guy liked to eat well, so perhaps La Cabaña, which was very trendy at the time. Only rich people and tourists went there. I remember that the supreme son of a bitch asked for "baby beef," and "omelet surprise," and I don't know what else. My parents had never been there before, and, of course, I hadn't either. It was extremely expensive, well beyond our means.

Elisa: That son of a bitch ordered dessert and all!

Miriam: And my parents took him a bottle of Chivas Regal as a gift.

Elisa: Had you suggested that?

Miriam: I don't know. My mom said, "We have to treat him very well" or something along those lines. [*Laughter*] My mom would have built a monument to him! She had no idea what went on inside the ESMA. All she knew was that he was the man who had brought me back when she thought she was never going to see me again.

Munú: Of course. The alternative was that you'd be dead.

Miriam: That's when he explained to my parents why I wouldn't be allowed to go abroad. My parents kept bringing this up during the *visits* and every time they had any contact through me. They wanted to send me to New York to live with an aunt. They said I'd be fine there, that I'd start a new life, blah, blah, blah. So the Tiger explained to them that Admiral Massera needed me in Buenos Aires. [*Laughter*] I was very capable, good with languages, and the admiral had a project and he needed me. And sending me abroad wasn't a good idea, since my former compañeros might find me and execute me as a traitor. "You know what violent people they are," he said.

Munú: They always used the same old lines.

Miriam: He also asked them to rent an apartment for me so that I'd be living alone, because if the navy let me go home to live with them, I was at risk of being kidnapped by another branch of the armed forces. The ESMA stood by its own actions but couldn't answer for what the army did. And if they kidnapped me and took me to the Campo de Mayo, who would get me out of there? That was the friendly advice he gave my family over dinner.

Munú: He wanted to keep on running your life, to dominate you for as long as he could.

Elisa: What perverse minds they had!

Adriana: Did you know that I went to Ushuaia[9] with Abdala?

Elisa: I can't believe it!

Adriana: We were already out. Ana and I were in Buenos Aires. I must have still been working with them; I don't think I'd gone back to school yet. I

---

9. Ushuaia is a city in southern Argentina, in the Tierra del Fuego province.

166

don't remember exactly when it was, but one day ABDALA proposed that we take a trip to Ushuaia.

Munú: For what?

Adriana: A one-day pleasure trip. [*Laughter*]

Munú: Did you know it was a pleasure trip?

Adriana: No, I talked with my mom about it just the other day. My parents remember a lot of things that I don't. They are my memory, because mine is pretty well ruined. I asked my mom why they took us to Ushuaia, and she said, "Because ABDALA wanted to show you how beautiful our country was so you wouldn't go to Peru." So obviously I had already decided to leave. It must have been in late 1979, because I'd been discussing it with MARCELO. The idea was that they would forget all about my humble personage. I had a German passport and a German language diploma that would enable me to do university studies in Germany without taking any sort of exam. But I didn't want to go there, because I intuited that I would never return to Argentina. My roots are German—I learned to speak that language first and then Spanish—so there was a strong family issue. I chose Peru because I didn't want to go to a country where there were a lot of Argentine exiles. I later discovered that some of the Mothers [of the Plaza de Mayo] were living there, and one of them had been kidnapped. They took her through Bolivia, and she disappeared. Anyway, it seems that I'd already decided to leave and ABDALA was using that argument to persuade me not to do it.

Miriam: I can't believe he would take you to Ushuaia for that!

Adriana: My mom says that was the reason. I can't come up with any other reason. I really don't know why he took me.

Munú: We should add that ABDALA was a navy pilot.

Cristina: Yes, and remember that when he talked about what it meant to fly, he would say he left earthly things behind, he dreamed, he was a passionate aviator. I remember hearing him say how wonderful it was to soar into the sky, into the great beyond.

Adriana: He took us by car to an airstrip near Ezeiza, I believe. We climbed aboard the plane, and he showed us the cabin.

Munú: Was it a small plane?

Adriana: Yes, we went to Ushuaia, we had coffee, and we returned to Buenos Aires.

Miriam: Now we know that they threw our compañeros into the sea from navy aircraft. That image came into my head just now.

Adriana: Another time, BLONDIE took another compañera and me to the movies and then to The Embers to eat onion rings. The stupid things you remember. I don't remember the name on the fake passport they used when they took me to Mexico, but I do remember the fried onion rings.

It was more out of context to eat onion rings than to travel with a fake passport.

Miriam: I think all of this had to do with their wanting to show us the joys of capitalism. It was as if they were telling us, "Look at all you're missing. You could dress well, go to shows, travel, eat at nice places, and you wasted your life being involved in the militant cause, concerning yourself with the poor, the disadvantaged. Why? For what, when all of this was within your reach?"

Munú: You think that showing us all that was part of the *recuperation process?*

Miriam: I think so. I'm convinced that it explains so much madness. In my mind, it's the only way to explain why they kidnap you, torture you, and then take you out to dinner.

Cristina: ABDALA wanted to demonstrate that he was different from some of the other members of the Task Force, especially TIGER ACOSTA. It was a different style within the same system.

Munú: When he was still with the SIN, he often brought pastries when he came to the ESMA to visit his prisoners.

Elisa: It was the same as the French perfume that the marinos brought for us prisoners to use.

Munú: What's that?

Elisa: I remember, in Capucha, the smell of the rats and the scent of French perfume.

Adriana: They were looking for the feminine side.

Elisa: With shackles, darling! Shackled, but wearing French perfume!

Miriam: They wanted us to show them—

Elisa: That we took care to be very feminine women!

Adriana: They couldn't abide my shoes.

Munú: They made one compañera throw hers away and buy new ones.

Adriana: They threw mine away, and I had hidden in them a poem by a woman named Kati, which was lost. When I was in Capuchita, Veronica had given it to me to save, because she had a feeling they were going to kill her. I wasn't even aware of when they took my shoes. I felt so bad for not having taken better care of the hidden treasure I was carrying around. It was like losing a vestige of a compañera's life, like letting it die.

Miriam: We had to look elegant, as if we cared about our appearance. They noticed it when we went out too. When they'd take me out to dinner, I'd be thinking, "Right now there are compañeros in Capucha who are eating boiled meat with stale bread that the rats have run all over, and here we are dining with the torturers in Los Años Locos." At the time, I didn't really understand why the marinos were doing it. All I knew was that I felt bad, that I hated them. It nauseated me to sit at the same table with them, and I found it repugnant to have to pretend that I was *recuperated* and that I didn't resent them for having killed the people I loved.

Elisa: Was that something you were able to articulate after you were out, or was it that clear to you in the moment? Maybe at the time what you felt was a vague discomfort.

Miriam: It was just the raw feeling. I'm not sure I could have stood to analyze the true magnitude of what was occurring. I would have gone crazy.

Elisa: Yes, you felt like you'd rather go back to the ESMA, to the concentration camp, than sit in that upscale restaurant. As a kidnapped person, the camp was where you belonged.

Munú: Everything was so much clearer when you were in the Basement or in Capucha. You knew: that is the oppressor, and I am a captive. When they took you out, they turned the whole situation around; they put you in the place of an equal. They took you out, sat you down beside them, and gave you the same food. I imagine it caused us an enormous amount of confusion.

Miriam: And we behaved in a submissive manner in both situations. For me it was a test; that's what it felt like. If you flunked, they'd *send* you *up*. They were always watching us.

Elisa: In order to pass, you had to laugh, act as if the things they said were funny. But all the while inside you were wondering, "What am I doing here?" You felt out of place.

Miriam: I think when they took us out, they were trying to tell us, "You young, desirable, middle-class women were wasting your time playing guerrilla while all of this, this life of pleasure, was within your grasp. You have chosen the wrong path, young Argentine women!"

Elisa: Do you really believe that's what they thought?

Munú: Do you think they really cared whether we thought that?

Miriam: If not, then why did they take us out?

Munú: I have no idea!

Elisa: Because they were bored.

Cristina: It was part of the discipline.

Elisa: When they put you in that place, even though you didn't kick and scream, you felt bad. It was a punishment. The conflict it caused inside you played in their favor.

Munú: They were still subjugating you.

Miriam: I don't understand. Are you trying to say that they did it as a reward, as a perk, as if to say, "You have demonstrated that you are *recuperable*, so we're taking you out to dinner"?

All: No!

Cristina: It was a perverse game.

Munú: It was a mishmash! There was the guy who cried, repented, and then tortured again; he took you out to dinner, and then he brought you back again and sent you to Capucha. It was completely arbitrary!

Elisa: We were subjugated; we were disappeared. We were people who didn't exist and people they took out to dinner! There is no rational explanation. What happened defies logic or, I should say, has its own perverse logic.

Cristina: Taking us out played a role in that systematic *recuperation* plan, as did hundreds of other episodes we endured.

Miriam: That's what I'm saying. Within that *recuperation process*, their idea was to get this across to us: "Look at what you had at your disposition. And you were missing out on it by thinking about social justice and the poor!"

Elisa: It was probably a form of indoctrination. "Why can't you eat well? Why can't you dress like young ladies instead of wearing those blue jeans? Why can't you use sophisticated French perfume?"

Miriam: I remember that my kidnappers from the air force went to my mom's house, and a few days after that they went to the place where I'd been living, which was a room in Villa Madero with a sheet of metal for a roof. When they came to visit me in my cell, they said, "But that's incredible. How could you have put up with that shit hole—the roof was a sheet of metal, and it leaked—after having lived in that house!" They were very impressed by the crystal chandelier with the fringe in my mom's house. "You had that chandelier, fit for a palace, and you went off to live in a little room in Villa Madera!"

Munú: I think we can agree that someone who didn't share our way of thinking or our convictions would find it hard to understand why a person, at age eighteen, or twenty-five, or thirty-eight—

Elisa: Would decide to change her life.

Munú: Of course. You lived a certain way up until a particular moment, and then you suddenly decided, "Now I think this way, and since I'm a consistent person, I'm going to live over there!" It wasn't easy for other people to understand it.

Miriam: The nice clothes, the makeup, the jewelry—for us to use them was a sign that we had renounced our ideas. The TIGER gave me a silver bracelet for my birthday—with the perverted twist of calling me to his offices at midnight. I thought he was going to send me to Capucha because he'd caught me out with Laurita during a family *visit* after he had expressly forbidden it. Instead he gave me a silver bracelet in a velvet case: "Michi, I found out it was your birthday, and we didn't give you a gift. Here, take it." I'm sure I went pale, expecting them to *transfer* me for having disobeyed. He made me wait for hours, alone in a meeting room in Jorges. Hours. I would never have imagined the reason. And he knew very well that I thought it was for something else.

Cristina: Mmmmm!

Elisa: I always missed out! They didn't give me any presents! [*Laughter all around*] I feel fortunate to have been spared that as well.

Miriam: I don't think I ever lost a bracelet faster in my whole life. It got lost right away!

Adriana: Speaking of gifts and perversions, I always remember that one day BLONDIE went into the stall where I slept with some other compañeras, and he gave me a magazine. "You'll like this. Read it," he said, and he gave me *El Eternauta*. I'd never heard of it. I read it cover to cover. BLONDIE gave me a book by [Hector German] Oesterheld, a compañero they had murdered, in which he describes a group that organizes to mount a collective resistance against an invisible enemy who sends beings to invade the Earth and whose lair is on the corner of General Paz and Libertador.

∾

Miriam: Adriana, what was the story about your trip to Mexico?

Adriana: I was working in RUGER's parents' house, on Zapiola and Jaramillo, where they had installed all the materials and typewriters they'd taken from the Fishbowl. My job was to classify newspaper articles. I'd left the ESMA on April 24, 1979, and that's where I worked. And on top of all that, this nightmare of a trip came up.

Elisa: Were you together at Zapiola?

Miriam: No, by the time Adriana got out, the TIGER already had sent me to work in MASSERA's press office, on Calle Cerrito.

Munú: When was the trip?

Adriana: In May 1979. I don't recall exactly how long I was there, but I have one of the postcards I sent to my parents, and it's dated May 15, 1979. Someone had to go to Mexico with two guys who were traveling—we didn't know exactly for what, but I'm sure it wasn't to visit the Mayan ruins. A deployment like that must have had a very special objective, probably an evil one. At that time, I didn't think they could actually kill or kidnap a compañero living abroad, although now it's clear that they could. The denial mechanism was very effective at helping us endure the extremely dangerous situations that we were constantly placed in. Someone had to go with two monsters: GERONIMO and the CAT.

Miriam: Oh! GERONIMO! He had his own particular way of behaving. He ended up working with Yabrán, as a lot of them did.[10]

Adriana: We decided among ourselves that it would be best to send someone who didn't have kids, to minimize the cost. The trip was risky.

Miriam: They could have decided to kill you at any moment; you could have become an inconvenient witness to something.

---

10. Alfredo Yabrán was an Argentine businessman in the telepostal sector who committed suicide when he was about to be arrested for the murder of photojournalist José Luis Cabezas. He hired ex-oppressors from the ESMA, including FEDERICO and PALITO (both aliases) to work in his companies.

Adriana: Yes, but I don't remember seeing it that way at the time. I guess I was in denial. Otherwise it would have been unbearable. We were trapped: we couldn't refuse, because we knew that essentially we were still in just as much danger as we were on the first day in Capuchita.

Elisa: Who were the potential candidates?

Adriana: Those of us who had evaluated the situation: Andrea, Lucy, Diego, and I. It had to be a woman who could serve as cover, to pretend that it was a couple taking a trip. La Flaca had been there too, but she wasn't even a possibility, because this happened after she'd had the seizure and they'd left her at home. La Flaca was "outside of the program," and we made sure not to speak of her, because we didn't want to remind them. Cristina couldn't go either, because she had a reputation for being rebellious. [*Laughter*] Andrea had a baby, so we proposed that I be the one to go. The marinos gave me a phony passport.

Munú: They also gave me a set of phony documents when I left for Venezuela, supposedly so that I would have a fake identity in case the Montoneros wanted to kill me for having survived. I traveled with my own documents. I destroyed the phony ones when I returned to Argentina. I was afraid to bring them and have them found on me. I wonder whether anyone saved them. They were the ones I had made. I have a photograph, taken in there, of me making the original in order to forge the official identification card. My photo album is as haphazard as life itself! We made all the documents: the official identification card, the national identity document, and the passport.

Elisa: How did you make the documents?

Munú: The compañeros who worked in the photography lab would make about a 50-cm by 70-cm enlargement of the design on the official identification card. I would use a Rotring tip with black ink, a little brush, and a little bottle of white tempera paint to fix the errors in the enlargement. Then we would reduce it to its normal size and make the galleys, and Roque and Chiquitín would print it in the Liberty building. We all agreed that we didn't have very sophisticated technology to work with. It was really prisoner labor. We spent more than two months working in that area.

Miriam: They used those documents to move around inside and outside the country, and they equipped their OPERATIVES with them so they could spy on and kidnap people.

Munú: They used them, but they also gave them to some of us, gratuitously in my case. I think they were useful for other compañeros, at least I hope they were.

Elisa: What was the objective of the Mexico trip?

Adriana: I don't know. Now, after so much time has passed and with the mixture of facts and fantasy, I'm not sure whether it might have had something to do with Pelado,[11] who had escaped in July 1978 during the World Cup. I think that was my conclusion afterward, but the truth is that I'm not sure. I sent postcards to my parents. I called them on the telephone. I wanted them to know every minute that I was all right. I knew that the rest of the compañeros from Zapiola and the other "departments" were going to be on alert, because their security was also in jeopardy. We were all like parts of the same body, a pretty abused body at that. It was so clear that the compañeros who had stayed behind were hostages that even though I had the address of my mother's aunt in Mexico and I could have asked her to take me to the German Embassy to request asylum and denounce my illegal entry into Mexico, I didn't do it. In the first place, I was afraid the compañeros would suffer reprisals. In the second place, when I went to my aunt's, I rang the doorbell of the wrong house. When no one answered and I returned to the hotel, I confirmed that the number I was looking for was 44 and not 40, where I had gone. The subconscious had taken over. Who knows what would have happened if I'd seen my aunt? She probably would have pressured me to go to the embassy, and I would have gone to Germany. It would have caused a huge commotion, and they might have killed the compañeros still inside and those outside too. I remember the impact of those first denunciations made by ESMA survivors in France, how we talked about them and suffered the consequences of them. Those of us who were still inside had the feeling they were going to kill us—if not today, then tomorrow. There was a sense of imminent and extreme insecurity and an increased sense of uncertainty, a sense of total danger. Those guys went crazy, and we felt, on one hand, admiration and relief because someone had taken the lid off the pot and, on the other hand, fury because they seemed to have neglected to take into consideration our situation as hostages. That's why in Mexico I felt as though I couldn't take a false step and I had to go back, the same way I had come, to avoid screwing anyone else. I was as much a captive as if I'd been in Capucha, even though I was freely exploring the Mexican crafts markets.

Munú: Did you travel on a regular commercial airline?

Adriana: Yes, a regular airline with a layover in Panama. We arrived in Mexico, and from there we flew to another town and went to a luxury hotel. They apparently had interviews with some contacts—I imagine they must have been milicos too—to acquire weapons or something like that. I have that memory, but now I'm not sure whether it was something I imagined or something I managed to overhear.

---

11. Pelado was a kidnap victim in the ESMA. He escaped in July 1978, during the World Cup soccer tournament, when they took him to the Paraguayan border so he could *finger* compañeros who might be trying to enter the country.

Munú: What were the sleeping arrangements?

Adriana: I was in my room, and they were in theirs.

Munú: The conduct of—

Munú and Cristina: "Gentlemen of the sea."

Adriana: Yeah, yeah. Although during the night, one "gentleman of the sea" made an incursion into my room. All I remember is that I was in the bathroom washing some kind of fruit I'd bought at the crafts market. We'd come back from dinner in the hotel dining room, and the guy knocks on the door. I tell him to come in, we make small talk for a minute, and then he starts acting stupid. I can't remember whether he tried to take me to the bed to go at it or what, but—

Elisa: Ah!

Adriana: And with a knee to his "parts," he left offended, hurling insults at me.

Elisa: Who was it?

Adriana: The Cat. Looking back, it was a huge risk, because they could have liquidated me. But I wasn't even conscious of that at the time. Besides, I think our connection with them was such that in a way we intuited what we could do or say and what we couldn't. We were all living in the same subworld, with some explicit rules and a lot of others that weren't so explicit. I could, for example, go to the crafts fair on my own while they made their contacts. I wasn't anxious about it, but I was in a constant state of alert. It was probably even worse than the days before we *fell*, because I didn't know where the danger might be coming from there, and, besides, I was in an unfamiliar place. I also didn't have a sense of being protected by them, not at all. I guess they figured I wouldn't do anything foolish.

Elisa: Could they have been looking for Pelado?

Adriana: I don't know. Maybe there was another objective. After that we went back to Mexico City.

Munú: Oh, so everything you were describing happened in that little town.

Elisa: So why did they go to that town?

Adriana: I don't have the faintest idea. It was a tourist area, and the hotel had a swimming pool. I actually got into the pool! I have an image of the room with all the trappings—the television; the movies in English; the commercials, in Mexican Spanish, about fleas and dandruff; dinner in the restaurant—ass perfect.

Miriam: And you, the hostage, thinking they were getting organized to bust Pelado.

Adriana: Then we went back to Mexico City, and there they made the sleeping arrangements as if we were a couple.

Munú: Oh!

Adriana: In the same room, with a double bed, with Geronimo.

Munú: No! No way! [*Exclamations from all*]

Elisa: And what happened?

Adriana: He didn't so much as hint at touching a hair on my head. Even so, I didn't sleep the whole night.

Munú: How long did you sleep with that guy?

Adriana: How long was I in Mexico City? I don't remember. It's an amorphous time, a lump of time that—I don't know. Maybe it was a week. I slept in a nightshirt, petrified, on the left side of the hard, double bed, and I think I dozed off in a state of alert. I guess I must have been in some sort of denial that allowed me to get through the situation. He wasn't the type to mess around or get chummy, and that must have helped to distinguish who was who.

Munú: How horrible!

Cristina: How repulsive!

Adriana: At one point, we walked over to the Autonomous University where there are some beautiful murals, and he told me the story of his niece. He said his brother was a terrorist like me. So was his sister-in-law, according to him. They were both involved in militant action in the western zone. I asked him what names they had gone by, and I don't remember what he answered. I had been part of the health unit of the *West Column*, and I was very interested in knowing who they were. I have a feeling I didn't know them. He said that they had *fallen* in another branch of the armed forces and that he hadn't been able to do anything about it and that he wouldn't have anyway, because they were subversives and he didn't recognize the guy as his brother. But he had the girl, because he was her uncle and he had to take responsibility for her. What he never told me was that his sister-in-law was also pregnant. He didn't talk about that with me. Anyway, what he did tell me was enough to turn my stomach. I was indignant, and I felt incredibly helpless.

Munú: Had they *fallen* in another branch of the armed forces or in the ESMA?

Miriam: She gave birth in the ESMA, but the air force had kidnapped her. Her name was Hilda Pérez de Donda.

Elisa: Maybe they took her there from another camp.

Miriam: The baby disappeared. It's not clear who ended up with the baby.

Adriana: The other memories I have of Mexico are touristy things, of going to see a church with a shifting foundation, Rivera frescos, the ruins, of the names of the avenues—La Reforma, La Revolución—those suggestive words.

Munú: But what did they do? What exactly was the *operation* they were working on?

Adriana: I don't know. They'd go out.

Munú: Did they ever take you along as cover?

Miriam: Of course, so it wouldn't be so obvious that they were an intelligence group.

Munú: I don't know why two guys are an intelligence group and a couple isn't! [*Laughter*]

Adriana: At one point we were in a record shop looking at albums and cassettes, and suddenly one of them came in from the street all agitated.

Munú: Do you remember whether they were armed?

Adriana: I never knew. It seems there was an appointment. One of them was in the record shop, and the other was outside. We had to go to somewhere.

Munú: Ah!

Adriana: And in the middle of it all, GERONIMO grabbed my arm as if to drag me outside and take me with him. I managed to free myself, and I started chatting with the guy in the store. They ran out, and I stayed there. After a while they came back, reproaching each other because he'd gotten away.

Miriam: Ah!

Elisa: Who got away?

Adriana: I don't know. Someone they needed to talk to. Clearly they were waiting for someone there.

Miriam: And they took you to the appointment without offering a clue as to what was going on.

Adriana: I really don't know any other details. They must have had some information and some time to kill, because we went to the Sun and Moon pyramids, to some park, after which—and after calling my parents every day, collect, to tell them that I was in good health, physically speaking, of course—we returned. I don't remember anything else.

Munú: Wow!

Adriana: Of course I had my little moments of resistance. For instance, I bought two cassettes by Pablo Milanés and Silvio Rodríguez that weren't available in Argentina; I bought a book by Mario Benedetti, *The House and the Brick*, which talks about exile. I did that kind of thing, always in secret, of course, because if they'd caught me, they'd have discovered that actually—

Miriam: You weren't so *recuperated* after all.

Adriana: Not much. Just think about the type of relationship we had with those guys that they didn't even check what you took with you or brought back. Deep down, they knew we were still wearing the *hood*, in terms of denial, and that there was a pact between us to "behave ourselves," recognizing that, in a way, we were all hostages.

Miriam: What an incredible story! What would have happened if you'd said you weren't going to Mexico? [*Sighs all around*]

Adriana: Now I see that they could have killed us, but at the time it didn't even occur to us to say no. We weren't in a position to negotiate. Some of the compañeros, such as Diego and Lucy, were able to accomplish certain things, like getting us out of the ESMA, for example, and going to work in Zapiola or in the press office, the ultimate concession. They helped some of us. I want to tell you about a conversation I had with Lucy when I was in Dorado, the office where we had to transcribe *tapped* phone conversations—which of course we always pretended not to understand—and make photocopies. I was translating a dossier into German. Lucy told me that Diego was asking for me, that he needed me in Zapiola, that it was essential. I responded that I didn't want to leave the ESMA and still be connected, working with Massera. She got angry, and it was the only time in my life that I saw her irritated with me. She stood up to me, and she said that I shouldn't try to leave disconnected. I had to accept that the extrication process would be gradual. I should be grateful at least to be able to leave that place, which was more dangerous than being in Zapiola, and I should resign myself to leaving step by step. If I didn't accept the alternative and stayed inside, they could kill me. She brought me back down to earth, gave me a strong dose of realism in that completely insane world. I now realize that the two of them invented strategies to get people out whenever they could.

Miriam: You know what they made me do once while I was with the air force?

Munú: What did they make you do?

Miriam: They made me sit down at a desk in front of a video camera, wearing a wig, all made up, and wearing glasses. They made me write something about what my native land meant, what God meant, and the family. I had to read it on camera. It was surreal.

Elisa: They wanted you to demonstrate that you were *recuperated*.

Miriam: Right. I guess they thought we had no faith whatsoever, no respect for anything. I can't remember what I wrote, but they were moved by it. One of them said, "I wish some of my men thought like you."

Munú: We definitely thought a lot better than his men.

Miriam: You know what the problem was? They had a terribly prejudiced view of us. They thought we shit on our family, on our native land, and that we didn't believe in God. This played in my favor, because I didn't have to lie in what I was saying. Besides, the nationalistic discourse of the Montoneros was oddly in sync with theirs in that regard.

Munú: Absolutely.

Miriam: They also told me that the fact that I'd called every day to find out how my dying grandmother was doing and that they had *hooked* me because of it had played in my favor. They weren't used to keeping people alive for so long.

Munú: The fact that they had to keep you there for so long, supposedly because they wanted to *hook* your friend, created a kind of relationship they hadn't experienced before. They always had people who passed through, spending only a couple of days there.

Miriam: Yes, although only rarely did anyone speak to me. I spent ten and a half months there, in solitary, in the dungeon, almost always alone. A few weeks after they taped the video, they opened the door and said, "Congratulations, girl, today you were reborn!" I guess that, after watching it, the chiefs had decided that they weren't going to kill me.

∽

Liliana: Do you remember when they took us to the villas?

Miriam: I went only once, shortly after I got to the ESMA, to THUNDER's parents' villa in Del Viso.[12] I remember that was where I found out, to my surprise, that FRAGOTE was actually a marino and not a prisoner.

Liliana: Do you remember whether it was Mother's Day?

Miriam: It must have been earlier, because they took me to the ESMA in March 1978. I remember swimming in the pool.

Munú: Those must have been two different trips.

Liliana: They took us to the villa in October 1978 for Mother's Day, and Chiche was in bad shape. I didn't realize that her children had been kidnapped by the army.

Munú: We weren't aware of it, because we were in the Basement. The people in the Fishbowl knew.

Liliana: I remember that we swam in the pool, and she spent the whole time off in a corner, with Quica beside her. I found out later that, during those same days, her children were in the hands of RIVEROS.[13]

Munú: Do you remember an Australian pool?

Liliana: A beautiful pool, behind the house.

Elisa: I'm not sure whether that was the Del Viso villa. I have the notion that I went somewhere with a pool, but I was no longer in the ESMA in October 1978.

Liliana: The thing is that I went to that villa more than once.

Miriam: I went only once.

Liliana: Do you remember that the men had organized a soccer game?

Miriam: Yes.

Liliana: But they probably did that all the time. That's why it's hard to know when it was.

---

12. Del Viso is located in the northern zone of greater Buenos Aires.

13. General Santiago Omar Riveros is currently in custody and being prosecuted by the federal justice system for stealing children. He was convicted by an Italian court for the kidnapping, torture, and murder of eight Italian citizens.

Miriam: Or volleyball?

Munú: The women played too. I went only once for Mother's Day, but my memory is very foggy.

Elisa: It seems as though it was very common, because when I *fell*, on September 21, 1977, they were all coming back from a villa, prisoners and oppressors.

Miriam: Yes, you said they went to see you, and they were all tanned.

Elisa: They went on another occasion, before I was on the *staff*. Capucha was practically deserted. I can't remember the exact date. Another time they took me because a reporter from England was going to visit the ESMA. They wanted to show him that, contrary to the denunciations abroad, there weren't any concentration camps in Argentina, so they took us out of there.

Miriam: That was in March 1978. They were going to put on a show.

Elisa: They took us to the villa, but they brought me right back, along with some of the other compañeros, because they had a few extra police costumes. They needed a relatively large woman and a tall man; I'm not sure whether they brought Chito or Beto. We had to dress up as jailers. In other words, they took us to the villa, we spent two hours there, and they brought us right back to the ESMA.

Miriam: It was a costume to you, but they were actual uniforms! [*Laughter*]

Elisa: I'm not sure whether the others spent the whole day at the villa. They made four of us come back. And the people from the *mini-staff* were already there, in uniform. They gave one to me and told me I had to stay in the Fishbowl, in the archive, which was where I usually worked. They told the reporter that it was a press office that had been set up to improve Argentina's image abroad.

Miriam: Run completely by police, in a navy establishment.

Elisa: Exactly. That was the famous ESMA that caused so much confusion. The world was saying there were prisoners, but it wasn't true! It was a place with offices and police officers.

Munú: Did they take photographs?

Elisa: No.

Miriam: Did you see the reporter?

Elisa: Of course, and I also saw a woman, Berta, with whom I later worked in the Foreign Ministry. She was the official translator for the visit. It had been organized by the Foreign Ministry Press Office, which by that time was in the hands of the navy. Since the reporter was coming to Argentina, they invited him to visit the ESMA.

Miriam: Was it just one person?

Elisa: Yes, he was from the London press—Fiscman, Feiscman, something like that. And the official translator was a Foreign Ministry employee.

Liliana: Someone you hadn't met before.

Elisa: I didn't know her.

Munú: So the *mini-staff* was there and a few others?

Elisa: A few others, brought back from the villa.

Liliana: I'm wondering whether that was the time they made Jorgelina and me dress up as police and left us in Dorado.

Elisa: They sent me to the Fishbowl.

Liliana: Do you remember whether Jorgelina was in the Fishbowl?

Elisa: No, she wasn't there.

Liliana: So it probably was the same occasion.

Miriam: A few days later, there was an extra police shirt in the storeroom, and they gave it to me because I didn't have any clothes.

Elisa: What happened was so strange. This woman comes to the archive—

Miriam: To the ESMA, accompanying the reporter?

Elisa: Yes, she came with everyone else: the officers, the reporter.

Miriam: ESMA officers? The torturers?

Elisa: Yes, the torturers—

Miriam: Who were accompanying the English reporter, to show him that there wasn't any torturing going on in the ESMA and that you were police, not prisoners. They were confident that they had us so subdued that no one was going to wink, make a move, that no one was going to shout out something in English to the reporter, that no one was going to try anything. How pathetic!

Elisa: Berta—the translator—and I looked at each other intently. After twenty-five years, I still remember that look. They put on the whole circus, they talked, they commented, she translated, and they inspected. They talked about the nuts and bolts: where our information came from, the magazines we had—*Somos Gente, Siete Días*—newspapers from across the spectrum, everything that was in the archive. They were there for just a short time, and they left. Later, when they took me to work at the Foreign Ministry, I ran into Berta again.

Munú: Those same eyes.

Miriam: Did she recognize you?

Elisa: I don't know. In all the years we worked together, the only thing she ever said to me was, "You have such sad eyes."

Munú: I'm sure she always knew who you were.

Elisa: I think she knew everything from the very beginning. I think she always knew that we were prisoners dressed up as police, but she never gave the slightest indication of it.

Miriam: What would have happened if one of the prisoners had yelled something to the reporter?

Elisa: They would have *sucked* him *up*! What was to stop them?

Miriam: Wouldn't he have had connections in the British Embassy?

Elisa: Well, then they'd just have to put up with the international conflict later. Didn't they kill Elena Holmberg?[14]

Miriam: And Hidalgo Solá, the ambassador to Venezuela, no less! Maybe you're right, Elisa. They killed that little Swede, Hagelin, the French nuns. So many!

Elisa: Sure, what did they care.

Munú: It's just like asking why, when they let you go to your house, you didn't leave, why you didn't make a denunciation. When you went on a *visit*, you could go to any embassy and tell all, and yet you went back to the ESMA.

Miriam: Getting back to the subject of the villas, what other villas were there? There was an island in El Tigre.[15] Did you ever go there?

Munú: When I was working on the outside with the group that fixed up houses, the officers talked about an island where they were doing some renovations so they could take captives there when the Inter-American Commission on Human Rights came, which occurred in late 1979. They came to visit the facilities and write a report. None of us was in the ESMA by then, but they took the compañeros who were there and the survivors later denounced it. People know about the island.

Liliana: I went with fat JUNGLE to rent an island in El Tigre. I don't know what they used it for. He took me along for company, and they rented it completely legally. He created some forged documents for me, and the owner never knew that she'd rented the island to navy personnel from the ESMA.

Munú: *Legally*, but with forged documents. [*Laughter*]

Liliana: She thought she'd rented it to a couple made up of fat JUNGLE and me. We left in a coast guard boat. The woman was waiting for us because they had set it up through the real estate company. We looked at the house, the island; everything looked fine to us. I don't recall what happened then, whether or not we went back to the real estate office to close. I never went back to that island. And I never went to any other villa, other than that one with the pool where we spent Mother's Day, where I think I went several times.

Munú: It seems as though we're always talking about the same villa.

Liliana: I remember that ABDALA's people spent a summer at a villa near La Plata. They came and told us they'd rented it for a month. They were people who had been *sucked up* by the SIN. The outings to the villa were organized by JUNGLE, who was full of ceremony and protocol.

---

14. Elena Holmberg was a Foreign Ministry official who was kidnapped and murdered by the navy.

15. El Tigre is a municipality in the northern part of greater Buenos Aires. A delta carries the same name.

Miriam: When I went to the Del Viso villa, they had cakes and barbecue.

Liliana: Yes, it was Pantagruelian. They barbecued and took cakes for the afternoon. They were the same cakes that fat JUNGLE always took when there was a birthday party. I don't know where they got them; I think they ordered them from the ESMA kitchen. They took them in wooden boxes with several layers [*Laughter*], and in each layer there was a different kind of cake: chocolate, caramel. He loved having a cake for every preference. I never saw those wooden boxes again in any bakery in the world. In other words, they were a navy invention.

Cristina: I was at the Del Viso villa once with Adriana and Andrea; I guess it was that one, in that area. They took us by a roundabout route, and we spent the whole day there. There was a volleyball court.

Miriam: I remember the volleyball, and I remember that the prisoners slaughtered TIGER ACOSTA's team. [*Laughter*]

Liliana: And in the late afternoon they'd take out the guitars, and TIGER ACOSTA would sing zambas, old zambas.

Elisa: And at night—

Liliana: It was all over.

Munú: And the return to the ESMA, where everyone went back to his or her place again—all of us to Capucha!

Liliana: In the evening someone would bring out a guitar, and the guitar playing began, and the TIGER would sing those zambas from the forties like "La López Pereyra," very folksy. It was strange; the guy wasn't that old.

Miriam: My question is this: at that moment, would everything come to a halt in the ESMA, would they stop *sucking* people *up*?

Liliana: A guard would stay behind.

Miriam: Ah! Others stayed too. Did only a few officers go?

Elisa: Didn't I mention that they had gone to the villa on the same day they *sucked* me *up*? Everything went on as usual.

Munú: I don't understand why they did it.

Miriam: I don't either—whether it was because they enjoyed it or for our recreation.

Munú: Isn't it just like when they took us out to dinner?

Miriam: No.

Elisa: It was a much more costly deployment, taking twenty captives to a villa.

Miriam: Going out to dinner was more selective.

Liliana: This was massive. Four, five, six cars would go.

Elisa: It was a deployment. I still say I lucked out of having so much contact. I listen to you, and I can't help but feel that it was just one more form of torture, whether it was going with them out to dinner or to the villa.

Munú: I don't think it had any different objective.

Miriam: Different from the one we never could figure out.

Cristina: Yesterday I was out driving on the road early in the morning, and I remembered that when they took us out, they always came back through Palermo.[16]

Munú: At top speed.

Cristina: At an impressive rate of speed, like 160 km per hour. It was another ostentatious display of power, of testing the limits.

Munú: They brought us back by way of Palermo and also the Coastal Highway, and as we were arriving, the whole sequence of asking to enter the ESMA began. "Selenio" was the name they used to identify themselves, and they'd call the guard from the car to open the gates so they could go in without stopping. They said they were afraid that the Montoneros would fire on them with an anti-tank rifle. It went something like, "Selenio, Selenio, we finished the match with two bishops," and I don't know what else. They used chess terms. It had to do with the types of cars and the number of people arriving.

Miriam: Do you remember any other excursions?

Cristina: I remember they took me to El Tigre once. We were in a boat, Andrea, Adriana, Tito. BLONDIE took us.

Munú: They took you on an outing?

Cristina: Yes, there was a visit or something going on in the ESMA, and so they took us out to spend the day somewhere else. For whatever reason, and no matter how complicated it may be to try to analyze it, those guys spent twenty-four hours in there; their lives transpired in that place. That's why, even in the context of the project they were upholding, they channeled their personal needs there too.

Miriam: In other words, you think the outings were part of their own recreation?

Cristina: That was one of the reasons.

Elisa: Exactly. And since they were already there, they tortured you a little bit more.

Munú: They didn't go home. They could have, and they didn't.

Liliana: I remember that sometimes Jorgelina and I would be in Dorado, and along would come FRAGOTE asking MARIANO's permission to take us out for pizza.

Munú: To go out.

Liliana: Sure. Or MARIANO would get four or five of us together and take us to a movie. Or he'd tell the ANT to do it. Do you remember when the theaters were broadcasting the World Cup in color? I remember the ANT taking us to a movie theater to see the soccer games.

Munú: That's when they *sucked* me *up*; in other words they did both activities at once. The same thing happened to Elisa. She *fell* while others were coming back from a villa.

---

16. Palermo is a residential and park area of Buenos Aires.

Munú: Did you all know about the house? Did I ever tell you about that?

Miriam: That they forced you to sell it?

Munú: Right. The house where Peter and I lived in La Plata was in my name. I had the deed. When I *fell*, they took me to a place outside the ESMA, presumably to a notary's office. FRAGOTE, with his innocent little boy face, took me. I'm not sure the notary even knew I was *sucked up*. They made me sign a power of attorney authorizing FRAGOTE, who was using a fake ID, to sell it. I investigated the situation when I came back to Argentina. Since I didn't have the deed, I had no way of knowing which lot and division it was. So I went there with my lawyer, and I showed him which house it was. They started to search for it in the Property Register.

Elisa: The house was just as you'd left it?

Munú: Yes, I saw it only from the door. They couldn't find it in the Property Register. I wanted to go to the notary's office right away to look for the information, but the lawyer advised against it. He said we shouldn't pursue the matter at that particular moment; we should wait a little while. This happened right in the middle of the trial of the juntas.

Miriam: I wonder who has it?

Munú: There are people living there now, because I always go by it. It's like a ritual. I usually go by there whenever I go to La Plata. Maybe someday I'll go and tell the neighbors and whoever's living there all about it.

Elisa: How long did you live there?

Munú: About two years.

Elisa: So people in the neighborhood knew you.

Munú: Of course. The next-door neighbors would let us use their telephone, and Peter would watch soccer games on TV with the neighbors across the street. Two years ago, when I started making inquiries again, I found out that the history of the place doesn't appear in the Property Register. The information was lost, and the only available information is from recent years. That history can be reconstructed. The house stood vacant for a long time, but now it's occupied. My understanding is that when the marinos took possession of a property, they usually conducted several fake sales in between.

Miriam: Of course, to create distance.

Munú: That way, the trail was erased or at least confused. One fraud would sell it to another fraud, and he'd sell it to another fraud, and a fifth would buy it, ostensibly in good faith.

Elisa: But who ended up with that house?

Munú: The ESMA in principle. Someone told me that one of the notaries who created those powers of attorney testified in CONADEP.

Elisa: A notary testified and said that they brought people from the ESMA Task Force to him to create the power of attorney?

Munú: I have no idea what he testified about. There were a whole lot of houses in that "real estate office" that belonged to the ESMA or to some members of the Task Force. A lot of them were partially destroyed, they shot them up with bullets during the raids, and then they fixed them up to sell them. They put some of us prisoners to work on the renovations. We had an architect, a construction foreman, a carpenter, and two bricklayers, and I was in an office adding up lime and sand vouchers.

Miriam: So they got the house and the renovations for free. The amount of money they must have made on everything they stole! What crooks!

Munú: They kept our houses, our cars, our books . . . our children.

Elisa: And the lives of our compañeros.

∽

Adriana: Who was the compañera who choked on a piece of meat and almost died?

Munú: The *Chaqueña!*[17]

Adriana: Oh! Was it you, Liliana? Incredible. And to think that now you're sitting here right beside me. Tell me. What happened?

Liliana: A piece of meat got stuck in my throat.

Munú: But you nearly died. That's what I remember. There was a huge uproar.

Liliana: I don't think it was that bad; true, it got stuck, but I don't think it went down into my windpipe.

Munú: Still, they said you almost died of asphyxiation. There was a huge commotion, and they took you somewhere.

Liliana: The ANT took me. What I find surprising is that the emergency room doctors at the hospital acted as if that piece of meat had gone down into my windpipe.

Adriana: If it had gone into your windpipe, you must have turned blue.

Liliana: I don't think I turned blue; I was probably coughing. They put me to sleep in the emergency room, and I don't know what happened. The first thing they did was give me a shot and put me to sleep. When I woke up, it was gone. I'm not sure whether they actually extracted the piece of meat from my windpipe or just said, "No, there's nothing in her windpipe; take her back."

Elisa: After the pain had passed, did you feel anything?

Liliana: The pain went away after several hours. It was a very strong pain in the upper part of my chest. I'm convinced that the piece of meat had got-

---

17. *Chaqueña* means "woman from Chaco."

ten stuck in my esophagus. It had happened to me before, and the pain was the same.

Adriana: And those of you who were in the ESMA, what do you remember?

Munú: We were all sitting at the table, in the Basement, having lunch.

Liliana: And I said, "Oh!"

Munú: And suddenly you started to cough as if you were choking, and we were hitting you on the back—paf paf paf—and you kept on coughing. In a total panic, we called LITTLE PAUL, and they took you away. You went alone, with none of us to accompany you.

Liliana: They took me in a car. When we got to the Navy Hospital,[18] they sat me in a wheelchair and gave me oxygen. They took me like that to another hospital.

Miriam: It's so strange—so much concern about saving our lives.

Adriana: It's perverse, but death had to come when they wanted it to.

Liliana: You had to die whenever they decided and not a moment before.

Adriana: As if a piece of meat were going to have more power than they had!

Liliana: I have the feeling that when we were in the car, I couldn't bring myself to tell them I was fine, that I'd just had a scare. They'd put on such a circus that I was afraid I'd be punished. They took me to another hospital, the Udaondo,[19] for gastroenterology, and the whole way there in the car, the ANT was communicating by radio. I heard him say, "We're not going to make it."

Munú: Then it was true that you were dying, Liliana!

Liliana: Oh, no. But that's what they thought.

Adriana: It was the same fear they had when La Flaca had her epileptic seizure. They never went back to her house to get her after that. Brave people!

Munú: First they destroyed us, and then they tried to heal us. They wanted to fix my ankles, because I had some torn ligaments from the torture. They put some kind of ointment on them, wrapped them, and put them under a heat lamp. In their eagerness to fix me, they ended up burning me!

Adriana: They took me to the dentist. It was the first time in my life that a dentist gave me anesthesia. From the time I was a little girl, I'd gotten used to having everything done without it; I couldn't believe it.

Miriam: They took care of us right there in the ESMA. I went to the dentist there too.

Liliana: They pulled out my wisdom tooth.

Adriana: Mine too, and it didn't hurt.

---

18. This refers to the Argentine Navy Hospital located in the Parque Centenario neighborhood in the city of Buenos Aires.

19. Udaondo refers to a municipal hospital specializing in gastroenterology located in the Barracas neighborhood in the city of Buenos Aires.

Miriam: I remember that the dentist asked questions that I could hardly answer with my mouth wide open: "You're here?" And I answered, "Yes, I'm here." And he asked, "But here? Why did you get involved so young? How old are you?"

Cristina: "And you, so old." ·

Miriam: No, he was a young guy; he couldn't have been more than twenty-seven or twenty-eight years old.

Liliana: Like the psychologist.

Adriana: The psychologist in Ramos Mejía.[20] Now there's a character I'd like to know about—who he is and where he is now. He saw me at a clinic.

Miriam: You mean they took you to a clinic? You mean they took you to a psychologist?

Liliana: I think he was the same one who came to the ESMA, the skinny one with glasses.

Elisa: Blondish.

Liliana: Blondish, tall, skinny. I don't know why he met with me at the clinic. They took me there a few times to talk to him.

Miriam: And why did they take you there?

Liliana: I don't know why. Ask TIGER ACOSTA.

Miriam: But did they say, "We're going to take you to a psychologist"?

Liliana: Yes. [*Laughter*]

Miriam: When was this?

Liliana: Shortly before they released me, after the famous interview with the TIGER.

Miriam: There was an evaluation to see whether you were ready to leave.

Liliana: Of course. He said it seemed to him that I was a person . . . how did he put it?

Munú: Who decided to cry. When Liliana decided to cry, you had to hold on tight.

Liliana: He said something like I blew my problems all out of proportion. [*Laughter*]

Munú: Of course, that's why you cried, because being disappeared wasn't really a problem. [*More laughter*]

Liliana: He said I exaggerated my problems a lot, that I wasn't even-tempered. He said I had a personality problem.

Miriam: Unlike him. The TIGER was normal. [*Laughter*]

Liliana: So he wanted me to see a psychologist.

Adriana: Being kidnapped in the ESMA was the most normal thing in the world apparently.

Liliana: What problem could I possibly have? The TIGER said, "You have to

---

20. Ramos Mejía is in greater Buenos Aires.

understand that things happen all the time. People go through all kinds of things during their lives. You're going to leave, and at the first minor inconvenience, you're going to have these same reactions, which, I think, are all out of proportion."

Elisa: Why? What did you do? Did you cry? Did you scream? Did you fight?

Liliana: How should I know? I don't remember what I did.

Munú: Every once in a while, she'd have a crying fit, and she'd start saying she wanted to go to Chaco, she wanted to go to Chaco, and she'd cry and cry. And do you know what would happen? They'd take her to Chaco!

Liliana: I think that the TIGER wanted me to go to the psychologist so that the psychologist would send a bill. He didn't intend for him to decide whether or not I could leave.

Adriana: Those guys didn't believe in psychologists, even if it had been a father confessor.

Liliana: Sure. I think they had an arrangement. He owed him a favor, and so the other guy would have said, "Send me a few patients." Nothing else occurs to me. They took me there twice.

Miriam: What did the psychologist ask you?

Liliana: I'd really have to rack my brain to try to reconstruct the interviews.

Adriana: But they wouldn't have told the guy . . . or did he know about the kidnappings?

Elisa: He used to come to the ESMA! They set up an interview with the psychologist for most of us, at least in my time. After Nose escaped, they apparently decreed that we all needed a psychological evaluation.

Munú: To see whether we were *recuperable*.

Elisa: To determine our level of *recuperation* and progress. That was how it seemed to us, based on the questions the psychologist asked us. You had to get up your courage and create a cohesive picture or story. I sweated through that interview!

Liliana: You thought anything you said might be used against you.

Munú: Your life was on the line!

Liliana: Someone should track down that psychologist.

Munú: My interview was in Dorado.

Elisa: Mine too. There was a desk, and the guy asked a few questions. Mine lasted about thirty-five minutes.

Munú: Didn't the rest of you have interviews?

Miriam: I didn't. It appears that I was quite normal.

Liliana: The information that guy must have.

Elisa: I remember that during the interview he asked me what I was doing there, what I did before, how I felt, whether I got along well with my coworkers at the job I was doing.

Liliana: The guy conducted the interview just as if it were a normal situation.

Elisa: First there were the questions, and then came the test: he showed me colored sketches of trapezoids and triangles.

Munú: MARIANO came to take me to an interview. "With a psychologist?" I said. I'd probably been in for about two or three months. I more or less had an idea about what was going on, to the extent that anyone could understand it. He laughed about the situation, as if to suggest to me that it was a step that had to be taken to be included in the *recuperation process.* I remember the little sketches, the tests, perfectly well. One of them asked, "If you weren't a person, what would you like to be? If you belonged to the mineral kingdom . . . ? If you were part of the plant kingdom . . . ?" When they got to the question about what I'd like to be if I were part of the animal kingdom, I practically vomited the word "Bird!" "Why?" Then he got it. "Of course. For freedom," he said.

Miriam: As you can see, the boy was very well educated! [*Laughter*]

Adriana: And he stopped the session there, because it was over! That was all he had to give!

Elisa: The story of the psychologist caused panic in the Fishbowl.

Adriana: Naturally. You'd feel his piercing stare; you were afraid that he'd see through you and that your story was in danger of being uncovered. The guy was going to know what you were feeling deep inside.

Munú: I went into it very naively; I went in to talk very calmly. Besides, I didn't have any experience with psychologists.

Elisa: I remember how nervous the compañeros were.

Adriana: They never took me, never even brought it up. I *fell* in August 1978, and I never saw him.

Munú: Another thing MARIANO told me before going to the interview was that the guy was afraid of us. He laughed about it.

Adriana: There isn't an ounce of sense in what we're talking about.

Munú: But that's how it was! Who could find any logic in all of this?

Miriam: The Russian started therapy during one of the family *visits* when they left him at home. And that son of a bitch of a psychologist apparently tipped off the ESMA; he called ABDALA in Los Jorges.

Liliana: What? The psychoanalyst he went to see?

Miriam: Yes, he must have had some contact with the ESMA. The guy told them; he must have been scared.

Munú: Another son of a bitch!

Liliana: He should have told him not to come back—anything.

Adriana: My ex started therapy after having been kidnapped. He wanted to do it with the psychologist he'd been seeing before, but he said no because he was too afraid—which is understandable.

Liliana: He had a right to be afraid and not to want to do it.

Adriana: There were many cases of analysts who were kidnapped because they had compañeros among their patients. And in several cases, their files were taken in order to retrieve intelligence data.

Miriam: Well, ABDALA called in the Russian. We all thought they were going to discipline him, send him back to Capucha. But instead he said, "If you have problems, we can provide you with a trustworthy psychologist from the force. It's someone who won't divulge anything; he's one of our men."

Adriana: What a guarantee!

Munú: I just took it for granted that all of us inside there had been taken to the psychologist.

Adriana: In other words, some people went to the psychologist, and others didn't. Even now we can be surprised. We discover parts of the story that happened right in front of us and we didn't know it. This piecing together of the puzzle with the scraps of our memories never ceases to amaze me.

∽

Miriam: And what do we know about the rapes?

Elisa: They happened. I remember one compañera's story about two girls who were with her. And they raped one of the girls.

Miriam: A GREEN?

Elisa: Yes, in Capuchita.

Munú: They were people who'd been kidnapped by the SIN.

Elisa: Yes, but the GREENS were the same ones who were with us. Didn't any of you ever hear stories about rape? I was told that they raped Jorgelina, and people talked about it at the time.

Munú: Oh! They raped Jorgelina?

Elisa: Yes.

Munú: How cruel! I saw an incident, but I can't say for sure that it was a rape. I always assumed it was, since one of the people I saw was one of those really son of a bitch GREENS.

Miriam: What did you see? A struggle?

Munú: No, I saw the compañera, thrown down on the floor in Capucha, and two GREENS. The really detestable one was on top of her, and the other one was standing there as if he was keeping watch. When I went by there with LITTLE PAUL, who was taking me up to sleep, they didn't even care. I assumed it was a rape, since that GREEN was one of the higher-ups and really nasty. He would make the captives jog wearing their *hoods,* so they'd bang their heads against the ceiling beams.

Miriam: And you didn't tell anyone at that moment?

Munú: No one, not even a compañero. I thought it was a rape, but I didn't know how she saw it. Maybe she did it as a way of trying to survive. No one survived because of that, as far as I know, but she couldn't have known that. I never knew who she was. I never saw her face.

Miriam: One thing I always remember is how some of the marinos were disgusted by the behavior of certain compañeros. One day a militant *fell*, and he gave them quite a bit of information about houses and *appointments*, which they used to *suck up* a whole bunch of people. There was a lot of commotion in Dorado. OPERATIVES went from one place to another; it was chaos. The milicos went up and down, all armed. They brought in compañeros incessantly to torture them. The Basement was convulsing. Late that night—I might have been in the Fishbowl—BLONDIE came in, completely exhausted and pissed off, and he said, "I just came back from a battle in one of the houses that son of a bitch *sang*, and in the hallway, when he saw me returning, he said, 'BLONDIE, I was worried about you. I thought they'd given it to you.'" Then BLONDIE said, "He's a shit. He *fell* just three hours ago. I should have squashed him like a worm!" Even BLONDIE was pissed off by the sleaziness of a guy who turns in his compañeros and, within three hours of *falling*, feigns concern for one of the oppressors.

Munú: What the militant did was very bad, but BLONDIE didn't show himself to be any better in the Malvinas, did he? When they asked him whether he surrendered, he didn't hesitate; he didn't wait for a single bullet. He heroically turned himself in! I find it more despicable every day. It's easy to ask others to resist.

Miriam: What infuriated him was that attitude of feigning concern. BLONDIE had a lot of respect for La Cabra because she was tough—respect between soldiers, an acknowledgment of the enemy's valor.

Elisa: That happened a lot, and the marinos often spoke admiringly of the heroism of the compañeros.

Munú: They demanded that the captives stay tough and withstand their torture, but they never showed themselves to be like that.

Elisa: PACO used to say he admired Chiche because they'd tortured her as they'd never tortured any woman before, and she'd faced it valiantly.

Munú: They admired someone who resisted more than someone who said, "Well, okay—"

Miriam: "Let's sit down. Let's make a deal. I'll turn in . . ."

Munú: Their attitude was similar to that of a rapist: if you don't resist, you deprive them of the opportunity to be a rapist. If you say, "Let's go to bed; let's have a good time together," you confound him. He needs your resistance, your panic. These guys did the same thing: if you *fell* and gave them all the information, then what role did that leave them? They were the ones who dragged it out of you through torture; they became your owners.

Elisa: They didn't always see it that way. They said, for example, that Gabriel was crazy, because he didn't want to negotiate the kidnapping of his wife and children in order to—according to those supreme sons of bitches—save her.

Miriam: Some did it. They turned in people in exchange for not having anything happen to their wives. It was a negotiation: her life in exchange for information on other compañeros.

Munú: There was no guarantee that it would turn out like that.

Elisa: When they *sucked up* Gabriel, they took him to his house, and they asked him to call his compañera on the building's intercom system so she would come down and they could kidnap her. Since he refused, they went up to the apartment, opened fire, and killed her and another compañera. Nothing happened to the kids—physically.

Munú: In their minds, it was bad for you to provide information on compañeros without putting up some resistance, but it was okay for you to turn in your wife so they could kidnap her, torture her, and who knows what else.

Miriam: That offer was made only to male militants. It never happened the other way around. To my knowledge, they never offered a woman the chance to give information in exchange for her militant husband's freedom.

Elisa: Not even when the woman was higher up in the Montoneros Organization than her husband.

Miriam: I was thinking that the issue of the disappeared triggers a certain degree of insanity in a lot of people. A lot of characters have come out with phony, invented histories about what happened in the ESMA, particularly with regard to the corpses, the famous burials. In one woman's denunciation, she said that her husband had been police chief at a precinct on the coast[21] during the dictatorship. According to her, the corpses showed up on the beach, and they were ordered to hide the bodies in the local cemetery. Others make up stories about how they know places where there were mass burials of "NN,"[22] which were not verified later. A lot of people tell tales, and they don't realize how much their fabricated stories hurt the families of the dead. Adolfo Scilingo[23] is an example. He must have participated in a *flight*, but none of us remember him as a member of the Task Force. The marinos' policy was to involve officers who weren't assigned directly to the war against subversion. A decision had been made, probably

---

21. This refers to an area in Buenos Aires Province known for its Atlantic coast beaches, one of the country's tourist attractions.

22. "NN" stands for "no name" (i.e., anonymous).

23. Adolfo Scilingo was a naval officer who acknowledged his involvement in the ESMA Task Force and in the death *flights*, during which captives were thrown—alive but sedated with pentothal—into Rio de la Plata.

by Massera, that they should *get their hands dirty*, as the Tiger used to say. So they called them in and made them participate in a couple of compromising actions so that internally they'd be linked to the "dirty war."

Munú: Later on they couldn't go out and denounce it or claim they hadn't been involved.

Miriam: When Scilingo was on Mariano Grondona's[24] television program, he referred to Pelusa, a fictional character—literary license—from the book *Recuerdo de la Muerte*. He talked about Pelusa's situation as if it had really happened and he had witnessed it.

Cristina: And in the book, that character wasn't a real person?

Miriam: That character went through a situation similar to that of a compañera. Scilingo talks as if he had seen Pelusa, a person who never existed! Miguel Bonasso created her to describe what had happened to a captive without revealing her name, to protect her. I think Scilingo is a big storyteller. He read everything that was published about the ESMA, and then he talked about it as if he'd been an eyewitness.

Munú: Scilingo must have been one of those marinos you saw only occasionally but who wasn't always with the Task Force.

Miriam: Those visitors.

Munú: The ones they called Rotativos.

Cristina: They were there *legally*.

Miriam: Some of them were professors at the school; they slept in the Officers' Casino, and you ran into them from time to time.

Munú: They looked at us in horror when we passed them on the stairs. They'd stare at the wall or look the other way. I think our response was completely different. I remember walking up those stairs and staring at all of them, one by one.

Miriam: But we went downstairs *hooded*!

Cristina: Or with the *mask* on!

Munú: Toward the end, when I went upstairs to sleep—usually around three or four in the morning—I had the *mask* on, but I'd have it pushed up almost onto my forehead, and I could see them. The Rotativos had to participate for a short time so they would feel somehow implicated, as you were saying, and wouldn't go out and denounce things. That way, they created a sense of corporate identity with the Task Force. I remember once they took me on an *expedition* with La Cabra, and they took us to the southern zone. There were three marinos in the car that I was in. The guy in front, whom I'd never seen before, started asking me questions about my life: what I did, where I was involved in the militant cause, whether I was married, and so on. When we got back to the ESMA, this came up in a conversation with Mariano, and he rebuked me, because, according to

---

24. Mariano Grondonas was a journalist, a political pundit.

him, I wasn't supposed to answer questions from anybody. He called the guy in and punished him. Apparently, they weren't privy to a whole lot of information, and they weren't allowed to ask questions.

Miriam: Naturally. They came to *get their hands dirty*, as the TIGER said. They came to *get them dirty*, not to take away information. It was prohibited. The Task Force despised and distrusted them.

Munú: Scilingo must have been one of those guys.

Miriam: They didn't have much contact with the detainees; they spent more time with the OPERATIVES. They took them out to *suck* people *up*, but they didn't hang around Capucha or in the areas where we worked.

Munú: Of course, the OPERATIVES took us on the *expeditions*.

Cristina: I heard that, some time before I was detained, a guy went in totally drunk and was talking to some prisoners. It appears that he talked too much, and because of that they decided to *transfer* all those people. I'm not sure whether he was a TEMPORARY or not; it was a guy who usually wasn't there.

⌇

Cristina: Do you remember whether the GREENS were armed?

Miriam: Only the one at the entrance to the Third Floor and the Basement. No one went in there armed. It's the same in jail cells. Police officers aren't allowed to go in armed.

Munú: I saw fat JUAN CARLOS go into Dorado, take his weapon from his waistband, put it on the table in front of MARIANO, and say to me, with his weapon standing right there in the middle of the table like a vase, "You're all a bunch of sons of bitches who are going to fuck us over; you should all be *sent up*. I tell them so." And he was right!

Liliana: Of course he was right.

Miriam: Because we talked. We were able to testify and tell the truth.

Munú: In fact, we are sitting here now talking about things they never wanted anyone to know. One time when I was really afraid was when fat JUAN CARLOS took me to the police station to get a passport. I was going to Australia, and two days before my departure they had denied my visa, stamping it "visa denied." I reported my passport lost, and I had to stay another month to get another one. I went with fat JUAN CARLOS in one of those macabre Ford Falcons. He really moved in those cars; he loved having everyone see that he was a member of the *gang*. He never tried the modesty of the coupe. [*Laughter*] He was overjoyed at having people realize he was a "heavy." I remember thinking in the car, "This guy's going to say that I tried to escape and kill me." Then, in the Police Department, I applied for the passport, and he wandered around without letting me out of his sight. It was totally absurd: I was afraid he would kill me, but actually he was there to "take care of me." He belonged to the Task Force that had *sucked* me *up*, and he was guarding me so that I wouldn't be *sucked up* by people from the federal police, which at the same time was the institution that he legally belonged to. Get it?

Liliana: Yes, it was part of their internal struggle, between the armed forces and the Task Force. He also took me to get an ID card.

Munú: And was it like that?

Liliana: Yes.

Munú: Did you go alone?

Liliana: Yes, with him.

Munú: It was terrifying for me.

Miriam: Speaking of weapons and strange situations, do you remember once when they took us to Los Años Locos for dinner? I was in the car with Mariano. All of a sudden he said to me, "Take this; I'm tired of carrying it around," and he pulled his 9 millimeter from the holster and gave it to me. "Put it in your purse," he said.

Liliana: But was he doing it deliberately? Was it a provocation? A failed act? What was it?

Miriam: It was a test. I'm sure the gun wasn't loaded. If you wanted to take off, they'd bring you down. It was a lesson for everyone. "Terrorist Gunned Down on the Northern Coastal Highway." After we arrived, I remember that I went to the bathroom with two compañeras. I said, "Girls, check this out," and I showed them the weapon in my purse. One of them said, "That son of a bitch." The other was speechless.

Munú: They left me alone in a car with weapons. I don't know who it was they wanted to see or *suck up*, and they took me along so I'd be in the car with one of them, with an Operative. It was at a turnoff on the Pan-American Highway.[25]

Miriam: So they'd see that there was a woman with them, and no one would get suspicious.

Munú: To everyone else, we looked like a couple talking. When I look back on these things, I can't help but feel anxious, and I guess it will be that way for the rest of my days. I can understand it, but I can't stop the anxiety. We were parked on the shoulder of the highway. About 100 or 150 meters ahead there was a turnoff, a dip, and another vehicle was there. The Operative with me clearly was covering anyone who might come down the highway and turn off there. At one point he got out of the car and went over to the others. But before he left, he said, "Leave the radio on, and if nothing happens, I'll call you to come with the car." Suddenly, there I was . . . with a car.

---

25. The Pan-American Highway is in greater Buenos Aires.

Miriam: And no registration. What if the police stopped you, and you didn't have your registration! [*Laughter*]

Munú: With a car, a radio that those sons of bitches were going to call me on, weapons on the floor. Presumably they were going to have a shoot-out with someone they wanted to kidnap. And I was just sitting there, alone, anxious, and with all the fantasies you might expect. Suddenly the radio spoke up and said, "Bring the car here."

Miriam: No! And?

Munú: And nothing. They didn't say, "Go on home." [*Laughter*] I had to turn off the radio, start the car, and drive to where they were, which I did like an automaton. Luckily they didn't find whoever it was, and nothing happened. And from there, back to the Basement of the ESMA.

Miriam: What a horrible situation! They've done so many outrageous things to us, and yet we never cease to be amazed.

Elisa: But there were exceptions among all those bastards. Do you remember my telling you about the Green who was a friend of Gabi's and who wanted to marry me? He was just like another prisoner. He was the only Green you could talk to; he was closer to the *sucked up* people than to the marinos.

Munú: I talked to the Greens a lot, and they'd tell me the stories of their lives. One of them told me that he'd fallen in love with a girl who had recently *fallen*. He showed me a poem he'd written to her. Some of them fell in love every other day. Since I stayed alone in the Basement with the guard on duty until four or five in the morning, they'd usually come lean against the door where I worked, and we'd chat. Many of them had grown up in absolute poverty, in the countryside. I made pacts with several of them that I'd cover for them or that they'd cover for me. I also did things like that with some of the Peters. That speaks to a degree of trust. But some of the others were terrorists and did horrendous things.

Cristina: Some of them didn't understand what was going on there at all. Some were psychopaths, and others brought you a little yogurt to eat in Capucha, undoubtedly stolen from the Officers' Casino.

Miriam: I think that because I spent so much time in solitary and didn't have relationships with other prisoners, I developed a kind of emotional bond with one of the air force guards, a guy about my age who treated me better than the others. He brought me the newspaper, the Bible; he talked to me about God. When I got to the ESMA, I turned totally toward the compañeros. It was a huge relief.

Munú: It was very clear who was who. You were with your peers, the compañeros who were part of the *recuperation process*, all the time, and you related to them differently: you had to be careful with a few of them; you established a relationship of respect and solidarity with most of them; and then there were some, a select few, who were the friends you talked to, shared things with—fears, complicities. The relationship with the GREENS was different. Up to a point, you could meet up and talk about X or Y and you might agree or not, but you were always aware of who he was and who you were. You were always weighing what you said and how and when you said it, even though you didn't always do it consciously. When we talk about a fond relationship, we do so in the context of knowing the fundamental division between those who were with one band and those who were with the other.

Liliana: But that doesn't mean you could avoid the flow of affection.

Munú: And besides, I think it's healthy to accept it. I think the situation with the officers was different—at least it was for me—and more complex. Even though they were all part of the same annihilation project, I can't deny that different kinds of relationships formed that are very hard to describe. When you see the same people every day for months; when your life depends on them and you feel, wrongly or not, that spaces have opened up in your daily existence, tiny cracks where you might have an influence and obtain some favor for yourself or for another compañero; when the person who tortured you and continues to subjugate you is the same one who lets you talk to your family in order to bring them a modicum of tranquility, someone you can tell things to and obtain a response of "you can say this to me but no one else," and you know it's true; when you think he could have destroyed you more, and he didn't do it . . . Nothing is easy to explain; nothing is absolutely linear; the gray areas exist, and they are overwhelmingly profound. It took me years to unravel this knot, to get past the barrier of "gratitude" and arrive at the overall image I have now, even though I acknowledge individual behaviors. From the outside, it's easy to conclude that everyone was there by choice: they were all part of the same project, and therefore they are all one and the same. It isn't quite as simple to arrive at that same conviction based on our experience, from the standpoint of those of us who were in there. And perhaps there are conflicting feelings that will be with us for life. What seems healthy to me now is not to be afraid of those feelings, to try to get beyond them or live with them in the healthiest way possible, in as much peace as possible. I always remember a reflection by Primo Levi that goes more or less like this: "Those who were not there can never fully enter, and those of us who were can never fully leave." I'm convinced that it's true.

∾

Cristina: Once the GREENS started to "play around" with the detainees. It was nighttime. They forced the prisoners, who were shackled and probably handcuffed, to walk downstairs one by one while they counted. And if they didn't reach the bottom before they finished counting, they beat them terribly. It was horrific! The rest of us couldn't see what was happening, because we were *hooded*, but we heard the whole thing. We knew that the skinny guy wasn't going to make it, that there was no way out for him. It was either going to be the tremendous blow when he fell down the stairs, or the sadistic punishment meted out by the GREENS.

Munú: Were you in Capucha?

Cristina: I was in Capuchita.

Munú: And they didn't make you go down?

Cristina: No, just the men. I didn't know them. They had sent me back to Capuchita.

Munú: You'd been in the ESMA for a long time by then.

Cristina: Right. I was already familiar with the camp and the few rules that governed it. Despite being immobilized and punished, I had some maneuvering room that the other compañeros lacked. So, as we listened to the macabre jokes of the GREENS and the cries and screams of pain of the prisoners, I was becoming more and more upset and infuriated, until finally I exploded into a stream of obscenities that came out of me in a guttural voice that even I didn't recognize. I raised my *hood* a little, and I looked at the GREEN, a guy named DANY, and I kept yelling at him something about how shameful it was to attack a defenseless person. Of course, they pounced on me in a fury, and while one pressed my head down hard with his boot, another one started kicking it. So I screamed in pain, and I shut up.

Liliana: Didn't any officer hear the noise and come?

Cristina: Not at that moment, no. But later—I don't remember how much time had passed—they came looking for me.

Munú: And they took you to talk to whom?

Cristina: To MARIANO. I talked to MARIANO. They took me downstairs, and they decided to put me in a little cell at the far end of Capucha.

Munú: You hit a GREEN?

Cristina: How was I going to hit him when I was shackled and *hooded?* He hit me; for a while I felt that something inside my head was putting pressure on my skull, which felt as if it were going to explode any second. Then someone gave the order to take me out of there, and I ended up in that cell-like stall. And they all came parading in—MARIANO, naturally, BLONDIE, and even GERÓNIMO—to see how I was doing.

Miriam: What was that episode when you were punished, when they took you back to Capucha after you were already working. Was it because you read the 1,000 Cases?

Cristina: Early one morning, I was in Dorado, which was deserted, and I wanted to try to see the files, to see whether I could find out anything about certain people. So I opened a cabinet they'd told us not to touch.

It was a file cabinet with numbered hanging files, which were the 1,000 Cases. We thought they contained information from other camps. The files we had access to didn't give exact information about people's fates. And I started to read those files; I took them out, and I saw that there were transcripts of interrogation sessions. In one file, I was able to identify a session involving a compañera from San Fernando,[26] and in another I was able to identify that of my compañero's first wife. I started reading, although I didn't manage to see very much.

Elisa: So they were interrogations that had been conducted somewhere else?

Cristina: I wasn't able to figure out where they came from; it wasn't very organized or very clear. You had to delve into it and weave the strands together and understand the references. That's what I was doing when—

Miriam: Why were they called the 1,000 Cases?

Cristina: I don't know. Later on, I mentioned it to Strassera,[27] and he looked into that file, but I don't know.

Liliana: They were numbered from 1,000 on.

Munú: We were from 0 to 999.

Liliana: I think that's right; that was because the kidnapped were numbered from 0 to 999, and then they started over. The 1,000 Cases included all kinds of external information or matters or sometimes a case. For example, Case 1,037 wasn't a person; it was a file of a denunciation. They weren't always people. They were things to investigate, miscellaneous things.

Cristina: Well, I'll finish telling the story. I was reading, and in came the Ant, who had a tortuous relationship with me. He was from the coast guard, an NCO, a photographer. He was an unscrupulous sadist who kept photographs of a compañero's son and used them to extort money from him.

Miriam: The Ant came in and saw you.

Cristina: He saw me, and there was a huge scandal. He was in his element, calling me on the carpet. But the worst part was facing Mariano's reaction. I thought it was all over.

Liliana: Because you had betrayed his trust.

Cristina: And so they sent me back to Capuchita again.

Munú: To Capuchita, sent by Mariano.

Cristina: By Mariano shouting the whole way.

Munú: It was atrocious when he shouted, impossible not to be afraid. I don't know how there could be so much violence in a voice.

Cristina: He would go totally berserk.

Munú: I saw him several times when he was going down to torture. He'd go down shouting and banging on the doors where we were working. He'd

---

26. San Fernando is in greater Buenos Aires.

27. Julio César Strassera was a prosecutor in the trial of the juntas.

bang on the doors and shout, and that's how you knew he was going to torture. His eyes would pop out of their sockets—I always remember that—like the transformation of the werewolf.

Cristina: In the early days, when I was in one of those little rooms in the Basement, he'd come in all the time. He'd burst in and shout at me in different tones of voice, "Don't you feel like a snot for having been one of the Montoneros?" And I'd say no. I'll never forget it. That would start a conversation in which I would explain to him the reasons that I didn't feel, and would never feel, like a snot. This could lead in any direction: a more or less civilized conversation or a screaming fit. He'd come in every day and shout the same thing at me, sometimes totally beside himself. And once, he caught me at a bad moment, and I said, yes, I felt like a snot. I was worn out, and at that moment I felt as though I didn't have the strength to withstand so much pressure. I suspect that even he didn't believe me. Even now it's hard for me not to show what I'm really feeling.

Munú: But you didn't feel like a snot for having been part of the Montoneros. You felt bad for other reasons.

Cristina: Of course. I defended my militancy at all costs to avoid losing a locus of support removed from all that insanity. It was a way of holding on to my center. Saying what I thought—as much as I could—helped me keep my sanity. Obviously I couldn't always do it. The business of the 1,000 Cases occurred in the context of that sort of connection. Mariano sent me to Capuchita, and that's where I was during the whole episode when the Greens decided to "play around" with the detainees. There were several of them, but one of them was a true psychopath. He was very young, and you saw him in that position of power, playing around with human beings, like someone betting on a horse race. The air was thick with the tension of not knowing who the next victim would be.

Munú: Do you remember who else was in Capuchita then?

Cristina: I remember the Rat and Carnaza; it was a later group. I saw them again afterward, shortly before I left. I shared a sort of dormitory with them in Capucha.

Elisa: Do you know what became of them?

Cristina: Both of them survived. I know they were there for that episode, because we ran into each other later, and we talked about what had happened. They told me the marinos had set that Green straight; they put him in his place. There were some internal rules, even in the insanity of the camp. The Greens couldn't do whatever they wanted to us. There were certain limits, even though the officers might decide later to torture and murder us. Those were functions of the chiefs, not of their own *perejiles*.

Elisa: It seems to me that all of those terrible things happened more in Capuchita than in Capucha.

Munú: That's because Capuchita was a harsher punishment than Capucha.

Elisa: Not always. In my time, the captives in Capuchita were the people who'd been *sucked up* by the SIN.

Miriam: It wasn't a harsher punishment at that time at least.

Elisa: There was also less supervision by the officer corps. It occurs to me that the officers were more on top of the GREENS' behavior in Capucha than in Capuchita. The rape cases I knew of happened in Capuchita.

Munú: Because the ESMA people wouldn't keep as much control over the people from the SIN.

Elisa: I don't know. The ESMA people were in control. But to the GREENS, who had little understanding of the relationship between the people in the Fishbowl and the officers, we also represented a form of control. What I'm trying to say is that if they ordered something out of line, they were afraid their superiors would hear about it from our mouths.

Munú: There were certain things the GREENS couldn't do with us. The officers placed limits on the violence they could exercise.

Liliana: When the captain's in charge, the sailor isn't. They, however, could do whatever they wanted to us.

Elisa: Naturally. In Capucha there were some very violent GREENS and others who treated us better; they would let us talk to people who'd just *fallen*, for example. There were some, like the famous GRANDFATHER, who wouldn't even let a fly move; you couldn't even lift your *hood*. Those were the ones who later committed those barbaric acts that Cristina was describing in Capuchita.

Cristina: There was one GREEN who was a very sweet guy. He'd bring me things. He was from a small town in Buenos Aires province. I remember him feeding me a yogurt that the compañeras had sent to me. He was like that with everyone, not just with me. You could see he was a sensitive kid, and it was obvious that he was very unhappy in that situation. He talked to me about his plans, about how he was thinking he might go live in the country. Right after I *fell*, I spent several days in isolation—I don't know where, downstairs, thrown down on a mattress, recently tortured. They took me out of the Basement to some place I can't specify; it was probably Capucha. It had walls on the sides, and it was a very narrow space with a mattress or something on the floor. I was in a kind of fog. They'd brought me a piece of beef or chicken, and I couldn't eat. So the GREEN came over and asked me why I wasn't eating, and I told him that my stomach felt closed up. He started to laugh about my stomach being closed up. He had a knife in his hand. What he did was to hold the knife to my stomach and say he was going to open it up for me.

Munú: But didn't you panic?

Cristina: No. It was an incredibly unpleasant scene, but I didn't panic. I realized he was joking.

Munú: Ah, so you were sure he wouldn't do it.

Cristina: I didn't feel in danger of having him stick the knife in me. But I went crazy. I had an attack. I was completely distraught, and I started to let it all out to him—that they'd killed my compañero, and what was he laughing about when he didn't know what it was like to be in that situation, so how could he joke like that? You see what happens when you let things fly without filtering them through your brain?

Munú: And the GREEN must have been thinking, "Why did I have to go and make that joke!"

Cristina: He was petrified. I imagine him with that little knife in his hand. I couldn't see his face; I remember the darkness, undoubtedly because of the *hood*, although the image I can evoke is of darkness inside and outside the *hood*. But the skinny little thing didn't say a word and didn't bother me anymore. I just lay there crying, totally fucked-up. I ran into him afterward, and I could tell it was him by his inflection. A lot of them were from the provinces and had slightly different accents. I think he was from Córdoba. I ran into him in other situations, and it was obvious that the guy had acquired a certain respect for my pain, something like that.

Liliana: You'd caused a reaction; he'd become humanized.

Cristina: He was just a kid; he was eighteen years old.

Munú: You weren't much older than that.

Cristina: Yes, I was twenty-four.

Munú: Hmf . . . that old!

Cristina: But at that age it's a big difference.

Miriam: What could those kids, who were barely eighteen and had no political education, understand about what was going on around them?

Munú: Nothing. I remember one saying to me, "They brainwash us before we come here. They tell us that you're all terrorists, that you don't care about family—not your own or anyone else's—that all you want is to destroy everything and kill people, and that you put bombs everywhere. So we come here expecting to face terrifying people, and little by little we get to know you, and we realize you aren't like that. You're just normal people, and we can talk."

Miriam: And where did they do this brainwashing?

Elisa: In the Navy Mechanics School, and they paid them more.

Munú: They gave them credit for the whole year, course credits.

Elisa: They had tons of benefits.

Munú: They paid them more, and they could use the money to rent a room among two or three of them.

Elisa: And help their families.

Munú: That's why they chose to face those monsters—us.

Miriam: But it seemed like a good deal.

Elisa: In their minds, the officers were also monsters, because they ran them ragged and they mistreated them.

Munú: I remember situations of complicity with the GREENS, when we looked at each other and knew we'd pulled something in which both of us were involved.

Elisa: I remember the decent guards who would let you speak with the compañeros in Capucha. You'd go around without the *mask* and without the *hood*; you could go up and talk to the captives.

Munú: That too was an act of complicity.

Elisa: Yes, but I remember that even though the people in Capucha benefited from the more permissive guards, in general they maintained a respectful distance. Once, in Capucha, a compañero and I were trying to talk using signs. The guard noticed the effort we were making to communicate, and he offered to take us to the bathroom so we could talk in peace. I communicated this to the compañero, and he got upset and made me understand that I had to say no for my own safety, because on another occasion that GREEN might want to take me to the bathroom to abuse me. Anyway, you could feel the difference among the guards. Some let you raise the *hood* but wouldn't let you speak. And you couldn't do anything with the bad ones.

Miriam: You didn't even blink.

Cristina: When I was in the Basement, on two occasions they let me see compañeros who were in what had once been the infirmary, across from where I was. A GREEN—I don't recall which one—took me. I asked him to.

Elisa: There were instances of complicity, a sort of tacit agreement.

Munú: Of course. With the PETERS too.

Elisa: No, not for me, not with the PETERS. They scared me to death!

Munú: For me, yes. I always talked to Cafati the Turk, and the PETER usually was aware of it. Sometimes, he even joined in the conversation. It all depended on which PETER was on guard duty. The first time I saw the Turk, on my birthday, I didn't even ask to talk to him. The PETER offered it.

Liliana: Do you remember which PETER it was?

Munú: I can remember his face perfectly, but not his name. He drank a lot, but when he wasn't drunk, we got along pretty well. PETER HEAD was the one I got along with the best.

Elisa: And PETER MARBLE?

Munú: No, I got along terribly with that one!

Elisa: And PETER PEPPER?

Miriam: There was one called PETER PARROT.

Elisa: PETER PARROT!

Liliana: Weren't the PETERS in charge of the GREENS?

Munú: The GREENS and the LITTLE PAULS.

Elisa: They were career NCOs.

Liliana: And the Ant and Mocho—what were they?

Elisa: Police, NCOs from the coast guard.

Miriam: The Gustavs were the drivers, the Little Pauls were the Peters' assistants.

Munú: The Little Pauls were also Greens. The Greens and the Little Pauls were under the Peters.

Miriam: The Peters were called that because they had the keys, like Saint Peter in Heaven. What an affair! Comparing that hellhole to heaven. And the Little Pauls were the Peters' assistants. They were in the Greens' hierarchy.

Munú: Yes, they were the ones who took us upstairs and down, between the Basement and the Third Floor, and they brought us food. The Little Pauls were moving all the time—they couldn't sit down—whereas the Greens couldn't leave their guard posts.

Liliana: The Gustavs were drivers, but under what circumstances? They weren't the drivers for the *operations*.

Miriam: No, they were used only for day-to-day things—administrative stuff, errands, shopping.

Munú: They'd take you to run errands. A Gustav was driving me the day we crashed. He was a very young Gustav known as Little Boy, and he remained at the Tiger's side until at least 1983. He took me to find an apartment to rent. They were going to let me out of the ESMA. I was going to have to live alone and work with them under supervised release. They sent me out to rent a place for six months. I wasn't familiar with Buenos Aires. The Gustav took me to the real estate agencies they had selected. I went two or three times. He had a weapon in between the two seats. One time, we were in traffic, and the car in front braked suddenly and—bam!—he rear-ended it. He went crazy; he jumped out of the car as if he were going to eat the other guy alive. The bumper was barely scratched. And the shouting started. I was sitting in the car. At one point he came back and made as if to wave the gun through the window. When I saw his intention, I grabbed the gun and put it on the other side. I hid it from him. I didn't want any more trouble than there already was.

Liliana: The Green shooting it out with someone in the street—it wasn't in your best interest.

Munú: I moved the gun from in between there before he could grab it, and I said, "No. Go over there and work it out. Calm yourself down." It would seem that I had a clearer sense of how things were. I was a very good student; I had learned something.

Liliana: And how did the Gustav react?

Munú: He reacted well. He went over and talked to the guy.

Liliana: He took out the fake card, the fake papers; he took out everything fake he had on him.

Elisa: The fake insurance—"Would you like my information? Here."

Liliana: When the other driver went looking for him to pay the insurance . . . Well, he's still looking! [*Laughter*]

Munú: The GUSTAV took care of everything and returned to the car. I put the gun back in its place, we took off, and his personal tragedy of having to face the TIGER began. He thought the other guy had gotten hold of some piece of information that would identify him.

Liliana: He'd left some evidence behind. He was terrified.

Munú: He had to go and say, "I crashed the car and got into a dangerous situation."

Elisa: He was panic-stricken at having to face the TIGER.

Miriam: But you, waving the gun at the kid!

Munú: I have several stories like that. I always got into situations involving weapons. And it's not something I enjoy; they actually make me feel unsafe. I remember telling him how he could make up a story for the TIGER. You tried to be nice to the lower-ranking milicos, because they were the ones who sometimes allowed you a few perks. So we decided what each one of us would say about the incident. Of course, the shouting wasn't going to be part of the scene, much less that I had waved the gun!

Miriam: At one point, Munú, you mentioned something about PETER HEAD.

Munú: Yes, PETER HEAD came from the South, and he'd been in another camp where they apparently treated people a lot worse than in the ESMA. There was no *recuperation process*.

Liliana: In the South, in a navy camp?

Munú: That's my impression.

Miriam: That would be Bahia Blanca.[28]

Munú: It could be. He came from the other camp, and when he got to the Basement, there was a problem with Serafo. The PETER said something to Serafo, who answered him as if he were just anybody. But the PETER regarded it as insolence, and he punched him so hard that he lifted him off the ground. This PETER was a big guy, and he had a huge head—that's where HEAD comes from—and Serafo was a skinny little guy. Later they laughed together about the episode.

Liliana: Isn't PETER HEAD the one who beat the Engineer at chess? Remember how the Engineer was always playing chess? And he was practically a genius, unbeatable. He spent hours playing chess with other prisoners, four or five brains, one of whom was Tano. They'd play through the night, and this PETER HEAD would watch them. One day he told the Engineer

---

28. Bahia Blanca is a city in southern Buenos Aires Province.

he wanted to play, and the others, laughing their heads off, let Peter Head have a turn.

Miriam: Sure. Some of the prisoners, the intellectuals, were patronizing too. Shit-eating zumbo! This was something they had in common with the officers, although they didn't voice it out loud.

Miriam: The game lasted for hours. And Peter Head beat the Engineer!

Liliana: And what was the story with Peter Head and the strike?

Munú: One day I was in the Egg Carton, standing in front of a file of photos from the newspaper *Noticias*. I spent a lot of time looking at the photos in that file. Our history was recorded there. Suddenly Peter Head rushed in with his hands in the air, making the "'V' for victory" sign, which was one of our symbols of that time; it was the "we shall overcome" sign, the "Perón will return" sign. And he was yelling out, "We won, Flaca; we won; we won." I didn't know what he was talking about, so he showed me the newspaper where there was an article about the first strike against the dictatorship, which, if I remember correctly, was by the railroad workers. The strike was going fine, and, well, we'd won, he and I! I don't know how, but he and I had won the strike.

Miriam: Peter Head was including you in this "we won" of his?

Munú: Totally. He included me even more than himself, in any case.

Liliana: He had decided to ally himself with the railroad workers.

Elisa: But had you talked to him beforehand?

Munú: Yes, many times, but not about that. Anyway, he knew who we were and what we advocated. You had to do no more than glance through that file to know where we were coming from—from participating in all the strikes. I think that as an NCO, he felt as though the officers looked down on him. So at some level we were both the underdogs, sort of like equals—totally unequal equals, because he had spent several years of his life as part of the Task Forces.

Elisa: He was looking for allies.

Munú: We were equals beneath the officers, without forgetting that he was a Peter and I was a captive. In a way, with his thing about wanting to win the strike, he was also on this side. He wasn't part of the power elite; he was one of those trying to make a better life. He played during his guard duty, and I covered for him several times.

Liliana: I saw him playing chess.

Munú: I don't know whether it was chess, or checkers, or cards. He played with the compañeros in the dining room, and I worked next to the entrance to the Basement. He couldn't sit down and play with the prisoners; he wasn't supposed to. So, if some officer came in, I had to call him. I had to yell, "PETER!" as if I needed him for something, and he'd know to grab the walkie-talkie and come walking out, stop the game.

Liliana: I was really afraid of the PETERS.

Munú: The only one who scared me—or, rather, made me sick—was PETER MARBLE.

Elisa: I had a very good relationship with the GREENS, but I was terrified of the PETERS.

Munú: Did you know the HEAD?

Elisa: I'm not sure. He's the only one I can't place.

Miriam: PETER HEAD probably spent more time in the Basement.

Munú: He probably felt more comfortable there.

Miriam: The PETERS' job was to patrol around, but some of them spent more time in Capucha or someplace else.

Elisa: The PETERS found the people in the Fishbowl to be very patronizing. They didn't have much of a relationship with the people in the Fishbowl.

Munú: Of course, because some of the compañeros there were doing more intellectual work, at a level that was out of their reach. We forged or printed documents; we made things by hand; everything we did in the Basement more closely resembled the *dog pack*. [*Laughter*]

Liliana: They called the builders the *dog pack*.

Munú: Sure, the construction group.

Liliana: Fermín, Bichi, Mantecol, Chiquitín.

Miriam: Later Em, Roque, and Chiquitin moved to the printing group, which was a little more sophisticated.

Munú: But in any case, downstairs we were always doing manual activities, whereas the people upstairs did more intellectual things. I think PETER HEAD felt more comfortable playing cards with Serafo and doing idiotic things with Tito than going to the Fishbowl. When PETER MARBLE got pissed off, it was horrible. Once on the Third Floor, when he was taking me to sleep in the middle of the night and no one was awake, he tried to grab me, to fondle me. I remember shoving him hard, and I told him to get his hands off me and to quit fucking around. You knew you had a certain space, that there was no danger of being killed for that. And he took it, but he threatened me. He said he was going to make me pay for it. I think they knew that if we reported that type of behavior to the officers, they wouldn't approve of it.

Elisa: They were afraid.

Munú: He threatened me, but I was holding that card.

Elisa: He was testing you to see whether you'd tell anyone. If you didn't, it was a point in your favor, a point of alliance.

Munú: No, no alliance was possible with PETER MARBLE.

Elisa: But you didn't report it to MARIANO.

Munú: No, but I warned him about the possibility that one of the PETERS might try to accuse me of something.

Miriam: The officers were the only ones who had the right to make advances to the women prisoners.

Elisa: And the PETERS knew that very well.

Cristina: And this would have clued them in that they couldn't go a centimeter farther.

Munú: Because of that, PETER MARBLE got me in trouble. He said, "Now I'm going to make you pay."

Liliana: And you remember that he made you pay.

Munú: He made me pay. I had told MARIANO, "I had a problem with a PETER, and he's going to try to screw me over." I didn't tell him who it was or what sort of problem it was. When PETER MARBLE got me in trouble—I don't remember what for—MARIANO ordered him to take me to his office. He asked me what was going on, and I reminded him that I'd warned him that some problem was going to come up. PETER MARBLE was behind the partition trying to hear. MARIANO pretended he was scolding me, but I knew he was doing it to avoid undermining his authority. After the scolding, the MARBLE took me back to the Basement. He saw himself as the winner, and I was thinking, "I really shit on you!" There I was, an accomplice to the officer man! I hear what I'm saying, and it gives me the shivers.

Cristina: How horrible.

❧

Miriam: They say that the ESMA was total chaos at the beginning and that the TIGER went in to establish order. Instead of killing people in such a disorderly way, they did it only through the *transfers*.

Munú: There must also have been some sort of change in the behavior of the milicos.

Elisa: The ESMA had the worst reputation on the outside. That's why, when you *fell*, they'd ask you where you least wanted to be in the world.

Miriam: Everyone thought it was the cruelest of all the concentration camps.

Elisa: At first, in 1976, they said that there was no restraint at all. The GREENS had total control over what happened to the prisoners. No one placed any limits on their cruelty.

Miriam: They were seventeen- or eighteen-year-old kids with absolute power over the lives of the captives. They were practically children, with all the malice that a child with no boundaries is capable of unleashing. People said that when they had the captives lying down on the floor of the basement, the GREENS rode over them with a motorcycle.

Elisa: Yes, that was one of the things people said. They even said that the one known as the GRANDFATHER was the instigator of that practice, and the rats in the vagina, and the saws to cut off your fingers and hands. You heard those things. We can't be certain they were lies.

Munú: Inside no one talked about that, except in a joking voice.

Elisa: They'd say, "That constant sawing noise you hear is because we are always under construction so the prisoners will be better off."

Munú: When I *fell*, the radio was on in the Basement day and night. But you could also hear the saw—sssssssss. At first, I didn't know I was in the ESMA, and I didn't know what they said about the ESMA either, but I had heard stories that they cut off appendages with a saw during the torture. And the two things that I heard were the saw and, suddenly, shots—bam! bam!

Elisa: And what was it?

Munú: The automatic pistols they used to put in nails. They were building—probably Bichi and Mantecol.

Elisa: Ah!

Munú: They were building the new little rooms, redistributing. They did it all the time; I have no idea why. They were always moving things around, changing the way the space was distributed.

Cristina: They probably wanted to disorient people. None of the few people who were released would ever be able to describe a building that was changing all the time. Or maybe it was another one of the many things in there that had no logical explanation.

5

A Foray into the Outside World

It is among ourselves, the survivors, that we can talk. For us, paradoxically, it is a happy thing. We talk about what happened, joking, laughing.
—Simone Weil, survivor of the Bergen-Belsen Nazi extermination camp

The ESMA had a system of family *visits* for captives who had been selected to work. The oppressors returned them to the outside world for a few hours and allowed them to have contact with their loved ones, at first under armed guard and later seemingly alone. Before leaving the ESMA for the first time, the detainees already knew that their fellow captives remained behind as hostages. It was an unwritten code. Escape during a *visit* could mean the massacre of the other prisoners and savage reprisals against the escapee's family. Making the disappeared "reappear" benefited the marinos in two ways: First, it averted the presentation of a writ of habeas corpus, which would expand the number of victims of the dictatorship. Second, it gave the detainee hope that the possibility of survival and freedom was more than just an empty promise.

Munú: Right now, I can't remember what I knew about the *visits* when I was in the ESMA. I must have known something, because when they took me to my house, I didn't have the fear of heading toward the unknown. They were going to take me on a *visit* to my hometown, Guaminí,[1] to see my family, and since there had been some talk around town about my militancy, the marinos decided that the meeting should take place in the countryside so no one would see me. They made me telephone before we left, and I must have told my mother that I wanted to talk to her and my brothers, so they should meet me in the country.

Elisa: How long had you been kidnapped when they took you?

Munú: Good question. If only I could only answer it. I guess about three months.

---

1. Guaminí is a rural area in Buenos Aires Province located 500 kilometers from the federal capital.

Elisa: You had to figure it out based on whether it was summer or whether it was cold.

Munú: I *fell* on June 19, 1978. I remember writing letters from the ESMA that the marinos would read and then send. It was a ritual I had with my family, and I made an effort to keep it up. My family never imagined that I was kidnapped, not even when I called them on the telephone. The marinos would take me outside the ESMA to place the call.

Elisa: You're saying that your family knew nothing of your kidnapping and disappearance?

Munú: No, nothing.

Elisa: Didn't they think it was odd for you to go to the countryside?

Munú: Yes, it was very strange. By then my compañero was disappeared, as were two cousins of mine. I'd told my mother that if I ever *fell*, they should give me up for dead. I was very clear about that, and I'd conveyed it to them. When I called her . . . the whole situation was abnormal! They lived 500 kilometers away, and the only information they had about me was what I told them by phone or in my letters. My saying that I was going there and that they should meet me in the countryside led them to make some pretty wild assumptions. I hadn't gone to visit them in about two years for security reasons.

Elisa: Oh! A long time.

Munú: My father had died in Buenos Aires, and I couldn't attend the funeral in the town because of the rumors going around. They had raided a few houses, including my parents' home. When they raid a house in a town with a population of twenty-five hundred, the whole district knows it. One day an anonymous letter arrived, which was obviously from the police, given the way it was written. It was like a police dispatch.

Cristina: Unmistakable.

Munú: That happened while my father was still alive, in late 1976 or early 1977, and the *visit* was in late 1978. My mother sent it to me at the time. They were writing to notify my father that a guy who claimed to be a friend of his daughter's had denounced her to the police. They gave his first and last names and his alias, and it couldn't have been anyone else but El Loco. I had warned my parents about how things were, but they didn't believe me. It was very hard for them to distrust someone they'd known forever and who'd been my friend besides. Basically, a lot of things were keeping me from going back there, for security reasons. Getting back to the *visit,* MARIANO took me, and we got caught in a huge rainstorm. You had to take dirt roads to get to the house, and we ended up getting there around one in the morning.

Elisa: Did your family have a country house?

Munú: It was the house where we'd all lived. We arrived; it was dark. I knocked, I opened the door—it was always unlocked—and went in, and a guy who worked there stood up. He looked at me as if he were seeing a ghost, and he told me that my family had waited for me until late, but they'd all left. So we headed for the town. I don't know how we avoided getting stuck in a ditch. "The man of the seas" didn't drive very well in the mud. [*Laughter*] We got to the town, and MARIANO said he was going to sleep at a pension. He dropped me at the house and left. I went in, and there were my mom and my two brothers. They seemed confused to me. I showed up happy as a lark! I didn't want to worry them. I felt as if they were removed from it all, without the benefit of the information that you could get here, and basically I figured that if they were going to kill me, my family would find out when it happened. Horrendous! That was my thinking, and I was trying to give the impression that I was fine. Now I can see that I overdid it. It was important to me to let them know that I was a prisoner. There'd been an article in a magazine—*Gente* or *Siete Días*—about a "*Recuperation* Farm," where militants could supposedly turn themselves in and be well treated. I hope no one believed that. I told them that I was at one of those farms, that I was a prisoner—not kidnapped—and that I was okay. My mother, who probably didn't believe me, asked, "What do you do all day?" and I told her that I did translations from French.

Elisa: Did your brothers believe you?

Munú: I don't know. I never asked them. I always assumed they did. I was going through an extreme situation, and I was trying to protect my family by hiding the truth. It hurt. I had to hide what I really felt from the people I loved most.

Elisa: But since you had a cousin who had disappeared from a neighboring town . . .

Munú: They took her away one day, and she never came back. But I was there, talking to them. I told them that one of the people from the place where I was detained had brought me and that the idea had been to go to the country where no one would see me, so there wouldn't be talk that might put them—put my family—in danger. Judging from what MARIANO told me, the fear was that the army based in Pigüé[2] would show up and there would be complications. I don't know whether or not that was true. I remember that I acted happy, and my brothers and my mom were looking at me strangely. I slept there that night. MARIANO and I had agreed that the next morning he'd go back to the countryside on his own and I would go there with my family, but since it was still raining, we weren't going to be able to get there. So the next morning, we had to go to the pension to tell him not to go to the countryside. I decided that it shouldn't be one of my brothers, for fear that he'd get nervous and, since he was armed, start

---

2. Pigüé is in Buenos Aires Province, 70 kilometers from Guaminí.

shooting at them. The best thing would be to send my mom. I told her where he was, the color of the car. "What's his name?" she asked.

Elisa: And what did you tell her?

Munú: I have to admit that I didn't know his name, much less what ID he'd have on him or under what name he'd registered, so I told her to ask for the guy with the yellow coupe, and off went my mother. Naturally, she got to the pension and started with "Hello, how are you? How's everything?" and asking for the boy in the coupe. "Oh, he's in the room at the end of the hall; go on ahead." And my mom went to wake up that "boy." Later MARIANO told the other marinos, laughing, that my mother had knocked on the door and he'd grabbed his weapon, and my mom had said, "I'm Munú's mother, and I've come to talk to you." He let her in and got back into bed. My mother went into the room and sat right down on the bed to talk about me. I can just imagine what a pathetic scene! My mother also told me about this incident, but without seeming troubled or amused, as if it were the most normal thing in the world. MARIANO had become my savior in my mother's eyes. My death had stopped weighing on her shoulders. I'd told her that they were going to hold me for a while and after that they'd let me go abroad. So in a way, he was the one who had given her back her daughter; he had rescued her from death.

Cristina: Were you able to tell her that they'd kidnapped you, that they'd tortured you?

Munú: Not at the time. They talked in the pension, and according to MARIANO, my mother explained to him why I had gotten involved in that type of political militancy, that I had always been concerned about poverty, and that I had done it because I was a good person. According to my mother, MARIANO told her that I was too good, that I'd been misled and that's why I'd joined the militant organization, but that it had been a mistake and he was going to help me in any way he could. Both of them told me their version, and they both thought I was wonderful. The only minor difference was that one of them had given birth to me and the other was someone who had devoted the past several years of his life to kidnapping, torturing, and killing people. At the end of the conversation, my mother explained how to get to the house. He came to lunch, and my in-laws came, and we all ate together. My torturer was sitting at the table with my family, using our cups, our plates.

Elisa: Were your nieces and nephews there?

Munú: No. My mother was there with her three children, my sisters-in-law, and him. It was all very bizarre. MARIANO was enjoying himself so much there that . . . well, I didn't want to go back to the ESMA for obvious reasons, but neither did he. It's as if he saw himself as a friend who had taken me on an excursion. I feel as if they not only took me off the street and put me in the Basement but they also violated the most intimate thing, some-

213

thing that was truly mine: my parents' house. And that's how it was the three times they took me there.

Elisa: And your mom and your brothers never realized that you were a disappeared person?

Munú: Only afterward, when they let me leave the country and I went to Venezuela. But they never knew the details.

Elisa: And they never asked you about it again?

Munú: They had a general idea. I think it's very hard to face a loved one's horror and pain. I also believe that my mother always knew everything. During that time, there were several years when we saw very little of each other. Then I was kidnapped in the ESMA. And when I came back from Venezuela, my mom was very ill. I went to see her frequently, but it didn't make any sense to tell her the details. She died a year after my return. The ones who asked questions were my nieces and nephews. Probably when the emotional relationship is slightly more distant, it's easier to assimilate the other person's pain. An aunt isn't the same as a sister. I don't know; that's what I think.

Cristina: Besides, your nieces and nephews didn't live through that period. It's harder for someone who lived through it.

Munú: One of the things I want to talk about is to what extent we were conscious, or not, of the possibility that they might kill us while we were in the ESMA. I don't remember living with that feeling on a daily basis, although I did things that would indicate otherwise. Since my father had died, they were dealing with the inheritance. The first time they took me there, I told my mom and my brothers that they should go to the notary and draw up a broad absolute power of attorney—I'm getting upset just talking about it—so that in my absence they could sign anything on my behalf. The next time I went, I signed the power of attorney. I knew perfectly well that if I disappeared, they were going to have a big mess on their hands, and they weren't going to be able to proceed with what they were doing.

Elisa: You were a woman condemned to death, and you were settling your affairs.

Munú: Right. Well, taking a deep breath, let's go on. They took me to my hometown three times, and here in Buenos Aires I think they took me out twice to the home of some friends. They left me there overnight. It was the same in the town. On the way back from Guaminí, we'd take General Paz[3] all the way to the ESMA. When we got to General Paz, I'd start to get very upset, and I couldn't talk. So MARIANO would start in on his speech:

---

3. General Paz is a beltway around the city of Buenos Aires that serves as the dividing line between the city and greater Buenos Aires.

"Well, don't put on that asshole expression! There are a lot of people worse off than you!" Apparently it bugged him to have to put me back in the ESMA after he'd spent two days with my family. It's all so complicated.

Elisa: Didn't they ever leave you there alone?

Munú: They left me alone in my house, but they stayed in the town.

Elisa: Of course, for one night. Did MARIANO always take you?

Munú: No, he took me twice, and once an OPERATIVE took me.

Elisa: And did he go to your house?

Munú: No. I contacted him by telephone, and I told him what I was going to do and where I was going to go. He didn't come near me; he kept an eye on me while I was with my family, but he also made sure to go everywhere I went. Since I didn't go out much, I guess no one in the town figured it out, but it was common knowledge that I came and went in a coupe with a guy who looked like an asshole. There was a lot of gossip going around in Guaminí: "Look at Munú, always so worried about poverty and now she shows up in that car." And I couldn't talk, couldn't tell; it was gut-wrenching, and nothing could be done. I ran into some old friends I used to go out dancing with every weekend, those grand old hometown buddies, and I went up to say hello. They looked at me in disgust, backed away, and said, "You're acting strangely; what are you up to?" I used to talk politics with these people, take them literature to read, magazines sold in newsstands that weren't available there. They wanted to get involved, and they invented things to do in the town. We had a shared history, and they knew what my beliefs were. Their coldness toward me was a powerful kick in the gut, and I remember saying to them, "Some day I'll tell you about it." They thought that I'd been disloyal, that I'd sold out, that I'd betrayed the ideals of our adolescence.

Elisa: Did you see them afterward?

Munú: Yes, of course. They're from the town, and I always go there. I suppose it's different for people who've always lived in the city, where you don't know your neighbors so well. There you know everyone from birth; you know what each person has done, who your friends are, who your relatives are, who your boyfriend was. There was a time when they said so many— and I mean so many—things about me. The guy who worked with the intelligence services didn't know anyone else, so he blamed me for everything: I was the one who had placed all the bombs, killed all the dead. Can you imagine how my family felt? When I came back from Venezuela, I regained people's affection little by little. People know that I denounced what happened, that I participated in the trial of the juntas. Some people asked me about it. *Never Again* was circulating, and parts of my testimony were in it. In 1987 I painted some murals with teenagers from the high school, over the opposition of some of the local politicians who continued to denounce me. Fortunately the kids and their parents didn't pay any attention to them. They told me about it, so I confronted my detractors, and the people defended me. It was very important to me.

∾

Elisa: I'm going to tell you about my first *visit*. It was three months after my kidnapping, before New Year's Eve in 1977. I *fell* in September, and they let me contact my family in December. They told me that fat JUNGLE would take me to meet just one person, whom we would pick up and take somewhere else. We weren't going to go to my house.

Munú: One person in your family?

Elisa: Yes. I called my mom, we went by my family's business to pick her up, and we went to the Northern Coastal.[4] They took off my shackles to go to that meeting, to that interview. I'd worn them constantly up until Christmas 1977.

Munú: They took off your shackles and your handcuffs?

Elisa: I was no longer handcuffed. I was still wearing shackles, and they took them off for me to go meet my mom.

Munú: Was JUNGLE there?

Elisa: Yes.

Munú: In a bar?

Elisa: It wasn't even in a bar. In the car.

Munú: You talked on top of the car on the North Coastal with fat JUNGLE present?

Elisa: Yes. Of course, I couldn't talk about anything except the weather, the heat. So you know what I did? After a half hour I asked JUNGLE to take me back again because I felt worse than I did in the ESMA. How can anyone bear such a situation? A torturer, a kidnapper, acting like Mr. Nice Guy and taking me to meet with my mom—I felt that I couldn't connect with the world. I preferred to go back to the familiar, to the meaningful looks among my compañeros. My mom was so happy to see me that she couldn't understand the looks I gave.

Munú: You couldn't tell her anything about what was happening or what you were thinking.

Elisa: My mom thought I looked great. "You're doing so well!" she said. What was I going to do? I wasn't about to show her the shackle marks!

Miriam: Didn't she ask you where you were staying?

Elisa: My mom saw that I was fine, period. She told me my sister was engaged and other family matters.

Miriam: She didn't ask why you hadn't called? She probably knew. She knew that they'd *sucked* you *up* and that it was a real miracle that you were alive.

----

4. The Northern Coastal is an avenue that runs alongside the Río de la Plata in the northern part of the city of Buenos Aires.

Elisa: I have to explain something here. There was a GREEN, a really good kid. He was the one who wanted to help Gabi escape.

Cristina: Ahhh!

Elisa: He said he was in love with me. I asked him several times to call my house, and he did, so my mother knew where I was. She knew because the GREEN would call her on the telephone.

Munú: And she faked it beautifully.

Elisa: Of course. She didn't say a word to me because in between the call announcing our get-together and the meeting with JUNGLE on the Northern Coastal, the GREEN had contacted her and told her not to ask any questions. He'd warned her—

Miriam: To just listen. To keep her mouth shut.

Elisa: The meeting didn't last more than forty-five minutes.

Munú: What did it mean to you to leave the ESMA, to be back on the street? Had you seen it before?

Elisa: I'd seen it, because they'd taken me on the *expeditions*.

Munú: Were there a lot them during that time?

Elisa: A lot! And I had the misfortune of running into people I knew. I always saw the father and brother of a friend of mine from inside the car. The fear was that they could make you get out at any corner, and I was panicked at the very thought that someone might come up to me—to have to look the other way, to feel the anguish of having them see you.

Cristina: Of course.

Elisa: That *visit*, even though it was the first, was inconsequential. I wasn't ready to leave the microclimate of the ESMA. Let's say it was a protocol *visit*, so they could see that I had a family. The second time they took me to my house. My parents had a business downtown. A friend of mine, Petisa, was always going over after work to see my mom, and she had to put up with my father, who blamed her for what was happening to me.

Miriam: You who were such a good girl!

Elisa: Right. "It's your fault my daughter . . ." he'd say. Even so, Petisa kept on going over to drink *mate* with my mom. I love her; that's how she is. So she found out that they were going to take me for a *visit*. I was going there for lunch; they'd leave me there all day Saturday, and they weren't sure whether they'd be picking me up that same night or the following day, Sunday.

Munú: Were they going to leave you alone in your house?

Elisa: They left me alone there.

Munú: How long had it been since you'd *fallen*?

Elisa: This was in February 1978, five months after. A half hour after they dropped me off at home, my dad came home from the shop with Petisa.

She was crying! She told me she'd gone to a fortune-teller who had told her that I'd had problems with my hair.

Miriam: We've got to go see that fortune-teller. She knew about that scalp infection you had!

Elisa: It was very moving. My mom had fixed chicken and rice. Petisa couldn't finish her meal because my dad threw her out, and I stayed there.

Munú: How did he throw her out?

Cristina: He got angry.

Elisa: My dad started in with the same old thing, and to avoid an argument, she got up and left.

Cristina: He must have felt that she was encroaching on his space.

Elisa: I never tried to understand it. To me it was a mortal wound; it was my first *visit*, and I would have liked it to be a little more harmonious.

Miriam: What had they told you? That they'd pick you up at a particular time?

Elisa: That evening or the next day. I arranged to meet Petisa somewhere else. In the afternoon I went out and called all my friends to tell them not to say hello to me if they saw me in the street.

Cristina: You told them that on the telephone?

Elisa: Yes. The first day I went out. It was weighing on me heavily. I was tortured by the thought that someone would see me and approach me during an *expedition*. I also had the telephone number of a compañero in Capucha.

Miriam: And did you call?

Elisa: Yes. A woman answered, and I told her that her brother was in the ESMA. She hung up without a word. I still remember the number.

Munú: Didn't you ever call back?

Elisa: I called a number of times, and they never answered again. Once, during a *visit*, I went to see a friend who'd been a militant, and together we went to the home of an acquaintance who knew I'd been kidnapped. The poor girl had an attack! I'm talking about July 1978.

Munú: The World Cup . . . when I *fell*.

Elisa: Exactly. Well this girl reacted almost violently.

Munú: Let's just say she understood things very clearly.

Elisa: Very clearly. "Listen to me; you have one foot in and one foot out," she said. "How do you know they aren't following you?"

Miriam: And how did you feel about it? Did you understand her?

Elisa: Yes, I understood. It made me angry, and I told her off. I said to my friend, "What are you doing with this gal?" But I did understand, and she was right.

Munú: Sure.

Elisa: I ran into her a long time afterward, and I really didn't have any bad feelings. She said, "You were always so omnipotent." We didn't realize what was happening. At the time we thought we had some control over reality, when we didn't even have any control over our own lives.

Munú: There was also that omnipotence of youth.

Elisa: My efforts were focused on pretending that nothing had happened, that everything was just as it was before. I was so crazy that I couldn't see that everything already had happened to me. What else could happen to me? That compañera was right, but in our case it was more insanity than omnipotence.

Munú: Of course she was right.

Elisa: Maybe it was an act, something like, "I can deal with this myself"—in the same way that the compañeros would tell me that after the ESMA I should leave the country, and I'd say, "No, I'm staying here." Although it's true that financially I had absolutely no means of going, I also didn't make any effort to try. I thought of the ESMA as just one more thing, and I managed to survive several years like that.

Munú: Were you in a relationship when you *fell?*

Elisa: No. The relationship showed up later, during one of those excursions, when I had one foot in and one foot out. He was the friend of a friend of mine, and now he's my husband.

Munú: That guy was half suicidal. You were in the ESMA, and he became your boyfriend.

Elisa: He was half suicidal, along with other friends who were aware of my situation and invited me to their homes anyway. And when you and I went out with Chito, Miriam?

Munú: You left the ESMA together?

Elisa: No, we met up on the outside!

Munú: What do you mean you met up on the outside?

Elisa: Saturdays, when we were both on a *visit*, we'd meet up in the evening and go out. No one knew, but we'd go to the movies, to Cosmos 70.

Miriam: I remember going to see *Close Encounters of the Third Kind* at the Gaumont.[5]

Munú: You'd meet up outside? They'd take each of you to your homes, and then you'd meet up? You're crazy! [*Laughter*] It would never have occurred to me.

Miriam: And she introduced me to one of her friends to see whether I liked him, but nothing happened.

Elisa: Yes! And I introduced Chito to La Negra, a friend from high school, and he went out with her.

Munú: How nice! You found boyfriends on the outside for prisoners in the ESMA so they'd have something to dream about! This woman never ceases to amaze me.

---

5. The Gaumont was a chain of movie theaters located in downtown Buenos Aires.

Miriam: There were problems with getting together on the outside. Once they found out that I'd met up with Laurita. She was about to leave the country; they were about to release her. I was still in for a while longer. This would have been in late 1978. We had become buddies, and she wanted me to meet her daughter. The little girl was two years old and adorable. We were chatting, half hidden in a pizzeria in Olivos,[6] when in comes GONZALO, the coast guard OPERATIVE, and he tells us that there was a huge brouhaha because the TIGER found out we were seeing each other on the outside and he was furious. Laurita, who had a dark complexion, turned white.

Elisa: When Viki was on a *visit,* I even went to her house. Didn't you know anything about this, Munú?

Munú: I never knew people met up on the outside!

Elisa: Didn't you ever get together with anyone?

Munú: They took me out only a couple of times in Buenos Aires.

Miriam: Of course. Because they took her to the provinces.

Munú: I was with my family, and I went out with them.

Miriam: Elisa had friends who were still alive. I didn't have anyone left! I started calling, and they were all dead.

Elisa: You called people too, Miriam?

Miriam: Yes. After the first *visits,* I needed to know how my friends were. My two best girlfriends were dead. They killed them when they *busted up their houses,* when they were nine months' pregnant. Their husbands were dead too. I started calling a friend of my boyfriend's, Alejandro, a guy from Dámaso Centeno High School. I never found him. "No, Alejandro isn't here," they said. I tried calling at different times, until finally his mother asked me who I was. I bluffed; I told her I was a friend from college, and I wanted to register with him for the next term. Then she told me in a sad voice, but in a tone meant to console me, "No, dear, Alejandro is gone for good."

Cristina: Mmmmm.

Miriam: I remember crying in the street, because I'd called from a pay telephone. I cried for him, for his mother, for myself. I cried for all the dead. One day, I happened to run into another guy from the same group, which had been decimated really—it was a massacre. He was so happy to see me. We sat on a bench in the square and looked at each other. He said, "Flaca, I can't believe you're alive! When I tell the guys I saw you, they're not going to believe it. We'll all get together; this is wonderful!" He told me they'd all stopped militating, but one of them was collaborating with the Mothers of the Plaza de Mayo, which had recently formed. I called

---

6. Olivos is in greater Buenos Aires.

him about getting together and having a big gathering, the reunion. But he never answered my call. They didn't trust me.

Munú: Fear broke the bonds of trust.

Elisa: I remember that Miriam and I would go sunbathing during the *visits*.

Miriam: Yes. We had an enormous need to feel the sun on our skin. It was vital. We hadn't felt it for so long! We'd go to the place that is now the Ecological Reserve, and we'd stay there for hours. It was an urgent need. During the entire year that I was kidnapped in the air force, I spent just ten minutes in the sun: one day on the terrace, wearing the *mask*. The doctor had recommended it, the same one who treated you after the torture sessions.

Elisa: What we did was a big secret. The marinos couldn't find out.

Munú: When I said you were crazy, I was thinking about how hard it was to relate to other people, even when we were out but still working with them.

Elisa: It was very hard for us to start new relationships. We couldn't tell just anyone what was happening to us. And those who knew wanted to know only so much, and then they didn't want to hear any more about it.

Miriam: When we were in the ESMA, we couldn't meet with other people! You couldn't answer even the simplest questions: Where do you work? Where did you go on vacation? Have you seen such and such movie? We had no shared codes with anyone, except for others in the same situation. It was the world and us. Tell the truth to whom? It was impossible, and besides it was dangerous for the others.

Elisa: Nonetheless, the people we saw tried to be part of our lives. I remember once, when we met up during a *visit*, Chito went with me to Petisa's house. We needed to see how we related to those who hadn't been through our experience.

Miriam: I went to Petisa's house too, but I think it was after we started working on the outside. At that time, only people who'd been our friends from before could join our meetings, our talks, and that was it. There weren't many. I always remember, Elisa, that your husband would turn white and start to sweat whenever he heard us talking about the ESMA.

Munú: When you went on a *visit*, weren't you afraid to be out on the street? I was. The first time they took me on one, here in Buenos Aires, they left me overnight, from Saturday to Sunday. I remember the recommendations: "Don't even set foot on the street, because although now you're in the ESMA, tomorrow you could end up somewhere else, and who knows whether you'll ever get out of there!" I didn't go outside, not even to see what it looked like. Nothing! I stayed inside the house the whole time.

Cristina: I didn't go out either, but I don't remember that it bothered me much. It was actually painful for me to *visit* places that were full of memories. It was like living a life that I couldn't recognize as being mine; I avoided it. That's why I didn't even consider the possibility of being kidnapped by a different branch of the armed forces.

Munú: Even afterward, when we were outside and we had to keep working with them—from February to June in my case—I was afraid of being *sucked up* by other milicos, even though they'd given us that telephone number in case we had any problems. You were supposed to say, "Look, I'm already *sucked up*. Call this telephone number in code." But in the meantime they'd already have me *hooded,* in the trunk, and being beaten. I wasn't interested! I really was afraid to go out. I went out as little as possible and only as far as the bus stop.

Miriam: I was *sucked up* by the air force and then the navy. I had only the army left to go. There wasn't much risk. [*Laughter*]

Cristina: When they started leaving me with my family for several days, my friends would come over, but I wouldn't go out. Later, I had no choice but to start moving about in order to go to the job they'd assigned me, but I would go back and forth directly. I almost always read during the trip in order to avoid looking out the train window. I found it hard to recover my ability to concentrate on what I was reading, and I practiced on Agatha Christie novels. That's why I preferred to stay home with my family or have friends over.

Elisa: Your friends would come over when you were on a *visit?*

Cristina: Yes, and besides that, some really crazy situations occurred during those *visits*—for instance, when they forced my sister and brother-in-law to marry in a civil ceremony.

Munú: The marinos?

Cristina: Yes. They'd had only a church ceremony. They always pressured me about my sister, telling me they were going to kidnap her because she had militated. I couldn't stand even the thought of her being taken to the ESMA. And on top of that she was pregnant! MARIANO kept up the pressure on this issue until they decided to get married. And the marinos were there at the Civil Registrar's Office.

Elisa: Why did they want them to get married? I don't get it.

Miriam: Everything is incomprehensible.

Elisa: They had you kidnapped, and they were holding her hostage.

Cristina: Something like that.

Elisa: They forced them to get married during a *visit?*

Cristina: During one of those family contact *visits.* I had written a long paper arguing why it didn't make sense to take my sister to the ESMA. MARIANO was always insisting they were going to get her, so I decided to write it to convince them otherwise.

Elisa: Was your sister a militant?

Cristina: Yes. She had militated at the school where she was studying, but to distract their attention from her, I talked about how very young she was and how little time she had militated. But they didn't care about that!

Miriam: They took fourteen-year-old kids.

Munú: The issue was to keep on subjugating.

Cristina: The marriage was an example of making the absurd seem natural: for us, I think, by denying their presence in order to get through the situation and for them as another show of power, a ridiculous way of imposing discipline.

Elisa: What year was that?

Cristina: 1979.

Munú: With every passing day I consider them even bigger bastards! They took over everything—as if they were so legalistic! Cristina's sister was married in the church and not civilly, so they had to legalize the situation!

Cristina: Everything legal!

Munú: A compañera's son used her last name, and they changed it to the last name of his father, who had been disappeared for a year and a half, because . . . how could she be a single mother!

Elisa: They did that?

Munú: They made up a fake life story for him. They created a phony document with the name of his father and the face of a marino, who went to the Civil Registrar, acknowledged him, and forged the signature.

Miriam: God! [*Painful sigh*] The oppressor acknowledged the baby by masquerading as the disappeared father.

Cristina: Besides that, when my sister got married, BLONDIE was there and MARIANO was there at the Civil Registrar.

Munú: Oh no!

Elisa: I can't believe it!

Cristina: It was four blocks from my parents' house. And our friends went anyway, out of affection for my sister and my brother-in-law.

Munú: Of course, it was the marinos who were out of place, not the friends!

Miriam: What did your sister say about it? Did you explain it to her?

Cristina: Naturally! My sister was actually the only one who knew how things were.

Elisa: How was it that she agreed to get married?

Cristina: When I *fell*, my sister and brother-in-law went to the coast. They kept their distance because they weren't sure what was happening. Later, the first time they took me to my parents' house, I did my best to explain everything necessary to Cecilia so there would be someone on the outside who knew the truth. At the time, she was the only one I could confide in about what had happened. My little sister, Claudia, was only fourteen years old and had already spent a long time living in uncertainty and fear, ever since we'd had to *vacate* the house. I couldn't leave my parents with so much anxiety. After I finished telling her everything, she started crying, and she kept saying over and over, "Don't die! Don't die!"

Elisa: Meaning that she understood everything.

Cristina: She understood what she could.

Elisa: How much time passed between the time you *fell* and your being able to talk to your sister?

Cristina: I don't remember the time frames. They were shorter in my case because everything was shorter. It must have been about two months.

Elisa: And why did BLONDIE and MARIANO go? To see what?

Cristina: Are you looking for a logical answer? Let's just say that it was a display of power. We were all hardened. Everyone was trying to make the best of the situation—a situation that was completely forced—although I think there was a lot of denial on our part.

Elisa: How did your parents take it?

Cristina: Well, they just put up with it. My parents had believed they were never going to see me again. After one or two brief *visits*, I was out of touch for a long time, and communication was broken off again when they sent me back to Capuchita as punishment. My grandmother died then, and several other things happened so that by the time I reappeared on the scene . . . The marriage was ludicrous, but compared to everything else, it was the least of my family's worries.

Munú: Right. The alternative was that you were dead. If you were alive, everything else was secondary.

Cristina: And besides, to get married . . . My sister and I talked about this. They didn't care whether or not they got married. They hadn't done it before for security reasons, but now they were expecting a baby. Certainly if it had been possible, they'd have chosen to do it, but they wouldn't have invited the marinos!

Munú: They must have regarded it as something that would help you. I always wonder why they weren't scared, why they didn't leave the country.

Miriam: And what if the marinos interpreted that as an act of rebellion and killed Cristina? They might have thought they were going to denounce what was going on in the ESMA from outside the country or go back to militating. I definitely think you wouldn't be here to tell the story. The TIGER would have *sent* you *up*.

Cristina: My sister and I had shared a lot of things. Before I *fell*, we went all over together, the way people did in those days. We got by as best we could and supported each other through the loss of so many beloved compañeros and the increasing deterioration of the project we had upheld in our militancy. Then we both got married at right around the same time. We didn't do it legally, but a priest friend of ours presided over a ceremony of sorts, which wasn't recorded in the books.

Munú: In the ESMA, you lived in constant fear that they would *suck* her *up*. I don't know whether you ever talked to her about it, but she probably realized it.

Cristina: And there we were, trying not to do anything different. We kept our movements to a minimum, trying not to take any risks. It was essential to me that they not *suck* her *up*, to save her from being put in there. I felt that they had absolute control over the situation.

∽

Munú: For years the ghost of when the moment would come was heavy on my mind. As I was running from one place to another, getting out of one fix and then the next one, I was finding out about all those around me who had *fallen*, so I knew it would happen to me at some time. When I *fell*, after the first few days, I felt something like relief.

Elisa: The same thing happened to me. I felt that nothing worse than that could ever happen to me again.

Munú: Death was worse, and that could happen! That was the next place where you drew the line.

Elisa: That's where the insanity of after, of how to survive, comes in. But the ghost of not knowing where to live, where to sleep, of knowing they could *suck* you *up* any second had vanished.

Cristina: Ah yes! We lived as if we were wearing armor. There wasn't even time and space to cry for those who were absent. I still preserve the image of being out in the street when I found out that a compañero, my first boyfriend, had *fallen*. The person who told me immediately added that I shouldn't cry, that it wasn't a good idea for security reasons. It seems really harsh, but the risk was there. That compañero was looking out for me, although for me it was incredibly hard to swallow that pain.

Munú: We spent years like that!

Miriam: Always looking over your shoulder to see whether a green or any other color Falcon was pulling up next to you, never able to sleep well at night, arriving at an *appointment* a few minutes late and finding the pools of blood left by your own compañeros who'd been gunned down, running into the *gang* there and taking off with your eyes filled with tears—these things happened to me repeatedly.

Elisa: Maybe that's an explanation for why we went out and got together on the outside. It had happened; we had *fallen*. We were already—

Cristina: On the other side, on that side that I'd always imagined as dark—an unknown quantity, but definitely evil.

Munú: Besides, outside you met up with other kidnapped people, people you really had things in common with at the time, and not just anything!

Elisa: We'd go to the movies; we'd have coffee; we'd meet on street corners; we'd laugh and everything.

Munú: We also laughed inside!

Elisa: But not before. The fear we had before *falling* had vanished. We were already meeting up during the *visits* by the time you *fell*, Munú.

Munú: You were already—

Cristina: In the next stage.

Elisa: We had turned the corner.

Munú: Just when it was all beginning for me!

Miriam: For us, the *fall* was the beginning of a new stage. For most people, however, falling into the hands of those murderers was truly the beginning of the end.

∿

Miriam: I had my first family *visit* two months after they took me to the ESMA. Before that, I'd been kidnapped in the air force.

Munú: How long had you been there?

Miriam: I was there for ten and a half months. [*Sighs*]

Munú: Did your family know anything?

Miriam: My family knew I was alive, because I'd been forced to call them on the telephone several times from there. They'd put me on one extension and listen from the other telephone. And I'd say, "Mom, stay calm; I'm all right. I can't tell you where I am."

Elisa: Did they also do that to keep your family from presenting a writ of habeas corpus? Did your mom know you'd been *sucked up?*

Miriam: No, my mom didn't know. She thought I was in hiding, underground. "Are you okay? Do you need anything? Where are you?" she'd ask. "Mom, I can't tell you." I'd say. "Are you healthy? Who are you with?" she'd ask. "I can't tell you," I'd answer. She thought I was free. The situation was such that when I called her from the ESMA and said, "I can't tell you where, but I'm detained," my mother exclaimed, "Thank God!"

Munú: In those situations, the mothers drew the line at alive or dead, nothing else.

Miriam: Right. My mom told me that when she read the newspaper and saw that there'd been a skirmish—

Elisa: She thought that it was you.

Miriam: And on top of that, a lot of friends of mine that she'd known since they were little had died that way, gunned down.

Munú: It had been a year since you'd seen her.

Miriam: Exactly.

Munú: You'd called her before, but you'd never told her that you were detained.

Miriam: Right. Sometime around October, the air force guys who were holding me called her and told her to get everything ready because I was going to the United States.

Munú: But was that true?

Miriam: I don't know whether or not it was true. Once they brought a passport application to my cell. I filled it out, gave it to them, and they never brought the passport to me. They also went to my mother's house to pick up a bag of clothes.

Munú: So it seemed perfectly feasible.

Miriam: Right. They also called her to ask for money.

Elisa: And you knew it?

Miriam: Nooo! They did all that themselves. I was in solitary, shut in a cell.

Elisa: How did they identify themselves to your family?

Miriam: They didn't, but afterward, when I saw my mom, I asked her, "What did you think? How come you didn't realize I was detained?" And she said she thought they were my compañeros from the militant organization who were helping me flee the country.

Munú: Of course. Why would she think you were detained when a young guy in jeans and a checked shirt showed up—

Elisa: And told her, "Miriam needs clothes."

Miriam: "She needs clothes and five hundred dollars." It seems that they really did think about letting me go abroad. I think they asked her whether I had a passport. My mom said no, and that's when they application process got complicated, and they decided not to send me anywhere. They had kidnapped me because they were looking for one of my best friends from high school, the daughter of a very high-ranking air force officer. She was in the militant organization and had participated in an important *operation*. Of course, when she went underground, I never had any more contact with her. And that was lucky. When I *fell*, I had no idea where she was. During the torture they kept saying, "We're not interested in you; we're interested in your friend. Tell us where she is." They probably thought that maybe someday they were going to find out that my friend was in a particular place, and they were going to take me along to look for her, to identify her. Maybe that's why they kept me alive and isolated for so long instead of taking me to the Seré Mansion.[7]

Elisa: Oh, lucky for you!

Miriam: They never took me to the Seré Mansion or put me in with the other air force prisoners. They left me there. The house where they held me was very strange, old, with the blinds always closed. Even today it's exactly the same as it was then. It's located at 632 Virrey Cevallos, two blocks from central police headquarters. I go by there a lot, and I always feel a chill run up my spine and the temptation to go knock on the door.

Munú: Were you and a skinny guy who escaped the only ones there?

Miriam: Yes, Osvaldo López was an air force corporal accused of sabotage,

---

7. Seré Mansion, or Villa Seré, was a clandestine air force detention center, located in Morón, in Buenos Aires Province.

who escaped over a wall more than six meters high. He broke down the door to his cell and left. He tried to get me out, but the door had a heavy chain with a lock. It was impossible. We didn't speak, but sometime before dawn I heard him touching the lock, and I could sense his frustration. We met many years later. We embraced. I think that minute united us forever. Anyway, they always *sucked up* people who would spend only two or three days there. They kidnapped them, shocked them with the *electric prod*, and then took them away—maybe to Seré Mansion—or they killed them; I don't know.

Elisa: Didn't you ever see anyone else there besides Osvaldo?

Miriam: No, and I never saw him either. In that place, which belonged to the Air Force Intelligence Service, I never saw the face of any captive. I only heard voices. There were just two cells. They never had more than three prisoners there at once. I was in my cell, without handcuffs, but chained, and with a padlock on the door; another was in the cell across from mine, handcuffed; and a third was in a room down below, tied to a bed. At least I think so, because I could hear them using the *machine*.

Munú: So what happened to your friend?

Miriam: The milicos found out she'd been killed in the southern zone. They killed her during an action by the provincial police, who were after a common thug. When uniformed men entered the boardinghouse where she was living with her husband, he got a rifle ready. The police saw him through the window, and there was a shoot-out. They thought they were thugs. When a grenade flew, they realized that wasn't the case, and they called in the Combined Forces.[8] They even sent an artillery helicopter. They died there; that's how it all ended. The milicos told me all about it in great detail—there in Virrey Cevallos—to mess with me, I think. It happened in October, twenty years ago now.

Elisa: If she'd *fallen* alive, they would have torn her apart.

Miriam: My two best friends died pregnant and about to give birth. One of them, Patricia, was twenty, and the other, Norma Matsuyama, was eighteen and full term. They killed her in April. Do you remember the shoot-out on New York Street, in Villa Pueyrredón?[9] It was on the first page of *La Nación*. Adriana Gatti, the daughter of Gerardo Gatti, the Uruguayan labor unionist, was also wounded. She was only seventeen, and she was pregnant too. Her boyfriend had just *fallen*. She was *under wraps* in my friend's house. There were two pregnant women there.

Elisa: Was she alive when she *fell*?

---

8. Combined Forces was the *operational* name for a coordinated action by the three armed forces.

9. Villa Pueyrredón is a neighborhood in the city of Buenos Aires, near the northern boundary with greater Buenos Aires.

Miriam: She was alive, but she died afterward in Alvear Hospital. She was six months along.

Elisa: When you were in the air force, what did they say to you—that they wanted your friend in order to *recuperate* her? Wasn't the father involved?

Miriam: *Recuperate* her? No!

Elisa: But what did Patricia's father think? He was a high-ranking officer!

Miriam: I have no idea what Patricia's father thought! Do you think that once they found out he had a daughter in the Montoneros Organization, they'd give him the time of day, regardless of how high-ranking he was?

Elisa: That guy went to *visit* you there, where they had you *sucked up*.

Miriam: I don't know whether or not he went to see me. Why would he have wanted to see me?

Elisa: So you could give him an explanation. He probably thought that it was your fault, that his daughter was a good girl and you had pushed her into the militant organization. Wouldn't that be typical of a father?

Miriam: Someone who was very important in the air force came to see me in the cell once. They wouldn't let me take the *mask* off. The man disguised his voice. He asked whether they had treated me well, how I was. But I don't think it was Patricia's father. It might have been Agosti or someone they thought I might recognize, someone who appeared in public.

Elisa: Did you know that girl's father?

Miriam: Since I was twelve.

Munú: It's very likely, if they had allowed it, that he would have wanted to talk to you.

Elisa: Your whole situation in the air force was very strange.

Miriam: Yes.

Elisa: What do you think about it now? Don't you know what happened?

Miriam: I don't think I'll ever know.

Munú: Didn't you ever go talk to the girl's father?

Miriam: No.

Elisa: Don't you think he had something to do with what happened to you?

Miriam: With my kidnapping?

Elisa: With your being alive.

Miriam: I don't think so.

Elisa: You had everything against you.

Miriam: I think that once they realized that I was totally useless to them, the concern was what to do with me. They didn't want to release me or kill me, so they sent me to the ESMA.

Munú: Why would they be worried about killing one more person?

Miriam: If not, then how do you explain why I'm alive, when they killed almost everyone? There were virtually no survivors from the air force.

෨

Miriam: Getting back to the issue of the *visits*, as I said before, I had my first *visit* two months after I got to the ESMA. But the one I remember most is the time we crashed.

Munú: That was a lot later, because I was there by then. I remember it perfectly.

Miriam: I was with the ANT in one car, and HUNCHBACK and someone else were in another car, behind us. They were on some kind of mission. By coincidence, the two cars left at the same time and were heading in the same direction. We crashed at the corner of Santa Fe and Juan B. Justo. It was terrible; the car was totaled. My head smashed into the windshield, and, in the midst of the torrent of glass and blood, I had a nervous attack—I couldn't stop screaming and crying. They all drew their weapons, they drove away a medical student who wanted to help, and then they put me in the car behind us and took me back to the ESMA.

Elisa: I can just imagine the expressions on people's faces, and particularly that student's.

Miriam: The compañeras had instructed me to get dressed up. They said the marinos liked it when we fixed ourselves up, when we acted feminine. La Negrita, Ramiro´s compañera, had lent me a blue velvet blazer, and someone else had given me a white blouse.

Munú: This would have been your second or third *visit*.

Miriam: Right. The only thing I remember about the first one is that they didn't leave me there. They left me there for two or three hours, and they took me back inside again. What surprised me most about the day of the accident is that I was more worried about the blazer than my injuries, because La Negrita had asked me to take good care of it. I'd told her not to worry, and then I got blood stains on it, so I was thinking, "Oh, poor girl!"

Elisa: Didn't they take you to the hospital?

Miriam: No. They gave me stitches in the Infirmary in the Basement, and a few days later they took me to the Naval Hospital, because some glass had been left in the wound and it had scarred badly, leaving keloids. They took me, passing me off as a friend of the daughter of the ESMA director, CHAMORRO. I was looking at them all in terror. I didn't care how it had scarred; I didn't want any treatment. To me, the whole thing seemed horrifying and ridiculous at the same time.

Munú: Their insistence on providing treatment for us—it seems this wasn't the only place where it happened. When my cousins *fell*, they had wounded one of them in the leg, and they put it in a cast. People who saw him in the Banfield Pit[10] said he was wearing a cast. After that, they killed him. They fixed you up, and then they murdered you.

---

10. The Banfield Pit was a clandestine detention center in the southern part of greater Buenos Aires, in the Lomas de Zamora district.

Miriam: Just like the Nazis. They were they ones who got to decide when they would hurt you, when you would die.

Elisa: They treated you because they had absolute and total power over you. It's all so crazy. Miriam, let's continue with your *visit*.

Miriam: Well, on the day of the accident, I got to my house later than arranged.

Elisa: Of course. Because you'd gone back to the ESMA.

Miriam: I went back to the ESMA, they treated me, and then they took me and left me there for about four days. I remember that my face was swollen, disfigured. My mom and I went out in the Once neighborhood, and people stared at me because I looked like a monster. I was totally covered with bruises, cuts, bandages.

Munú: I remember you in the Infirmary with that gash and how worried you were about what had happened and whether you were going to have a scar. They were also worried about how it was going to heal.

Miriam: I don't remember being worried about the scar. I don't think I cared about it at the time.

Munú: But you did care about the jacket.

Miriam: I was very worried about that stained blue velvet jacket. When my mom saw me, I looked like a mummy! I had a bandage here. [*Indicating the jaw*] I had another here. [*Indicating the forehead*] And I had another here. [*Indicating the nose*] The only parts of my face that were visible were my eyes and part of my mouth. "What happened? What did they do to you!" my Mom asked, and I said, "Shhh, be quiet!" She thought they'd beaten me up. In the end, they left me there for three or four days, and then they came back to get me. I can't remember whether they told me when they were going to come back, whether I knew for some reason.

Munú: They'd have called you.

Miriam: Those things . . . those details . . . Yes, they would have called me, because otherwise how would I have gone out without worrying that they'd come back and not find me there. Leaving the house when they left you for a *visit* was a serious infraction.

Munú: The times they took me for a *visit* here in Buenos Aires, they'd tell me more or less when they'd be back to get me. When was the accident?

Miriam: It must have been in September. I wonder whatever became of La Negrita and Ramiro?

Munú: They were among the first to leave; it must have been around October 1978. They were SIN *suck-ups*, ABDALA's charges. I remember that ABDALA would come down to the Basement every week. He'd come to see his *suck-ups*, and he'd bring them pastries. I don't know why they made us stay in our offices while he was there. Sometimes they brought people down—I guess it must have been Bubble and Merque—and they would all meet in the Egg Carton.

Elisa: I think he sometimes went upstairs to see them.

Munú: And when did they let you out of the ESMA?

Miriam: In January 1979.

∽

Munú: Adriana, did you know that they were left alone during the *visits* and they'd meet up on Corrientes Street? It was dangerous. Did you by any chance carry a sign saying, "I've already been *sucked up*."

Elisa: What would have happened if the marinos had found out that we met up and went out together? It was forbidden! We were so oblivious, Miriam!

Cristina: Oblivious in what sense? The whole situation was anomalous.

Adriana: You went around the city. People saw you. How is it possible that people in the street were unaware of what was happening to us? It was as if you were carrying a little sign saying, "I'm kidnapped," and no one noticed. When they took me for a *visit*, I had an absurd and incredulous feeling that I've never felt again, but I'll never forget. I saw kids dressed like little boys and girls, but I had the impression they weren't children at all, that they were adult midgets dressed up like little dolls. My perception was totally distorted during my first *visit*.

Elisa: When they took you to your house, did a lot of them go along?

Adriana: No. I think there were two of them, but I don't recall who they were—fat JUNGLE and MARIANO, I think, but I'm not really sure.

Elisa: Did they leave you there?

Adriana: No. They stayed the whole time. My parents were there, but I couldn't speak with them alone. At one point, my mom took me to my room to ask me a couple of things, and we spoke in German. My parents were there, my sister, and my niece. Last year I was talking to a friend, and she told me that she'd also been in the apartment and that I'd greeted her and we'd talked.

Munú: And you don't remember?

Adriana: I don't remember anything. She told me that I'd seemed lost, totally confused, very thin. I probably weighed ninety-nine pounds. I was wearing Víctor's pants; he must have been very thin, but they were big on me. It was the first time I'd seen people again, seen the street. And I had that deformed perception of the kids.

Munú: Did they continue to take you on *visits*?

Adriana: They took me a couple of times. At first, they told me they would take me for my birthday, on October 12. But that *visit* never happened. By then it had been two months since I'd *fallen*.

Munú: And were you working?

Adriana: No! I was in Capuchita. I was very high up. I started working during the fourth month, in January 1979.

Munú: What do you mean by "high up"?

Elisa: Closer to heaven than—

Cristina: Closer to the harp than to the guitar. [*Laughter*]

Miriam: Closer to the harp than to the *visit*.

Adriana: The only thing I did for my birthday was push-ups, a gift from the GREENS. And I had wet bricks on my mattress.

Munú: What?

Adriana: They put wet bricks on the mattress; I had to spend the whole day on the wet mattress.

Munú: That was a punishment?

Adriana: The punishment for the fact that it was a special day or for wanting attention. The present from the GREENS was to humiliate me with their sadism. They knew it was my birthday and that I was expecting them to take me to see my family. They'd told me they would, and naively I'd believed it.

Munú: Had you already called on the telephone?

Adriana: I think I talked to my parents. I don't remember exactly, but evidently I did, because afterward my mother wrote a story about the cake she'd made, as she did every year, for my birthday. I'd asked her to make me an apple cake. My parents were expecting me. Apparently there actually had been the promise of a *visit*.

Munú: You had disappeared two months before, and your family knew nothing?

Adriana: They knew. Moreover, my dad *fell* with me. [*Silence, sighs*] My dad had taken me to the apartment where I lived with La Flaca to move a cradle. That day we were moving to a house lent to us by friends of my parents, to take care of her. And when I got there, they were waiting for me. I remember only that when I put the key in the door, which was at the far end of a covered passageway, the door opened from the inside. Everything was dark, and they grabbed me by the hair. There was a scream that I later learned was mine, pistols to the head, men screaming orders, the *hood*, the handcuffs, my body hitting the ground, and boots on my body. I hadn't spoken German for a long time, but I was thinking in German something like, "So this is what it's like, then, when they kill you." And finally came a sensation that was a mixture of equal parts terror at imminent death and relief, just as when, after a lot of suspense, you get to the end of the nightmare and you no longer care whether or not it's a happy ending. When my dad heard the screams and the shots, he took off running. They fired on his car, and they kidnapped us both. We communicated a couple of key words in German.

Munú: They took him with you to the ESMA?

Adriana: Yes.

Munú: To the Basement?

Adriana: I guess he would have been in the Basement. They took everything he had on him: money, watch, glasses—not his ID. Then they let him go.

Munú: Who *sucked* you *up*?

Adriana: I don't know.

Munú: Didn't you recognize anyone later?

Adriana: I didn't see anyone. The house was dark when I entered.

Elisa: And afterward, when they interrogated you?

Adriana: Co was at the interrogation. I thought I was with the federal police, because I had the idea that only the police force had female personnel. It never occurred to me that she could be a compañera, and I have no memory of what she might have talked to me about in that place. MARIANO was also there. He was calculating for me how much time they would give me, *through the front door*, for illicit association, document forgery (although mine weren't forged), and the other charges, and he was saying that I'd spend a thousand years in the clink. He didn't tell me where I was, but he did say that they would send me *through the front door*. Ca took photographs of me—full face and profile. He made me take off the *hood* and the *mask*, and when he ordered me to open my eyes, he'd ducked behind the camera.

Elisa: How long was your dad there—one day, two?

Adriana: He was there for a few hours. They took him in his own car, and then they let him go—I don't know where. I have no idea how he got home, and for a month afterward he couldn't bear to go out; he was totally disoriented and fearful—imagine!

Munú: Besides, he knew he had left you behind in that place.

Adriana: Yes. In conclusion, I did not go home on October 12. I don't remember exactly when my first *visit* was. What I do remember is that I was *walled up* when they took me out, and when we got to Libertador, they let me open my eyes. They told me where I was, and as I watched people passing by and not paying any attention to me, I thought, "What's wrong with them that they don't realize? Can't they see it in my face?" It was the strangest feeling.

Munú: They also took me out *walled up*. They themselves had told me I was in the ESMA, and later, the first times they took me out to dinner, they put the *hood* over my head when we left and when we returned. Why would they do that?

Adriana: It was to act out the story for the benefit of other people.

Elisa: Of course. For the outsiders: the marinos who weren't in the Task Force and the GREENS.

Miriam: The other marinos at the Navy Mechanics School knew we were kidnapped but not that they took us out to dinner and took us for *visits*. They weren't aware of the sick relationship they forced us to have with them.

Elisa: Probably not.

∽

Miriam: Why do you think we didn't escape when they left us alone in our homes? Any human being would have had the impulse to flee when the marino or police officer in charge of taking them left. It's clear why we didn't escape during the first few *visits*: we were accompanied. The guys stayed with us, and they were armed. But it's hard to understand why we didn't do it when they left us on our own for entire weekends toward the end. Why didn't we go when in reality we knew that our survival wasn't guaranteed when we returned to the ESMA—to the contrary.

Munú: It was never guaranteed.

Miriam: The tide could have turned after Pelado's or Nose's escapes, or when they killed LAMBRUSCHINI's daughter,[11] and TIGER ACOSTA could have said, "We're doing these people a [quote unquote] favor by sparing their lives, but no more; they're all going to be *sent up*." Or there could have been a coup within the coup, and they could have decided that there would be no more survivors—not even the few there were.

Elisa: One of the things that stopped us was the possibility of reprisals against our loved ones, against our families. And the other thing that was going around in our heads was that, if one person escaped, everyone else's life would be in jeopardy. I don't know whether it was the same when you all were there.

Miriam: Yes, absolutely. It's macabre, but it was real. Those who remained inside were like a warranty.

Munú: When they left you alone in your house, the other prisoners, people you cared about, were hostages.

Elisa: Yes. In fact, a short time ago, when fat JUNGLE testified before Judge [Adolfo] Bagnasco in the trial for the theft of minors,[12] he said that he'd had a car accident during an *outing*, and he'd left his weapon. He was with Quica, and she didn't flee. When Viki called her on the telephone to ask her about it, she said, "How could I escape when everyone else's life would be in danger!" It never even occurred to me.

Munú: It didn't occur to me either, and I think it was the same for many others.

Elisa: I couldn't even imagine escaping, even though I knew that no one's life was guaranteed, and I understood everything that was happening at the ESMA.

---

11. Paula Lambruschini died in a 1979 attack on the home of the Lambruschini family, just as her father was to take over as commander of the navy.

12. The theft of minors case was initiated by the Argentine courts to investigate the existence of a systematic plan to steal children born in captivity during the military dictatorship.

Miriam: I had heard about the massacre of the Tarnopolski family. Sergio was twenty-one years old and a draftee. He had to do his military service in 1976, as an aide to TIGER ACOSTA. When the marinos found out that the guy was a militant—according to them, they caught him setting a bomb on the inside—they *sucked up* his whole family: his parents; his wife; and his fourteen-year-old little sister, Betina. It was no coincidence that the milicos at the ESMA quietly spread the story around. They wanted to terrorize you, and they succeeded. They told you about it in a tone that suggested, "If they find out I told you this, they'll kill me, but I'm telling you anyway so you'll know how to handle yourself inside here."

Elisa: The entire Tarnopolski family passed through the ESMA. Did they kill them all?

Miriam: Yes, except for Daniel. He's the only one who survived. He lives in France. He was the only one left. When I was in the ESMA, my brother was thirteen and my parents lived here. Any attempt at escape would have had to include my whole family. I couldn't leave them alone. I was certain that they'd *suck* them *up* if I escaped and that they'd kill the compañeros inside there too.

Elisa: Are you referring to what you thought when you were on a family *visit* from the ESMA or the air force?

Miriam: The ESMA. Before that, in the air force, I never had a *visit*. The only thing they allowed me was one telephone call to say that I was fine and to prevent anyone from looking for me. It wasn't until I got to the ESMA that they started to tell me about the family *visits*. At the same time, as I was saying, they started to talk about how the marinos had killed entire families. I'm not sure whether I really understood that they might kill all the other captives if I escaped or whether I was mostly afraid they would *suck up* my family.

Elisa: But did you actually think about it? Did you consciously think about escaping?

Miriam: Yes, I thought about it. I seriously considered it when they left me home on my own. Especially when I realized that apparently I wasn't under surveillance. I could go a few blocks, take a bus, and nothing happened; no one stopped me.

Munú: I think you felt it more than thought about it.

Miriam: Your attitude about it also had to do with what was occurring in the country. What was required in order to escape?

Cristina: To be able to go somewhere.

Miriam: You had to have an infrastructure, as Pelado had in Paraguay, where presumably people were waiting for you, where you'd have a house to hide in. Here, in this country, a fugitive from the ESMA—where would I have gone? To an uncle's, a cousin's, a compañero's or ex-compañero's? They'd all *vacated* their houses and gone underground. There was no rear guard anymore, no organization to go back to. Go back where? Escape to where? And who would have put up with having you in the house with those murderers out looking for you? The alternative was to leave the country but with what papers? We didn't have ID or a passport; we didn't have anything.

Elisa: Right.

Miriam: And on top of that you ran the risk of running into a *finger* and being *sucked up* by another branch of the armed forces or by the navy again, because if you escaped, they'd reinforce the borders to prevent you from leaving the country. And if they *sucked* you *up* again, you were dead for sure.

Munú: You mentioned Pelado's escape, which was at the border, but Nose's was still inside the country.

Miriam: The organizational structure was still in place then. Nose had somewhere to go back to.

Munú: How did that escape happen?

Elisa: Nose was a very persuasive compañero, an operator. He convinced an officer that he had to put some envelopes in the mail. The officer—I can't recall who it was—assigned a GUSTAV to take him. Nose convinced him to go to a post office downtown. When they got there, he told the GUSTAV that instead of wasting time looking for a parking spot, he should drive around the block while he went in. The GUSTAV had to go around the block several times! Nose had taken off!

Munú: Had he planned it, or had he just seen the opportunity?

Elisa: He'd planned it. He'd talked to El Sordo beforehand. They held El Sordo in the Basement for a long time before they killed him. Nose asked him for a contact on the outside, because he was planning to escape.

Munú: Elena told me that she also thought it was necessary to escape, and she had even discussed it with Pelado.

Miriam: So what happened after Nose escaped?

Elisa: It was crazy at first; there were *expeditions* all over the place. The slogan was "Find him, or else find him." The people from the *mini-staff* started doing interrogations to find out about contacts, family, relatives. Those of us on the *staff* acted all disconcerted, but most of us were really thrilled. Those were days of all-out mobilization. Besides, it was a mortal blow to the TIGER: it just had to be Nose, one of his chosen ones. Then the atmosphere quieted down a little; they started acting very sure of themselves, as if to say, "He's going to *fall* any day now." A few days later Nose called La Chinita, a compañera who had already gone home, to find out how everything was on the inside, whether there had been any reprisals. That day the marinos got us all together and said, "He's a son of a bitch! He shit on all of you and on everything we're doing!"

Miriam: So they wanted you to think that Nose escaped without caring what might happen to you all; that was the message.

Cristina: The marinos used to say things like that to the detainees; they were ways of breaking our spirit. They struck where they knew it would hurt.

Elisa: Yes. When things happened that had such a strong impact on us and disrupted the day-to-day routine—for instance, when they killed Gabi, or Ricardo, or Loli, or in this case—they would take four or five of the most important captives in the Fishbowl out to dinner and give them all the relevant explanations. Always taking care to preserve their good name and honor naturally: in Gabi's case, they said the army had pressured them; in Loli's case, the pressure came from the force itself. And in Nose's case, they said that those escapes caused widespread irritation, and the high command of the armed forces was asking for all our heads. Then those four or five compañeros would convey the message. We all knew it wasn't an apology, as the marinos tried to make it out to be. We knew they wanted us to remain calm so that we would continue to produce.

Miriam: When Pelado escaped, they told us about it directly. The TIGER went to the Fishbowl and said that he talked to baby Jesus every night, and baby Jesus told him who stayed and who was to be *sent up*. He said that bastard Pelado had shit on all of us, and they were going to find him. I think that Nose already had *fallen* again and they'd put him on display.

Munú: I *fell* right at the time of Pelado's escape, and they put Nose on display after that. I was already there.

Elisa: Munú, you were already there when they brought in Nose's corpse?

Munú: Yes.

Miriam: I'll never forget that night. They brought the bullet-ridden corpse in the back of a pickup. They parked it in the yard and made everyone who knew him, all the prisoners, walk past it and look at him.

Elisa: Did you see him, Munú?

Munú: No, they didn't take me, because I didn't know him.

Miriam: I didn't either. I watched the scene from the third-floor dining room window: the parked pickup and the prisoners filing by the back of it, looking at Nose's bullet-ridden corpse. I could see their faces but not the body. That night I remember that I had the worst liver attack of my life. I was moaning, "I want to die," and I was crying, and the compañera who slept next to me said to me terrorized, "Please be quiet, Michi; calm down, because they'll kill you." We were in Capucha, and I was screaming because my head was splitting in two. I didn't care about anything at that moment. To sleep, death, not to feel anything anymore, ever again, was a relief. I asked a GREEN to call a doctor, and a nurse came in with a shot. Now I think, "How could I let them give it to me!" But, well, the medicine calmed me down, and I finally fell asleep.

Cristina: I wasn't there then, but later I heard MARIANO talk about that incident, about what it meant, that it had been a "symbolic" gesture.

Miriam: And it was. How were we going to escape? At that time, there was no well-oiled organization waiting out there to give us a fake passport, cash. There wasn't anything!

Cristina: Something similar happened to me. They put a lot of pressure on me in the ESMA, mostly through my sister but through my parents as well. I came from the North, where I'd had serious disagreements with the organization over the militaristic approach it had adopted. By then I had experienced everything we've talked about here: the exhaustion, wandering the streets with nowhere to go, seeing how the compañeros *fell*. You looked for work even though you were underground, because there was no organization to support you, to give you a place to stay or even the most basic elements of survival.

Miriam: No, there was nothing.

Cristina: And you had to carry on however you could in the midst of the disaster. And those conditions hadn't changed. Under those circumstances, escape to where? For what purpose? And the people left behind? Make a denunciation? Where? In Argentina? Impossible.

Miriam: But besides that, to make a denunciation in 1978 . . . I think the first time I uttered the word "disappeared" out loud was in 1981, when I got to New York. And I said it fearfully, looking over my shoulder to see whether they were coming to kick down the door.

Elisa: The collective message was the matter of the hostages. It had been ingrained in our conversations and our daily lives: if you escaped, you screwed all the rest. I remember discussing this with the other prisoners.

Munú: You thought collectively, not individually. I remember that the first compañero they allowed to talk to me was Gabriel. One day, when I still didn't even know I was in the ESMA, they opened the door and brought him in. He sat down at the other end of the Infirmary. He gave me tips on how to function, and he said there was a pact about not trying to escape: "Either we're all saved, or no one is saved. One person's escape can mean death for everyone."

Elisa: That was the doctrine; it was the Bible.

Munú: We kept operating under the same philosophy we had in the militant organization. You were able to move forward because you knew the compañero behind you was watching your back. In any activity you did, no matter how small, you knew that someone else was there, and you placed all your trust in that someone. Our head functioned as a collective: one did one part, someone else did another, and we went along like that, and together we faced the same danger. So, with that belief, which I considered sacred, it never would have occurred to me to escape; I didn't dare even think about it. It was the same thing that made me ask, when I went to

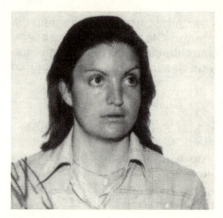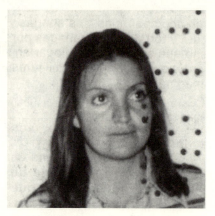

Above left: Photograph of Liliana Gardella taken inside the ESMA in November 1978.
Above right: Passport photograph (supervised release, April 1979).

Venezuela, whether there were compañeros from the organization there, so I could tell them who I was. When I told them who I was, what I had done, and where I was from, they responded, "If you make a denunciation, we'll believe you." And right then I said, "I'm not going to denounce anything until I know that every last person inside the ESMA is free, because each person is important to me." And I continued, "The most important things that need to be known are already known. What could I tell? Five more details. Everyone already knows that there are kidnapped people, disappeared people. The little bit that I would add could mean death for the people still inside there lying on a mattress, who still have a chance to get out alive. I'm not going to go there; you can do whatever you want." The first testimonies appeared two or three months later. I remember how panicked I was for those who were still kidnapped.

Elisa: Cristina, were you in Buenos Aires?

Cristina: Yes.

Elisa: And what was the impact of the denunciations?

Cristina: A huge uproar. I remember wondering, "Okay, so what now?" But I wasn't completely conscious of all the implications.

Munú: Were you out or in?

Cristina: I was out, but I came and went. I didn't sleep in the ESMA any longer, but they'd show up at my house unexpectedly and take me somewhere without telling me why. In that sense, for sure, it was almost the same as being inside.

Munú: Then ABDALA traveled the world over trying to stop us, to keep us from making denunciations.

240

6.
Babies in Custody

I'm going to tell you the story of your coming into this world
in the subsoils of fear, upon a table,
at noon on a day in springtime,
on the meeting day.
On the meeting day, I'm going to tell you
the story of this incomplete sister,
the story of your absence, of the hollow in every birthday,
every New Year, every diploma, every vacation, every burial.
                    —Mariana Pérez Roisinblit, "El Cuento,"
                 February 4, 1999, dedicated to her brother Rodolfo,
                              born in the basement of the ESMA.

A clandestine maternity ward operated in the ESMA. Pregnant women were taken there, even from other concentration camps. Until these prisoners gave birth, a few of the kidnapped women—taking advantage of the tolerance of certain guards—accompanied them, sustained them, and at the same time took refuge in their exceptional kindness and strength. Deceived by the marinos, most of these women never suspected that their babies would not reach their families or that instead they would become the war booty of members of the military. It was a fate too cruel to imagine.

Elisa: Liliana, didn't you *fall* in Mar del Plata with the pregnant women?
Liliana: During the same period but not at the same time. Liliana Pereyra
    fell, and so did Patricia de Rosenfeld, Walter's wife, the mother of the little
    blond boy who was born afterward in the ESMA. Did anyone ever find
    out anything about his parents, about Walter or Patricia?
Miriam: Some things are known: the Forensic Anthropology Team found
    Liliana's body. She was shot to death after giving birth.
Liliana: Where did they find the body?
Miriam: In Mar del Plata.
Liliana: Pati and Liliana were kidnapped around the same time that I was, in

November 1977, when they were both a few months' pregnant. They must have been about three or four months along.

Elisa: Pati was the last pregnant woman I saw while I was in the ESMA. It was before they emptied out the Pregnant Women's Room on the Third Floor. I'm sure they sped up a lot of those deliveries. They induced them because the World Cup was approaching and they were afraid that international organizations or journalists would conduct inspections of the ESMA. I also remember Cristina Greco, who was taken to the ESMA from the air force sometime around February 1978. She was very worried because she'd been kidnapped and released a few months before and she'd *fallen* again and PETER MARBLE had recognized her. She was in Capucha for a short time, and I met her there when she had her baby. They took them both away.

Munú: The Pregnant Women's Room was the one under Capuchita?

Elisa: Yes, under Capuchita.

Munú: A large room.

Elisa: When the *mini-staff* people were still in the ESMA, before they let them sleep on the outside, they slept in that room—up until February or March 1978. At that time, the pregnant women were held in a room across from there, in a space we later used as a dining room. After the *mini-staff* stopped sleeping in the ESMA, they moved the women there. That's where Pati, Lili, and Bebe were. I'm certain that Pati was the last pregnant woman to stay there.

Miriam: Did any of you know that they didn't turn the babies over to the families?

Liliana and Munú: No.

Elisa: Yes, people suspected it.

Miriam: Did you suspect it?

Elisa: At first, such atrocities seemed unthinkable. The fact that they separated them from their parents was punishment enough.

Miriam: Personally, I never imagined anything so horrible, never.

Liliana: I was never able to accept that people were dead. I felt the same uncertainty about the babies that I felt about the rest of the disappeared. It took me years to accept that they were dead and years too to accept that the babies weren't with their families.

Elisa: The rumor going around in the Fishbowl and Capucha was that they ended up in the hands of officers who couldn't have children. There was even talk of a list of officers who wanted them.

Miriam: I never heard that in the ESMA, never.

Liliana: I didn't either.

Elisa: Miriam, did you think they gave them to their families?

Miriam: Of course. Because they made each compañera write a letter to a relative, usually to her mother or mother-in-law, asking her to raise the child with love until they could be together again. It calmed them down.

Elisa: They bought clothes for them. Fat JUNGLE bought a layette for every baby, under orders from the marinos. That's what led me to conclude that they were given to families the marinos knew. Otherwise their efforts to make sure the babies were well dressed didn't make sense. That's why I was surprised at two cases I found out about later: Emiliano Hueravillo, the little boy who showed up at an Orphans' Home, and Patricia de Rosenfeld's son, who was restored to his family. A little while ago a compañera and I were talking about that case. She thought that none of the military men wanted him because he was of Jewish descent.

Munú: There are other children of Jewish descent who are disappeared.

Liliana: Is that the only case from the ESMA of a restored baby?

Miriam: No, Mo and Pe's children were too, although it's a different type of situation; it isn't the same, because they were part of the *mini-staff*.

Munú: They left those babies with their mothers. They never took them away. In the Rosenfeld case, they disappeared the mother and left the baby with her family.

Liliana: Yes. They didn't always do the same thing.

Miriam: In most cases, they killed the mother and disappeared the baby. There were a few exceptions.

Elisa: Liliana's baby was never seen again, whereas Patricia de Rosenfeld's baby was turned over to her family. The grandmother who received him was so terrified that she didn't tell the paternal grandparents. So they kept looking for the baby even after she had him.

Miriam: Was it the marinos themselves who took him there?

Elisa: Someone from the ESMA took him.

Liliana: It's so strange—isn't it?

Miriam: They must have thought the baby was sick or something like that. Otherwise it's inexplicable. I'm not persuaded by the version that they rejected him for being Jewish.

Elisa: Quica and Chiche tried to intervene a lot on Patricia's behalf. She was the only pregnant woman left by that time. They kept insisting that they should let her go; they talked to the officers for a long time. The marinos insisted that they wouldn't let her live because her husband was disappeared; there was no chance that she could remain alive. That's what they told Chiche, what the TIGER told her.

Miriam: And the baby—why do you suppose—?

Elisa: I think they must have given the baby to his grandmother because of the family's persistence. I found out about this when I was working in my parents' business. A Grandmother of the Plaza[1] came by, and she asked me whether I knew the boy. So I said, "I rocked Sebastian." And she said that the child was very upset, so I wrote him a letter telling him what I knew about his birth, his mother's hopes, how much his mother loved him and took care of him. In the letter I told him about the history that I had shared with his mother during part of her pregnancy inside the ESMA. Around the same time, Viki went to visit him, and she gave him a bracelet that had belonged to his mother. Later they told me the other part of the story, about how the other grandparents had been looking for him because the grandmother who had him had kept silent. Several years later, the same grandmother who'd acted as go-between called me again to go over the story and verify it, because when they took Pati from Mar del Plata to the ESMA, they took her compañero, Sebastian's father, to La Cacha.[2] According to the testimony of survivors from that camp, he had said that his son, whom he'd never seen, had remained in Mar del Plata, and this created some confusion. We can't cast doubt on the few things that we know for certain! Our denunciation has always given the location of Sebastian's birth, because we knew him! We were with him and his mother! Fortunately, the boy knows the truth. He's not confused about it.

Munú: I wonder how it was that his dad was transferred to La Cacha and why he would have been left with the idea that his son was in Mar del Plata. A lot of detainees were transferred between camps.

Miriam: Yes. My case was unique, because I went from the air force to the ESMA, but not for interrogation. Other people were taken from camp to camp to get information out of them, to torture them again months after they had *fallen*. They did it to compare statements, to see whether the captives were lying to them.

Munú: I remember the case of Patricia Roisinblit, who was brought from another *chupadero*. She got there just a couple of days before her baby was due, so they held her in the Basement, in the Infirmary, for about twenty-four hours, and then they took her up to the Third Floor.

Miriam: Yes. They brought her from the air force; she told me herself that she'd been in the air force. We talked about it a lot, because the place

---

1. This refers to membership in the Association of Grandmothers of the Plaza de Mayo, an organization of mothers of disappeared persons searching for their grandchildren who were born in captivity and/or who were in the hands of the military, their associates, or people who—unaware of their real roots—adopted them in good faith.

2. La Cacha was a clandestine detention center located in the area of Lisandro Olmos, near the city of La Plata.

where they held her, a house in the western zone, also seemed to be an operations center where there weren't any other *sucked up* people, just like the house where I'd been.

Munú: Do you remember that they put her in a little room?

Miriam: It was in the Storeroom, on the Third Floor, where they kept their booty from the raids, under the staircase that led up to Capuchita. It was a luggage holder with no ventilation.

Munú: Yes. Next to what used to be the Pregnant Women's Room. She was there for a few days, and they took her downstairs for the delivery. Then she spent about three days with the baby.

Miriam: In the Basement, in the Infirmary?

Munú: Yes, in the Infirmary, and that's when—

Miriam: Ah! That's why I never saw her again.

Munú: Of course. That's when they sent Andrea and me to take care of the baby and her, to help her wash and take care of him. Everyone asked them to bring José, and they never did.

Elisa: Who was José, her husband?

Miriam: Patricia's husband—José Manuel Pérez Rojo.

Munú: A lot of people knew him, and they asked them to bring him to the ESMA.

Miriam: But it was no use. They said they couldn't, because it wasn't their jurisdiction; he was in the hands of a different branch of the armed forces. That's what MARIANO told me.

Elisa: This was at the end of 1978?

Miriam: In November. I knew Patricia and her husband; he was my *responsable* in the Western Province. The last time I saw her on the outside, she was pregnant with Mariana, her eldest daughter. In the ESMA, I'd visit her in the little room. I tried to persuade her to ask to stay. I told her that she'd have a better chance of surviving and that afterward it would be possible to ask them to bring José. I could neither assure her that she would live if she remained in the ESMA nor tell her—because I didn't know—that the air force would kill them both. What I never imagined, at any time, was that they'd steal the babies, that the newborns would never get to their families. It was too horrible to imagine.

Munú: I had seen her downstairs, and I'd also duck into that little room when I was upstairs. It was very hot out, and it was unbearable in that dingy little room. We'd leave the door open, even though it wasn't allowed. Until they brought her, I hadn't realized how the ESMA operated with respect to the pregnant women. I knew there had been some there, but I didn't know whether they had been *transferred*, whether they were from the ESMA, or whether they also brought them in from other *chupaderos*. Those things had been going on for a long time before Patricia's arrival in November 1978.

Elisa: Not for a long time but for months. The last pregnancy had been in April of that year, and you *fell* in June. That's why you hadn't seen any, but there were a lot of them.

Munú: Patricia's little boy was born on November 15. The baby was born in the Infirmary. A doctor named MAGNACCO assisted her. Quica and Andrea helped with the birth, and afterward they also let you in, Miriam. Patricia named him Rodolfo in honor of a *fallen* compañero.

Miriam: Yes. I went in as they were cutting the cord. She had a rash on her face from the exertion; she asked them to put the baby on her breast. She was happy. The doctor told her she'd done a good job, and she responded that she had done better during her previous delivery.

Munú: I saw her for two or three days afterward, until they took them away. They were in the Infirmary where I had slept for five months. I was very familiar with the place, and now she was there with the baby. It is a terrible and incongruous scene: a *chupadero*, a kidnapped woman, a newborn baby, me, and the uncertainty about what would become of our lives—so connected, one on top of the other, life and death superimposed. I talked a lot with Patricia; actually she talked a lot. She told me what it was like in the *pozo*[3] where she and her compañero had been and her enormous fear of being tortured when she got back there. She never said she was afraid that they'd kill her. What I remember most is her desire to live, her plans, the house she dreamed of having for her family. One day I was taken downstairs and they were gone. It was a pain unlike any other, an invasion of sadness. Rodolfo's grandparents and his sister never stopped searching for him.[4]

Elisa: In the cases I was familiar with, they also took the mothers away right after the babies were born. When I was there, it was forbidden to go into the Pregnant Women's Room. We always took precautions to make sure no one would see us.

Munú: A couple *fell* around that same time. The girl was in the advanced stages of pregnancy. They tortured him a lot. It all happened in the Basement—that's how we lived.

Miriam: Women in labor, with the tortured, with the dying.

Munú: They put her in a little room, and they put him in the Infirmary. Later they took her there too. He suffered around three cardiac arrests. LITTLE APPLE, the doctor, would get his heart beating again, and they'd keep on torturing him. The girl delivered soon after, and they let her go with the baby. They were there for only a couple of days.

Miriam: But they didn't let him go?

---

3. "*Pozo*" is a term used synonymously with concentration camp.

4. In 2000, Rodolfo was found living with the family of an air force intelligence agent.

Munú: They kept him inside. What I don't know is what happened afterward.

Elisa: Who was he?

Munú: They called him Luis. I guess they must have been released, and they have the child with them. The child was born, and he was with her in the Infirmary.

Miriam: Don't you remember who attended the birth? I don't recall that situation.

Munú: That's because she never went upstairs; all of this happened in the Basement. Maybe Liliana can remember something.

Liliana: I remember the episode and the couple, but I don't know the girl's name. I also had the impression that they released her, but you never know whether or not such things are true.

Elisa: Víctor and Lita *fell* with their twenty-day-old baby. In his denunciation, he testified that they tortured the baby.

Miriam: Yes, they used the *electric prod* on his little leg.

Munú: He says in his testimony that a certain PIRANHA, from the coast guard, came into the place where they were torturing him, holding his baby by the feet, and they told him that if he didn't collaborate they were going to smash the baby's head against the wall. And they gave the baby an electric shock. [*Silence and sighs*]

Miriam: When I testified before Judge Bagnasco in the case of Patricia Roisinblit's baby, I took pains to emphasize that they had a whole system in place for the pregnant women; her case hadn't been an exception. A lot of women captives gave birth in the ESMA, and pregnant women were even brought in from other camps. Her baby's birth was, it's true, the only one that I witnessed, and she was the only pregnant woman with whom I was in close contact. I testified that other detained women had "permission," to accompany the pregnant women. Viki explained to me that this "permission" wasn't all that explicit. How was it, Elisa? You always talked with them.

Elisa: You went in when the GREENS who were on duty at the time let you. At first it was terrible, but I think the security measures and isolation were relaxed over time. When I *fell*, the pregnant women were locked in a room. When they had to use the bathroom, they had to bang hard on the door from the inside so the guard would open it. It was impossible to speak with them. That was when María José was there, and the two Susanas: Silver de Reinhold and Pegoraro. I knew Susana Silver from the Law School. I saw her in the bathroom, and she told me that certain guards would let me go into the room. I wasn't able to do it while I was in Capucha, but it was easier once I started to spend time in the Fishbowl. Anyway, by

Above left: Elisa Tokar, working in the Foreign Ministry (supervised release, February 1979). *Above right*: Elisa with Miriam, on the occasion of Miriam's marriage to another kidnapping victim (supervised release, August 1979).

then there weren't any locks in the way, just a closed door. In other words, when I went to the bathroom, and the guards weren't looking, I'd always try to go in. I found that I needed to see them; they connected me to life, to tenderness, and they always kept going. They had incredible strength. They took any garment that came their way, and if it was wool, they'd unravel it and make it into clothes for their babies. That's how I met Laurita, Susanita's daughter; Federico, Liliana Pereyra's son; Juan, Alicia Alfonsín's son; and Sebastian, Pati de Rosenfeld's son.

Munú: A lot of babies were born in the ESMA. The two births while I was there happened in the Basement, but from what you say, they were upstairs before that.

Elisa: We were there at two different periods. Most of the pregnant girls I knew were upstairs on the Third Floor, others were in the Infirmary in the Basement, and they took Susana de Reinhold to the Naval Hospital for a caesarean.

Miriam: Were there medical clinics in any of the other buildings at the ESMA?

Munú: I don't know. When they brought in people who were wounded, they said they took them to the Naval Hospital, and when Liliana choked, that's where they took her too.

Liliana: How many babies do you think were born in the ESMA?

Miriam: Quica says that she witnessed seventeen births, and there must have been others that she didn't witness.

Munú: The pregnant women were the most horrifying part! It was the possibility of death delivering life!

Elisa: Now we are able to see it as the most horrifying part. At the time, going into the Pregnant Women's Room was like a balm. Entering that room after the tense atmosphere in the Fishbowl was like a caress. Despite the anguish that enveloped them, they seemed like a hymn to life, always doing things for the people in Capucha, for their children. They took bread crumbs and made all the pieces of a chess set, and when they found out that one of us was going on a *visit*, they'd send us embroidered figures to frame. More than once, even the GREENS went to ask them for some piece of handiwork to give to their girlfriends. The strength of those women was enviable.

7

Freedom and Beyond

> We emerged from the camp stripped, robbed, emptied out, disoriented—
> and it was a long time before we were able even to learn the ordinary
> language of freedom.
>
> —Jean Améry, *At the Mind's Limits:*
> Contemplations by a Survivor on Auschwitz and Its Realities

Freedom did not come to all the survivors in the same way. Many were forced
to remain in the country under supervision, working in places that were under
navy control, still subjugated. The control did not cease even when at last they
were able to go abroad. And most were stricken with guilt: "Why are we the
only ones who lived?"

Miriam: They let me out in January 1979.

Elisa: "Out" in quotation marks.

Miriam: Yes, supervised release. I had to work in RUGER's parents' home, just
a few blocks from the *chupadero!* They were no longer living there, and
RUGER let the house be used to relocate all the materials—books and
files—from the Fishbowl.

Munú: But you didn't have to go back to the ESMA to sleep—that was
important.

Elisa: That's for sure!

Munú: I started sleeping outside of the ESMA in early February 1979. You
were already doing that, Miriam. Almost everyone had left the Fishbowl,
except for fat Casildo, who was being punished and had been put in solitary somewhere else. There were new people in the Fishbowl.

Elisa: I started working at the Foreign Ministry in July 1978, after the World
Cup. Sometimes they took me to my house to sleep, and sometimes I had
to sleep in the ESMA. After a while, they didn't take me back there anymore. That must have been in October 1978.

Miriam: Who was at the Foreign Ministry?

Elisa: There were people from the *mini-staff*, but they didn't take us to sleep in
the ESMA at the same time. Sometimes they'd come for them, and other
times they'd come for me.

Munú: After they let me leave the country, for a long time I lived in fear that they'd come looking for me again, that they wouldn't leave me alone. They were like a ghost that kept pursuing me. And in fact, they made their presence felt more than once. They gave some of us tickets and visas to leave the country. People leaving the ESMA who had writs of habeas corpus pending had to sign a statement to the effect that they'd been off having fun somewhere for a period of time and that's why they hadn't turned up. Others had to write letters expressing repentance. Even though I had to keep on working with them, I wrote a letter of "gratitude" before I left the ESMA. It was part of my conscious or subconscious survival strategy.

Elisa: Was it actually a strategy, or is that how you see it now?

Munú: It was a strategy. It was one of the things I did to show that I was *recuperated*. Most of us who left the country sent back a postcard or letter saying, "We arrived fine. Everything is in order. Good-bye." It was like an ending; it was our way of making the break.

Miriam: New life.

Munú: Yes.

Miriam: Those of us who left the ESMA between the end of 1978 and the beginning of 1979, after MASSERA retired, were forced to sign a ridiculous statement saying that we'd turned ourselves in voluntarily—in the ESMA precisely!

Munú: That also took place. I left in February, but they didn't force me to sign.

Elisa: Me either.

Miriam: You had left a few months before.

Elisa: But I was still under supervised release, working with them.

Miriam: It's not really clear why they let some people leave the country and not others. At one time, we thought that the ones who left were in danger of being *sucked up* by another branch of the armed forces because of their status within the Montoneros Organization. Some had very well known surnames. But I don't know. Whether or not the TIGER made you stay ended up being as arbitrary as everything else. They let Liliana leave right away, and they made the rest of us stay here and work for different periods, longer for some of us than for others. It's baffling. And we had a hard time reestablishing ourselves, either in Argentina or abroad, after having lived through that inferno.

Munú: Our militancy was so intense, penetrating every instant, every place, every circumstance of our lives. Being without the militant organization left us disoriented. And you had to reestablish yourself, but out of defeat, out of the loss of the compañeros, out of tragedy.

All: It was impossible!

Adriana: I think the older compañeros had a harder time of it. Those of us who were younger had the chance to embark on something new—to study, to do something else. We were all broken, but being twenty wasn't the same as being forty.

Munú: You're right. I agree with what you're saying, and I also think that the compañeros who had children must have found it harder to keep going, even though they had an incentive of incalculable value, especially at the emotional level.

Elisa: It was hard for everyone to adapt, to face the reality of the times. I have friends who never went through the experience of being a disappeared person and yet they too were disappeared in a way, just by virtue of having remained in the country. They had been involved in the militant organization to varying degrees, and they had to change their whole life plan. The fear was such that JUP supporters left the university and people known for their trade union activities changed jobs.

Adriana: I remember that in 1979 and 1980, we got together a group of friends and set up phone trees to let each other know about cultural evenings that we were organizing. It was careless, but it was a carelessness that kept us alive. We would get ten people together, all friends or friends of friends, and we'd set up a movie club, cultural events, conferences, recitals. A lot of people went to them.

Cristina: We tried to connect people or groups doing interesting things with large groups of people that we assembled en masse, within the realm of what was possible in the moment. It was rare to find such opportunities at that time.

Adriana: One of the girls put together an Andean music group, and we promoted it.

Cristina: We even traveled together to different provinces.

Adriana: Then I went to Peru. When I returned in September 1980, I got together with the group again until I moved to the South in 1982. In part, that's what kept us alive; it connected us to others and to an activity that was militant in one way or another.

Cristina: We did what we could. During that period, getting together for a cultural evening meant a lot, and we'd end up playing the guitar until dawn. We all needed to be with others.

Adriana: I remember it as a magical time.

Munú: What do you mean by "magical"?

Adriana: That an atmosphere of solidarity, of affection, of equanimity was created.

Cristina: The group we were telling you about formed in 1979, when I was still under what we call the period of "supervised release," so I was involved only indirectly at that point. In February of 1980, I went to Santa Fe Province to finish my degree. I was trying to distance myself from the sadness I felt in Buenos Aires and above all from the constant threat that the marinos might ring my doorbell and take me away for interrogation, which had already happened. Ana and I had met inside, and we planned to go to her hometown. I spent six months living in her grandfather's house, her "Nono," a marvelous person I'll never forget. On Friday night, Ana and I, along with some of her sisters or friends, would go to a nearby town where there was a sort of general store, and we'd play guitar and sing with the people who went there. When I returned to Buenos Aires in the mid-eighties, we planned a trip to that town with the group that organized the cultural evenings. I remember there were seventeen of us, plus the young children of some of the compañeros in the group.

Adriana: All young couples with kids, and we'd all take care of them.

Miriam: There wasn't any more repression by then?

Cristina: Of course there was, but I think that the need to do something, to be together, was more powerful. Although there was certainly a degree of denial, we were always careful about certain details in order to avoid trouble. That's why we were very discreet at first, inviting people only by word of mouth. We sponsored activities with nongovernmental organizations, courses and workshops. We would show movies, which were followed by discussions. Once we invited one of the directors, and we put him in the audience just like any other spectator. Then, at the end of the discussion, we surprised everyone by introducing him. Later, since the activities were free, we even announced them in the newspaper *Clarín*.

Adriana: We got together with people who hadn't been *sucked up*, people who had been involved in the militant organization and had then gotten out.

Cristina: There were also younger people who had nowhere else to go to play a little guitar, have a discussion, or listen to a talk.

Adriana: Some people had been close but had never joined the militant organization. It was a combination of broken people and others who were more or less whole, and we were able to build a history together.

Munú: Miriam and Elisa, did you two also get together with people?

Miriam: We'd get together with Chiquitín, who had been with us in the ESMA, and with his friends, who'd been in prison. We had little kids, and we had a good time. We'd go to Elisa's house and make pizza, or we'd come to my house or go to Chiquitín's. We were a group of couples, all former militants, extremely frustrated, with no desire to do anything new. We were just trying to survive the moment.

Elisa: We were very focused on our relationships, the family.

Miriam: Elisa got pregnant right away, and so did I.

Elisa: I barricaded myself in my house. I felt that it was the only safe place on the entire planet. It wasn't easy to stay in Argentina. The memory of those who were no longer there was with you constantly, and it was compounded by the fear that reigned in the streets. I remember once, in 1981, I was driving in the car with Néstor and Ceci, who was just a few months old, and when we turned onto our block, we ran into a police operation involving fifteen to twenty armed men at the entrance to the building, which had only four occupied apartments. Immediately I thought about the pregnant women in the ESMA, about the chance that they could take Ceci away from me. The memory is still painful. Néstor dropped us off a couple blocks away and went back to see what was going on. The whole operation had to do with a neighbor who'd complained about the noise level. Only after Néstor came back to get us was I able to breathe again; the terror was still inside me. We didn't sleep at home that night.

Miriam: I left as soon as they gave me the passport, in April 1981. Juan, my eldest son, was already fifteen months old. I had wanted to leave as soon as I got pregnant, so I'd gone to talk to ABDALA. I explained to him that I was going to have a baby and that my aunt was waiting for me in New York, with a house and a job. I went into the ESMA to ask his permission to leave the country. I don't recall whether or not Roque was with me. We'd gotten married in August 1979, after asking ABDALA's permission for that too. Sometimes people ask me why I asked for his permission. We were so conscious of the fact that we were on supervised release that it never would have occurred to me to do anything without telling him. On my wedding day, we were celebrating at my parents' house when something sinister happened. The doorbell rang, and there was a gift for me: a combination vacuum cleaner and buffer from Admiral MASSERA. It was so weird! It fell apart almost immediately. It kept falling apart, and after a few months it didn't work at all.

Elisa: At least they didn't go to your wedding!

Miriam: ABDALA received me in Los Jorges, and he gave me a big speech. He said he knew that I had a new life and I was expecting a baby, and he gave me permission to leave. He said they'd go with me to get a passport. Fat JUAN CARLOS took me to the police to fill out the application, and two days later some compañeras who had been kidnapped in the ESMA gave a press conference in Europe.

Munú: And of course that gave rise to a period of uncertainty and fear, just as in 1979 when another group of compañeras gave the first testimony—in Paris, in the Parliament, I believe—about the horror they'd endured in the ESMA.

Miriam: Those of us who were still here were thrown into complete turmoil—total panic, telephone calls, speculation about reprisals. The specter of the marinos' reaction was always present: What would become of us, those of us who were still within their grasp? A lot of people were still inside. There was the specter of death and of *transfer*. Because of that, they retained my passport until April 1981. When I asked where it was, they said, "It's been misplaced," and when they finally gave it to me, it was the same passport that I'd originally applied for, dated the previous year.

Adriana: They'd held onto it themselves!

Munú: Because of those first testimonies given by the compañeras in Paris, ABDALA traveled the world looking for us in order to convince us not to make denunciations. I know they were in Europe trying to contact the people living there, but they didn't succeed. When I was in Venezuela, Diego called me at work one day. I was so happy; I thought he'd gotten out. We met, and he told me no, he was still with the marinos, and they intended to contact everyone who'd been in the ESMA and was living in Venezuela. Their assessment was that the testimonies had begun because the Montoneros Organization was pressuring us. They were there to support us and to tell us that we shouldn't be afraid of the Montoneros, because they would protect us. I couldn't believe what I was hearing! I was still capable of surprise! I told Diego that I wasn't going to meet with the marinos and that I wasn't going to give them the addresses of the other compañeros either. I also reiterated to him what he already knew—that I wasn't going to testify publicly as long as any kidnapped compañeros remained in the ESMA.

Miriam: And what happened?

Munú: I suppose that when I met with Diego, some marino was watching the whole thing. I went alone and took no precautions; apparently I hadn't learned my lesson. The next day, I met with the other compañeros and told them what had happened. We decided that they all needed to go along in solidarity with those who were still inside. We believed that any chance they might have to follow in our footsteps depended largely on our behavior. They made an appointment to meet with Diego, taking certain security precautions. Our political relationships were such that we could raise the alert in case they made any attempt to kidnap or put the squeeze on us. And the whole thing left us with the bitter feeling that the story continued even though we were in a different part of the world. And poor Diego had to go back with them.

Miriam: When did that happen?

Munú: I think it was in November 1979.

Elisa: Your story notwithstanding, Munú, it was very different for those who were able to extricate themselves from the marinos. The ones who couldn't—those of us who had to continue working with them—had to keep up the pretense. We had to hide from them the fact that we saw each other, that we met outside their control, which was strictly forbidden.

Munú: Who was still working with them at that point?

Miriam: Of our friends, not counting the *mini-staff*, Roque and Chiquitín worked at the daily *Convicción*, Elisa was in the Foreign Ministry, and I was in the Social Welfare Ministry. Anita, the Duke, and Co also worked there. It was constantly drilling inside your head! You wanted to break free, and you couldn't. They wouldn't give Roque and me the documents we needed to leave.

Liliana: In December 1978, they sent me to Chaco with my family. Then I went back to the ESMA for four or five days, and they sent me home again. I spent the holidays in Chaco, went back, and after January 8, I never returned again. I'm still very confused about this final period.

Elisa: And you were in there until when, Munú?

Munú: February 1979. They let me leave the country in July 1979. I was born—I left—in early February. In this case leaving and being born are the same thing.

Liliana: You emerged from the shadows.

Elisa: You had to stay in Buenos Aires.

Munú: Yes. The first few days of February, I went to live in an apartment on Ugarteche and Cabello, near the zoo. "Quite an area isn't it?" said the TIGER, and I didn't have the faintest idea, because I didn't know that it was a swanky locale.

Elisa: Had you rented a place there?

Munú: Yes, they rented a place for six months. They paid it all up front so they wouldn't have to put up any collateral. I lived there until July, working in their real estate company, and after that they let me leave. Bishop Grasselli[1] helped me get a visa to leave the country.

Miriam: You and others, right?

Munú: I know of some cases. The first time I saw him, the marinos took me to a place. I couldn't remember the address, but based on the description I gave afterward, I found out it was the Mater Dei Hospital.[2] Caggiano[3] was there; he was extremely ill, critical, and Grasselli was taking care of him. I remember crossing a courtyard and coming to some sort of a chapel. Grasselli was there in a room, and the sick man was behind the door. There we all were, a "jolly bunch." Grasselli welcomed me and started in with his views on how the army was worse than the navy.

Liliana: Why did Grasselli take care of the visas? I never understood that part of the story.

Miriam: He must have had connections with the embassies.

Munú: Maybe not all of them. All the cases I'm familiar with involved Venezuela. At that time, Venezuela had a lot of visa requirements. Grasselli got me a forty-five day visa to attend the Conference of Religious Women

---

1. Emilio Teodoro Grasselli was private secretary to Adolfo Tortolo, then vicar general of the armed forces. Grasselli's office was in the Stella Maris chapel in the Liberty building.

2. Mater Dei Hospital is a well-known, very exclusive private maternity hospital in the city of Buenos Aires.

3. Antonio Caggiano, cardinal primate of Argentina and former vicar general of the armed forces, died in 1979.

I-don't-know-what. In other words, he was sending me to a conference, a church event.

Liliana: He invented church-related activities.

Munú: I went twice to the Argentine Bishop's Conference, which is on Suipacha between Marcelo T. de Alvear and Santa Fe, to pick up the visa. The first time I went it wasn't ready and I had to go back again. Grasselli gave me a letter he'd written and signed with his own hand so that, once in Venezuela, I could go see a priest, somone called Nardi, who lived in a little town where the compañeros who had left the ESMA for Venezuela were living. I think everyone ended up seeing him.

Liliana: They went to see the priest referred to them by Grasselli?

Munú: Right, and the priest would help them find a job, get them settled. I told Grasselli that I didn't want to see anybody, that I needed to leave that history behind, and he wrote that in the letter. The priest, Nardi, read it, and the first thing he asked me was, "Do you want to see them?" "Of course," I said, and he took me to visit them. I had made up an elaborate story for the marinos. I told them I was going to marry my boyfriend in Australia. [*Laughter*]

Elisa: And they believed you?

Miriam: Did you want to go to Australia?

Munú: I wanted to go anywhere to get away. The story about the boyfriend just came to me, how I wanted to be with him and that's why I was going to go to Australia. It's not that I wanted to go, but it was a possibility.

Elisa: What boyfriend?

Munú: I'd had a boyfriend at the university, and he'd moved to Australia.

Elisa: And you wanted to go to him.

Munú: It's not that I wanted to, but it was to my advantage to say so. He was in Argentina a month before I left, and the marinos knew it. You had to give a reason for wanting to leave instead of continuing to work for MASSERA. So I made up the story of how I wanted to marry my former boyfriend and have a house with curtains and flowerpots. The truth was that I wanted to go anywhere! But the Australians denied my visa.

Elisa: How did you face the desperation? Did they tell you why they denied it?

Munú: No. In order to issue the visa—now all the irritation is coming out—they made me buy a round-trip ticket to and from Australia, which isn't cheap. Later, the marinos paid for my ticket to Venezuela, as they did for many others, out of a navy checking account, a fact that I included in my denunciation to CONADEP. They ended up covering my fare to Venezuela! How did they justify those fares? Anyway, I'll go on with the story about the Australian visa. I took everything to the consulate to apply for the visa, and it was denied—after I'd purchased the round-trip ticket!

They stamped my passport "visa denied." My mom went with me; I was
supposed to leave four days later.

Elisa: So what did you do?

Munú: I had to report that my passport was lost, because with that stamp
in it, it would have been hard to get another country to give me a visa. I
had to go through the whole process again with fat Juan Carlos at the
police headquarters and stay here for another month, with all that that
implied. That month was terrible for me. The marinos who had been our
kidnappers were being transferred outside the country, and different marinos were taking over in the ESMA. In fact, the one who let me leave was
Abdala, who had replaced the Tiger. This complicated my departure
tremendously, and they almost sent me back in there. The Tiger was still
around, and Mariano said that he didn't want me to spend a single day
in Argentina if he wasn't in the country.

Elisa: What did he mean by that—that they might come after you?

Munú: It seems that the Tiger wasn't very fond of me, and Mariano was
worried about it.

Miriam: Why do you say they almost sent you back in there?

Munú: Because the Tiger had told me that he would decide in September, or
sometime after that, whether or not I could leave. It was July and Abdala
was letting me leave. One day before I left, I asked to go to the ESMA to
say good-bye. I thought that kind of behavior would show them that the
recuperation had worked and they would keep things moving forward. I
wanted to go, but it was hard for me to leave the others behind. It was the
same as the time I couldn't leave La Plata. In the ESMA, Abdala gave me
a long speech, and I didn't know how to take some of the things he said.
"You live outside the ESMA, but you'll feel free only when the plane takes
off, when we don't know where you're sleeping. I love you much more than
you can ever love me, because I'm one of the people who killed your husband, your friends. The most I can be for you is the good enemy."

Elisa: He said those things to you?

Munú: Yes. Then I asked to go down to the Basement to say good-bye to the
compañeros. I was in Los Jorges, and when I started to walk down that
long, wide hallway, the Tiger appeared at the other end and started to
curse me out at the top of his lungs: "I knew that you were a bitch and
that you were going to shit on us!" and the like. I was petrified. An officer I
didn't know came out of an office and stood in front of me, placing himself
between me and the Tiger. He was huge, and at that moment I felt that
he was protecting me. The guy didn't say a word; he just stood there. The
Tiger lowered his voice, and with the sarcasm we all knew very well, he
turned the situation into a joke for my departure. It was pure horror. That
was the final proof that we were more than just the ESMA's *suck-ups*; we
were the property of one band or the other. The Tiger couldn't stand to

have someone else make decisions about us. We were his quota of power. Our lives were part of their internal struggles.

Elisa: What a story! They really could have left you inside. So you met Bishop Grasselli when you applied for the Venezuelan visa?

Munú: Yes, that's when they put me in touch with him.

Miriam: The marinos took you.

Munú: Only the first time. I went on my own after that.

Elisa: So when they denied the Australian visa, you decided that the curtains and flowerpots were in Venezuela.

Liliana: "Please," you said, "just send me anywhere!"

Munú: I told the marinos that they had denied the visa from Argentina to Australia because a lot of Argentine women had gone there and tried to stay, but I assured them that coming from a rich country like Venezuela—Venezuela was rich at the time—they wouldn't deny it. So I proposed a layover there, in order to continue on to Australia. I don't know whether anyone believed it, but they got me the visa.

Elisa: And you went to Venezuela.

Munú: They took me to see Bishop Grasselli. He talked to me about the army guys. He said they were stupider, more ignorant than the navy guys. He said they'd committed a lot more atrocities. He also told me that he'd helped some—I can't recall the word he used, whether he said subversives, guerrillas, terrorists, or what—who were just small fry, *perejiles*, and because they were *perejiles*, he'd helped them cross the river into Uruguay: "The same way that I denounced others because they were responsible for those who militated in the first place, I helped some, and I denounced others."

Liliana: How does one react to such a comment?

Elisa: "Exactly what are you saying to me, Bishop?"

Munú: It was so awful. I didn't know whether I should say yes or no—once more the "nothing" face. He was aware of everything that was happening, and he didn't even try to hide it. I think that a single misplaced gesture or word from me he would have told to the ESMA. It is incredible how some men of the church could act like that, and I'm sure they still do.

Elisa: I remember one day they took me from Capucha to the Basement, and going down the stairs I stumbled against a huge black cassock with a violet sash. I couldn't see much at the time because I had the *hood* pulled halfway down. But later, when I was in the Foreign Ministry, in comes Ne to introduce me to TIGER ACOSTA's first cousin, and there was the same cassock and the same violet sash I'd seen a few months before. I agree with you, Munú.

Cristina: We've sometimes wondered if we'd recognize the TIGER if we saw him now. In 1997 or 1998, I don't remember exactly, I ran into him in the subway. I couldn't believe it! I got on—I don't remember at which station, but I think it was Scalabrini Ortiz—to go to Callao. I didn't realize it right away, but something caught my eye, and I turned, and there he was with his back to me. The car was full of people; I saw his reflection in the windowpane of the door, and I couldn't stop staring at him. "It can't be!" I thought. I went crazy! How could he have been in the subway! I couldn't stand the suspense, so I moved back to get closer and to try to hear his voice.

Miriam: Which is unmistakable.

Cristina: He was chatting with another guy. I leaned back in order to hear better, and they stopped talking. I was in a completely altered state. I was thinking I couldn't get off without knowing for sure. I started to observe his gestures, to recall how he wrinkled his nose, and gradually I confirmed it. "What do I do?" I thought. We always talk about how they're free, but to see evil TIGER ACOSTA[4] right in the middle of our everyday life, on the way to work . . . At one point I moved back, I heard him, and it was the TIGER! I watched him from the side. If he'd seen me, I wouldn't have been able to refrain from saying something to him. I have to confess that I felt the screams in my throat, but I couldn't scream and alert the other passengers. I felt a mixture of nausea and terror. His hair was completely white. His face used to be more angular, but it had filled out.

Liliana: Like swollen? Bloated?

Cristina: With less tension in his expression. Wouldn't he be around seventy now?

Elisa: How old would you say he is now?

Miriam: He was thirty-eight years old when we were there.

Liliana: He was thirty-eight in 1978?

Miriam: Yes.

Liliana: He can't be so young still. How horrible! He's never going to die! To live, to coexist with TIGER ACOSTA for twenty years, thirty . . . !

Miriam: BLONDIE was twenty-seven.

Elisa: BLONDIE was younger. The TIGER was a lieutenant commander, so he had to have been forty.

Miriam: I ran into the TIGER three times and FEDERICO once.

Elisa: Is FEDERICO the one who followed you?

Miriam: In 1995 I was called on to be a poll officer for the presidential elections. Since I wasn't going to be able to be there, I had to go the courthouse with a letter of justification from my employer at the TV station.

---

4. JORGE EDUARDO ACOSTA was later arrested (1999) and charged with the theft of minors.

When I crossed Corrientes and got on Paraná, he appeared on the sidewalk in front of me. He started walking alongside me and invited me to have hot chocolate. "Do you remember me?" he said. "How's your family? Would you like some hot chocolate?" And I replied, "How could I not remember?" He went on, "Are you well? Is your family well?" At the time, he was working with Yabrán in a security agency near the courts.

Liliana: That guy was a terrible sadist.

Miriam: I remember that it was around the time of Scilingo's testimony, because I asked him when he was going to talk, and he said he would if he thought it would do any good. He'd take a microphone, and he'd talk for an hour and a half, but he didn't think it would do any good. I told him I thought it would do a lot of good, because there were still a lot of people who didn't know what had happened to their disappeared relatives. So he said it was an issue that should be discussed. And I answered, "What you people did is an outrage. I think they should open a Museum of Horror in the ESMA so everyone will know about the atrocities you committed." And he said no, it wasn't like that and, well, it would be best to sit down and discuss it over coffee.

Elisa: Mmm.

Miriam: By then I couldn't hold back the tears. I was becoming increasingly indignant, and I said, "Go sit down with someone else, because I'm not about to sit down and drink coffee with any of you people." And I left crying tears of rage. I saw the TIGER in 1991, during one of the marches against the pardon. I was with the marchers from Plaza Congreso. We got to the corner of Corrientes and Callao, and when we turned onto Corrientes, I split off and continued on alone down Rodríguez Peña toward Lavalle, because I had to go to Radio Splendid. The march was just a block away. When I got to the corner of Rodríguez Peña and Lavalle, I glanced into a bar and I saw, sitting at a table, three guys and the back of a neck. "That's the TIGER!" I thought. I stood there looking in the window, and right at that moment he turned around and saw me. It drove me into a state of total confusion; I didn't know where to turn. I was thinking to myself, "Where am I? What do I do? Where should I go?" It didn't for one minute cross my mind to yell, to call to him, "Torturer, murderer." I thought people would be indifferent; they'd think I was crazy.

Liliana: He saw you.

Miriam: It took me about five seconds to react, and I left. When I went to bed that night, my teeth were chattering; I was grinding them, I was trembling, and I had a nightmare: I was with a beautiful baby. I was changing his diaper, and the baby cried and cried, and when I opened his diaper, he'd been castrated!

Elisa: Oh! No!

Miriam: It was the worst nightmare I'd ever had in my life; it symbolized the impotence I felt at that moment. I saw him again walking down the sidewalk of San Martín theater, with a cell phone, wearing a suit, accompanied by a woman wearing a silk dress, who looked like an executive. Another time, on a Sunday, I was taking the kids to the movies, and a gray car stopped at a traffic light at the corner of Rodríguez Peña and Corrientes. I looked at the driver, and it was the TIGER. And there I was with the kids! I felt repugnance; it was like a sacrilege to run into him, a man who was death, when I was there with my kids, who were life. Fortunately, I never saw him again after that.

Liliana: Once I had to put up with FEDERICO sitting right next to me in the subway.

Miriam: And did he speak to you?

Liliana: Of course!

Cristina: Oh, Liliana, please!

Liliana: It was in March or April 1985.

Elisa: Shortly after you came back?

Liliana: Right, and the trial of the juntas was starting.

Cristina: God!

Liliana: He saw me, and he came over and sat down. He started chatting with me as if we'd both worked together at the Nation's Bank, like someone who runs into an old friend and starts asking about her life: Had I finally married Tano? Did we have any kids? Were they loud as he'd said they'd be, since they were Italians? It was awful. The whole way—from one subway station to the next one, where I got off—he was sitting there beside me chatting, and I was just looking at him.

Miriam: It's revolting to run into those people, to share physical space with them.

Elisa: Did you feel intimidated by them?

Liliana: I don't know. I wasn't scared at all. I was paralyzed but not with fear.

Elisa: The only encounter I had was in 1981, and it was no coincidence. The marinos had sent me to work in the Foreign Ministry. After that, the air force people came in, and I was still working there, totally disconnected from the world, as if it were a regular job. Then, after I had my daughter, I stopped working. One day, I went out to do some shopping, and all of a sudden PACO and FRAGOTE appeared from the opposite direction. They started asking me questions about my life. They knew that I had a daughter and that my father had died. So I thought, "They've been following me." It was terrifying! I asked them how they knew, and they said they'd gone to my dad's store—they'd already known where it was, because they'd taken me there on one of the *outings*—and they'd found out. It was an unlikely story, because my mom would have told me if someone had gone there looking for me. I felt that I was being pursued. They knew everything that had happened to me! Even though I never saw them and had no ties, they knew the most important things that had happened to me, and besides they knew where I lived. It clearly was not a chance encounter.

Cristina: They called me on the telephone in 1985.

Elisa: No!

Cristina: On January 8, 1985, at two o'clock in the morning.

Elisa: Who called you?

Cristina: I don't know; it was an anonymous phone call. The trial of the juntas was approaching, and I was working for SERPAJ[5] and with the Student Center at the university. I had an episode, an attack that I can't explain. Once again I had that horrible feeling that I represented a danger to everyone who knew me. It sounded to me like MARIANO's voice. He said that I was a loudmouth and that they weren't going to let me live any longer; they were going to kill my whole family. Putting two and two together, I figured that the intimidating phone call was because of the upcoming trial.

Miriam: It must have been.

Cristina: They didn't make it sound like reprisal for something I might do in the future; it was more like a warning of what was to come because of what I had supposedly already done.

Miriam: The marinos brought a lawsuit against me twice, once in 1985 and again in 1987. In one, the Guzzetti[6] case for the attempted first-degree murder of the vice minister of foreign affairs, in an anonymous letter shoved under the door of Judge Fernando Archimbal's courtroom, they accused me of having participated in the attack, even though they knew very well that it was a lie. They knew who was really involved, because they had killed that woman in the ESMA. One of the witnesses was none other than ABDALA's wife. And naturally she accused me! When I went to testify in court, and they showed me a file full of photographs of people. I had to say whether or not I knew them. Supposedly, the file included photographs of the people involved in the attack. I knew only one person. She was a friend of mine in the United States, an Argentine woman who had lived in Brooklyn with her husband since 1976. When Roque and I were in exile in the United States, she'd come over to the house often, we'd go to her house, or we'd go out together. And her photograph was among the twenty or thirty there—the photograph from her police-issue ID card! So I was thinking, "The marinos followed me; they were keeping track of who I saw in New York, and that's why this photo is in here. This photo is a message: 'We've been following you all these years. We've never stopped watching you.'" They must have taken all kinds of measures because of the

---

5. SERPAJ, the Peace and Justice Service, is a human rights organization.

6. The vice minister of foreign affairs was a naval officer who was seriously wounded in a Montoneros operation.

trial of the juntas. They prepared entire dossiers on some of the witnesses who testified. In my case, since I didn't have a real police record, they concocted one for me. They called Cristina on the telephone. They must have been working intensely to block the testimonies.

Adriana: They also filed a lawsuit against me in 1987, just before the Punto Final law, and it automatically resulted in an arrest warrant. I was pregnant, and my parents didn't know whether or not to tell me. As soon as Manuel was born, I went to Buenos Aires with my two children to have the warrant rescinded in the San Isidro court. They knew it was trumped up. After several years, in October 1989, they exonerated me of all charges against me in that case, which had already been dismissed. But later on, in the nineties, they wouldn't give me a passport, because the arrest warrant was still pending at the federal level. This story is never going to end.

Miriam: That was the second lawsuit they brought against me. We were both on the list! They accused us of kidnapping a businessman. In a letter— also anonymous, of course—they denounced thirty-two people to Judge Alberto Piotti. Twenty-five of them were disappeared—in other words, dead—and the rest were almost all survivors of the ESMA! The first time they filed suit was to keep me from testifying at the trial of the juntas. The second was perhaps an act of reprisal for having done it anyway.

Munú: I returned to Argentina for the first time in 1984, and I gave my testimony to CONADEP. I'd come for only twenty days, and when I wanted to leave, the police wouldn't give me back my passport. They said it had been misplaced, and they sent me back and forth from one office to another. When I went back with a congressman, it suddenly reappeared. This happened to me every time I renewed my passport, up until just a few years ago.

Miriam: Most of us have that problem with our passports. I got used to it after a while! At first I took lawyers from the human rights groups with me when I went to get it. After that I started going on my own.

Elisa: When compañeros who had been disappeared would come up to me after I was released and say they were going to make a denunciation, I didn't want to hear anything about it. I didn't want to listen, or see, or hear, or even think about it. I preferred to keep on pretending that nothing had happened to me.

Miriam: I was consumed with guilt—guilt over being alive, over having survived. Being an ESMA survivor isn't the cause of the guilt over being alive, but it exacerbates it. I think all of us who were involved in the militant organization are dragging around the general guilt that the others are dead. Besides, each person has his or her own individual guilt for various reasons: for leaving, for getting away, for suggesting that a friend join the militant organization. I thought I'd never be worthy of participating in a grassroots movement again, because I felt so guilty for having worked for the navy. I couldn't acknowledge that I had been kidnapped, that it was slave labor.

Liliana: Right.

Miriam: I thought I wouldn't even be able to join a homeowners' association, for example.

Liliana: It's a feeling of being broken off from the world, of being left on the other side.

Miriam: I thought, "I am unworthy to sign the minutes of a homeowners' meeting. Who am I to testify against the marinos when I worked in the ESMA?" I couldn't. I couldn't stand the guilt. I remember when Viki wrote me from Madrid, in 1982 or 1983, when CONADEP began its work. I had started to give testimony with great difficulty. Viki sent me a thirteen-page letter about why I shouldn't feel guilty and why it was important that I give testimony. And I argued with her. "But no, I should have died. I should have taken the cyanide *pill*. They took it out of my mouth and from then on—"

Liliana: None of it should have happened.

Miriam: From then on, everything I did was wrong. I shouldn't have even flipped on a light switch in the ESMA. It was a terrible feeling of unworthiness.

Elisa: Were you able to overcome it?

Miriam: Yes.

Elisa: I keep on dealing with the guilt as best I can.

Liliana: You keep going in circles with it. It comes and goes.

Elisa: It's always there. I can't contain it.

Liliana: What happens is that since you're able to recognize it, you just keep dealing with it. I remember a feeling of encapsulation. When they'd take me out or take me to see my family, I'd see the people in the streets, or I might run into someone I knew, and it was as if there was a glass wall between us.

Elisa: Between your friends and you?

Cristina: Or between you and anyone on the outside?

Liliana: Between me and anyone else, except for my family. I had a different kind of bond with them, which enabled me to endure it better. I had a feeling of estrangement from everyone else that lasted for a long time. I remember that in Italy, for instance, the few times it occurred to me to participate in a march where exiles would get together to protest something that had happened in Nicaragua or El Salvador, or the pacifist mobilizations, I felt ashamed!

Elisa: Did that happen to you too, Cristina?

Cristina: Yes. It still does; it isn't as strong as before, but I feel it. At first, I felt that I couldn't go the marches organized by the Mothers of the Disappeared. I couldn't assimilate the slogan of bringing them back alive, because it reminded me that I knew it was impossible. I didn't have a place there; I felt strange because I knew and I was alive. I couldn't testify in CONADEP, I guess because I was overwhelmed with guilt. At the trial of the juntas I went to the courts, and I told them everything I knew, thinking that some piece of information I had might contribute some new element. I talked to Strassera about the 1,000 Cases, a matter that seemed to interest him. But I couldn't give formal testimony. I was only able to ask that they let me know if there was some piece of information that required my testimony in order to accuse an oppressor, because that was my limit and in that case I would have testified no matter what. I was overcome with shame even more so after I wasn't able to testify on that occasion. Those feelings, however, never kept me from participating in any social or political activity, which I did from the moment I left the ESMA, despite the marinos' prohibition and their subsequent threats. But I was totally blocked on the issue of human rights. It wasn't until a few years ago that I was able to start working specifically on human rights and to testify publicly about what I knew and had experienced.

Liliana: Now I've entered a new phase, although I think it's actually the same one in disguise: now I'm in an "it isn't worth protesting anything" mood. I have a feeling of—

Elisa: Indifference, skepticism.

Liliana: Yes, skepticism. I think what I did was mask the unworthiness with skepticism, which, underneath it all, is really more of the same. And I realize that it's more of the same, because what's happening to me is an illusion. It has a high cost. It isn't that I'm indifferent.

Cristina: Or that it doesn't faze you.

Liliana: Right, I act like that and then I kick myself, which means it isn't really like that. In Europe I couldn't do a thing—not a thing!—and it was because of that feeling of unworthiness that stays with you, that asking yourself why they let you live. Instead of leaving you in that condition, it would've been better if they'd killed you and solved your problem once and for all. Those bastards schedule your torture to last until you're eighty years old!

Elisa: My first reaction was to hide in my house. I didn't work. I almost never went out, and when I did go out, it was always with a very limited group of people. I started to realize what was happening to me around the time of the trial of the juntas.

Liliana: The trial was very hard on everybody.

Elisa: To me it meant facing up to the fact that I couldn't testify. I just couldn't. I couldn't.

Liliana: And those around you didn't help much either.

Elisa: No, not at all.

Liliana: Neither the people who'd never gotten involved nor the world of the militant organization. No one took care of us. That's the feeling I have, that no one took care of us.

Elisa: We were all in a bad way. It wasn't that you expected someone to come and persuade you, but I needed a letter, as you said, Miriam, or someone to talk to me. The trial opened my eyes. I began to realize that this wasn't my life, so I asked for help, and I was able to start living in a different way. I started to recognize that I was still a victim and that there was an enemy, a victimizer. Even now, these are still just words, in part because underneath I still find guilty attitudes in myself. I think some people found that testifying in CONADEP was a relief: a before and an after. I don't know whether that was your experience, Miriam, or whether you were able to make the break before that.

Miriam: I felt calmer after I testified to CONADEP in New York. Maybe people who were exiled in places like Spain or Mexico and kept in touch with other survivors were able to talk more about what had happened to them.

Elisa: That's what I think, and that's why I found it strange the other day when Munú was saying that in Venezuela they didn't talk about it, about how it had been for them, how they felt. I thought that if I had left the country, maybe I would have understood it all better.

Liliana: I felt relieved only after I finally was able to testify and tell everything I knew. It was only then that I freed myself, when I started to feel that I had finally committed.

Elisa: It happened to me when I testified at the CELS[7] and again about ten years ago, when we wrote an article about the pregnant women, which was published in the newspapers. I needed for my name to appear, to begin to reconnect with life through a testimony. The first thing I did when I left the ESMA was to look for people associated with kidnapping victims I knew had been *transferred* and tell them that they were gone. I was always terribly afraid when I did it. When I left to meet with Mrs. de Fidalgo,[8] I fell apart, and I couldn't keep the appointment. I composed myself afterward, but it was incredibly hard. This lasted a long time, and I think it still isn't really clear to us that we were victims.

Liliana: No, and not to society either!

Elisa: Two Sundays ago I ran into a compañero from the militant organization, someone I hadn't seen in twenty-one years. The first thing he did was whitewash his image and tell me all about how he'd behaved like a real

---

7. The CELS, or Center for Legal and Social Studies, is a human rights organization.

8. Mrs. de Fidalgo was the mother of a young disappeared woman who had been kidnapped by the navy.

militant and how he hadn't *sung* about anybody. I just stood there staring at him, and I was thinking, "What is he saying to me? How can he come to me with a militant explanation after all that's happened?" Guilt is a recurring theme. It seems as if, because I'm alive, I carry the weight of all the dead on my back. You carry them with you; they are in your soul.

Cristina: I want to be very honest, even if it means exposing my human limitations. One of them has been my inability to place myself squarely in the position of a victim, by virtue of having been "chosen" by an officer who, after demonstrating that he was capable of torturing and murdering an infinite number of times, decided not to continue torturing me or pressuring me to go out and *mark* compañeros, after a couple of attempts at which I returned in a deplorable state. An escape valve built into the repressive system itself? An opportunity to cleanse one's guilt? A sophistication of discipline? I don't know, but I can't deny that it happened and that it weighs on me.

Munú: I've never been able to do something with my life without explaining my past. When I got to Venezuela, I said, "I come from such and such a place, and I want to talk to people from the militant organization." And I spent the whole next night talking about who I was, my behavior, what I had done and not done. There were a lot of Argentines where I worked, but I didn't relate to any of them. At one point, some Venezuelan friends told me that the Argentines wanted to publish a communiqué in the newspaper denouncing us as navy intelligence agents. I remembered that the marinos in the ESMA had told us that would happen.

Miriam: They wanted to do that?

Munú: Yes. So I went to the little town where the other compañeros were living to tell them. They had been there longer, and they told me that the same thing had happened before and only time would prove us in the right. They said that with time we'd stop being perceived as the bad guys.

Adriana: But not completely.

Munú: After that, every time I met an Argentine who acted friendly toward me, the first thing I'd say to him was, "You invite me to your home because you don't know who I am." Once, one of them said to me, "What exactly is it you think I don't know about you?" and he told me my own story. He knew as much as I did. He asked himself, "Could the forty of us here in Venezuela who are trying to do something to promote democratization in Argentina be so important that the navy would assign us six intelligence agents? I doubt it." After a few months, they apologized to me for what they had said. But it wasn't until 1982, during the Malvinas conflict, that for the first time they invited me to participate in the meetings of Argentine exiles. And then there was a complete turnaround; they were seized with remorse, guilt. Everything that happened to us happened because we stayed in Argentina. And the ones who had left, instead of helping us, kept on kicking us.

Liliana: We are moved and mobilized—not only because we are moved by these conversations but also because Judge [Baltasar] Garzón's trial in Spain for the Spanish citizens who disappeared in Argentina and the trial over the stolen minors here mean that our kidnappers are closer than ever to prison and these issues are being covered by the media and discussed by people in the street every day.

Elisa: It's a permanent fixture of everyday life.

Liliana: So let's really be moved!

Miriam: Let's forge ahead. It doesn't make sense to try to protect ourselves from the shock.

Elisa: I think it's no coincidence that we chose this moment to start having these conversations.

Liliana: Evidently we've reached a stage at which there is a powerful need to talk.

Munú: I think most people are at the same stage.

Liliana: Maybe not most people.

Munú: The passing of time has made it possible. A process has taken place that enables people to have a different perspective. Now they dare to ask, to open themselves up, to try to understand how it was. Before they would say, "How terrible! How terrible!" and that's as far as the investigation went.

Elisa: It's a very special time for those of us who shared this history. There is a collective mobilization. A huge number of people went to the meeting convened by the Association of Former Detainees-Disappeared.[9] Judging from how they talked, it was clearly the first time in twenty years that some of them had met with other people with whom they shared a common history. I still say it has a lot to do with the trial in Spain.

Munú: It isn't happening only to those of us who spent time in the camps or to friends or relatives of the detained-disappeared. I observe a generalized awareness, another way for the general public to hear about the issue. During the trial of the juntas in 1985, it was all still so close, and there was still a lot of fear. Right now the press is reporting that those guys were also thieves. They're not saying only that they destroyed us or tortured us. Although there are still people who say, "Well the guerrillas killed people

---

9. The Association of Former Detainees-Disappeared is an organization of people who were kidnapped by repressive forces during the dictatorship. The meeting mentioned was held in early 1999.

too, and if the military hadn't stepped in to stop them . . ." But it turns out that not only did they kidnap and murder; they also stole. This weighs on people, as does the subject of the kids. They are child stealers!

Liliana: They were the lowest of the low.

Munú: Twenty years ago, democracy arrived just as the lid was starting to come off the pot. Lots of things happened; there was a flood of information. I don't know whether or not people believed that the stories we told at the trial of the juntas were true.

Elisa: And you're saying that people couldn't see because so little time had passed?

Munú: It's just that you sat there and said so many things that the listener probably thought, "How could all that be true?"

Liliana: Sort of like a defense mechanism because they couldn't bear the guilt. They probably felt guilty for not having realized what was happening at the time.

Elisa: That's very true. They closed the door. They didn't want to know any more.

Cristina: I also think you had to surmount the barrier of horror. When so many blood-curdling testimonies started to become public, it seemed incredible; it was very hard to process it all. One day in 1983, a colleague at the university—without knowing my history, which was very hard for me to share at that time—said to me, out of the blue and very upset, that she felt terrible when she started finding out what had happened during the dictatorship. She said she couldn't understand how she could have lived all those years without realizing what was going on around her.

Munú: Of course. Now it's discussed in a different way. People talk about the babies, about the search for the children who were born in captivity or stolen during the kidnapping. It seems to me that now no one doubts the truth of what we were saying years ago. Only now is there a generalized consciousness, the possibility to believe.

～

Elisa: How are you all affected by the arrests in the trial for the systematic stealing of babies? How do you feel about fat Jungle's arrest?

Miriam: Happy. I'm delighted!

Elisa: I guess I've been gradually toning down the volume. I was much more excited about the arrest of Videla or Massera than about fat Jungle and not because I think he's any less culpable than the others. I still haven't read much about his arrest. The newspapers barely paid any attention to it. I've only just realized that he's really in custody. What has been exciting for me personally is that I feel that I've settled an account with history. When I read my name in the newspaper, I felt as though I truly "appeared."

Miriam: You reappeared!

Elisa: Right. It was very exciting for me to be able to testify at the trial over the stolen babies and have my name figure as one of the direct accusers. In a way, it helped me settle a debt I owed for having been unable to testify at the trial of the juntas. At that time, when the prosecutors summoned me, I went to talk to them immersed in anguish. I felt as though I couldn't recreate the story; I couldn't remember anything.

Munú: A lot of people weren't able to testify at that time.

Adriana: Society expects you to feel better than everyone else about the arrests that are happening now. People familiar with the history will call you up and say, "Isn't it great!" It's sort of like they're congratulating you.

Miriam: Yes. That happened to me.

Adriana: It's a way of showing solidarity and reminding you that you have a lot more stake in it than everyone else. According to the political analysts, this would be the positive side of globalization, in the sense that now that those murderers are no longer useful to the system, it discards them, knowing that if more are needed, they can be found. Oftentimes the things that happen, seen through the lens of history, have causes or determining factors that aren't exactly what one would like from an ethical standpoint. There's probably a lot more negotiation going on than justice per se. On the other hand, it's still a real blow.

Munú: The trials of the juntas were held in 1985. When they tried to prosecute anyone other than the commanders, there was a military uprising that led to the Due Obedience and Punto Final decrees. They rose up here; they rose up there. Democracy trembled supposedly. Now they are arresting them, and the armed forces, unwilling or unable to do otherwise, are letting it happen. Like any institution that belongs to a system, it moves ahead with those who serve its purpose, and when they are no longer useful, it abandons them. That's why [Augusto] Pinochet and MASSERA can be imprisoned today, which isn't to say that tomorrow other men won't take power and repress with the same savagery. Those guys aren't useful to them anymore. They have a bad public image. In any event, it means a lot to us that they are in prison.

Elisa: You feel better knowing that you won't run into them in the street.

Adriana: Things have changed, Munú! Historical cycles are different from people's individual life cycles. What was good during a particular period suddenly isn't good anymore. If you mentioned Che Guevara in the seventies, they disappeared you. But now Diego Maradona[10] can lift up his shirt and show off his Che Guevara tattoo and say it's a patriotic symbol, and nothing happens to him!

Munú: Sure.

Adriana: When I testified at the federal court, the judge asked me why I

---

10. Diego Maradona is a famous Argentine soccer player.

hadn't testified before, and I told her that it wasn't only because I distrusted the justice system but also because of guilt. It's a very complicated subject: the guilt over being alive, the fear that they'll point you out in the street and say, "If you're alive, there must be a reason! Who did you inform on? Who did you betray?" There's the fear that some mothers, when they see you, will accuse you of being alive when their children are not. You're a bearer of life when so many people are dead. You're the image of possible betrayal, even though you know intimately what really happened. Had I testified at the trial of the juntas, I would have had to say that I was a militant, but I was afraid they'd end up prosecuting me for illicit association, as they did during the dictatorship.

Elisa: To me, not testifying was an outstanding debt that I have now paid. The guilt went around and around in my head when I couldn't tell how they tortured me, which compañeros I had seen and in what conditions. I was carrying it all on my back and had no way to communicate it. When we *fell*, we had a history, a life experience, and we reacted accordingly and as best we could. But the people on the outside also collaborate in heaping guilt on us.

Munú: The "if they took them away, there must be a reason" in the time of the dictatorship, and the "if she's alive, there must be a reason" afterward have a lot in common.

Adriana: I also told the judge that, and it made a strong impression on her. She asked me how the breaking-down mechanism worked inside, and I explained how it felt when you didn't know whether a compañero was still a compañero or whether he had stopped being trustworthy and how demoralizing that disjunction was. If you made a mistake, the error could be very costly. Once, in Capucha, a kidnapped compañero told me something I'll never forget, "I don't want to leave here alive, because my father will be so ashamed: I'm the idol, the son who sacrifices himself for a just cause. How can I go back?" In other words, it was all or nothing for us, life or death. And all of a sudden, we have to rediscover life.

Munú: I feel the guilt of being alive while the others are dead. Who doesn't? Raise your hand if you don't! But I began to feel that guilt long before I *fell* in the ESMA. I've been dragging it around ever since people started to die, and it didn't end when they stopped dying! But besides the guilt, there are other people's suspicions, which I think will always hang over the survivors.

Elisa: It will last forever.

Munú: I would pose a question to every single person who is suspicious: Do you know who provided information to try to find the kidnapped children? What did they use to build parts of the legal cases? They used the testimony of the survivors, "traitors and suspects all!" We go, we put our bodies on the line every time we relive that story, and we testify; it hurts, but it does us good. And now MASSERA and JUNGLE are going to end up in jail! And why? In large part because we survivors keep on going in and testifying. And when we leave the courts, some of the people who should be right there beside us still say we are suspect. If we'd all been erased, I wonder what history could have been reconstructed; probably part of it would have come out but much less than what is actually known. We are suspect for being alive.

Adriana: It's very perverse.

Munú: One way or another we are still putting ourselves on the line, out of our need to speak for the thousands who aren't here, to help people understand how it was—and our desire to break chairs over heads! A while ago, when I was offered the opportunity to meet one of the oppressors face to face, I said I wasn't going to be able to talk to that guy, because I would break a chair over his head, and then to top it off they'd prosecute me for his injuries!

Adriana: The people who knew us from before don't have that suspicious attitude. I worked in the Neuquén province for ten years. In October 1989, when the local paper published a full-page story about my rejecting the pardon, some of my colleagues came up to me and said, "It's a good thing I didn't know about your past before, because I would have been very biased, and I probably wouldn't have given you the time of day. But now I see things differently." These are normal, everyday people who suddenly start to reflect on their own biases.

Munú: Getting back to what we were talking about before, MASSERA's arrest in the case of the babies stirred up a lot of very powerful things in me. I was happy about it, but I was also very distressed. I saw his face, and somehow it put me right back inside the ESMA. The next day, when Pinochet was arrested in London, I was so happy that one would think it was Pinochet who had kidnapped me instead of MASSERA.

Adriana: The Pinochet matter is a political happiness, but with MASSERA it's visceral. It happened to us; it's something else altogether.

Cristina: I was euphoric the day Pinochet was trashed in the newspaper for what he really was and is, a genocidal dictator who should pay for his crimes. In the case of MASSERA and his henchmen, of course I think they should spend the rest of their days removed from the society upon which they inflicted so much harm. But for a long time, my having been part of that history, and being alive, created internal contradictions relating to the guilt of having lived side by side with those individuals and having survived.

Adriana: No one can comprehend the relationship that existed between them and us, when they tortured and subjugated us and at the same time took us out to eat or on a boat trip on the Paraná Miní River[11] in El Tigre, when they told us that they wanted to separate from their wives or confessed to us that they wanted to leave the navy but they didn't know how to wash dishes or make their beds and they'd never be able to get any other job because they were completely useless and their life was laid out for them. Those same people, the enemy, are people you lived with one way or the other, involuntarily, of course. That discourse suddenly makes them more human within the perversity, the sickness of it all. The same perversity that was inside that place, with all those nuances that didn't exist anywhere else, is reverberating here on the outside and especially now, when they are being sent to prison.

Miriam: That doesn't happen to me. I don't feel any sort of contradiction. And although I wouldn't give them the death penalty (as a lot of people would), I think they have to pay for what they did. They spilled too much blood, even if they did decide that I would live.

Cristina: No one is saying otherwise!

Munú: Of course not! There's no contradiction there.

Miriam: I am absolutely delighted to see them behind bars! I am convinced that the TIGER must be imprisoned.

All: We all think that!

Miriam: The PUMA, MARIANO, RUGER, GERÓNIMO, HUNCHBACK, FEDERICO—all of them.

Elisa: I feel a little bit like Munú was describing. I feel happy and distressed at the same time. Intellectually, I'm happy that he's in jail, but I'm also deeply distressed at having been part of that history and at the fact that this history of kidnapping, death, and disappearances happened here, in our country—at having been a witness to so much horror.

Munú: It's very complex. No one is denying that those people have to be jailed; otherwise we wouldn't have testified. But there are other things at play as well. You believe you're alive because some people made that decision. They had a part in the deaths of a lot of people but also in your being alive. They're just like COLORS, or JULIAN THE TURK, or any of the other ones I never met, but they had a face, a voice; there was a relationship; they took us to our houses. So my joy over the arrest is intermingled with my distress when I relive the story every time I see one of them.

Adriana: That's the issue!

Munú: Another situation that gives me a strange feeling is the issue of persecution. Those guys have to go and testify, and I'm sure they're afraid, so they're ending up in the position we were in, of being afraid of what might happen to them. Without the fear of death, obviously. At some level, I probably recreate my own experience.

---

11. The Paraná Miní River is a river used widely for recreational purposes.

Miriam: It gives me a sense of immense satisfaction to imagine the Tiger, that murderer, terrified and in a state of alert!

Cristina: Trying to escape! Did you see that wily, psychopathic grin in the photograph?

Munú: They haven't changed. I hope they've never had a peaceful night's sleep!

Miriam: Don't even doubt for a minute that they slept like little angels. I don't think they feel any remorse, at least he doesn't.

Adriana: They cannot be among us!

Elisa: There should be no possibility of running into them anywhere.

Adriana: Of being exposed to having it all stirred up for you again.

Miriam: How have you all been affected by Magdalena Ruiz Guiñazú's[12] documentary on the ESMA and in general the fact that this issue is so prevalent in the media right now? There are moments when I get tired of it, when I feel mentally drained.

Elisa: It raises expectations in me. Maybe because it's a story that I'm reliving now.

Munú: I have conflicting feelings: the feeling of constantly reliving everything; the feeling of being under constant scrutiny, exposed, and not just when it's one of us but also when the others appear on the air, the Tiger Acostas, the Marianos, and the rest. They're all there in my memories of the ESMA, the compañeros and the marinos. I think it made a difference that we didn't just throw up our hands, and I also have a sensation of risk. I think it's good that the issue isn't forgotten. Now people are more capable of understanding, because at the time of the trial of the juntas, it was impossible to digest such a torrent of information. There were days and days of taking in horrible, unbearable information.

Elisa: Now people pick certain things and talk about them, analyze them, and are able to process them, but one at a time—before it was all at once. The attention is still focused on things that were said a long time ago; people still haven't assimilated them.

Munú: The same thing happens to all of us with these issues! Even we forget things we knew before! Other people aren't the only ones who've developed defense mechanisms against the horror. There comes a point when it's just impossible to absorb any more. That's why I always try to put myself in the place of people who stayed in Argentina.

Elisa: They'd enjoyed the World Cup, democracy was returning, a climate of

---

12. Magdalena Ruiz Guiñazú, an Argentine journalist who was a member of CONADEP, produced a documentary entitled "ESMA, the Day of the Trial," which was aired on television and was viewed by a large audience.

peace was needed, and suddenly some clown sits down in front of them and starts talking about torture and death.

Munú: Sometimes I feel that it's harder for me to talk now than before. It comes out of a different part of me; it's more painful.

Miriam: I think there's a phenomenon in which one "pulls down the shade." For example, during the trial of the juntas, when my mom read my testimony, she said, "But you never told me they tortured you."

Elisa: "No, I was out dancing, Mommy!"

Miriam: And I said, "Yes, I did tell you!" but she kept insisting that I hadn't. She had the typical reaction of someone who can't bear something and therefore refuses to listen and pulls down the shade.

Munú: I think your mom's reaction was typical.

Miriam: And besides, there was a saturation effect in the eighties—too many testimonies, too much horror! People couldn't; they just couldn't.

Elisa: I'm wondering what it was like for you all recently when you went to testify in this case of the stolen babies. I saw their surprise at what I was saying, their gestures, as if I was telling them something they didn't know.

Miriam: I was alone with the guys at the court, and they asked me questions as if for the first time, as if I were back in CONADEP. They asked me for descriptions of the ESMA, its internal workings. I had to check the calendar to see if we were in 1984 or 1998. At one point, when they asked me to draw a map of the ESMA, I said: "I'll do it, but it's going to take several days if I have to tell you everything. I thought I was here only to testify about the babies who were born there." So I suggested that they read the trial of the juntas, since everything was laid out there in detail. They hadn't even looked at it!

Elisa: They're thirty-year-old kids who were fifteen when all this happened.

Munú: But they're investigating the minors stolen during the dictatorship . . . !

Miriam: Judge [Luisa] Riva Aramayo, who was in charge of the proceedings for the reconstruction of the historical truth,[13] confessed to me that she'd tried on several occasions to read the trial of the juntas and had to stop because it upset her too much; it overwhelmed her. I remember thinking, "Oh my God, she gets overwhelmed and doesn't read the mother of all cases." And if she doesn't read it because it upsets her . . .

Munú: Presumably, she'll take her time and read it.

Miriam: All of this exhausts me. I'm tired, not because I think the oppressors should be left in peace. To the contrary, I'm exhausted by the incessant public debate over this issue, which should be resolved by now. In 1987,

---

13. The reconstruction of the historical truth was an investigation launched by the Argentine justice system twenty years after the military dictatorship to clarify past crimes and the fate of the disappeared. The federal court was in charge of the investigation, which did not have any prosecutorial objective.

when my eldest son was seven years old, I had to testify in the kidnapping-for-ransom case they brought against me to harass me for testifying on behalf of the prosecution at the trial of the juntas. "My son's going to turn eighteen, and he's going to subpoena me to testify," I said, as if I were joking. It's exhausting! And I'm still going to court to testify. Now it's for the stolen babies.

Elisa: I didn't go through that phase. When you started testifying, I was still in Capucha wearing the *hood*, even though I was no longer in the ESMA. I didn't testify in 1985; I couldn't.

Munú: She was still—[*Laughter*]

Miriam: Still wearing the *hood*.

Elisa: I've taken it off.

Miriam: Little by little, you gradually raised it.

Munú: During that period, most of society was wearing the *hood*.

Miriam: My brother was twelve years old when they kidnapped me. He was in the seventh grade. He was afraid to go out alone; he suffered from nerves; he chewed on his duster coat.

Munú: While you were *sucked up*?

Miriam: Yes. He was young, and it was very hard on him. He told me that when he watched the documentary "ESMA, the Day of the Trial," he went off to cry. He was with a relative who said, "Well, the terrorists also set off bombs and killed people. The Montoneros went to where my dad worked to steal communications equipment; they stuck a pistol in his stomach, and he had to give them everything." Obviously they didn't hurt him; they took the devices and left. So my brother explained that state terrorism was different and that there were places, like Italy, where guerrillas were fought using other means. "When you talk to Miriam about this, I ask you to do so humbly," he said. The documentary is useful for that sort of person, because it isn't a subject the person knows about. That's why I think that, even though it's exhausting, it's good for the new generations.

Elisa: It opens their minds. It connects them to a history that is unfamiliar to them, a history of young people committed to their ideals.

Miriam: This exhaustion has a flip side. In my own family, there is someone who doesn't know, who didn't listen, who didn't register it.

Munú: That's right. In that sense it's useful, and that's what's most important to me, but at the same time I can't help feeling used. I'm referring to the media, which seems to discover a particular issue all of a sudden. I remember in February 1999, when I came back from a family vacation, they had discovered that there was a real estate agency inside the ESMA that sold the stolen houses.

Miriam: Yes, yes. It was all news.

Munú: They use it as filler for magazines, on screen, in the newspapers. They discover the news, and then they call us. The paradox is that we know they're using us to an extent, yet that's the space available to us, and we have to take advantage of it. It's the price we pay for helping to keep the discussion alive.

Miriam: I think the same thing must happen to World War II survivors.

Elisa: Exactly.

Miriam: I was struck by a report by Federico Andahazi, author of *The Anatomist*, where he talks about being a descendent of a Hungarian who saved a lot of Jews in Budapest and had to flee the Nazis. One of the things he saved that belonged to his grandfather was a newspaper clipping from 1960 when he and Emilie Schindler were honored, which is to say that Schindler's story was already known in 1960, and yet we're only just hearing about it through [Steven] Spielberg's movie!

Elisa: Forty years later!

Miriam: The same thing has to happen in this case. In other words, every so often, a new generation emerges for which everything that has gone before is a surprise. Thirteen years ago, people who are now twenty-five were completely unaware, and now they know. And in another five years, the same thing will happen all over again—meaning that we have . . . [*Laughter*]

Elisa: For a lifetime!

Munú: We're going to be going around with our little canes. Do any of you feel as if you're being used?

Miriam: Sometimes, when I testify in the courts, I feel that some judges compete among themselves over these human rights cases. They want to polish their image, which is pretty dirty, that's for sure. Or they even want to build a political campaign for themselves on the blood of the dead or the pain of the grandmothers searching for their grandchildren.

Munú: I agree with some of what you're saying about the judiciary. And regarding the media, it's as if every five years this story becomes news again, and they pounce on it. Evidently torture isn't the breaking news anymore; now it's either the children who remain kidnapped or property theft.

Elisa: It's what gets people's attention. The theft of babies has aroused more emotions in people than the kidnapping and torture. And it's logical that it should. These kids have grown up living a lie, and in a way they're still kidnapped.

Munú: There is no question that it has been and will continue to be the most emotional aspect. The stealing of houses shows the perpetrators to be common criminals.

Miriam: And the stage of dealing with the thefts is still to come. Only recently have they begun to talk about Nazi gold, the gold stolen from the Jews, when it's something that everyone has known about forever.

Elisa: Fifty years after the fact!

Munú: I think those crimes have a statute of limitations.

278

Miriam: I don't know. If that's true, no one paid any attention to those cases when there was still time because they had stolen our lives.

Miriam: Inside the ESMA, no one, not one compañero, ever gave me an orientation or welcome speech or an induction into that collective survival project. I acted more or less through imitation. I didn't have a very good understanding of each person's role there.

Elisa: I was with people on the inside who testified as soon as they got out, but I didn't want to let on that I was aware of it. Now I remember things that are no longer useful after twenty-two years. At the time, no one explained to me why I should testify, and I am still upset about it.

Miriam: I don't understand what you're trying to say.

Munú: Elisa is talking about the time of the trial of the juntas; she persists with her guilt over not having testified then.

Elisa: My guilt and the fact that no one told me why I should testify, as with that letter from Viki that you mentioned, Miriam.

Munú: No one told me either.

Miriam: When I testified at the trial, we were seeing each other all the time, and I just assumed that you had a reason for not doing it and that it deserved respect. Each person has his or her own rhythm.

Elisa: The thing is that no one took off my captive's *hood*! No one told me to open my eyes! Looking back, I feel that what I needed was a little push.

Munú: No one can take off a *hood*. Just as we all reacted differently on the inside, and we survived as best we could, we also kept on surviving after we got out, and our responses were different. Some were able to testify in 1979, others in 1984, others in 1990, and others in 1995. Each person did it when he or she could, and there must be people who still haven't been able to do it or who told only one-tenth of what they know or who remember only one-tenth of it but will remember more in a year and will tell it. It seems to me that these are still survival strategies.

Miriam: Some people were able to testify right after they got out, and others waited for years, and some people haven't been able to do it yet!

Munú: And no one is better or worse!

Miriam: You gave up everything for the project, for the militant organization. And it didn't succeed in transforming reality, and it cost so many lives, and it created a profound internal crisis in you. I felt guilty over the death of my friends. I remember the case of my boyfriend who, frankly, I pushed to keep on militating. When he wanted to stop, I put my foot down and said, "I'm going on with this, and if you don't, then we'll separate." They killed him, and I'm alive. All this makes me feel extremely guilty. We failed to see the obvious, that we were utterly defeated, that they had run right over us. If I'd realized what was happening in 1976, I would have agreed to leave when my boyfriend Juan's parents told us that they knew people who could get us to Brazil and my mom offered to send us to Israel. But I said, "Not a chance; I'm going to keep struggling for the *fallen* compañeros." Maybe a lot of lives around me would have been saved if I hadn't been so unyielding then, if I'd brought them together and told them I was going to stop militating.

Elisa: Would they have followed you? No! That's the omnipotence of thinking you would have gotten through to them.

Miriam: I don't know. It was a crisis I went through; it wasn't even regret.

Munú: People decide for themselves. We joined the militant organization based on our individual need to participate in that project, and the decision to leave was also a personal one. No one pushed anyone in or pulled anyone out. You can influence people, but you can't decide for them.

Miriam: When I was in exile in the United States, I didn't mention that I had been in the ESMA. Only two or three people knew, people from the human rights groups. It was because it was so hard to explain the fact of having been kidnapped and having survived. And it was even harder because there weren't any large groups of exiles in New York as there were in Mexico, or Spain, or Italy, or France. Certain countries had larger groups of exiles. There were only a few of us there, some who had left Argentina for economic rather than political reasons or to study or work, and they became human rights activists out of conscience or because one of their relatives had disappeared.

Munú: It seems to me that, from the standpoint of the deterioration, it was one thing to *fall* in 1976, another thing in 1978, and quite another in 1980. Your level of deterioration in 1976 was much less than in 1978.

Miriam: Not to mention 1974 or 1975! The people who *fell* then almost never *sang*.

Elisa: They never *sang*, and they really fucked them up! But you had something inside you.

Miriam: That fire, that certainty of victory, the feeling that Utopia was within your grasp.

∾

Elisa: Miriam, you're purple.

Cristina: What's wrong?

Miriam: Well, this has been a very special week for me. I'm editing the pieces from "Cutting Edge Stories of the Century," on survivors of Nazism.

Munú: Of course, they're broadcasting your stuff on TV.

Miriam: Besides that, some colleagues from "In Two Voices" are putting together a documentary on the pregnant women, on the kids born in captivity, and they're trying to get an interview with MASSERA to ask him questions about it. So while I was working on the Auschwitz piece and the Warsaw Ghetto piece, one of the producers came up to me and said, "Miriam, when you have a minute, could you look over the interview questions for MASSERA?" [*Sighs all around*] I went to the bathroom, and I sat down on the toilet and I said, "That's enough! So much horror!" I wanted to make myself very, very small; jump into the toilet; and pull the chain!

Munú: When I was watching the news program, I wondered what you were feeling, talking about the survivors when, in a way, you're one of them.

Miriam: Well, except for the disparities—we weren't six million.

Munú: But you're you. Each person has his or her own experience, regardless of whether four people or six million people were in the same situation.

Elisa: Did you relate?

Miriam: Inevitably you relate. There's one part that I couldn't include in the story because even though it was very important to me, I understood that other aspects would have more impact on others. I was interviewing Francisco Wichter, a survivor from Schindler's list, and at one point he said, "They say that those of us who survived are the lucky ones. Lucky how? They liberated us. Liberated us from what? Why us? And the others? They liberated us from everything, our family, our home. They liberated us from the dreams of our youth!" [*Sighs*] "And we're still dragging around this weight that we'll never be able to leave behind!" Everyone tells you, "You were lucky." Lucky how? And the others? Why us?

Elisa: I really identify with that! At one point, when I was able to start reacting and realizing everything I'd been through, I thought, "I'm alive. And for what?" I felt paralyzed, as if I had amnesia; I was mentally incapable of testifying. Only after I was able to start talking about what happened to me, to reconstruct my own history, did I feel as though I "appeared."

Munú: Was that many years later?

Elisa: Many years later!

Munú: The man Miriam interviewed is still saying it now.

Elisa: After fifty years!

Munú: That's a long time.

Elisa: Is he the same one who told you that it did him good to keep talking about it?

Miriam: He was able to do so only in 1993, after the Spielberg movie. He'd held his silence all those years. [*Exclamations all around*] He said that when he saw Emilie Schindler, his savior, in a televised report and realized she was in Argentina, he became completely confused. He didn't know where he was.

Munú: The same confusion that invades us!

Miriam: He said he went out onto the balcony, and people were talking to him, and he didn't know whether he was at home or in Poland or where he was.

Munú: That's what happens to you when you run into the oppressors. Now

I realize that the subconscious mind has no sense of time! You see them, and the past comes crashing down on you; you can't think.

Cristina: I had a similar experience. Standing there in the street and—

Miriam: And not knowing what to do or which way to turn!

Cristina: Yes, completely disconcerted. In 1980, when I was living in Santa Fe, I finished the teaching degree that I hadn't been able to complete because of the coup. I had to do the classroom practicum, and one day, duster coat over my arm, I stopped short at the corner, disoriented and in a daze. What was I doing in that place, heading toward a school? How had I gotten there? I didn't recognize myself in that role, when just a year before I'd been wearing the *hood*.

Elisa: Munú, do you also experience these states of confusion?

Munú: The same as all of you. When I'm very disturbed by a situation, I don't understand what's happening, and I don't know what I'm supposed to do. Once I had an experience that was something like splitting into two. I was conscious and I perceived what was going on around me, but something completely different was going on in my head, and if I spoke, it was about what was happening inside me. There was an episode in the street. A group of people were chasing a girl who supposedly had thrown rocks at a house. When they caught her and called the police, I tried to intervene. The whole pack against that defenseless little thing triggered inside me the situation in the ESMA, and I entered into a state of total confusion. I was with friends, and I couldn't explain it to them. I tried to speak, but the things I said didn't have anything to do with what was going on around us. I realized it, and without hesitation I let them take over; they even had to tell me when to cross the street. It lasted for hours. By the next morning it had passed, but I felt as if I'd been beaten up. It was very strange.

Miriam: You live a normal life until something—sometimes sharp like lightning and sometimes diffuse like fog—hits you or envelops you, and the camp reappears.

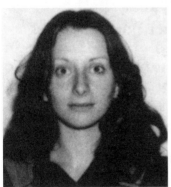

Top: Miriam Lewin, pregnant, and Anita, another captive, working in the Social Welfare Ministry (supervised release, September 1979). The sticker on the window reads, "Los argentinos somos derechos y humanos" (We Argentines are right and human), a slogan used by the Argentine military government. *Bottom*: Photographs of Miriam taken in the ESMA, 1978.

8
The Jewish Holocaust

The prisoners of the ESMA experienced firsthand the similarities between the procedures and conduct of the Nazis during World War II and the Argentine Navy during the military dictatorship. The selection of prisoners for slave labor, often based on skills but sometimes lacking any apparent rationale; efforts to encourage betrayal and the emergence of a caste system among the prisoners in the camp; systematic, organized extermination; propaganda techniques and efforts to conceal the massacres from the general population are not the only points of convergence. Similarities are also apparent in the wounds that the few survivors bear and in the difficulty some of them have faced in giving testimony about the suffering.

Miriam: I returned from my visit to Poland very disturbed. I found parallels between the organization of the concentration camps and ghettos and that of the ESMA. Let's start with the ghettos, in other words the neighborhoods where the Nazi's confined the Jews. There was a Jewish Administrative Council, which had a lot in common with the *mini-staff*. The Jewish Administrative Council, or *Judenrat*, performed an appalling function in the ghetto. It was in charge of not only administering scarce food and resources but also, in some cases, providing lists of deportable people to the Nazis; in other words, the Jews themselves decided who would end up in the gas chamber. Some councils resisted, however: the president of the Warsaw Ghetto Council, Adam Cherniakov, committed suicide rather than assume that responsibility. In contrast, [Mordechai Chaim] Rumkowski, president of the ghetto council in Lodz, which was an industrial city, called a meeting when the Germans started to require quotas of children to be deported. He said, "We have to hand them over, because if we don't, they're going to come and they're going to take anyone they want. On the other hand, if we do it in an orderly manner, first giving them the mentally retarded children, then the palsied children, then the orphans, then . . . Fathers, Mothers, hand over your children! In order to save ourselves, as many as we can, we have to hand over the children."

Munú: Did you read that somewhere?

Miriam: Yes. In a book I borrowed—a memoir of the Lodz Ghetto.

Munú: Primo Levi talks about that, and it's awful; it makes you sick to your stomach.

Miriam: Concentration camp prisoners who were put to work, who were useful, had a better chance of staying alive, the same as in the ESMA. There were *kappos*, whose role was comparable to that of certain compañeros we knew in the *mini-staff*. And then there was the *Sonderkommando*, the people who classified all of the prisoners' belongings—organized the "Storeroom," in ESMA slang—and worked in the kitchen and the laundry.

Munú: Of course. They were forced to work, just as we were.

Miriam: The role that the milicos designed for the *mini-staff*, the role of the *kappos*—which was meant to turn them into the eyes of the milicos and the executioners of their peers—existed in the concentration camps. And life was extremely precarious, even for those who worked. There always came a day when the Nazis would send the entire *Sonderkommando* to the gas chamber. In other words, the Tigers woke up one morning and . . . It was very painful for me to see the Jews in the role of collaborators.

Liliana: They used people, as in all wars.

Miriam: You're saying it's something that happens in all wars—but with such strong similarities?

Liliana: Not just in wars but during occupations too.

Munú: Whenever one group of people is held hostage by another.

Miriam: But with such a similar organizational structure?

Liliana: Yes. That's what the Spanish did with the Aborigines; there's a tendency to exploit the conquered.

Miriam: As manual labor, yes. But I'm still struck by the parallels. The Nazis set up Therensienstadt near Prague in order to hide the truth about the massacre. It was a "model" ghetto, where cultural life was encouraged; it had music, conferences, theater. It was used for propagandistic purposes; the Nazis filmed it to show off their "happy" Jews. It was like the "subversive *recuperation* camps" that—even though they never really existed—the Argentine milicos conjured up in newspaper articles every so often.

Munú: I recently read some books written by survivors: *The Drowned and the Saved*, by Primo Levi, an Italian Jew who survived and then ended up committing suicide, and *Literature or Life*, by Jorge Semprún. They talk about and even analyze that experience. Semprún couldn't write, or talk, or do anything for many years—around forty. He said that he needed all that time in order to be able to write and that if he'd forced himself to think, to reflect from the very beginning, he surely would have committed suicide. So he puts life before literature. He affirms that he was able to live—

Liliana: Thanks to what he didn't write?

Munú: Because instead of trying to think and stir it all up right away, he respected his own timing. The books talk about the fact that there were Jews who had to push others into the ovens, in exchange for nothing more than a little extra food.

Miriam: Yes.

Munú: Knowing that doing so in no way guaranteed their survival. It meant only—

Liliana: A little more food while they were alive.

Munú: A little more time alive. They knew they'd be killed in the end anyway, since they had witnessed greater horrors than the rest.

Miriam: And a few days ago, I found out that my great-grandparents died in a camp.

Munú: How?

Miriam: The other day we were celebrating my cousin's daughter's fifteenth birthday. My uncle, my father's only living brother, was there. I asked him how they felt when all that was going on in Europe. There were a lot of Jews living in other parts of the world, in the United States, in Canada, here in Argentina.

Munú: And what did they do? How did they react?

Miriam: At first, no one knew anything. Exactly like what happened during the Process [of National Reorganization], no one thought that something so horrible could be going on. Who could have imagined that they were murdering six million people—who had done nothing! It wasn't a war in which Germans and Jews were facing off with weapons. He told me that the first time they saw corpses and photographs of what was happening in the camps was in 1945.

Liliana: When the Allies started to go in.

Miriam: There were five siblings in my grandmother's family, four sisters and a brother. The first four emigrated from Poland around 1928, before the war, to different countries: the United States, Canada, and Argentina.

Munú: That's incredible!

Miriam: The youngest sister stayed behind in Poland to take care of their parents, who were too old to emigrate. This sister was fourteen years old when the others left. Later she got married and had a little girl. My uncle says he remembers when my grandmother received the letter saying that her parents, her sister, and her little niece had been taken to the camps. My grandmother read it and started to cry and scream. Her brother-in-law, her sister's husband, was the only survivor. Last Friday, I learned that he came to Argentina after the war to live in my grandmother's house. He had lost his own parents, his in-laws, his wife, and his three-year-old daughter.

Liliana: Oh!

Miriam: And here he married another survivor. In the early fifties they emigrated to Israel, and he died there in the seventies. Apparently they kept in touch for a long time. I just found out all this because I happened to ask! I don't understand why my family hadn't talked about these things before. There can't be so much silence for so long. Ours, after leaving the camp, didn't last that long. We didn't talk about it at first. I was afraid even to utter the word "disappeared." When I was in exile in the United States, I jumped the first time someone asked me in a normal voice whether I had been disappeared. But that was different. How could such a tragedy not have been discussed in the family!

Munú: Maybe they talked about it, and you didn't pay attention at the time because you were so young.

Miriam: I don't think so. The truth is that the trip to Poland really hit me hard.

Munú: Semprún describes the odor of the crematorium in such detail that I thought I could smell it; how the trees around it shriveled and the birds didn't sing. The ovens rarely stopped working.

Liliana: That's what they say, that it was constant.

Miriam: In Treblinka, they killed 650,000 people in one year.

Munú: How do you describe to someone else what it's like to smell that every single day? When I talk about the ESMA to someone who wasn't there, I get the feeling that the person is hearing a story, can get the idea, but is still a long way from the actual experience. We had to keep track of so many things at once to make sure nothing changed. Now just thinking about everything that went on in a single minute in the ESMA is beyond me.

Miriam: In the Majdanek Camp in Lublin, the ashes of the murdered are practically out in the open, under a dome-like structure. It's a museum now. Visitors go there to cry and to pray; it's always full of candles lighted in homage. The Germans used human ashes as fertilizer; they buried them or scattered them in a nearby field. When the allies arrived, they gathered them up, built a receptacle and placed them there. The barracks were there, the administrative offices, the ovens. The concentration camp was located quite close to the city, in plain view.

Liliana: That has always intrigued me. I've never read anything about what life was like in the city and whether the people there wrote about what happened in the camp.

Miriam: The camps were hidden and isolated in Germany, but not in Poland. Evidently the Nazis didn't care about concealing their existence. They were worried that people would find out about the extermination of millions of people in Germany, but not in Poland. They called it the trash heap of Europe. Did any of you ever think about the fact that the ESMA was on Avenida del Libertador, also in plain view?

Munú: The comparison is too strong for us. I always feel as if the things that happened to other people are more dramatic than the things that happened to me. I feel as if I wouldn't have been able to endure them, when the fact is that you did endure things that, despite the differences, were also quite horrible. The fact that people played different roles in there and that they don't have a judgmental attitude, at least Semprún and Levi don't, should make us think. It's clear that they're all victims and that some of those victims did one thing and some did another. But they're all on the same side, despite those differences. I think it has to be made clear that the same thing happened in Argentina: some people were kidnappers, and others were kidnapped; some were victimizers, and others were victims, beyond the fact that within one group or the other some people behaved better and some people behaved worse. Before you start making value judgments, it has to be clear that some had all the power and the rest of us had absolutely nothing; we were subjected to all their pressures and arbitrary actions. When we talk among ourselves—survivors, or formerly disappeared persons, or whatever you want to call us—about our experiences, some people come down very hard on the issue of how the captives acted, and they equate the kidnapped with the kidnappers. I think this is gradually changing.

Liliana: It's dissipating.

Munú: There's more understanding. Besides, I think our coming from a militant organization that had very rigid positions ("If you do that, you're this; if you do the other, you're that") must also contribute to that rigidity.

Liliana: Yes.

Miriam: But I still think there are limits. I can't forgive the *mini-staff*, just as I can't forgive the *kappos* or Rumkowski from the Lodz ghetto. To me, they aren't on the same plane with Cherniakov, who killed himself rather than turn in his brothers and sisters.

Munú: Of course they're not on the same plane; that's not what I'm saying. I make a distinction between the ways in which different captives behaved. But I still say you should never forget that some were subjugated and others were subjugators, and after that you can start judging.

Cristina: Did you finish reading the books?

Munú: I couldn't. I got bogged down in both of them. I'll go back to them soon, but I'll have to start all over again, because I'm sure I'll have processed other things in the meantime. What happens is that I read a page and then go back ten days later and read it completely differently. Something has moved inside me.

Adriana: It helps me to read, to get rid of the sensation that no one else feels what you feel, that sense of aloneness. Once, when I was talking about the Nazis, my eldest son, who was about thirteen, said, "My four grandparents had to escape the Nazis, and you went through what you went through, so what's going to happen to me?" I had no answer to give him.

9
Political Prisoners

The dictatorship chose two venues in which to confine its enemies: the concentration camps and prison (prison was chosen when disappearance was not possible or practical for some reason). But there were many differences between the two. Mirta Clara is a psychoanalyst who spent eight years in the prisons of the Process of National Reorganization. She read the transcripts of the conversations compiled in this book. Later she met with the authors to analyze and compare forms of resistance, the relationship between the oppressor and the oppressed, expressions of sexuality in captivity, and the weight of death as an imminent possibility, in the official and illegal or unofficial prisons of the bloodthirsty Argentine regime.

Mirta: It took an enormous effort for me to read the transcripts. People who have been involved in any sort of militancy will realize that had they had ended up in a camp, they would have done the same as, or something similar to, what you relate—which isn't to say that everyone recognizes or accepts it right away. I think that reading about what you lived through, imagining the suffering you endured and continue to endure, leads to an uncomfortable question: What would I have done in the same circumstances? At the same time, I compared everything you described to the types of situations experienced in an official prison, and I came to the conclusion that they were two worlds with different features, united under a common objective. The irony is that it all took place under the same dictatorship. When we were in prison, we always wondered what would happen to us if they sent us to a camp—a place of absolute contradiction and ambivalence—and we were extremely apprehensive at the very thought.

Munú: People who were in prison, like you, can understand that we had to do certain things that we aren't happy about in order to survive. But what about the others?

Mirta: Not just those of us who were in prison but also those who stayed in Argentina and those who left should understand it. There's always a subconscious compromise that goes beyond what we would like. We wanted new possibilities for ourselves and for our country. We put a lot of passion into it. And none of it was possible. In the face of state terrorism, each person made an involuntary deal: each person who left made a deal to save his or her own life and those of husband or wife and other family members, leaving behind a project for the country that had been crushed. Each person who stayed felt alone and lost, tried to live a normal life, and couldn't continue to militate knowing that it would mean paying with his or her life. And those of us in prison—although we resisted the plans of the armed forces at first—later decided to "adhere" critically to what they told us, and we did what we could. In each scene of the dictatorial plot, there was always a "compromise" that enabled us to keep on living, to transcend what they imposed on us at the point of a bayonet. It was lucky that there was!

One of the differences between the camp and the official prison is that in prison we created an internal organization. It was a structured organization—part clandestine, part open—which the enemy tried to quash in its persistent attempt to break down the "modus vivendi" of the group that was "us." In contrast, that level of organization didn't exist in the camp, except in the little things. And that was because the kidnappers complied fully with the objectives of taking over and destroying the bodies and the possessions of the detained. In the camp, the oppressors used atomization, fragmentation. Each person sought to bond with others as best he or she could. You have shown how, day after day, you strove to create some kind of daily life together, which was precluded by that sense of "existing outside of time and space." And you talk about it because it was very important to you; it helped you survive.

There also was a difference between the ESMA and the prison in terms of the level of violence, except for the torture, which was our great equalizer. Unlike the disappeared, officially recognized prisoners were under the jurisdiction of not only the army but also the judiciary. Women detained for political reasons were treated like "ladies," and we were all together in the Devoto Prison, which was used as a showcase to the world in response to the pressures that were being brought to bear. As the denunciations became increasingly stronger, the repressive forces—along with the judges and international officials—toured the prison to refute the accusations, to show that we women prisoners were right there, that there were no disappeared.

That isn't to say that there were no reprisals: when the dictator, [Jorge Rafael] VIDELA, went to Córdoba, the Third Army Corps took three compañeras hostage in case anything happened to the "young master." Upon his return, they were sent back to the prison, and they described for us the horrors they'd suffered in the Menéndez dungeons. During a transfer from the prison to Federal Coordination, Teresa Di Martino was disappeared by the Interior Ministry, by the armed forces.

Miriam: What was the day-to-day treatment like? Were there beatings, disciplinary measures?

Mirta: There were violent situations, particularly at inspection time, once or twice a month. In the morning everything would appear normal, but suddenly you heard the "cavalry," and abruptly female prison staff would come in shouting and barking contradictory orders. They usually wanted to pat us down to see whether we were hiding political materials in unholy places. It was abusive. If they found something, the punishment was the "hole," the cell, solitary.

Munú: Although the official prison didn't guarantee your life, there was a much better chance of survival there. To me that's a major difference. We never knew whether we'd be alive from one minute to the next. In addition, there was the fact that no one knew where we were, or if they did, they had no access to us. As far as everyone else was concerned, we were disappeared. People walking down Avenida del Libertador had no idea that we were there, inside the ESMA, inside that building! It seems to me that the official prison offered a certain space for the detainees, a form of recognition: you were political prisoners of the dictatorship, and everyone knew it.

Mirta: Our male compañeros fell victim to prison executions, but not at the massive levels that occurred in the camps. The prison had its sinister moments. In 1978 the common prisoners in Devoto were crowded into one ward, and they "took it over." The prison guards surrounded them, firing tear gas. It was a tragic siege, in which sixty people died of asphyxiation and burns and many more sustained injuries of various kinds. We saw the whole thing, and we heard the screams through the windows. We expressed our solidarity with them, even from a distance. We used sign language to communicate with them before the repression began, and afterward we communicated with people from other sections about donating blood and helping them however we could. But we weren't allowed to.

As soon as the press reported the grim news, the Interior Ministry immediately issued a statement clarifying that "the criminal, subversive, terrorist women prisoners" were all safe. The only thing separating us from the common prisoners' section was a shared courtyard. Why didn't they eliminate us right then and there? I think that was when we began to understand that it was becoming increasingly difficult politically for them to just take us out and kill us. This was, as I said, in 1978. At the very same time, the camps were still operating as extermination machines. Despite the differences from the camps, there is no question that the prisons, too, aired their dirty laundry at times. They were part of the same repressive forces that used the same methods to solve social conflicts: in Devoto they killed sixty defenseless people in just one hour!

Elisa: A compañera who was kidnapped in the Bank once asked me how we'd managed to survive the constant confusion in the ESMA. She pointed out that we didn't have bars; in the prisons, and in other camps, the enemy didn't mingle with you.

Mirta: Just as there were different styles in different camps, in the ESMA the detainees were all together, but they were separated by level, by caste. At least that's how I interpreted what I read: they sought to create differences among the disappeared. They wanted to foster the "illusory" belief that there were different "positions of power." At the same time, the ESMA also wanted to co-opt the militants politically, and they wanted to appropriate in any way possible the money that had been accumulated by the Montoneros.

Elisa: In our conversations, we've talked about the insanity of the marinos in the Task Force, and we realized that it was virtually impossible to try to understand.

Mirta: But there is a method to madness that has to be deciphered in each unique situation. I think that in order to understand what happened in the ranks of the concentration camps of the armed forces, you have to keep in mind the overarching strategic goal, and from there the aim of the small redoubt that was the ESMA, and at the personal level the goal of each one of the murderers and thugs there.

Munú: I can't understand how someone can come to torture another human being. I find it unfathomable.

Mirta: As they were torturing me, while I was pregnant, and threatening to rape me, there was a guy sitting there sipping *mate*. I was able to see below the *hood* as he passed the *mate* to the people who were torturing me. All the other interrogators and/or torturers fit into the scene; they were there to do exactly what they were doing. But that guy seemed to me to be completely out of place. Sharing *mate* has the connotation of entering into the spirit of solidarity; it's a time of coming together, of sharing what one likes to participate in. They were enjoying another person's suffering!

Munú: We've often wondered why they let us live, and one hypothesis that came up is the strange relationship they had with us. Our faces had become familiar to them; they took us to our houses. Killing us would have been harder than when each of us had been merely a *hood*.

Miriam: We tried to understand why they didn't kill us, but who made the decision whether or not to kill us? We don't know who made the decisions. We don't know whether the TIGER just woke up in the morning and said, "Today I'll do a *transfer*" or whether he discussed it with MASSERA in the Liberty building, saying, "Commander Zero, I have a full floor; there are forty of them, so I'm going to do a *transfer*" and MASSERA signed the paper. We don't know whether we relied exclusively on their sympathy or antipathy. It's a complete unknown to us. Some people they had already "put to work" they later murdered—very few, but it happened. Others had blown up navy vessels with explosives or had carried out attacks against admirals, and they survived. Others collaborated in the sense of going out to *mark* people, and they killed them anyway.

Mirta: We, too, wondered constantly why they didn't kill us. What was the yardstick they used to decide how dangerous someone was? It clearly wasn't the same for people who had a court case pending or were under the jurisdiction of the National Executive Power, as it was for all of you who had disappeared off the map, in every sense of the word.

Munú: So the officially recognized prisoners also ask themselves the same question: Why didn't they kill us all?

Mirta: In my case, as in others, they didn't kill the women, but they executed our husbands, which makes it a pretty pathetic question. When the father of one of my prison compañeras, a widow like me, met with military personnel from the Second Army Corps, one of them told him that they didn't care about his detained daughter, because they had already gotten her husband! That's why, among all the motivations they might have had, I always add the gender issue, even though we didn't consider it at the time.

Miriam: They didn't kill you because you were women?

Mirta: What did we women represent in the social fiction of the repressive forces? The ideological and religious formation that takes place in a military institution compacted into the model of "tradition, family, and property" might shed some light on the matter. We were like their mothers, their wives, their lovers, except that we were dangerous because we were militants. We couldn't exist or think too freely. They detained us, and they "added" us to our male compañeros like appendages. They had to get to know us, spend time with us—in your case on a daily basis, and in ours very sporadically—in order to realize that we were autonomous individuals, with our own plusses and minuses. "We," the female prisoners, were a "rock" ideologically. We weren't going to give them a leftist political-ideological diatribe. But when some military person came to the prison and wanted us to tell him why we were detained, the first thing we asked him was whether he agreed with Martínez de Hoz's, or Siegaut's, or Cavallo's economic policies, a question that quickly infuriated him, because people in the military disagreed on this among themselves. We took advantage of the opportunity to sidetrack the interrogation, which we delighted
in doing. The important thing was to maintain our dignity in their presence, even if we had to refrain from saying everything we wanted to say to them!

At the highest level of explanation, there's a combination of causality and coincidence. Someone who had been kidnapped, a compañero who's now living abroad, spoke years later about having been the last person remaining in the Arana Pit[1] because they were going to close it down. One night they moved him out in order to kill him. The car broke down on the way, and the two guys who went for help were delayed. A third one was guarding him. The detainee started to say to him, "Don't kill me, and I'll never come back again." He kept repeating it over and over again until he convinced the oppressor. And he never came back to Argentina again! What they did was create an asymmetrical pact! It was like the dilemma of the master and the slave: the master remains so only as long as the slave doesn't rebel against him and defy him to gain his freedom.

Miriam: But he's alive! He can tell the tale!

Mirta: Yes. Luckily! That shadowy zone Miriam is talking about comes into it, in the sense that we have no way of knowing what their orders were, how many detainees they were supposed to have, each person's individual situation, the circumstances of the silencing of a disappeared person that conspired to save his or her life, and so on.

Elisa: There was a comparable number of male and female survivors from the ESMA.

Miriam: Yes, that's true of the captives from the *staff*. But remember that during the time we were there, when they *sucked up* large groups of small fry—*perejiles*—there usually was a chance that they'd release the women and retain the men.

Mirta: In Devoto, the milicos and prison guards had a very derogatory attitude toward us. We, like all women, were "ballbreakers." The men talked politics while we women remained silent, but we expressed ourselves in other ways. For example, when compañeras were *transferred* and were in situations where their lives were in danger, we organized pitcher-banging sessions. In other words, we took the pitchers of boiled *mate* and banged them on the bars, yelling to warn the other inmates in Villa Devoto. When Alicia País died from an asthma attack in the hospital, we organized a mass lunch boycott; we were even joined by the Graivers' aunt, who never liked to have very much to do with us.

On the issue of the kidnapped women who fell in love with their oppressors, I must confess that I am very critical of the way that some intellectuals and compañeros have approached it. I remember in 1984 and 1985, when this problem was being discussed, Eva Giberti[2] said something like this: "Until the day comes when we are unable to demonstrate that there was state terrorism against the whole of society, we cannot talk

---

1. The Arana Pit was a concentration camp close to the city of La Plata in Buenos Aires province.

2. Eva Giberti is a well-known Argentine psychoanalyst and academic.

about what happened between women captives and their captors." Now we are farther along, although a lot of work remains to be done on the issue of state terrorism. You have told stories of women detainees getting the milicos off their backs. Most of us have had the experience of resisting the kidnappers' "look," the "claims" they conveyed in one way or another, the many pressures ("I'll save your parents, and you'll go with me to the hotel"). Not one magazine article or book talks about everything that had to be overcome to keep it from becoming a mass response. More women resisted the pressures from the forces of power than gave in. No one ever talks about how we endured so many years without having sexual relations, without considering or desiring the oppressor in order to satisfy our needs, simply because he was there and was, at least in the jail, the only man we saw.

Munú: When we talk about women captives who had relationships with the kidnappers, I always wonder whether that might have been their way of surviving. In the camp, each person developed a persona, consciously or not, that contributed to his or her survival. They boxed us into a stereotype, and then we encouraged it.

Miriam: It's an issue that sparks people's curiosity. Relationships between prisoners and jailers have existed throughout the history of humanity, and they've been analyzed plenty. I think that essentially there was the possibility of two types of feelings toward the kidnappers as "men": either repugnance or the feeling of being protected by one of them. Maybe some compañeras became confused by the latter. This was clearer in the air force or in other camps, where the isolation was absolute. They tortured you; they didn't feed you; they didn't let you go to the bathroom; you shit on yourself in the cell; you vomited there; you menstruated and stained everything; you had no light, no air. And suddenly the guy took you to bathe; he brought you the Bible, a café au lait and two croissants; he asked you whether you believed in God, what you did on Saturday nights when you were free. It caused a bewildering feeling of gratitude. You might end up thinking, "This guy is a human being, and he's concerned about me." And this might make some women feel an attraction. In the ESMA, I took refuge in the compañeros, but maybe some women didn't feel safe being with the compañeros; it gave them a feeling of greater fragility and vulnerability. Maybe the relationship with the kidnapper gave them a certain feeling of safety, and that was probably encouraged: "Don't worry. I'll take care of you. I'll take you on a *visit* to your house. I brought you these clothes. Are you okay? What do you need?" And we also need to look at why they fell in love with us.

Mirta: Munú, to me that sad anecdote you told about Tiger Acosta was very graphic—when you asked him why they weren't home having dinner with their wives at that hour of the night instead of secretly taking disappeared women out to eat in the restaurants of downtown Buenos Aires. And he starts screaming. His response is to ask what they had to talk about with their wives. "You are the ones we can talk to. You talk about everything. You have an opinion on every subject." I think it struck me because it changed how I saw their opinion of you, of what you achieved by letting them get to know you as much as possible. And I thought about what this conflict against subversion was like. In the war against the indigenous populations, they were exterminated because they were different and they resisted colonization. In the Holocaust, Nazism "bought" the notion that it was necessary to prevail because of the Jews' supposed inferiority as a race. The colonists preyed on the black population to the point of extermination because they were of a different race, a beautiful one at that. But in this case, in this speech by TIGER ACOSTA, you can't help but think, "He wants what the other person is." They wanted everything you were; it's white reflected in a white mirror.[3] They had profound admiration for who you were as women under their cumulative domination, and it's what they would have wanted for themselves. These fissures in the sinister secret of the genocides show that theirs was a Pyrrhic victory, an infamous victory.

Miriam: Sometimes you fall in love with what the other person says about you. Maybe that happened to a kidnapped woman, based on the kidnappers' discourse. They'd say to us, "You are admirable, valiant, intelligent." On the other hand, those relationships were few and very ephemeral: once they were out in the open, once the situation changed, they ended.

Munú: Mirta, I don't know whether this happens to you all. We feel the guilt of being alive, although during the course of our meetings, the guilt started to shrink.

Mirta: That guilt is in everyone; it's in those who left, in those who stayed, in those of us who experienced imprisonment. I always say that some day we'll have to honor ourselves for what we are, for what we fought for and still fight for. What you're doing is part of that ongoing struggle.

Maybe you wouldn't have chosen each other if you'd met earlier. What unites you is that you were in an extreme situation. No one brought you together; it was your desire to challenge the mandate of terror, your mutual agreement during all those years of giving testimony to judges in the trial of the commanders on behalf of the children born in secret and disappeared, to journalists, to whoever asked. It's the chance to piece together the traumatic extreme situation through your daily life experiences. You

---

3. A trick or game of mirrors.

speak to us of your journey through a world that is inaccessible to our life experiences.

I'm not familiar with any groups of people who've been in camps and who talk about the things you talk about, in the way you talk about them, from your gut, never letting go of the contradictions and the ambivalence. This is not a polished tale from well-intentioned researchers. It's a spontaneous telling. The valuable thing about this work is that it represents an extension of the group militancy in this period of "daily post-camp life"— in the fact that you sought each other out, you met, and you're full of life, even as you carry the remains of the shipwreck on your backs. One could say that it's a triumph over state terrorism; a triumph over the concentration camps; a triumph of friendship, of solidarity, of the "we" that so many repressive forces wanted to and thought they had been able to destroy.

Bibliography

Benedetti, Mario. *Preguntas al azar.* Montevideo: Arca, Editorial Sudamericana, 1986.

Bonasso, Miguel. *Recuerdo de la muerte.* Buenos Aires: Planeta, 1998.

Calveiro, Pilar. *Poder y desaparición.* Buenos Aires: Ediciones Colihue, 1998.

CELS (Centro de Estudios Legales y Sociales [Center of Legal and Social Studies]). *Culpables para la sociedad. Impunes para la ley.* Buenos Aires: 1988.

CONADEP (Comisión Nacional sobre la Desaparición de Personas [National Commission on the Disappeared]). *Nunca más.* Buenos Aires, EUDEBA, 1986.

Gasparini, Juan, *Montoneros final de cuentas.* La Plata: De La Campana, 1999.

Herrera Matilde and Ernesto Tenembaum. *Identidad, despojo y restitución.* Buenos Aires: Abuelas de la Plaza de Mayo, Editorial Contrapunto, 2001.

Levi, Primo, *Los hundidos y los salvados.* Barcelona: Muchnik Editores S.A., 1995.

Semprún, Jorge. *La escritura o la vida.* Barcelona: Tusquets Editores S.A., 1997.

Verbitsky, Horacio. *El vuelo.* Buenos Aires: Planeta, 1995.

Acknowledgments

To all the human rights organizations in Argentina whose work has contributed to the construction of both our memory and the collective memory. To Mariana Pérez Roisinblit, Víctor Basterra, Enrique García Medina, Matilde Ruderman, María José Vásquez, Elvio Vitale, Ariel Lewin, Juan García Lewin, Julio Raffo, and Rafael Landea. To all those who read this book prior to publication and offered their suggestions and encouragement.

To Cristina, Elisa, Miriam, and Munú. (Liliana)

To Olga Wornat, Graciela Lewin, and Laura Bek for being there. To Norberto Colominas for knowing without having to ask. To Juan Luis and Diego, my loves and my sleepless nights. To Marta Diana, for showing me, through her book, that this story must be told a different way. To the staff of *Telenoche Investiga* for becoming my new compañeros. To the brave and honest judges and prosecutors. To Leia, who accompanied our conversations in canine silence. (Miriam)

To Viviana, to Elba Cuitiño, to Silda (with her family large and small) for being there. To all those who have helped me on my journey through life, often without knowing this part of my story. (Elisa)

To all those who, whether or not they knew it, braced my soul so I could set my voice free. To all those who are still unable to let loose their voices. (Cristina)

To my family, to María Elena Labín, Graciela Villanueva, Ana Alaniz, Asia and Mario Testa, Marimar Heras, Fernando Porta, Marimé Arias, Maco Somigliana, Rafael Landea, Matilde Ruderman, and Alejandro Inchaurregui because, by many different paths, they helped me keep going. (Munú)

About the Authors

Nilda Actis Goretta (Munú) was born in the province of Buenos Aires on October 18, 1945. She grew up in a rural area and went on to study mural painting at the Fine Arts School of La Plata. Her militancy focused on the most disadvantaged neighborhoods in the Ensenada region of Buenos Aires. She was kidnapped in Buenos Aires on June 19, 1978, and remained in the ESMA until February 1979, when she was given supervised release status: her oppressors knew where she lived and forced her to work with them. On July 16, 1979, the Argentine Navy issued her a prepaid plane ticket and allowed her to leave the country. Months later, in exile in Venezuela, she was still under surveillance. Following the restoration of democracy, she returned to Argentina to complete her degree. Currently employed in the field of public monument art, she enjoys her work, which she performs perched on scaffolding as she paints collective murals on the walls of Argentine cities and towns.

Cristina Inés Aldini was born in Lomas de Zamora on February 20, 1954. After leaving high school, she joined a Christian group and became involved in social work in the working-class neighborhoods of San Fernando. Later she taught adult education and turned to political militancy. Following the military coup, she endured repression and the loss of most of her militant colleagues. She was kidnapped on December 5, 1978, and was held prisoner in the ESMA until the end of May 1979. From May until December of that year, she was given supervised release status and was forced to work in an office that the Argentine Navy was preparing to convert into a press agency (a plan that never came to fruition). Eventually she was able to complete her studies in the province of Santa Fe, where she lived with the family of a friend she had met in the ESMA. In 1996 she joined a political organization and began working as a human rights activist. Until December 2003, she was a municipal official in the province of Buenos Aires, and today she works in public and private education.

Liliana Gardella was born on August 20, 1954, in the province of Chaco. After her graduation from high school, she went to Buenos Aires to pursue a degree in anthropology, but her studies were interrupted by her political militancy and the repression and exile that followed. On November 25, 1977, she was kidnapped in Mar del Plata and was subsequently taken to the ESMA, where she was held until January 8, 1979. She went into exile in May 1979, two months after the Argentine Navy contacted her at her parents' home and gave her authorization to leave the country. When democracy returned to Argentina, she was finally able to complete her degree. Today she works on social policy issues in the private and public sectors.

Miriam Lewin was born in Buenos Aires in 1957. She became politically active in the early 1970s, while at the Colegio Nacional de Buenos Aires. She joined various leftist groups, including the Peronist Youth [Juventud Peronista] just prior to entering the university's School of Economics and the School of Journalism of the Graphic Arts Institute. On May 17, 1977, at age nineteen, she was kidnapped in La Matanza by members of the air force. After being held in solitary confinement by the air force for nearly a year, she was transferred to the Navy Mechanics School. She remained disappeared until January 1979, when she was allowed to return to her family home. In April 1981, when she was finally permitted to leave the country, she moved to the United States. She became active in human rights organizations, and after democracy was restored, she returned to Argentina. Today Miriam Lewin is an investigative journalist. Her work has aired on some of the most prestigious award-winning gender programs on Argentine television.

Elisa Tokar was born in Buenos Aires on November 14, 1953. After graduating from high school, she worked and studied at the School of Law and Social Sciences. During that time, she became politically active, and later she joined the Peronist Worker Youth [Juventud Trabajadora Peronista]. She was kidnapped on September 21, 1977, and in mid-1978 she began forced labor under permanent guard at the Ministry of Foreign Relations. After a period during which she was returned to the ESMA each night, she was finally allowed to sleep at her family home. Following her release in late 1980, she remained in Argentina, where she gave birth to her two children. She currently works as a social psychologist at the AUN, a non-profit civic group that serves at-risk women.

That Inferno
Ese Infierno